Disseminating Behavioral Research

Annette K. Griffith • Tyler C. Ré
Editors

Disseminating Behavioral Research

 Springer

Editors
Annette K. Griffith 🆔
Behavior Analysis Department
College of Graduate and Professional
Studies- The Chicago School
Chicago, IL, USA

Tyler C. Ré 🆔
Behavior Analysis Department
College of Graduate and Professional
Studies - The Chicago School
Chicago, IL, USA

ISBN 978-3-031-47342-5   ISBN 978-3-031-47343-2   (eBook)
https://doi.org/10.1007/978-3-031-47343-2

This Springer imprint is published by the registered company Springer Nature Switzerland AG
The registered company address is: Gewerbestrasse 11, 6330 Cham, Switzerland

Paper in this product is recyclable.

"This summative guide to dissemination in the behavioral sciences provides a thorough walk- through of the writing and publication process that will be a very helpful reference across the field of behavioral science. Students and early career faculty will find the encouraging guidance on how to respond to reviewers especially useful, including the exemplar editorial letters and suggested feedback response recommendations. Additionally, even well-established behavioral scientists will find the chapter on non-traditional dissemination pathways provides critical information for widespread dissemination and consumption of research findings in the ever-changing landscape of online communities of practice and information sharing. This book fills a critical need in the effort to disseminate behavioral sciences to key stakeholders."

— Gretchen Scheibel, PhD, OTR, BCBA,
Assistant Research Professor,
University of Kansas

"Disseminating Behavioral Research (Annette K. Griffith, Tyler C. Ré, eds.) serves as a fantastic learning tool for new practitioners in behavioral analysis who wish to share their research findings or clinical efforts in broader public domains. Griffith and Ré have done a wonderful job in sampling a comprehensive cross section of potential areas where behavior analysts may disseminate their findings and then offer a set of guidelines as how to best achieve this goal. This book serves to bridge the practice to research gap in a way that is easy to understand and follow. It will serve as a valuable resource for both students and practitioners alike."

— John M. Guercio, Ph.D., BCBA-D, LBA,
NADD-CC, Clinical Director, Benchmark
Human Services

To my family – thank you for your unconditional support and encouragement.

– A.K.G.

To Eve and Liliana – thank you for pushing me to be a better husband, dad, and researcher each and every day.

– T.C.R.

Foreword

While behavioral sciences have several resources to guide research design and methodology, there is a lack of formal guidance in the publication and presentation process that goes beyond what we learn in graduate school. The importance of dissemination and publication in behavioral health and sciences is undeniable and demonstrates the social significance of the work we do. Unfortunately, there are many reasons why we have a research to practice gap. These include: (1) behavioral scientists are unable to conduct research due to competing job expectations, (2) it is difficult to implement controlled experimental research in applied settings, (3) if they are able to gather clinically significant data that are reliable and valid, they lack the time and resources to present or publish it, and (4) lack of success, or the fear of lack of success, that can make the task of writing a manuscript daunting. The authors of this edited book recognize these hurdles and have created a series of chapters that form a task analysis for writing up and disseminating research.

Although many organizations would love to be recognized as ones that conduct cutting-edge research, administrators are also faced with meeting the bottom line and the need for staff to provide direct, billable services which conflict with time spent conducting and disseminating research. So, it is important to recognize these conflicting goals and ideally discuss or negotiate for "release time" to conduct research in any position you take. One way to do this is to pitch to current and future employers that you can improve an organization's reputation by presenting and publishing research. Taking advantage of students in your midst can also help to foster research as projects are often required to meet graduate school requirements. Summer interns and undergraduate volunteers also allow staff some time to conduct and prepare research. Even small research groups and journal clubs can help teams develop ideas for research and foster a system of support for getting it done. Finally, there are foundations that fund small research projects that organizations can apply to, to help defray the costs of conducting research.

In this book you will see that each part tackles different aspects of the research dissemination process. Part I really helps to set the stage for developing a research approach to practice. Parts II and III break down this process so that anyone who is new to writing and submitting publications can take on the task. One particularly important element of this book is the part on how to get your research noticed. I appreciate that it is enough of a task to do the study, write up the manuscript, and get it submitted (and accepted). But what many of us forget to consider is how to make sure the information gets into the right hands, including practitioners in the field, parents and clients, and policy makers. I have found that as behavioral scientists we are often poor self-advocates, and our field is suffering from the lack of good public relations. Many anti-behavioral statements are based on false premises, so the more that you can do to reach the broader public, in addition to other professionals in the field, the more we can represent that our fields are not only evidence-based but compassionate and collaborative.

One note of caution is that it is critical that there is a clear delineation between what activities fall within the realm of the clinical work you are doing (and billing for) and the work that is done for research purposes. Be sure to clearly define what falls into each category and only bill for the appropriate services. Additionally, applied research must make sure that protocols are developed so that there are clear safeguards in place, that you recruit the help and support of an interdisciplinary team, and that you comply with all Institutional Review Board (IRB) requirements. If your site or program does not have its own IRB, it is critical to either set one up or identify an organization that you can affiliate with that has an IRB to provide support and guidance.

Now, enjoy reading this book created by a group of authors who have experience working in applied settings and getting their work disseminated. Learn from their advice and start your own research group so that you can have an impact in our field and one day you too may be able to reach the Holy Grail: dissemination to a large audience.

May Institute, Randolph, MA, USA   Jennifer Zarcone

Preface

In behavioral sciences, we have primary goals to describe, predict, and understand behavior, with an intent to address issues of social significance and interest (Cooper et al., 2020). Through the conduct of research, we advance our knowledge and gain information that can be used to facilitate progress in continued research and learning, policy development, and practice. A crucial component of the research process is the dissemination of research findings to key stakeholders, including the scientific community, funders, research participants, and the community at large (Marin-Gonzales et al., 2017). While the behavioral sciences have several resources to guide the research process, covering important topics such as design and research methodology (Cooper et al., 2020; Ledford & Gast, 2018; Kennedy & Edmonds, 2017), there has been a lack of formal guidance in our field on the best practices for dissemination.

Several fields, mainly in areas of medicine, have developed numerous and detailed resources dedicated to training and supporting their scientists and practitioners as they are encouraged to disseminate within their fields and to the larger public audience (Brazeu et al., 2008; Fowler, 2010, 2011). While these resources can be referenced and adapted for use by behavioral scientists, there remained a gap in information that was tailored to those who have sought to disseminate the results and interpretations of behavioral science within and outside of our fields. This gap served as the catalyst for this text, prompting us to develop a resource that could compile material to support our scientists.

The contributors for this text were selected due to their experience in dissemination and, in several cases, their experience in training the next generation of behavioral scientists on how to effectively disseminate their own work. We specifically sought out individuals with a broad range of experience and individuals with a positive and inspired vision for our field. We were so pleased with the content that they provided, particularly with the recognition that for several of the topics there were minimal resources available to help guide their writing, specifically from the fields of behavioral science. They have each produced chapters that provide a thorough foundation, detailed examples, and positive encouragement for those seeking to disseminate.

The intent of this book was to provide students and junior researchers in the behavioral sciences, individuals who may be newer to or just starting out in their research career, with some formal guidance on the best ways to share the findings and interpretations of their work. And while this book may indeed be most useful for those who are newer to dissemination, it is hoped that more senior researchers may also find the content useful, particularly those chapters that provide information on topics that extend beyond traditional dissemination practices and that consider dissemination from a global perspective. It is said that "Research is of no use unless it gets to the people who need to use it" (Whitty, n.d., as cited in Halbert, 2019), and it is our hope that the information provided in this text can assist in ensuring that the work that you are doing will reach those who need it, resulting in increased knowledge and understanding of human behavior and improvements in our collective wellbeing.

Chicago, IL, USA   Annette K. Griffith
                                                                                                  Tyler C. Re

References

Brazeau, G. A., DiPiro, J. T., Fincham, J. E., Boucher, B. A., & Tracy, T. S. (2008). Your role and responsibilities in the manuscript peer review process. *American Journal of Pharmaceutical Education, 72,* 1–3

Cooper, J.O., Heron, T. E., & Heward, W. L. (2020). *Applied behavior analysis* (3rd ed.). Pearson Education, Inc

Fowler, J. (2010). Writing for professional publication. Part 3: Following journal guidelines. *British Journal of Nursing, 19,* 1260

Fowler, J. (2011). Writing for professional publication. Part 6: Writing the abstract. *British Journal of Nursing, 20,* 120

Halbert, L. (2019, July 1). Don't let your research sit on a shelf! *National Institute for Health and Care Research: Research Design Service Blog.* https://www.rdsblog.org.uk/don-t-let-your-research-sit-on-the-shelf

Kennedy, T.D. & Edmonds, W. A. (2017). An applied guide to research designs: Quantitative, qualitative, and mixed methods. In An applied guide to research designs: Quantitative, qualitative, and mixed methods (2nd ed.). SAGE. https://doi.org/10.4135/9781071802779

Ledford, J.R. & Gast, D.L. (2018). *Single Case Research Methodology: Applications in Special Education and Behavioral Sciences.* Taylor and Francis. https://doi.org/10.4324/9781315150666

Marin-Gonzalez, E., Malmusi, D., Camprubi, L., & Borrell, C. (2017). The role of dissemination as a fundamental part of a research project: Lessons learned from SOPHIE. *International Journal of Health Services, 47,* 258–276

Contents

Part II Traditional Publication Preparation

Part IV   Getting Your Research Noticed

About the Editors

Annette K. Griffith, BCBA-D, is a Full Professor and Program Chair in the Behavior Analysis Department in the College of Graduate and Professional Studies at The Chicago School. She has worked in the field of behavior analysis for over 20 years, as a clinician, researcher, and administrator. Her current work is focused on training and development of doctoral-level students and on support for program faculty, specifically in areas of research and dissemination. Dr. Griffith's own dissemination efforts have included publications in peer-reviewed journals, book chapters, encyclopedia entries, and presentations at regional, national, and international conferences, in areas related to parenting and mental health. She was the 2023 recipient of the Award for Distinguished Research and Scholarship from The Chicago School.

Tyler C. Ré, BCBA-D, is an Assistant Professor in the Behavior Analysis Department in the College of Graduate and Professional Studies at The Chicago School. He earned his PhD in Applied Behavior Analysis and The Chicago School of Professional Psychology, his MA at the University of Missouri-Kansas City in Special Education, and his Undergraduate degree at the University of Kansas in Applied Behavior Science. Dr. Ré has 20+ years of experience working in multiple environments including public and private schools, residential facilities, center-based services, and higher-education working with both neurodiverse and neurotypical individuals across the life span. Through these experiences, he recognized the importance of effective and efficient staff training strategies to improve the outcomes for individuals receiving services and thus developed a passion for disseminating behavior analytic principles. He has served the field through participation in various scientific state and regional professional organizations, as an ad hoc reviewer to the *Review Journal of Autism and Developmental Disorders*, and published several journal articles and book chapters. His research interests include organizational behavior management, leadership skills, and multi-tiered systems of support.

List of Contributors

Leif K. Albright Department of Special Education, Manhattanville College, Purchase, NY, USA

Meredith Andrews Behavior Analysis Department, College of Graduate and Professional Studies, The Chicago School, Chicago, IL, USA

Meagan C. Arrastía-Chisholm Department of Human Services at Valdosta State University, Valdosta, GA, USA

Brittany Beaver Behavior Analysis Department, College of Graduate and Professional Studies, The Chicago School, Chicago, IL, USA

Kasey Bedard Behavior Analysis Department, College of Graduate and Professional Studies, The Chicago School, Chicago, IL, USA

Sara W. Bharwani University of Nebraska-Lincoln, Lincoln, NE, USA

Megan A. Boyle Upstate Caring Partners, Utica, NY, USA

Kylene Caquelin No Stone Unturned, Manhattan, KS, USA

Teresa Cardon Department of Educational Psychology, University of North Texas, Denton, TX, USA

Matt Cicoria Behavioral Observations Podcast; Positive Behavioral Outcomes, LLC, Newbury, NH, USA

Andrew R. Craig Golisano Center for Special Needs, SUNY Upstate Medical University, Syracuse, NY, USA

Katherine Davis Cornerstone Therapies, Huntington Beach, CA, USA

Julianne DiCocco Santa Clara County Office of Education, San Jose, CA, USA

Lucas Evans Missouri Department of Mental Health, Jefferson City, MO, USA

Tara Fahmie Severe Behavior Department, University of Nebraska Medical Center, Omaha, NE, USA

Susan Flynn Behavior Analysis Department, College of Graduate and Professional Studies, The Chicago School, Chicago, IL, USA

Yors Garcia Psychology Department, Pontificia Universidad Javeriana, Bogotá, Colombia

Alexandra Hamilton Oregon Research Institute, Springfield, OR, USA

Stephanie Hood Psychology Department, Marquette University, Milwaukee, WI, USA

Willow Hozella May Institute, Randolph, MA, USA

Jacqueline Huscroft-D'Angelo Oregon Research Institute, Springfield, OR, USA

Jessica F. Juanico Department of Applied Behavioral Science, University of Kansas, Lawrence, KS, USA

Estefanía Junca Psychology Department, Pontificia Universidad Javeriana, Bogotá, Colombia

Fan Yu Lin Philadelphia (Ningbo) Education Technology Co. Ltd., Ningbo, China

Amanda Mahoney Behavior Analysis Department, College of Graduate and Professional Studies, The Chicago School, Chicago, IL, USA

Shannon Martinez ABA Services, Firefly Therapy Clinic, Greenville, SC, USA

Neil Martin Behavior Analyst Certification Board, Littleton, CO, USA

Jacquelyn MacDonald ABA Inside Track Podcast; Applied Behavior Analysis Department, Regis College, Weston, MA, USA

Regis College, Department of Applied Behavior Analysis, Weston, MA, USA

Amanda Muñoz-Martinez Psychology Department, Universidad de los Andes, Bogotá, Colombia

Diana Parry-Cruwys ABA Inside Track Podcast; Applied Behavior Analysis Department, Regis College, Weston, MA, USA

Regis College, Department of Applied Behavior Analysis, Weston, MA, USA

Robert Parry-Cruwys ABA Inside Track Podcast, Department of Applied Behavior Analysis, Regis College, Weston, MA, USA

ABA Inside Track Podcast, Shrewsbury Public Schools, Shrewsbury, MA, USA

Raena A. Quinnell Step Ahead ABA, Omaha, NE, USA

Javid Rahaman Severe Behavior Department, University of Nebraska Medical Center, Omaha, NE, USA

Chrystal Jansz Rieken Behavior Analysis Department, College of Graduate and Professional Studies, The Chicago School, Chicago, IL, USA

Ashley N. Romero Little Leaves Behavioral Services, Weston, FL, USA

Rachael Schneider Autism Learning Partners, Buffalo, NY, USA

Michelle A. Sereno Behavior Analysis Department, The College of Graduate and Professional Studies, The Chicago School, Chicago, IL, USA

Henry Sessanga Speech, Language, and Educational Associates, Encino, CA, USA

Elizabeth Shaffer University of British Columbia, Vancouver, BC, Canada

Sean W. Smith Golisano Center for Special Needs, SUNY Upstate Medical University, Syracuse, NY, USA

William E. Sullivan Golisano Center for Special Needs, SUNY Upstate Medical University, Syracuse, NY, USA

Samantha Tackett Academic Center for Excellence (ACE), Division of Undergraduate Studies, Florida State University, Tallahassee, FL, USA

Jane Tammik Behavior Analysis Department, College of Graduate and Professional Studies, The Chicago School, Chicago, IL, USA

Kelly M. Torres College of Professional Psychology, The Chicago School, Chicago, IL, USA

A. Delyla Ulm Arizona State University, Tempe, AZ, USA

Dorothy Zhang Behavior Analysis Department, College of Graduate and Professional Studies, The Chicago School, Chicago, IL, USA

Part I
Introduction to Dissemination

Chapter 1
Introduction to Dissemination in Behavioral Sciences

Willow Hozella, Rachael Schneider, Jane Tammik, and Brittany Beaver

In any scientific endeavor seeking to improve the lives of organisms there must be a bidirectional relationship between those applying the science and those conducting research. This relationship aims to ensure practitioners implement evidence-based practices in the applied setting and researchers continue to explore hypotheses and experimental arrangements addressing pragmatic issues facing the practitioner. For such a relationship to exist, the practitioner must keep up with current research and the researcher must stay well-informed on what practices are being conducted in the name of the science. However, for both the practitioner and the researcher there is a basic repertoire to be learned beforehand. They must know about the types of scholarship available, the limitations of each, and the components that are most relevant to the task at hand.

If one wishes to disseminate a particular methodology, analysis, or conceptual approach, their verbal repertoire should not be limited to research outcomes, they must also be proficient in explaining how those outcomes were achieved and why the research being referenced is relevant. In this chapter, you will be presented with descriptions and analyses of a sampling of different types of academic scholarship so that you are more able to evaluate research critically and determine what types of research might best suit you endeavors. Academic scholarship can be categorized as either empirical scholarship or reviews of publications.

W. Hozella (✉)
May Institute, Randolph, MA, USA
e-mail: whozella@mayinstitute.org

R. Schneider
Autism Learning Partners, Buffalo, NY, USA

J. Tammik · B. Beaver
Behavior Analysis Department, College of Graduate and Professional Studies
at The Chicago School, Chicago, IL, USA

© The Author(s), under exclusive license to Springer Nature Switzerland AG 2023
A. K. Griffith, T. C. Ré (eds.), *Disseminating Behavioral Research*,
https://doi.org/10.1007/978-3-031-47343-2_1

Empirical Scholarship

Empirical scholarship is the study or research of a subject and the reporting on the results of this study. This scholarship might replicate previous research, report new findings on a topic, or discuss what a scientific field is doing to improve its scientific practices. However, not all research is conducted in a laboratory and there are types of scholarships that might not involve traditional research methods to show a causal relation between independent and dependent variables (e.g., book reviews, survey research, qualitative research, narrative reviews). However, empirical scholarship must be guided by scientific experimentation and observable measurable evidence as its primary topic. What follows will introduce the reader to a sampling of different types of scholarship, so that they can be savvy consumers of scholarly material and understand what options are available should they pursue their own scholarly activities.

Basic Research

The main purpose of basic research is to seek to gain knowledge and general understanding. With basic research, the knowledge gained is not required to demonstrate its practicality or solve a specific problem (Rubio et al., 2010). Skinner (1953) explains the basis for a functional analysis of behavior is prediction and control. In *Science and Human Behavior*, Skinner (1953) describes how prediction and control of an organism's behavior must be done within the confounds of natural sciences, and essentially this could be explained as the Experimental Analysis of Behavior (EAB). The Experimental Analysis of Behavior (EAB) explores the relationship between a dependent variable and an independent variable and its impact on behavior (Skinner, 1966), and is considered one of the branches of behavior analysis (Cooper et al., 2019). EAB dates to the 1930s and includes a set of methods and common subject matter (Lattal, 2013).

Cooper et al. (2019) defines the experimental analysis of behavior (EAB) as a natural science approach to study behavior as a subject in its own right. This natural science approach can differ from other approaches in behavior analysis because it includes basic analysis of scientific principles underlining behavior analysis. Five pillars of EAB include research methods, reinforcement, punishment, control by stimuli correlated with reinforcers and punishers, and contextual and stimulus control (Lattal, 2013). EAB is devoted to assessing the behavior of individual organisms through analysis of basic principles of behavior, including reinforcement, punishment, and matching law. The purpose of this research is to assess these core principles in behavior analysis to determine functional and controlling variables that may have an impact on behavior.

EAB is focused on designing, conducting, interpreting, and reporting on basic experiments (Cooper et al., 2019). EAB is made up of technological research that can then be applied or further investigated through replication and extension. Skinner led the foundation of conducting basic research to assess environmental variables in highly contrived laboratory settings in behavior analysis (Cooper et al., 2019). There are some features that set apart EAB from other branches of behavior analysis. These include rate of responding as a primary dependent variable, repeated and continuous measurement, visual analysis, and functional relations as the outcomes (Cooper et al., 2019). Research in the EAB includes clearly defined independent and dependent variables (Lattal, 2013). Responses can be clearly defined and objective and measurable considering the laboratory setting. These operant responses are simple by design, such as pressing a lever. The use of reinforcement and punishment to increase or decrease behavior are analyzed in contrived scenarios. Schedules of reinforcement are utilized and both antecedent and consequences are manipulated in order to determine what may evoke operant behavior.

This research is advantageous because of how controlled the research can be. Laboratory settings offer highly contrived situations using within subject design where it is unlikely that variables often found in translational and applied settings would arise and confound the study. This research can lead to translational research and applied research that can contribute to society by offering pragmatic technologies to applied settings. It can also further analyze concepts and principles in behavior analysis to build new knowledge and refine previous conceptual analyses. In addition, there may be ability to assess operant behavior in basic settings that may be unethical in applied settings. While ethics of all research is important, if research is being conducted in a clinical setting doing what is best for the client is most important. This can sometimes limit the bounds of applied research, making the trial and error of basic research advantageous. Critics of EAB have said that basic researchers are not always seeking to solve societal problems that can be translated and applied (Critchfield, 2011). Instead, this research is most often focused on theory and fundamental principles of behavior analysis, which is heavily made up of very technical language and complex concept (Critchfield, 2011). These critics recommend an increase in translational research to increase the link between basic science and practice (Critchfield, 2011).

An example of a seminal EAB article is the work done by Hernstein (1961) on concurrent schedules and the matching law. Hernstein (1961) conducted a study using three pigeons, two response keys, and a food hopper that supplied food for the pigeons on controlled schedules. This study made food available on two different variable interval (VI) schedules. The pigeons could switch between the keys throughout the course of the intervals. The results of this study found that the rate of responding percentages of the pigeons matched the reinforcement percentages. This led to the concept of the matching law, where response ratios are a function of reinforcement percentages. This one study led to many other conceptual and theoretical findings that have informed translational and applied research. This research has also informed practice on the use of reinforcement schedules in applied settings.

Translational Research

Discoveries, such as those by Hernstein (1961), must be translated to clinical contexts to determine the extent at which they can improve socially significant human behavior. Translational research is aimed at producing meaningful and applicable results that directly benefit human health (Translational Research Institute, 2022). Translational research takes basic science methodologies and utilizes them in applied settings to show that the results can be accomplished effectively outside of the laboratory. Translational research is bidirectional, meaning basic researchers can also take socially significant issues and study in a basic manner. Explore the addiction literature to see how basic research is exploring overdose issues. In behavior analysis, translational research is often conducted by replicating and extending experimental analyses to applied situations. Blending theory with practice can result in clinical innovations in the field, rather than relying on clinicians and their insights into problems and possible solutions (Critchfield et al. 2015). Blending basic scientific foundations to address clinical problems can lead to technological advancement in the field of behavior analysis.

Translational research can be seen published in the *Journal of Experimental Analysis of Behavior (JEAB)* or *the Journal of Applied Behavior Analysis (JABA),* as well as other academic journals outside of behavior analytic research. For example, *Clinical Pharmacology and Therapeutics* (Zerhouni, 2007), *The Journal of Hepatology* (Nevzorova et al., 2020) and *International Journal of Molecular Sciences* (Rudilosso et al., 2022) all feature articles discussing or presenting results from translational research. Benefits to this research are that applying concepts and outcomes of this research is much easier than experimental analyses. A clinician can take information from applying a concept or principle in behavior analysis to a common problem they face in the clinical world. For example, Mace et al. (2013) analyzed if differential reinforcement of alternative behavior has persistence strengthening effects on clinically significant target behaviors.

Like experimental research, translational research may be highly technical and complex, resulting in difficulty reading and applying the methodologies directly. In addition to this barrier, Critchfield et al. (2015) explained how basic researchers and applied researchers may not engage in one another's work, likely not resulting in much translational research. Even further removed are practitioners who are not engaging in research. There is a need for bidirectional translation, both basic research to applied research but also applied research to basic research. Mahoney et al. (2019) examined self- and cross-citations in the *Journal of Applied Behavior Analysis (JABA)* and the *Journal of Experimental Analysis of Behavior (JEAB).* They found that self-citations were low (*JABA* 40.1%, *JEAB* 28.7%) and cross-citations were even lower (28.7% *JABA* articles had a reference to *JEAB* and 27.5% *JEAB* articles had a reference to *JABA*). Therefore, there is an opportunity to increase the interaction between basic and applied research through translational research in behavior analysis (Mahoney et al., 2019).

While translational research is not in abundance, there is a growing body of literature (Mahoney et al., 2019). For example, Dozier et al. (2012) conducted a study to determine the effectiveness of two pairing procedures, stimulus pairing and response-stimulus pairing to condition praise as a reinforcer. They utilized two stimulus pairing procedures with reinforcement to determine if they could increase target responses. This research expanded upon basic literature in conditioned reinforcement while solving a socially significant problem, that individuals with developmental disabilities may not see praise as a reinforcer. Another translational study by Nevin et al. (2016) assessed the effects of signaled and unsignaled alternative reinforcement on pigeons and children. Through assessment of different reinforcement and extinction contingencies they found that less frequent DRA can reduce relapse, promotes outcomes, and infrequent signaled DRA can be a potential best practice for treatment of severe problem behavior.

Applied Research

Applied research seeks to take knowledge gained and apply or demonstrate its impact towards solving a specific problem (Rubio et al., 2010). Case studies are a type of academic scholarship more commonly seen in other disciplines, such as business and law and policy, however, they are also presented periodically in behavioral research (Crowe et al., 2011). Case studies can be described as an in-depth review of an issue, event, or topic of interest in natural contexts (Crowe et al., 2011). One way case studies can offer clinical insight is by looking at care over time and the factors involved that may contribute to this progress or lack thereof. This usually involves simple data collection methods such as interviews and use of secondary data to review and monitor behavior change over time.

An example of a case study within applied behavior analysis was conducted by Healy et al. (2008). Healy et al. (2008) conducted an evaluation of progress for a client after three years of intensive ABA services. They measured psychological assessments annually over a three-year period to monitor results achieved. They provided information on notes from assessments, summaries and results from psychological testing, minutes in attendance in mainstream classrooms, and raw scores from criterion referenced assessments. This review also included baseline scores in all areas. They demonstrated clinical gains across different skill areas over this time period. This type of scholarship can provide information for the use of multiple evidence-based strategies rather than assessing an isolated or a small treatment package in a short timeframe in typical single subject research.

A second type of applied research includes survey research. Survey research can be defined as a collection of information by asking questions from a sample of individuals (Check & Schutt, 2012). Survey research uses qualitative and/or quantitative research strategies to collect responses about a topic of interest from a sample of a specific population (Ponto, 2015). The foundation of behavior analysis is prediction and control, and observable and measurable behavior (Skinner, 1953). Since survey data are not a direct measure, survey research on its own may not offer as many pragmatic suggestions for practitioners consuming academic scholarship in the field of behavior analysis. However, there are many ways surveys can be included in applied research. For example, to identify a common practice, one might conduct a survey to determine the overall perceived frequency of the practice, as reported by those being surveyed. Additionally, survey research is frequently utilized in a wide variety of fields outside of behavior analysis such as neuropsychology (Marcopulos et al., 2020), otorhinolaryngology (Shakibayi et al., 2019), and educational research (Weatherford & Maitra, 2019)

Survey research allows many ways to recruit participants, collect data, and different methods of instrumentation (Ponto, 2015). Survey research can use both quantitative methods (questionnaire with numerical responses) or qualitative methods (use of open-ended questions), or a blend of both (Ponto, 2015). While surveys are frequently used in social and psychological research (Ponto, 2015), behavior analysis will most often incorporate the use of surveys with other direct types of measurement. Survey methods could be used for analysis of outcomes in social validity and overall satisfaction of results of the procedures. Although other types of research, such as qualitative research, are often used in applied settings, these are less common in fields such as behavior analysis.

Review of Publications

Research Reviews

The increased use of evidence-based practices has led to a variety of review types (Grant & Booth 2009). The use of reviews is observed across disciplines as they provide an overview of the current literature of a particular topic. Due to the rapid rate research is conducted, reviews on available research provide guidance to practitioners and decision makers (Tranfield et al., 2003). Practitioners and clinicians are constantly making decisions that affect the lives of the individuals they serve and their surrounding population. To follow the principle of doing no harm and providing the right support to individuals, these decisions must be based on the most current research. Literature reviews are conducted across disciplines to allow professionals to easily remain up to date with the current research in their fields. It would be nearly impossible for one individual to be fully knowledgeable of all the research on one topic, leading to the rationale and benefits of literature reviews.

Literature reviews are used to synthesize research on a particular topic and provide a comprehensive analysis. In behavior analytic research, the three most common types are narrative review, brief review, and systematic literature review. The type of review conducted will depend on the research question to be answered and the purpose of the research. Each type of review has its place in the literature and there are advantages and disadvantages to each. A literature review aims to answer more general and descriptive research questions. The types of reviews found include narrative review, brief review, systematic literature review, and book review.

Narrative Review

Definition and Purpose

A narrative review is a written document that supports an argument by presenting comprehensive evidence based in the literature to answer the research question regarding a particular area of study (Machi & McEvoy, 2022). This type of review is an older format, compared to a systematic review, as this review provides a summary and analysis on a topic of interest using a non-systematic approach (Gregory & Denniss, 2018). The purpose of a narrative review is to provide information and background of a certain topic to answer a specific research question regarding that topic. The main goal of narrative reviews is to provide the reader with an introduction to the topic and an overview of the literature conducted thus far.

Preparing a Narrative Review

As a narrative review uses a non-systematic approach, there are no formal guidelines to follow when developing this review (Gregory & Denniss, 2018). Generally, the first step of developing a narrative review is to identify the topic of interest and the question to be addressed. This question may stem from your workplace, experiences, or issues in the community. Once the topic is pinpointed, the authors begin gathering articles by searching databases. This search is comprehensive, but not as exhaustive as a systematic literature review. These sources are gathered to make a logical argument for your case using credible evidence and reasonable interpretation that does not exceed the established foundations and principles of the science. The final step is to further analyze the conclusions drawn by finding gaps in the evidence and suggesting alternative arguments. After the analysis is complete, results should be shared with others through publication and presentations (Machi & McEvoy, 2022).

Description and Uses

A narrative is meant to act as an overview of previous work and present a discussion surrounding the current research. The discussion focuses on gaps and limitations in current research, which may provide a rationale for future research. Compared to a systematic literature review, when reporting results of a narrative review, the methods used to gather, select, and evaluate the literature do not need to be described (Cochrane, 2019).

In addition to a narrative review acting on its own, a review may also be integrated into a study by providing context for the area of research (Efron & Ravid, 2018). Any research study will begin with a narrative review that serves as the basis for the current research question and direction of the study. This type of review introduces the research topic by exploring past findings and discussing the current knowledge on the topic. A quality narrative review will present a logical flow to why the current research question needs to be addressed and why the question being addressed is of social significance.

As with any research paper, a narrative review consists of an introduction, methods, results, and discussion (Moller & Myles, 2016). The difference is that the results are from previously published studies. The type of data collected on these included articles will be based on the research question and purpose of the review.

Advantages and Disadvantages

As with all types of work, there are advantages and disadvantages to this category of review. The main advantage to this review is that an overview of previous work on a particular topic is provided, allowing the reader to quickly obtain a summary of research on a topic interest. This type of review does not require a systematic approach to obtaining and analyzing the including articles, suggesting a few disadvantages. As mentioned previously, the search criteria and researcher's reason for conducting the review are unknown to the reader. Due to this lack of selection criteria, there could be biases when gathering research, creating a subjective pool of evidence. It is possible that researchers only selected articles that support their stance and omitted any articles from other parts of the literature (Grant & Booth, 2009). Furthermore, because the authors do not need to report methodology for identifying and collecting articles, the review cannot be replicated (Higgins, 2019).

Examples of Narrative Reviews

Narrative reviews are common across all disciplines as they can assist professionals in remaining up to date with the current research. Shortly after the outbreak of Coronavirus disease 2019 (COVID-19), a narrative review was conducted to summarize available information regarding the pathogen and current epidemic and published in a medical journal (Harapan et al., 2020). To integrate the knowledge on token economies gained from the laboratory and the applied field, a review of literature from both settings was conducted (Hackenberg, 2018). While in early and intensive behavioral intervention (EIBI), it is often recommended to complete receptive language programs before beginning expressive language, there is little evidence to support this. To address this question, a review was conducted on studies that recommend a simultaneous approach to teach receptive and expressive language skills to assess the evidence to support this approach (Petursdottier & Carr, 2011).

Brief Review

Definition

A brief review answers a narrow question including only research from the past five years (JABA). According to the *Journal of Applied Behavior Analysis* (JABA), a brief review is a written document that presents a summary of the recent research on a certain topic and offers areas for future research. Additionally, a brief review is 1200 words or fewer.

Description and Guidelines

As with all journals, there are specific guidelines to be followed for submitting a brief review to JABA. The review should concentrate on studies published in JABA within the previous five years. Before submitting a full manuscript, an abstract and list of references should be sent for review to determine whether this topic is already in press. Because a goal is to provide a timely analysis of recent research, strong attempts are made for the reviews to be published in the next issue.

Advantages and Disadvantages

As previously discussed, there are advantages and disadvantages to this type of review as well. This review covers recent literature within the past five years, providing the most up-to-date information. Because a goal is providing readers with the current research, an expedited review process is generally provided. Additional advantages include providing a brief, easy-to-read summary of a topic, allowing readers to navigate the current research quickly, and presenting a synthesis of current research on a narrow topic of interest. On the other hand, the most significant drawback is the review only covers five years, excluding the history and evolution of the research topic.

Examples of Brief Reviews

Brief reviews are also common across fields as they provide a succinct literature review on the most recent research on a particular topic. For professionals interested in a certain topic, brief reviews provide a short overview with relevant research. In the medical field, to examine the role the placebo effect plays in sports medicine, a brief review containing 12 articles was conducted (Beadie & Foad, 2009). Results from this review indicate psychological variables, including motivation, expectancy, and conditioning may contribute to the effects of medicine.

In behavior analysis, research over a span of five years was reviewed to assess the studies conducted on dementia in older adults published in JABA (Trahan et al., 2011). To address the socially significant issue of obesity, a brief review was conducted on behavior analytic research focused on interventions to increase physical activity and measurements systems for tracking physical activity (Van Camp & Hayes, 2012). With the increased use of technology to implement interventions across contexts, a brief review was conducted on technology-based training procedures.

Within the field of organizational behavior management, a review was conducted on the use of the Performance Diagnostic Checklist-Human Services (Wilder et al., 2020). This instrument is used to pinpoint variables that may contribute to poor employee performance and ultimately improve productivity in the workplace. Results of this review provide employers with an evidence-based tool to assess concerns in the workplace and implement strategies to increase desirable workplace behavior.

Systematic Literature Reviews

A systematic literature review is taking a systematic methodology (collecting, evaluating and presenting results) to assess multiple research studies in a specific area of interest (Pati & Lorusso, 2018). A systematic literature review (SLR) attempts to answer a more scientific question and provide a more comprehensive analysis when compared to a brief review. A systematic literature review collects all available evidence within predetermined inclusion and exclusion criteria to answer a specific research question regarding a topic of interest. The researcher uses systematic methods to provide an objective analysis of the included research, leading to more reliable conclusions regarding the topic. These methods include identifying a specific research question, specifying the range of the review, creating inclusion and exclusion criteria to determine eligibility of articles, searching for all relevant research without any bias, analyzing all research in an objective manner.

Purpose and Goals

Conducting an SLR allows researchers to develop more educated research questions by presenting results of current research and the limitations that still exist in the literature. The main purpose of a systematic literature review is to provide a comprehensive analysis of the current research in a particular topic to answer a specific clinical question. A few goals of an SLR systematic literature reviews are to provide results from the existing literature, identify limitations that still exist in this research area, and to present directions for future research.

Description

Systematic literature reviews were first initiated in the field of medicine and are associated with furthering evidence-based practices. Beginning in the 1990s, the medical field attempted to improve the quality of literature reviews by using a systematic, transparent, and reproducible method to collect and analyze current research (Tranfield et al., 2003). Specifically, a systematic literature review requires a clear approach to selecting articles within the literature to minimize the potential for bias and subjective results (Tranfield et al., 2003). This systematic method has since been adopted by other fields, including organizations such as The National Health Science Centre or Reviews and Dissemination (2001) and the National Institute for Clinical Excellence (2001).

Preparation

Similar to the previous types of reviews, the first step of a systematic literature review is to identify a particular area of study and develop a specific research question. These research questions should be detailed and attempt to answer a socially significant issue. Once the questions have been identified, a search strategy, inclusion criteria, and exclusion criteria need to be developed. Following which a search of the literature is conducted using the pre-developed method. Articles are then screened for initial eligibility usually through reviewing the title and abstracts. After which those articles are screened again by reviewing the full text to make a final determination for eligibility. Data collected from those articles are then synthesized and results are summarized based on the predetermined reporting methods.

Results of an SLR can be analyzed quantitatively or qualitatively. A qualitative review will summarize and interpret data collected from the studies included in the review and usually be displayed in a table. The information will be analyzed such that the meanings and implications can be presented. Qualitative results are presented in text summaries, while quantitative results will report using numbers and/or graphs. A quantitative review will still summarize and interpret the data collected from the included studies but will use quantitative analyses, such as statistical methods, to analyze and report the results.

PRISMA

Preferred Reporting Items for Systematic Reviews and Meta-Analyses (PRISMA) is an evidence-based protocol for reporting systematic literature reviews and meta-analyses. The primary use of this system is for reporting effects of interventions within reviews, but also can serve as the foundation for reviews that focus on alternative research questions. PRISMA is designed to assist authors enhance how they report results of their review and how peer reviewers and editors critique submitted reviews for publication. In 2009, a previously developed guideline, Quality of

Reporting Meta-analyses (QUOROM), was updated to reflect advances in systematic reviews and renamed PRISMA. Recent updates have been made to remain up to date with any changes in methodology and terminology within systematic reviews. Visual tools, including a checklist and flowchart, are available on the PRISMA website that can be viewed easily. These tools provide the basis for how to begin the search process, identify sources, screen obtained works, assess for eligibility, determine if inclusion criteria are met, assess results, report results, interpret findings, discuss limitations, and consider implications for practice and research and identify future directions for research.

Advantages and Disadvantages

There are many advantages to a systematic literature review. Specific methods are used to identify eligibility of articles and how those studies are selected, which are reported in the published manuscript. This reporting allows readers to critique the process used and allows for replication of the review. The methodological approach allows others to replicate the review process. This replicability also removes potential bias when obtaining articles, which provides a more thorough and objective analysis of the current literature.

While there are numerous advantages to systematic literature reviews, there are a few disadvantages to note. The goal of a systematic literature review is to answer a specific research question, which yields a narrow scope of the research and only provides support for the specific question asked. Therefore, additional questions related to the research area are not addressed and may require the reader to conduct additional research on that topic.

Examples

Systematic literature reviews are conducted across scientific fields as they provide the reader with a more comprehensive overview of all the literature on a certain topic. Systematic literature reviews have been conducted to assess the systematic literatures conducted on medical topics. A systematic literature review was published in 2017 of reviews on exercise in the cancer literature. The top cited systematic literature reviews in tuberculosis research were examined in a review to identify the most frequently cited works and establish trends in the literature (Zhang et al., 2017). Another systematic literature review focused on mindfulness practices for healthcare providers (Gilmartin et al., 2017).

In the field of psychology, an SLR was conducted on parent-based interventions for preventing and minimizing adolescent substance abuse (Kuntsche & Kuntsche, 2016). To better understand psychology practice in hospitals and provide models for future training and care, a review was conducted on the evolution of hospital practices from 1916 to 2017 (Kidd et al., 2020). Findings of this review provided an in-depth analysis of psychology in hospitals over 100 years and suggestions for best practices and policy changes.

In the education field, a review was conducted on the challenges to designing a blended learning environment within schools (Boelens et al., 2017). Interventions and methods behind teaching interactions should evolve over time and change to address the needs of the students. Another review examined empirical evidence for establishing creative learning environments, including the use flexible space, workspaces outside of the classroom, peer collaboration, and game-based approaches, providing implications for practice and directions for future research (Davies et al., 2013).

In behavior analysis, a review of all school-based experimental studies including students aged 0–18 published in JABA between 1991 and 2005 was conducted to evaluate the reporting of treatment integrity data (McIntyre et al., 2007). To identify the current knowledge and existing literature on the use of multiple schedules, as well as to provide implications for future use, a review on multiple schedules used to gain stimulus control over relevant responses in children of typical development and those with intellectual and developmental disabilities was conducted (Saini et al., 2016). Additionally, a meta-analysis of the use of non-contingent reinforcement on decreasing problem behavior was conducted by obtaining data and calculating the effect sizes of 55 studies (Richman et al., 2015).

To identify the extent to which determining the function of verbal behavior of children with autism would be beneficial, a brief review was performed. Research on functional analyses on verbal behavior was analyzed to provide guidelines for teaching procedures and directions for future research (Plavnick & Normand, 2013).

Within behavior analysis research, there is an area of study devoted to sports. To analyze current trends in studies on sports performance in youth, collegiate, and elite athletes, a review of translational and applied research was conducted (Luiselli et al., 2011). In the area of organization behavior management (OBM), a systematic review was conducted to understand the relationship between work and suicide by identifying studies that evaluate each to better integrate these two literature bases.

Conclusion

While there are several types of systematic literature reviews, each will provide an overview of literature on a specified topic. The type of review will dictate the method for obtaining and analyzing the results while the research question will suggest which type of review should be conducted. Researchers and practitioners need to remain up to date on the current literature to provide high-quality services and make evidence-based decisions. Reviews are an efficient way for professionals to assess the current literature and be aware of effective practices in a particular area of study.

Book Reviews

When an author publishes their book, it likely comes with a sense of accomplishment and pride that their work is now out for the world to see. However, not all books make valid scientific claims and not all books provide meaningful contributions to their subject or field. How would an author know that their contribution is seen, heard, or even understood? A book review is an excellent way for the author to know the impact, or message, the audience is likely to receive from their book. The purpose of a book review is to describe and evaluate the author's content, quality, and the significance of their book (Lee et al., 2010). To get a true assessment of the content, it is important that the reviewer be an expert with knowledge and experience in the subject, or topic, of the book (Gombeyaz, 2019).

A book review can benefit the author, reviewer, and the audience. A positive book review puts a spotlight on the author's work, potentially gaining more trust from the audience or reaching a new or unintended audience (Obeng-Odoom, 2014). The author's reputation as a writer or even within the topic the book was written about also stands to improve with a positive book review. Even a negative book review has a benefit to the author. Suggestions, faults, or inaccuracies identified in the book review can be considered when developing future editions of the book, supporting the author's success in that specific topic (Lee et al., 2010). For the reviewer, reviewing books gives the opportunity to strengthen important writing and critical thinking skills while also receiving a publishing credit which enhances their resume (Heyd, 2017). The audience benefits from book reviews as reviews can guide their decision-making with regard to what they read. The book review gives the audience information and an assessment of the book, to let the audience decide if it meets their reading preferences. This can help the audience avoid books that may not interest them and, as mentioned before, may guide the audience to a book they would not have previously considered.

For the field of behavior analysis, book reviews are not very common. For example, a keyword search of all issues of the *Journal for Applied Behavior Analysis* between the years 2012–2022 revealed a total of six book reviews published. For reference, each issue can publish anywhere from 15 to over 25 articles with four issues published annually. As the field of behavior analysis grows and continues to develop in different applications, the number of books written should be increasing as well. Thus, increasing the need for book reviews to be completed. The completion of book reviews will help highlight and develop (through critiques) various aspects of applied behavior analysis, moving our field further into relevance and application.

With so few examples and no clear definitive guidelines on how to write a book review, it can be daunting to think of how or where to start. Prior to writing the review, there are factors to consider regarding the book selection or how best to evaluate the book's contents. The following recommendations are suggested as a guide for the writer to create a meaningful book review.

Selection of the Book to Review

Any book selected for a book review should be carefully selected or considered by the writer. If the writer selects a book too quickly or without much consideration, they run the risk of complications further along in the process that will likely slow the progress down or result in abandonment of the review. To promote success, the writer should consider if they are part of the targeted audience for that book. The writer should have some connection to the material and contents in the book, whether that be expertise in the topic or invested in the opinion (or opposing opinion) expressed. The connection to the material will be significant when evaluating the contents and providing suggestions.

Reading and Evaluating the Book

It is recommended that the writer read and evaluate the book at the same time through active reading to encourage understanding of the messages and concepts that are being outlined by the author. Typically, the book being reviewed will fall into one of two categories opinionated books or subject/topic specific books. Opinionated books have a goal of convincing the audience of a specific thought whereas subject, or topic-specific, books have a goal of informing the audience of a subject or topic.

For books where the main message is expressing an opinion, the writer will want to understand and be able to articulate the main messages or arguments the author is trying to express. The writer should also evaluate how the author supported their opinion. This can be done by making a list or noting the supporting arguments or points made by the author throughout the book. An evaluation of the argument should be conducted by the writer to determine if the author effectively communicated their opinion or stance to the audience.

For books where the main message is informing the audience about a specific subject or topic, the writer should be assessing if the author was able to demonstrate their expertise in the topic. An assessment of whether the author covers all aspects of the topic necessary to fulfill the book's educational purpose should be completed. It would also be important for the writer to note what approach the author used to communicate the information and if it was the most appropriate approach to effectively communicate the message. The evaluation by the writer would determine if the book was effective in helping others learn more about the subject or specific topic.

Researching Outside Factors

Once the evaluation of the book has been complete, the writer should then conduct their own research on outside factors that could have contributed to the content of the book. Conducting author-specific research could provide insight into how the author formed their opinions or supported their arguments. Common research items could be where the author is from, their educational background, their work history, etc. All the author's experiences may have contributed to their view and the content listed in the book. Identifying those connections in the book review will help the audience understand the author's purpose and intentions with the book.

Conducting subject-specific research will help the writer become more familiar with the topic, or subject, to effectively evaluate if the author was successful in informing the audience about the topic. Researching the topic may also result in additional suggestions or informational misses for the author or audience to consider.

Writing the Review

When the writer has finished assessing and evaluating the book and completing any additional research called for, the next step is to start writing the review. The review should be written in an accessible way that does not assume the reader has specialized knowledge in this specific opinion or subject/specific topic (George & Dharmadhikari, 2008). When structuring the flow of the review, it is most common for book reviews to follow a relatively simple four-section format: introduction, summarization, evaluation and conclusion. This allows the audience to follow the writer through the review and organize the information the writer wants to present.

The introduction should introduce the topic or main message of the book. The introduction is not meant to be robust, but rather short and to the point to provide the audience an idea of what the book was trying to communicate and what to expect from the review. The reviewer should then summarize the main points of the book that supported the author's argument, or the information given about the subject. This summarization should explain to the audience what type of information they can expect to gain from the book. The evaluation section can be written more subjectively than the introduction and summarization, as it is here where the reviewer is able to voice their opinions and evaluation of the author's book. In this section, the writer should give their analysis of the author's message and if the author had successfully reached their goal of communicating that message. Outside research regarding the author or the subject itself is presented to support the argument the writer is intending to make regarding the contents of the book. The conclusion is a short summary of the main message of the book along with a short summary of the writer's arguments. The writer may note or offer suggestions to the author to support the further development of the argument or subject. A recommendation from the writer may also be made regarding the type of audience that would benefit from reading the book.

Conclusion

Book reviews can benefit all parties involved (reviewer, author and audience). The above recommended process is one way to structure a book review. However, there may be additional requirements depending on where the review is to be published. The reviewer should always consider the publisher, or at least be prepared to alter some parts of their book review to meet the standards required for publishing.

The opportunity to write a book review may be something an individual decides to take on or is asked to take on. Authors or publishers may reach out to individuals requesting they complete a book review, in hopes it will support their message and put a spotlight on their work. When contemplating writing a book review, it is important to consider the above process and assess the commitment involved prior to agreeing to write one.

Summary

The purpose of the preceding chapter was to introduce the reader to a sampling of key methodologies in behavioral science and to the ways these different types of scholarly pursuits may be disseminated. One of the most important considerations for disseminating science is that the dissemination should highlight the empirical nature of what is being discussed. Attempts at the dissemination of science are often met with critiques of what is presented, with the focus on what is weakest about the study, research, etc. This is an optimistic thing for science to address because unlike philosophical, political, or personal beliefs, science relies on observation and measurement. Additionally, science has a self-correcting mechanism in the replication and extension of research so that future researchers can focus their efforts on improving on what has been done in the past. The preceding chapter offers an overview of some common methodologies related to conducting research. It is our hope that the reader is more prepared to interact with research and disseminate it in an effective way because of the time and attention paid to this material.

References

Beedie, C. J., & Foad, A. J. (2009). The placebo effect in sports performance: A brief review. *Sports Medicine, 39*(4), 313–329. https://doi.org/10.2165/00007256-200939040-00004

Boelens, R., De Wever, B., & Voet, M. (2017). Four key challenges to the design of blended learning: A systematic literature review. *Educational Research Review, 22*, 1–18. https://doi.org/10.1016/j.edurev.2017.06.001

Check, J., & Schutt, R. K. (2012). Survey research. In J. Check & R. K. Schutt (Eds.), *Research methods in education* (pp. 159–185). Sage Publications.

Cooper, J. O., Heron, T. E., & Heward, W. L. (2019). *Applied behavior analysis* (3rd ed.). Pearson Education.

Critchfield, T. S. (2011). Translational contributions of the experimental analysis of behavior. *The Behavior Analyst, 34*, 3–17. https://doi.org/10.1007/BF03392231

Critchfield, T. S., Doepke, K. J., & Campbell, R. L. (2015). Origins of clinical innovations: Why practice needs science and how science reaches practice. In F. D. DiGennaro Reed & D. D. Reed (Eds.), *Autism service delivery* (pp. 1–23). Springer New York.

Crowe, S., Cresswell, K., Robertson, A., Huby, G., Avery, A. J., & Sheikh, A. (2011). The case study approach. *BMC Medical Research Methodology, 11*(1), 100–100. https://doi.org/10.1186/1471-2288-11-100

Davies, D., Jindal-Snape, D., Collier, C., Digby, R., Hay, P., & Howe, A. (2013). Creative learning environments in education—A systematic literature review. *Thinking Skills and Creativity, 8*, 80–91. https://doi.org/10.1016/j.tsc.2012.07.004

Dozier, C. L., Iwata, B. A., Thomasson-Sassi, J., Worsdell, A. S., & Wilson, D. M. (2012). A comparison of two pairing procedures to establish praise as a reinforcer. *Journal of Applied Behavior Analysis, 45*(4), 721–735. https://doi.org/10.1901/jaba.2012.45-721

Efron, S. E., & Ravid, R. (2018). *Writing the literature review: A practical guide.* Guilford Publications.

George, S., & Dharmadhikari, A. (2008). Writing a book review: Frequently asked questions answered. *British Journal of Hospital Medicine, 69*(2), M30–M31. https://doi.org/10.12968/hmed.2008.69.Sup2.28370

Gilmartin, H., Goyal, A., Hamati, M. C., Mann, J., Saint, S., & Chopra, V. (2017). Brief mindfulness practices for healthcare providers – A systematic literature review. *The American Journal of Medicine, 130*(10), 1219.e1–1219.e17. https://doi.org/10.1016/j.amjmed.2017.05.041

Gombeyaz, K. (2019). A guide for book reviews. *ULUM, 2*(1), 169–175. https://doi.org/10.5281/zenodo.3358594

Grant, M. J., & Booth, A. (2009). A typology of reviews: An analysis of 14 review types and associated methodologies. *Health Information and Libraries Journal, 26*(2), 91–108. https://doi.org/10.1111/j.1471-1842.2009.00848.x

Gregory, A. T., & Denniss, A. R. (2018). An introduction to writing narrative and systematic reviews--tasks tips, and traps for aspiring authors. *Heart Lung and Circulation, 27*(7), 893–898. https://doi.org/10.1016/j.hlc.2018.03.027

Hackenberg, T. (2018). Token reinforcement: Translational research and application. *Journal of Applied Behavior Analysis, 51*(2), 393–435. https://doi.org/10.1002/jaba.439

Harapan, H., Itoh, N., Yufika, A., Winardi, W., Keam, S., Te, H., Megawati, D., Hayati, Z., Wagner, A. L., & Mudatsir, M. (2020). Coronavirus disease 2019 (COVID-19): A literature review. *Journal of Infection and Public Health, 13*(5), 667–673. https://doi.org/10.1016/j.jiph.2020.03.019

Healy, O., O'Connor, J., Leader, G., & Kenny, N. (2008). Three years of intensive applied behavior analysis: A case study. *Journal of Early and Intensive Behavior Intervention, 5*(1), 4–22. https://doi.org/10.1037/h0100407

Hernstein, R. J. (1961). Relative and absolute strength of response as a function of frequency of reinforcement. *Journal of Experimental Analysis of Behavior, 4*(ISSUE), 267–272. https://doi.org/10.1901/jeab.1961.4-267

Heyd, M. (2017). How to write a book review- And why you should. *Journal of Hospital Librarianship, 17*(4), 349–355. https://doi.org/10.1080/15323269.2017.1366783

Higgins, J. (2019). *Cochrane handbook for systematic reviews of interventions* (J. Higgins, Ed.; 2nd ed.). Wiley-Blackwell.

Kidd, S. A., Styron, T. H., & Kazak, A. E. (2020). A systematic review of the psychology literature addressing hospital practice. *The American Psychologist, 75*(3), 316–328. https://doi.org/10.1037/amp0000498

Kuntsche, S., & Kuntsche, E. (2016). Parent-based interventions for preventing or reducing adolescent substance use — A systematic literature review. *Clinical Psychology Review, 45*, 89–101. https://doi.org/10.1016/j.cpr.2016.02.004

Lattal, K. A. (2013). The five pillars of the experimental analysis of behavior. In G. J. Madden (Ed.), *APA handbook of behavior analysis: Vol. 1. Methods and principles* (pp. 33–64). American Psychological Association.

Lee, A. D., Green, B. N., Johnson, C. D., & Nyguist, J. (2010). How to write a scholarly book review for publication in a peer-reviewed journal: A review of the literature. *The Journal of Chiropractic Education, 24*(1), 57–69. https://doi.org/10.7899/1042-5055-24.1.57

Luiselli, J. K., Woods, K. E., & Reed, D. D. (2011). Review of sports performance research with youth, collegiate, and elite athletes. *Journal of Applied Behavior Analysis, 44*(4), 999–1002. https://doi.org/10.1901/jaba.2011.44-999

Mahoney, A., Li, A., Curiel, H., Plattner, C., & Poling, A. (2019). Self-and cross-citations in the Journal of Applied Behavior Analysis and the Journal of the Experimental Analysis of Behavior: 2004-2018. *Journal of applied behavior analysis, 52(4), 1130-1139.* https://doi.org/10.1002/jaba.585

Mace, F. C., McComas, J. J., Mauro, B. C., Progar, P. R., Taylor, B., Ervin, R., & Zangrillo, A. N. (2013). Differential reinforcement of alternative behavior increases resistance to extinction: Clinical demonstration, animal modeling, and clinical test of one solution. *Journal of the Experimental Analysis of Behavior, 93*(3), 349–367. https://doi.org/10.1901/jeab.2010.93-349

Machi, L. A., & McEvoy, B. T. (2022). *The literature review: Six steps to success.* Corwin Press, ProQuest Ebook Central. https://ebookcentral.proquest.com/lib/tcsesl/detail. action?docID=6807758

Marcopulos, B. A., Guterbock, T. M., & Matusz, E. F. (2020). Survey research in neuropsychology: A systematic review. *The Clinical Neuropsychologist, 34*(1), 32–55.

McIntyre, L. L., Gresham, F. M., DiGennaro, F. D., & Reed, D. D. (2007). Treatment integrity of school-based interventions with children in the journal of applied behavior analysis 1991-2005. *Journal of Applied Behavior Analysis, 40*(4), 659–672. https://doi.org/10.1901/jaba.2007.659-672

Moller, A. M., & Myles, P. S. (2016). What makes a good systematic review and meta-analysis? *British Journal of Anaesthesia., 117*(4), 428–430. https://doi.org/10.1093/bja/aew264

Nevin, J. A., Mace, F. C., DeLeon, I. G., Shahan, T. A., Shamlian, K. D., Lit, K., et al. (2016). Effects of signaled and unsignaled alternative reinforcement on persistence and relapse in children and pigeons. *Journal of the Experimental Analysis of Behavior, 106*, 34–57. https://doi.org/10.1002/jeab.213

Nevzorova, Y. A., Boyer-Diaz, Z., Cubero, F. J., & Gracia-Sancho, J. (2020). Animal models for liver disease–a practical approach for translational research. *Journal of Hepatology, 73*(2), 423–440.

Obeng-Odoom, F. (2014). Why write book reviews? *Australian Universities' Review, 56*(1), 78–82. https://doi.org/10.3316/aeipt.201728

Pati, D., & Lorusso, L. N. (2018). How to write a systematic review of the literature. *HERD, 11*(1), 15–30. https://doi.org/10.1177/1937586717747384

Petursdottir, A. I., & Carr, J. E. (2011). A review of recommendations for sequencing receptive and expressive language instruction. *Journal of Applied Behavior Analysis, 44*(4), 859–876. https://doi.org/10.1901/jaba.2011.44-859

Plavnick, J. B., & Normand, M. P. (2013). Functional analysis of verbal behavior: A brief review. *Journal of Applied Behavior Analysis, 46*(1), 349–353. https://doi.org/10.1002/jaba.1

Ponto, J. (2015). Understanding and evaluating survey research. *Journal of the Advanced Practitioner in Oncology, 6*(2), 168–171.

Richman, D. M., Barnard-Brak, L., Grubb, L., Bosch, A., & Abby, L. (2015). Meta-analysis of noncontingent reinforcement effects on problem behavior. *Journal of Applied Behavior Analysis, 48*(1), 131–152. https://doi.org/10.1002/jaba.189

Rudilosso, S., Rodríguez-Vázquez, A., Urra, X., & Arboix, A. (2022). The potential impact of neu-roimaging and translational research on the clinical management of lacunar stroke. International *journal of molecular sciences, 23(3), 1497*. https://doi.org/10.3390/ijms23031497

Rubio, M. D., Schoenbaum, E. E., Schteingart, D. E., Marantz, P. R., Anderson, K. E., Platt, L. D., Baez, A., & Esposito, K. (2010). Defining translational research: Implications for training. *Academic Medicine, 85*(3), 470–475. https://doi.org/10.1097/ACM.0b013e3181ccd618

Saini, V., Miller, S. A., & Fisher, W. W. (2016). Multiple schedules in practical application: Research trends and implications for future investigation. *Journal of Applied Behavior Analysis, 49*(2), 421–444. https://doi.org/10.1002/jaba.300

Shakibayi, M. I., Zarifian, T., & Zanjari, N. (2019). Speech characteristics of childhood apraxia of speech: A survey research. *International Journal of Pediatric Otorhinolaryngology, 126*, 109609.

Skinner, B. F. (1953). *Science and human behavior*. Macmillan.

Skinner, B. F. (1966). What is the experimental analysis of behavior? *Journal of the Experimental Analysis of Behavior, 9*(3), 213–218. https://doi.org/10.1901/jeab.1966.9-213

Trahan, M. A., Kahng, S., Fisher, A. B., & Hausman, N. L. (2011). Behavior-analytic research on dementia in older adults. *Journal of Applied Behavior Analysis, 44*(3), 687–691. https://doi.org/10.1901/jaba.2011.44-687

Tranfield, D., Denyer, D., & Smart, P. (2003). Towards a methodology for developing evidence-informed management knowledge by means of systematic review. *British Journal of Management, 14*(3), 207–222. https://doi.org/10.1111/1467-8551.00375

Translational Research Institute. (2022). *What is translational research?* Retrieved from: https://tri.uams.edu/about-tri/what-is-translational-research/

Van Camp, C. M., & Hayes, L. B. (2012). Assessing and increasing physical activity. *Journal of Applied Behavior Analysis, 45*(4), 871–875. https://doi.org/10.1901/jaba.2012.45-871

Weatherford, J., & Maitra, D. (2019). How online students approach bracketing: A survey research study. *Educational Research: Theory and Practice, 30*(2), 91–102.

Wilder, D. A., Cymbal, D., & Villacorta, J. (2020). The performance diagnostic checklist-human services: A brief review. *Journal of Applied Behavior Analysis, 53*(2), 1170–1176. https://doi.org/10.1002/jaba.676

Zerhouni, E. A. (2007). Translational research: Moving discovery to practice. *Clinical Pharmacology & Therapeutics, 81*(1), 126–128.

Zhang, Y., Huang, J., & Du, L. (2017). The top-cited systematic reviews/meta-analyses in tuber-culosis research: A PRISMA-compliant systematic literature review and bibliometric analysis. *Medicine (Baltimore), 96*(6), –e4822. https://doi.org/10.1097/MD.0000000000004822

Dr. Willow Hozella is currently a Board-Certified Behavior Analyst (at the doctoral level) and Clinical Director at May Institute. Prior to joining the May Institute, Dr. Hozella served as an educational consultant for the Pennsylvania Training and Technical Assistance Network's Autism Initiative and School Wide Positive Behavior Support Initiative for 12 years, consulting in public school classrooms to train staff to utilize the concepts and principles of ABA in their instructional practice. Dr. Hozella has disseminated his work on a wide array of topics ranging from strategies to reduce problem behavior to teaching complex verbal behavior to individuals with autism.

Dr. Rachael Schneider is a Board-Certified Behavior Analyst, working with individuals with autism spectrum disorder and developmental disabilities across the lifespan. She recently completed her doctoral degree in applied behavior analysis at The Chicago School.

Jane Tammik   is a Board-Certified Behavior Analyst. She is currently completing her doctoral degree in applied behavior analysis at The Chicago School.

Brittany Beaver   is a Board-Certified Behavior Analyst and Clinical Supervisor at Achieve Beyond, supervising services for clients aged birth to 21. In 2015, she earned her Master of Arts degree in applied behavior analysis from Caldwell University, and she is currently working towards a PhD at the Chicago School. She has disseminated her work through publication and presentations at local and national conferences.

Chapter 2
Types of Dissemination

Susan Flynn, Lucas Evans, and Henry Sessanga

As you develop into a scientist and/or a practitioner, you will have an ethical (Behavior Analyst Certification Board, 2020) and professional obligation (Friman, 2014; Heward et al., 2022; Morris, 1985, 2014; Schillinger, 2010) to disseminate information to the public. Effective dissemination is a matter of effective behavior: the effective behavior of the disseminator to motivate, teach, or signal the effective behavior of the consumer. While this should be in the wheelhouse of behavioral health scientists and practitioners, effective dissemination has been a shortcoming and critical need (Becirevic et al., 2016; Critchfield & Doepke, 2018; Foxx, 1996; Lindsley, 1991; though see Normand & Donohue, 2022 for a counterpoint regarding the use technical jargon) that has real-world impact on those that need related services. For example, in the field of applied behavior analysis, dissemination impacts the consumers of the services (Chadwell et al., 2019) together with the policies that govern the practice (*Position Statement on the Use of CESS – 2022 – Association for Behavior Analysis International*, n.d.; *Resolution Opposing Applied Behavioral Analysis (ABA)*, 2021). In addition, professionals in any field are obliged to disseminate current information amongst their peers (e.g., Heward et al., 2022).

When you complete your manuscript, research study, or project, the next step is to disseminate what you have learned to the public. Accurate dissemination of your work is crucial. In particular, sharing your findings with the research community and relevant stakeholders potentially guides future research studies and affects

S. Flynn (✉)
Behavior Analysis Department, College of Graduate and Professional Studies
at The Chicago School, Chicago, IL, USA
e-mail: sflynn@thechicagoschool.edu

L. Evans
Missouri Department of Mental Health, Jefferson City, MO, USA

H. Sessanga
Speech, Language, and Educational Associates, Encino, CA, USA

© The Author(s), under exclusive license to Springer Nature Switzerland AG 2023   25
A. K. Griffith, T. C. Ré (eds.), *Disseminating Behavioral Research*,
https://doi.org/10.1007/978-3-031-47343-2_2

practice. Dissemination of research findings is critical in bridging the gap between research knowledge and practice, and it should be planned to ensure that the intended information is what the target audience receives.

There are various avenues through which to distribute your research. Some of the avenues are informal (e.g., conversations with your peers or colleagues, sharing your research findings with families), and others are more formal. Some formal avenues, the focus of this chapter, include publishing and presenting your research. These include publishing peer-reviewed and non-peer-reviewed journal articles, making poster presentations, undertaking conference session presentations, and disseminating through the media. This chapter describes each of these briefly and is meant as an introduction for the remainder of the book.

Publishing in Journals

Conducting research and learning something relevant to your field is a major accomplishment, and the results should be shared with the public. One of the best methods to disseminate your research is publishing in journals. Journals differ in terms of types of papers that are published, consumers of the material, types of accepted research methods, and quality. The first step in the publishing process is to select a journal for submission, based on these factors.

After selecting the journal, you then examine it for key information on guidelines for submitting articles for publication. This examination can be done by looking at a recent issue of the journal and scanning a similar article, and by reviewing the guidelines for authors section that is contained in the journal's editorial section. It is important to note that often you will have to meet certain page number restrictions, which means that you will likely have to trim down your thesis or dissertation to meet these requirements.

In preparing for submission, you will need to carefully follow the current American Psychological Association (APA) style manual and the journal's editorial guidelines. It is a good idea to have someone who is not familiar with your transcript to read it before it is submitted to the journal. After preparing your manuscript, the next step is to submit it together with a cover letter to the editor. Usually, the editor will notify you (the author) via email when the manuscript has been received.

The journal editor will scan the manuscript to see if it is suitable for publication in the journal. If the manuscript is deemed suitable, the editor will send the manuscript to three to five individuals to review the content for suitability. This is a type of professional peer review, and this process is typically conducted as a blind review (i.e., the reviewer cannot see who the authors are, as there is no identifying information provided to them). Following the review, a decision will be reached, and this may be one of the following: Accept the manuscript as is, accept the manuscript subject to revisions, reject the manuscript but invite resubmission, or reject the manuscript. The decision made by the reviewer(s) along with the reviewers' comments is communicated to the author by the editor via a letter. More detail on publishing is included in Chaps. 10, 11, 12, and 13.

Presenting

In addition to seeking publication of your research, you can consider presenting it to an audience. Presenting at a conference, whether local, national, or international – is an exciting opportunity. There are some things that you can do prior to and during the conference to make a great presentation. Preparations you can undertake may include ensuring that your slides are readable (e.g., not too much text), and rehearsing your presentation in front of your friends/colleagues or even in front of a mirror will assist you in having a successful and smooth presentation.

During the conference, it is important to dress as a professional (note that some conferences are more casual than others) and to find your presentation room in advance. You should present your research with thoroughness and integrity. More detail on conference and poster presentations is provided in Chap. 14. Below is a brief description of each type of conference presentation.

Conference Session Presentations

A conference session presentation will include the same components presented in your written study report/manuscript: Title, abstract, introduction, method, results, and discussion. This type of presentation opportunity can be either a result of a peer-reviewed proposal process, or as an invited speaker/keynote presentation. Typically, during the presentation, you present your study and answer questions within your allocated time.

Conference session presentations can also be a part of a symposium (i.e., a group of presentations that present research on a similar topic). This format reduces the amount of time in which you present, but you still follow the structure of an individual presentation. During these presentations, a session chair introduces the study, introduces the speaker, manages timing, and ends the session. In addition, there is often a discussant who summarizes the presenter's research findings.

Poster Presentations

Poster presentations at conferences provide an opportunity to disseminate studies in a way that is typically less "scary" than a conference session presentation. There is usually a general time slot during which conference attendees can view and listen to multiple poster presentations.

When presenting a poster, you prepare a visual display of the study (typically a printout of a PowerPoint slide) and stand near it. The visual display has the same sections (i.e., headings) as the written study report (and the conference session presentation as previously described). Conference attendees (e.g., professors, students, practitioners) walk by, look at the poster, read the information, and may ask questions. As the poster author, you need to prepare to give a 2- to 3-minute overview of your study. Furthermore, you should prepare handouts or include a QR code with the main points of your study, including references and your contact information for conference attendees who want more information. This format allows for brief conversations, as well as extended conversations with those who are extremely interested in your topic and study.

Peer Review Versus Non-peer Review

What Is Peer Review?

Peer review is a process in which your work is reviewed by professional peers who are subject matter experts in the area of your work or areas related to your work. Peer reviewers evaluate your work for its validity and significance. Peer reviewers are often peers within your discipline but may also be peers from related disciplines. For example, if a paper is written about an intervention within special education, the expectation is that individuals with a record of accomplishment of excellence in special education would review the work before it is accepted for publication. The idea is that through this scrutiny only verifiable findings that add significantly to the scientific knowledge base are recommended for publication to the public through scientific journals. Through this process, the quality of your scholarly works improves and offers credence to new knowledge production.

Peer review should serve as a tempering factor on any of the overstated conclusions, unwarranted extrapolations, conflation of association with causality, unsupported clinical recommendations, and spin that you may have inputted in your work, which often have negative impacts on the well-being of the community you serve. The peer-review process does not change the direction of your study, the hypothesis, or the study design, but it frequently improves your communication. There could be circumstances when the review leads to a need for you to revise or reverse research interpretations and recommendations. All such endeavors are aimed at enhancing the understanding of the readers of your published material and the population that is served. Consequently, material that is peer reviewed is often trusted by your readers, if they are aware of the stringent processes of an ideal review process.

However, like all systems, the peer-review process is fallible. Though the process is considered the gatekeeper of science, it is considered to move at a slow pace when compared with the rapid progress in research (Stahel & Moore, 2014). Among the challenges faced in the review process are situations when reviewers assess with unconscious biases (although blind reviews can often address these biases). Often, there is a tendency to view positive results as the correct outcomes and more exciting than negative results, often leading to a skew in the material that is recommended for publication. When your research outcomes present findings that are contrary to the norm, or if they are unique, there is a tendency for such material to be dismissed. Take note that the process can be skewed by the subjective views of the reviewers hence an inconsistency between the experts (Kravitz et al., 2010), which may lead to low levels of agreement among the recommendations of the reviewers (low inter-rater reliability). As such, even though your paper is reviewed, there is no guarantee that what is presented is the truth. However, despite the challenges of the process, without a peer-review process available from the scientific community, the quality of scientific publications may diminish (few people submit a perfect paper that is not improved by the peer-review process).

When reviewing papers, the subject matter experts take a conservative approach (tentatively assuming before reviewing) that your manuscript is devoid of any new knowledge unless the evidence provided is sufficiently robust to disprove this assumption. If this were to happen, a false null hypothesis is rejected, and the presented manuscript would be published. However, there is still a chance that an unsound paper is published since a Type 1 error might occur (Ioannidis, 2020). A Type 2 error is also possible, which involves rejecting the null that a paper has no new knowledge, yet it does (Bjork, 2019). It should be noted that as efforts are made to minimize the occurrence of Type 1 errors, this may lead to few papers being accepted for publication, but this also results in numerous good papers being rejected for publication (Heckman & Moktan, 2020). Such circumstances can impact your progress as a scholar since publishing prestigious journals may be the difference between promotion and failure (Lawrence, 2003). A change in basic assumptions concentrating on the content rather than the avenue is being promoted by the San Francisco Declaration on Research Assessment (2012) that recommended valuing what (quality of the content) and not where (the journal), a manuscript has been published, with the number of times an article is cited by others rather than journal impact factors being the more valuable promotion parameter.

Despite the benefits that come through the peer-review process, it impacts efficiency within the scholarly field. Most journals are expensive for readers to access, which means that much of the readership could be restricted to those with subscriptions to the journals in which you have published. In addition, the peer-review process is not transparent and the criterion for acceptance/refusal of a manuscript is not known and can be looked at as operating on a lottery system. Furthermore, the process can delay the time a paper gets published, especially if it is not accepted by the first-choice journal and is submitted to a sequence of journals, each of which will take months, or even years to decide (parallel submissions are not allowed). It should also be noted that the reviewers though may have a rubric to follow in evaluating manuscripts, their judgement may be viewed as subjective and hence differences of opinion become inevitable.

Peer-Review Innovations

Given the relevance of the peer-review process, there are several endeavors being undertaken to improve the process and among the innovations are:

Social media: The advent of social media including twitter, blogs, and other forms of social media has provided the advantage of transparency and involvement of a wider group of people (Ali & Watson, 2016). Many a researcher can use this model though since its still in a stage of infancy, it needs to be studied more, it is open to receive submissions from individuals that may not be competent in the subject under review which would adversely impact the validity of the material you publish.

Preprint: Another avenue that has arisen is the availability of preprints where material is availed to the public prior to expert reviews (Walker & Rocha da Silva, 2015). Preprints are scientific reports made available to the public without first going through the traditional peer-review process. Authors, in many cases, are simultaneously pursuing formal publication in a peer-reviewed venue. There has been an emergence of several preprint websites and institutional repositories such as arXiv eprint server, Scitation (https://scitation.aip.org), and SSRN (Social Science Research Network (http://www.ssrn.com), through which research results are disseminated in their primary form prior to publishing. This forum has been facilitated by some research funders that require that their grantees post their reports first on preprint servers before peer-reviewed publication (Kaiser, 2017; Sever et al., 2019). By using the preprint services, you may eliminate delays in publishing and provide free share, though you would not benefit from peer review, and hence the quality of your work would depend on your self-discipline. Using the preprints, you may be able to build your curriculum vitae by citing the preprints, hence boosting your career growth. You should, however, be aware that when you publish in the preprint avenues, that source retains the copyright, thus, rendering publication in a journal redundant or duplicate publication and this would be a copyright infringement by the journal under United Stated Law. Furthermore, as noted by Woloshin and Schwartz (2002), data presented at scientific meetings before a peer review often use formats that may exaggerate the perceived importance of findings. The rules against duplicate or prior publication may alter what scientists and clinicians, desiring to publish, choose to present at scientific meetings and in interviews before submission of their manuscript. To mitigate against such situations, presenters who want to avoid duplicate or prior publication because they plan to submit information to a peer-reviewed journal should not share their slides, materials or additional information with newspapers or tabloids before publication. In situations where a preprint is available prior to peer-reviewed publication, the author could engage the editor not to release information until completion of a peer-review process.

Technology: As a researcher, you have access to technological innovations, such as natural language processing, machine learning and other artificial intelligence tools are improving the peer-review process through facilitating tasks such as evaluating originality, validating statistics, and detecting plagiarism (Heaven, 2018). All these can facilitate your endeavors as a researcher. You can also use mechanisms that include collaborative review including manuscript assessment, interim referees, editors, and external readers who provide interactive comments leading to a consensus decision and a single set of revisions. In addition, you can use the portable review methods in which you could pay a company such as Rubriq, Peerage of Science, or Axios Review (Swoger B, Can you take it with you when you go? portable peer review, Scientific American. Available at https://blogs.scientific american. com/information-culture/can-you-take-it-with-you-whenyou-go-portable-peer-review/), for a review that they can submit with the manuscript to collaborating journals.

Non-peer Review

Non-peer-reviewed venues are exactly what they sound like: forums in which work is published without the formal refereeing of subject matter experts. This can allow for rapid dissemination of your work but provides little-to-no safeguards for consumers of this information. Non-peer-reviewed material offered to the public often includes conference presentations whose abstracts are often not peer reviewed. A systematic review showed that less than 50% of all studies accepted as abstracts went on to be published in full following presentations at a conference (Scherer et al., 2018). It is, therefore, important that abstracts and conference presentations are developed with as rigorous a process as that of a full publication because these may become the only source for a particular analysis.

Arguments for Preprints

The non-peer-reviewed preprints have several advantages, and these include free and near-immediate access to research results. There is also claimed acceleration of the progress of research by immediate dissemination without peer review. It is also assumed that manuscripts will be improved through the feedback provided by a wider group of readers alongside formal review by a few experts. In general, preprints are looked at as life savers as they circumvent the peer-review process that adversely delays the dissemination of research results (Abdill & Blekhman, 2019).

Arguments Against Preprints

Despite the great benefits that can accrue from the use of preprints, there are several faults in the system. Unlike safeguards mitigating against delivery of wrong or distorted information within peer-reviewed material, preprints are susceptible to erroneous material. This could put your publications at a path of providing flawed material to the public. It should be noted that through the non-peer-reviewed mode, there are continuous claims of breakthroughs and proven treatments based on preprints, followed by back pedaling after challenges and outcries, which impacts public confidence in the scientific endeavor. Silently retracted, withdrawn, or disappearing preprints are not sufficiently discussed by academics, but they constitute a fundamental threat to the integrity of open access (Teixeira da Silva, 2020a-Covid-19 papers). One of the challenges of preprints is that as they are being reviewed, the public is accessing several versions of the same paper making choice between the most up-to-date and current (with necessary revisions) hard to fathom. For example, in early 2020, there were retractions of two highly publicized Covid-19 papers in the New England Journal of Medicine (NEJM; Mehra et al., 2020a, b) and the Lancet (Mehra et al., 2020b) because of unreliable or non-existent data up to which those papers' analyses were based, and this should serve as an important alert to the biomedical academic community.

The use of retracted papers may constitute a public health risk because potentially dangerous and/or misleading information is released to the public, presenting them as clinically and academically valid studies. Lakens (2020) noted that academies must build their own defenses and strategies to certify the legitimacy of their research, because peer review even in top-rated journals may be fallible. There is a possibility of continued presentation of retracted documents due to the existence of unretracted copies on social media, third-party websites or pirate unrestricted access sites (e.g., Sci-Hub). Papers that cite retracted papers (e.g., Boulware et al., 2020) might themselves need to be corrected, while the metrics of these journals also need to be adjusted (Teixeira da Silva & Dobranszki, 2018).

Social Media/Online Dissemination

The internet has grown rapidly since the 1980s. It has revolutionized how we communicate, brought distant peoples into contact with one another, and has become ubiquitous in everyday life. Social media, particularly, has the perception of being a sort of new public square for discourse and democratized information even though they remain revenue-generating power houses (Franks, 2021). Online platforms have great potential for disseminating information about science to broad audiences. Online venues include social media sites like Facebook™ and Twitter™, content sharing websites like YouTube™ and Spotify™, blog hosting services like Wordpress™, pre-print servers, email listservs, and research-oriented social media sites like ResearchGate™ and Academia™. These kinds of online venues serve two functions, with some serving both in certain circumstances: dissemination to the public and dissemination to other professionals. Given the speed at which consumers can engage with online content and provide feedback to the content creators, online spaces, in essence, become sort-of verbal communities at scale. However, information online is often not peer reviewed, and there are some pitfalls when attempting to both disseminate and consume information online.

Dissemination to professionals online allows researchers to reach many fellow researchers and other professionals instantaneously. In venues when feedback is synchronous or nearly immediate, a genuine professional conversation can take place that could be considered real-time professional peer review. While there are frequently no standards for this sort of professional exchange, developing both a standard for providing critical and constructive feedback and representing quality based on feedback (to aid in critical consumption) could revolutionize peer review and move the scientific community closer toward the ideal of democratized and timely information (Stern & O'Shea, 2019).

Dissemination to the public allows researchers to reach our communities at large to share the latest findings in understanding a range of human and non-human animal behavior and how that connects with larger social questions, issues, and conversations. Reaching out straight to the general public also allows scientists and practitioners to advocate for the efficacy of evidence-based solutions based in areas of treatment of challenging life situations, organizational performance and conservation, and to advocate for increased legitimization of clinical practice.

In traditional media, there are usually clear discriminators of good information (signals such peer-reviewed journals; though see Grudniewicz et al., 2019 for a discussion of predatory journals) that allows a would-be consumer to easily pick it out from the background noise of information (irrelevant and bad information). Would-be disseminators, then, need only to be concerned about getting their work into established venues and can assume that relevant consumers are able to tell good information from bad and are motivated to seek out the kind of information being disseminated. This is not the case in online spaces such as social media, podcasts, and blogs. In online spaces, good information (the signal) is often drowned out by lots of bad or irrelevant information (the noise) and in some cases good information may be actively suppressed. There are several reasons why this might occur.

Traditional academic journals and professional conferences have peer-review committees that carefully curate and vet potential information before it moves forward into journals or presentations (though see Stern & O'Shea, 2019). However, in online spaces there is often a lack of standards regarding quality, tone, and content of the information shared. There are typically not referees with content knowledge of the science being shared—more often there are only site administrators that remove offensive or illegal material. The social response to online content may serve as an additional referee that in theory is a good idea, but again, there are no standards for this sort of feedback, which can result in either loosely structured well-intentioned activism or disorganized mobs that "shout down" information that people find inaccurate, offensive, or challenging to their identity narratives or accepted norms. In some cases, online activism is healthy and progresses our society toward a healthier more just state, and in other cases it is regressive and counter to the overall best interests (commonly called "trolling"). Furthermore, the volumes of content shared on these platforms is large and the velocity of the information is high, and platforms utilize behavioral algorithms to route content to users based on their preferences (measured through past engagement with the platform or other websites). This contributes to consumers being presented with an ever-filling, curated haystack with a smattering of needles

‿d throughout. This means that would-be disseminators must now not only ‿sider what sorts of information should be shared but also how to compete for the attention of the would-be consumer.

This is not completely new for the dissemination of information in any venue. All authors/presenters/speakers must compete for the attention of their audiences to induce a consumer to select the author's paper among the other in a journal issue, to select the author's book off the shelf, or select to sit in the audience seat and to keep attending to the work once it is selected. However, this is particularly severe in the online space, and there is a tendency to sensualize and dramatize titles, links, and descriptions (so called "click-bait"; Jung et al., 2022). Additionally, the need to be singled out among a multitude of voices and desire to communicate straightforward facts and actionable steps results in paring down of complex theories, phenomena and findings into bitesize chunks. There is value in taking this approach to increase accessibility and impact of information, there is also a risk of simplifying to the point of inaccuracy or overgeneralizing nuanced findings (Morris, 1985). The challenge to find the balance between accessibility and accurate representation is a noble cause and a worthy exercise for science to engage. This is not a new observation. Ogden Lindsley (Lindsley, 1991) noted that what was needed was a better language to serve as effective signals, which we not merely believed was effective but had been empirically validated. Behavioral scientists are only beginning to explore this area (Becirevic et al., 2016).

The intention is to not be overly pessimistic, and many examples of great dissemination of behavior science online abounds (*Practical Functional Assessment*, n.d.; *The Behavioral Observations Podcast*, n.d.; *The Daily BA*, n.d.; *ABA Inside Track*, n.d.; *Dissemination and Implementation of Evidence-based Practices*, n.d.). When you are preparing to disseminate information online, you should first determine who your audience will be. Will this be other academics? Will they be behavior scientists or other professionals? Will it be the general public? Will it specifically be families of individuals with intellectual disabilities? Answering these questions first will help you determine what you want to say and how you want to say it. The body of the content (in whatever modality you choose) should be clear and concise. Unnecessary technical jargon should be eliminated and replaced with more approachable words, especially when you are seeking to reach people outside of your field. You should simplify concepts to aid in communication but not to the point that they become uselessly simplistic. It is also critical to clearly indicate when you are speaking from the data and when you are speculating based on concepts, previous findings, or your own experience. The title and content description needs to covey quickly what you are trying to communicate. You should aim for something that will catch the eye of your intended audience without sensationalizing your content. More information on dissemination through social media and non-standard means can be found in Chap. 15.

Conclusion

Dissemination of science relies on trust between the disseminator and the audience, which constitutes a verbal community that depends on both speaker and listener behavior. To ensure you are most effectively disseminating your work, you must consider both the form of dissemination (publication, presentations, and social media) and the standards of the form (peer review vs non-peer review). You will need to weigh the PROs and CONs of selecting means to disseminate and you will need to tailor how and what you say to meet the different audiences.

References

ABA Inside Track. (n.d.). ABA Inside Track. https://www.abainsidetrack.com

Abdill, R. J., & Blekhman, R. (2019). Tracking the popularity and outcomes of all bioRxiv pre-prints. *eLife, 8*, e45133. https://doi.org/10.7554/eLife.45133

Ali, P., & Watson, R. (2016). Peer review and the publication process. *Nursing Open, 3*(4), 193–202. https://doi.org/10.1002/nop2.51

Becirevic, A., Critchfield, T. S., & Reed, D. D. (2016). On the social acceptability of behavior-analytic terms: Crowdsourced comparisons of lay and technical language. *The Behavior Analyst, 39*(2), 305–317. https://doi.org/10.1007/s40614-016-0067-4

Behavior Analyst Certification Board. (2020). *Ethics code for behavior analysts*. Author. https://www.bacb.com/wp-content/uploads/2020/11/Ethics-Code-for-Behavior-Analysts-210902.pdf

Björk, B.-C. (2019). Acceptance rates of scholarly peer-reviewed journals: A literature survey. *El Profesional de la Información, 28*(4), e280407. https://doi.org/10.3145/epi.2019.jul.07

Boulware, D. R., Pullen, M. F., Bangdiwala, A. S., et al. (2020). A randomized trial of hydroxy-chloroquine as postexposure prophylaxis for Covid-19. *New England Journal of Medicine, 383*, 517–525. https://doi.org/10.1056/NEJMoa2016638

Chadwell, M. R., Sikorski, J. D., Roberts, H., & Allen, K. D. (2019). Process versus content in delivering ABA services: Does process matter when you have content that works? *Behavior Analysis: Research and Practice, 19*(1), 14–22. https://doi.org/10.1037/bar0000143

Critchfield, T. S., & Doepke, K. J. (2018). Emotional overtones of behavior Analysis terms in English and five other languages. *Behavior Analysis in Practice, 11*(2), 97–105. https://doi.org/10.1007/s40617-018-0222-3

Dissemination and Implementation of Evidence-based Practices. (n.d.). CBT Radio. https://podcasts.apple.com/us/podcast/dissemination-and-implementation-of-evidence/id825798897?i=1000371807592

Foxx, R. M. (1996). Translating the covenant: The behavior analyst as ambassador and translator. *The Behavior Analyst, 19*(2), 147–161.

Franks, M. A. (2021, November 16). Beyond the Public Square: Imagining Digital Democracy. https://www.yalelawjournal.org/forum/beyond-the-public-square-imagining-digital-democracy

Friman, P. C. (2014). Publishing in journals outside the box: Attaining mainstream prominence requires demonstrations of mainstream relevance. *The Behavior Analyst, 37*(2), 73–76. https://doi.org/10.1007/s40614-014-0014-1

Grudniewicz, A., Moher, D., Cobey, K. D., Bryson, G. L., Cukier, S., Allen, K., Ardern, C., Balcom, L., Barros, T., Berger, M., Ciro, J. B., Cugusi, L., Donaldson, M. R., Egger, M., Graham, I. D., Hodgkinson, M., Khan, K. M., Mabizela, M., Manca, A., et al. (2019). Predatory journals: No definition, no defence. *Nature, 576*(7786), 210–212. https://doi.org/10.1038/d41586-019-03759-y

. ₍2018). AI peer reviewers unleashed to ease publishing grind. *Nature, 563*, 609–610.

⌐n, J. J., & Moktan, S. (2020). Publishing and promotion in economics: The tyranny of the ₌op five. *Journal of Economic Literature, 58*(2), 419–470. https://doi.org/10.1257/jel.20191574

⌐eward, W. L., Critchfield, T. S., Reed, D. D., Detrich, R., & Kimball, J. W. (2022). ABA from a to Z: Behavior science applied to 350 domains of socially significant behavior. *Perspectives on Behavior Science, 45*(2), 327–359. https://doi.org/10.1007/s40614-022-00336-z

Ioannidis, J. P. A. (2020). Coronavirus disease 2019: The harms of exaggerated information and non-evidence-based measures. *European Journal of Clinical Investigation, 50*(4), e13223. https://doi.org/10.1111/eci.13223

Jung, A.-K., Stieglitz, S., Kissmer, T., Mirbabaie, M., & Kroll, T. (2022). Click me…! The influence of clickbait on user engagement in social media and the role of digital nudging. *PLoS One, 17*(6), e0266743. https://doi.org/10.1371/journal.pone.0266743

Kaiser, J. (2017, March 24). *NIH enables investigators to include draft preprints in grant proposals.* Science Insider. https://www.science.org/content/article/nih-enablesinvestigators-include-draft-preprints-grant-proposals

Kravitz, R. L., Franks, P., Feldman, M. D., Gerrity, M., Byrne, C., et al. (2010). Editorial Peer Reviewers' recommendations at a general medical journal: Are they reliable and do editors care? *PLoS One, 5*(4), e10072. https://doi.org/10.1371/journal.pone.0010072. (http://tinyurl.com/2uukbc7)

Lakens, D. (2020). Pandemic researchers—Recruit your own best critics. *Nature, 581*(7807), 121. https://doi.org/10.1038/d41586-020-01392-8

Lawrence, P. A. (2003). The politics of publication. *Nature 422*(6929), 259–61.22. San Francisco Declaration on Research Assessment. https://sfdora.org/read/

Lindsley, O. R. (1991). From technical jargon to plain English for application. *Journal of Applied Behavior Analysis, 24*(3), 449–458. https://doi.org/10.1901/jaba.1991.24-449

Mehra, M. R., Desai, S. S., Kuy, S., Henry, T. D., & Patel, A. N. (2020a). Cardiovascular disease, drug therapy, and mortality in Covid-19. *New England Journal of Medicine*. https://doi.org/10.1056/NEJMoa2007621; expression of concern. https://doi.org/10.1056/NEJMe2020822; retraction https://doi.org/10.1056/NEJMc2021225

Mehra, M. R., Desai, S. S., Ruschitzka, F., & Patel, A. N. (2020b). Hydroxychloroquine or chloroquine with or without a macrolide for treatment of COVID-19: A multinational registry analysis. *The Lancet*. https://doi.org/10.1016/S0140-6736(20)31180-6; erratum https://doi.org/10.1016/S0140-6736(20)31249-6; expression of concern. https://doi.org/10.1016/S0140-6736(20)31290-3; retraction https://doi.org/10.1016/S0140-6736(20)31324-6

Morris, E. K. (1985). Public information, dissemination, and behavior Analysis. *The Behavior Analyst, 8*(1), 95–110. https://doi.org/10.1007/BF03391916

Morris, E. K. (2014). Stop preaching to the choir, publish outside the box: A discussion. *The Behavior Analyst, 37*(2), 87–94. https://doi.org/10.1007/s40614-014-0011-4

Normand, M. P., & Donohue, H. E. (2022). Behavior analytic jargon does not seem to influence treatment acceptability ratings. *Journal of Applied Behavior Analysis, 55*(4), 1294–1305. https://doi.org/10.1002/jaba.953

Position Statement on the Use of CESS – 2022—Association for Behavior Analysis International. (n.d.). Retrieved December 9, 2022, from https://www.abainternational.org/about-us/policies-and-positions/position-statement-on-the-use-of-cess-2022.aspx

Practical Functional Assessment. (n.d.). *Practical Functional Assessment*. Retrieved December 9, 2022, from https://practicalfunctionalassessment.com/

Resolution Opposing Applied Behavioral Analysis (ABA). (2021, July 22). Advocacy Monitor. https://advocacymonitor.com/ncil-resolution/resolution-opposing-applied-behavioral-analysis-aba/

Scherer, R. W., Meerpohl, J. J., Pfeifer, N., Schmucker, C., Schwarzer, G., & von Elm, E. (2018). Full publication of results initially presented in abstracts. *Cochrane Database of Systematic Reviews, 11*, MR000005.

Schillinger, D. (2010). *An introduction to effectiveness, dissemination and implementation research* (P. Fleisher & E. Goldstein, Eds.; p. 17). Clinical and Translational Science Institute.

Sever, R., Roeder, T., Hindle, S., Sussman, L., Black, K.-J., Argentine, J., Manos, W., & Inglis, J. R. (2019). bioRxiv: The preprint server for biology. 833400. https://doi.org/10.1101/833400

Stahel, P. F., & Moore, E. E. (2014). Peer review for biomedical publications: We can improve the system. *BMC Medicine, 12*(1), 179.

Stern, B. M., & O'Shea, E. K. (2019). A proposal for the future of scientific publishing in the life sciences. *PLoS Biology, 17*(2), e3000116. https://doi.org/10.1371/journal.pbio.3000116

Teixeira da Silva, J. A., & Dobránszki, J. (2018). Multiple versions of the *h*-index: Cautionary use for formal academic purposes. *Scientometrics, 115*, 1107–1113. https://doi.org/10.1007/s11192-018-2680-3

The Behavioral Observations Podcast. (n.d.). *The Behavioral Observations Podcast*. Retrieved December 9, 2022, from https://behavioralobservations.com/

The Daily BA. (n.d.). *The Daily BA*. Retrieved December 9, 2022, from https://www.thedailyba.com

Walker, R., & Rocha da Silva, P. (2015). Emerging trends in peer review—a survey. *Frontiers in Neuroscience, 9*, 169. https://doi.org/10.3389/fnins.2015.00169

Woloshin, S., & Schwartz, L. M. (2002). Press releases: Translating research into news. *Communicating to Readers, 287*(21), 2856–2858. https://doi.org/10.1001/jama.287.21.2856

Susan Flynn, PhD, BCBA-D, IBA   earned her PhD in special education with a focus on applied behavior analysis from the University of North Carolina at Charlotte. Before earning her doctorate, she spent 10 years teaching students with autism at the elementary and high school levels. Her professional interests include leadership and management, behavioral skills training, and expanding the field of behavior analysis to collaborate with other professionals.

Lucas Evans, PhD, BCBA-D   completed his doctorate in applied behavior analysis at The Chicago School, where he researched clinical practice, instructional design, and clinical decision support systems. He specializes in clinical decision-making, decision support technology, systems analysis, and systems design.

Henry Sessanga, PhD, BCBA-D, IBA   earned his PhD in applied behavior analysis at The Chicago School, where his research interests focused on culturally sensitive behavioral assessment. His current work specializes on assessment of human skill levels and developing capacity-building interventions.

Chapter 3
Ethical Dissemination

Kelly M. Torres, Meagan C. Arrastía-Chisholm, and Samantha Tackett

Previously, sole authorship was a common phenomenon in scholarly literature, which often overlooked individuals who were deserving of credit for their contributions in conducting or drafting the study. However, due to the emergence of research teams, international collaborations, advancements in modern technology, and a focus on interdisciplinary studies, co-authored publications have substantially increased over time (Cooke et al., 2021). As a result, the topic of authorship has become a widely discussed and debated issue within academia (Pruschak, 2021). Particularly, co-authored manuscripts are becoming more commonplace – resulting in researchers conferring on authorship order based on individual contributions. Collaborative research efforts often integrate distribution of tasks that align with the researcher's expertise and specialization (Pruschak, 2021) with the benefit of possibly reaching a wider audience through multidisciplinary studies.

The value of research may go unknown if dissemination does not occur. Still, researchers need to make several ethical considerations before sharing their work with the public. When including their name on a publication, authors take on the responsibility to disperse work that is inclusive of ethical and valid contributions to the field. Indeed, Ijzerman et al. (2020) cautioned that considerations for research dissemination should include the quality of evidence. For example, the general value of citations and impact factors of journals are frequently contested and vigorously discussed within the literature (Lawrence, 2007; Lortie et al., 2013; Wilhite

K. M. Torres (✉)
College of Professional Psychology, The Chicago School, Chicago, IL, USA
e-mail: ktorres@thechicagoschool.edu

M. C. Arrastía-Chisholm
Department of Human Services at Valdosta State University, Valdosta, GA, USA

S. Tackett
Academic Center for Excellence (ACE) in the Division of Undergraduate Studies at Florida State University, Tallahassee, FL, USA

© The Author(s), under exclusive license to Springer Nature Switzerland AG 2023   39
A. K. Griffith, T. C. Ré (eds.), *Disseminating Behavioral Research*,
https://doi.org/10.1007/978-3-031-47343-2_3

et al., 2019). Moreover, authors select citations, including their own, for numerous reasons impacting the number of times that a manuscript is cited resulting in inflated publication significance and visibility. Ultimately, the goal of research is to produce dependable knowledge and evidence (García-Pérez, 2012).

Garbage In, Garbage Out: Reliable and Valid Data

The first ethical consideration is to make sure that as much effort as possible has gone into generating reliable and valid data before making claims. If the data collected are not reliable, they cannot be valid. If such data are used to make claims, it is considered 'garbage in, garbage out' with the conclusions being questionable at best (Arias et al., 2020). In this section, we define reliability and validity and describe the various types of reliability and validity evidence. We also provide practical ways in which researchers can collect the most reliable and valid data.

Evidence of Reliability

Reliability is another way of describing consistency in data. Researchers want to look for consistency in data before making claims about trends or relationships. For example, whether an assessment is testing the same *construct* across time and participants is a matter of consistency. In research, a construct is a concept that can be described in terms of a theory and then measured as a variable. Reliable assessments are expected to result in the same measures of a construct for the same, or similar, people across administrations. For data to be reliable there must be a sense of consistency; and researchers can use a variety of methods to demonstrate the reliability of their data. There are many factors that affect reliability, including the number of items or tasks, the spread of scores, and objectivity across raters.

There are four major categories of reliability evidence: stability, equivalence, internal consistency, and consistency across raters (Zhu, 2013). *Test–retest reliability* shows stability of a measure over time. In other words, this type of evidence shows that a measure generates estimates that are very close to each other, time and time again. *Equivalent-forms reliability* demonstrates the consistency of data across forms of the same measure. This reliability evidence shows the equivalence of one version of assessment to another because they produce very similar data. *Split-half reliability* demonstrates how the data generated are consistent across items of a certain measure. For example, if a depressed person endorses high levels of depression when responding to one item in a depression scale, there should be similar responses elicited from the other items in the same scale. Within a scale this is often measured by Cronbach's alpha, but more recently researchers prefer to use omega to capture reliability of multivariate constructs (Hayes & Coutts, 2020). *Interrater* (or interobserver) *reliability* demonstrates consistency across raters (Watkins &

Pacheco, 2000). Again, if one rater endorses a client for high levels of depressive behaviors the same rating should be elicited from the other raters if the measure is reliable. Collecting multiple forms of reliability evidence may lead a researcher to more confidence estimates of constructs studied.

Evidence of Validity

As mentioned before, a test cannot be valid if it is not reliable. *Validity* is the degree to which a test or assessment measures what it is intended to measure. Tests that are poorly constructed or not thought out can often measure unintended outcomes. For example, a test that asks participants to type out directions to their childhood home in 60 seconds more likely measures a person's typing skills as opposed to their long-term memory. If such a poorly constructed test is used to make claims or come to conclusions, it is easy to see that the results would be useless for its intended purpose. That is why it is important to consider evidence indicating that a test is valid for the purpose for which it is being used (Kane, 2016). There are three types of validity evidence: content, criterion-related and construct validity evidence. To examine evidence of *content validity*, researchers should inspect the content of items or test criterion to make sure that they match the intention of the test. This is a minimum requirement for any test; at face value, it should appear to measure what it is supposed to measure. When the test is compared to an external standard, this type of evidence is often called criterion related. Within *criterion-related validity* evidence there are two subtypes: concurrent and predictive. *Concurrent validity* is the degree to which the test is correlated to measures it should be related to in practice. For example, a new measure of depression should be correlated to known measures of depression. Likewise, the new measure of depression should be correlated or predictive of other outcomes. For instance, a measure of depression could be predictive of self-harming behaviors. This would demonstrate *predictive validity*. *Construct validity* evidence demonstrates that a test is also related to other data as explained by theory. In one theory of depression, for example, depression is made up of symptoms, including low interest in daily activities, somatic symptoms, and negative affect. Therefore, a measure of depression would confirm that these different aspects are related to each other. A statistical test, called a factor analysis, would demonstrate evidence of construct validity. As with reliability, multiple forms of validity evidence should be collected before inferences about data can be made.

How to Ensure Reliable and Valid Data

There is always going to be some degree of error within the behavioral sciences; however, researchers can follow some practical guidelines to ensure that the data they are collecting, or on which they are basing their claims, are as valid and reliable as possible. In simple terms, we need to use or create valid and reliable measures (Heale & Twycross, 2015). For example, if using existing measures, check for the aforementioned types of validity and reliability evidence. Results from such statistical tests should be listed in the test manual of the instrument or in published work documenting its development. If creating an assessment from scratch, consider taking the time to gather all of the aforementioned types of evidence in the process and documenting that process meticulously. Additionally, the standard error of measurement can be estimated and researchers should be transparent about that estimate. All things being equal, the more reliable the assessment, the smaller the standard error of measurement (or the more valid the outcome). Test bias interferes with the validity of interpreting scores and should be reduced whenever possible by collecting validity evidence. Checking for differential item analysis, consulting with experts, and asking participants for feedback are just a few ways to reduce bias. Ultimately, validity (and reliability) is "assembled, negotiated, and transformed" by the researchers when they use their data to support their claims (Addey et al., 2020, p. 588). When in the role of research consumer, one should always critically evaluate the evidence of reliability and validity before considering the claims or outcome of the research (Hester et al., 2022).

Supported Conclusions

Once data are collected and analyzed, researchers need to develop supported conclusions to justify their claims and to effectively disseminate their findings. Specifically, presenting a clearly articulated and well-written conclusion provides researchers an understanding of the research problem, the significance of the study, how a gap in the literature was addressed, and new and expanded ways of considering the research topic. Integration of supported conclusions further reminds readers of the research strengths and helps to reiterate significant evidence that supports the researchers' claims and findings.

Conclusion drawing requires researchers to take a step back and consider what the analyzed data mean and its implications, as well as the responsibility of clearly articulating the theoretical or logical assumptions that underlie the research (Frechtling & Westat, 1997). For example, researchers studying the impact of response cards in classrooms to increase student participation and performance can draw logical and supported conclusions based on data that demonstrate greater occurrences of learners demonstrating their understanding through response cards and improved test scores. These conclusions can further be supported by prior studies that align with these findings and through theoretical foundations focused on student engagement and active participation.

Research conclusions demonstrate the importance of the study and the overall larger implications of the study. Therefore, this overview should be written concisely and include emphasis on the research problem, findings, and appropriate literature related to it. Well-written conclusions inform readers of the most salient key points of the study. Additionally, including evidence that supports researchers' conclusions also demonstrates how the study aligned with prior research. One example is research focused on the efficacies of interventions that highlight outcome data (e.g., socialization, communication, expressive language) and how the findings compare to prior studies examining applied behavior analysis interventions.

The conclusions drawn from research are important in reshaping or adding to the existing body of knowledge. *Supported conclusions* can further add to the literature through new research suggestions. Notably, research results are a highly important piece of the study and allow researchers to provide justified recommendations (LoBiondo-Woord & Haber, 2021). For example, researcher recommendations could include future research approaches and/or focuses, policy changes, effective treatment practices, and assessment and diagnosis considerations. Robust evidence that justifies the study findings allows researchers to demonstrate how they arrived at their conclusions and provide support of their research conclusions. Further, drawing conclusions supported by the research data demonstrate whether a theory or hypothesis is supported. Reporting clearly supported conclusions allow for the demonstration of sound experimentation and thorough data analysis. Frechtling and Westat (1997) highlighted that conclusions must be drawn from data that are found to be credible, defensible, warranted, and that can withstand alternative explanations. Precisely, the data should not "speak for itself" and researchers need to interpret their findings and draw meaningful conclusions. When writing supported conclusions, researchers should move beyond simple summaries of the research to encompass courses of action, key statistics and facts, and succinct statements that outline the importance of the study. These valid scientific conclusions will further explain significant findings and summarize the overall conclusions formed from data analysis.

Authorship Conventions

After completing the research study, the next step is to draft a manuscript and submit it for publication. Authors are responsible for verifying that all contributions are ethical, valid, and accurately credited prior to submission. However, authors regularly encounter issues related to determining authorship decisions given their impact on career and funding opportunities (Zauner et al., 2018). Specifically, authorship conventions are considered an essential aspect of career advancements (e.g., tenure, leadership positions) and can include academic and non-academic collaborators (Miles et al., 2021). For example, university faculty may collaborate with professionals in non-profit, government, or other types of settings on research projects. Nonetheless, authorship typically entails the substantial contributions related to conceptualizing the research design, analyzing and interpreting the data, drafting and revising of the article, and providing input on the final revisions and approval requirements necessary for publication. Cooke et al. (2021) contended that authorship conventions also encompass credit for research activities that have a direct or indirect impact on the research and accountability for outputs (e.g., reporting of research). Yet, scientific publications often contain co-authors with unequal contributions to the research and final manuscript (Dotson et al., 2011; Johann, 2022; Koepsell, 2017).

Typically, authorship of scholarly work encompasses individuals who contributed meaningfully and substantively to the intellectual content. Providing credit to everyone involved in the research is vital in ensuring an accurate reflection of appropriate authors and their contributions. Still, focus on authorship has been a continuing trend in research in ensuring that order of authorship is appropriately assigned. Especially given that the position of the author affects readers' perceptions regarding the contributions of the study and factors into institutional hiring decisions, awards, promotions, salaries, and performance evaluations. The first author listed in the byline is traditionally the corresponding author who put forth the most significant contributions with the remaining author list delineating how the group perceived contributions toward the final product. Basically, authorship provides conventions that are transparent and apparent evidence of who was involved in the study.

Authorship conventions and norms vary across research groups and cultures and considerations of what constitutes as author worthy (Jabbehdari & Walsh, 2017; Teixerira da Silva & Dobránszki, 2016). For example, Cooke et al. (2021) highlighted that biases toward author order occur from contribution types with technical contributions being undervalued in comparison to theoretical ones. Technical contributions could include editing feedback in comparison to theoretical input on the research design and process. When determining the order of authors, best practices involve developing a shared understanding among the collaborators early in the research process. Time allotted to each author's role and level of participation in the research is vital in developing clear expectations among collaborators. Additionally, negotiating authorship is an important component of conducting collaborative research. For instance, discussions reflective of who will draft document sections, collect and analyze data, and disseminate the findings are vital components researchers should address. Authorship conventions need to be agreed upon by all colleagues and within the mentor–mentee relationship between students and faculty. Although authorship order is typically acknowledged at the onset of the project, authorship roles can be adjusted throughout the project resulting in a renegotiation of the order of authors.

Faculty Student Collaborations

University-level students, particularly those enrolled at the graduate level, are increasingly involved in research collaborations. These scholarship partnerships should also follow best practices in establishing authorship conventions. This approach is vital given the increasing attention placed on the power differential that is inherent to the student and faculty relationship and the competitive and individual-centered process of promotion (Cooke et al., 2021). Academic bullying resulting from unfair crediting and distortion of authorship remains unreported for reasons associated with insecure feelings of position, poor recommendations or reference letters, and concerns related to fear of losing income (e.g., teaching assistant positions) (Mahmoudi, 2019). For example, graduate students may list their faculty advisor as first author on their own research (e.g., thesis, dissertation) even though they completed the majority of the work. Fear of challenging their mentor and uncertainty of fair research practices further exacerbate this problem.

Although mentoring students to serve as first author may possess unique challenges (e.g., lengthier writing process, decreased productivity, publications in lower-tier journals), Giuliano (2019) described strategies focused on providing effective writing instruction (e.g., copious feedback, formatting assistance, access to exemplar papers), explaining what authorship entails, and helping students find time to write as essential to scholarship projects. Graduate students often participate in research studies for professional development, career advancement, and to enhance their research expertise. Students also perceive these learning experiences as opportunities to network with experts in the field and develop professional identities. However, negotiating authorship is a daunting task for students with limited experience in discussing these roles and contributions to projects. When collaborating with faculty, students could consider who is the principal investigator of the study and the intellectual leadership and contribution of ideas to the project and document. These considerations help clarify authorship roles. Additional considerations occur when students participate in faculty research through paid positions or minor involvement in small tasks. Authorship may not be granted in these situations since the student's contribution did not result in substantial or intellectual impact on the study.

Citations

Guidelines from the American Psychological Association encourage thoughtful consideration about the purpose for citations and the number of sources to reference within one's work (APA, 2019). Citations are acknowledgements of others' scientific, creative, or conceptual work. It is ethical behavior to identify sources of insight, ideas, study design, or data, and to support the readers' access to the same resources. In most contexts referencing a couple of representative sources will be sufficient. Exceptions to this approach are various formats of systematic reviews such as literature reviews, dissertations, and appointed or authoritative panel reviews of research (e.g., National Academies of Science, Engineering, and Medicine). Rigorous reviews of research literature to identify the conceptual lineage or to summarize seminal and replicated findings will require extensive citations and references.

Best practice with using citations is to give credit to sources when paraphrasing, directly quoting, adapting/reprinting, or referring to another's data (APA, 2019). Two issues that may arise with citations are undercitation and overcitation. The APA guidelines caution writers to avoid undercitation due to the risk of plagiarism, even self-plagiarism. In contrast, outside the context of rigorous research reviews, the APA guidelines caution writers to avoid overcitation (e.g., citations with most sentences, lengthy citations). Examples of overcitation may include (a) more than four resources cited for a theory, concept, or research finding; (b) repeated citation of only one source; and (c) lengthy lists of resources that interrupt the readers' comprehension of the sentence. Exhaustive citations are unnecessary and risk overcitation for the purpose of one's work. Instead, writers should choose citations that best capture the theory, concept, or research finding.

Dissemination Through Open Resource Citations

At least since the Nuremberg Code (HHS, 2005), an outcome of the World War II war crime tribunal, research activity has been governed by ethical considerations throughout the design, implementation, and analysis processes (Farrow, 2016). Another ethical consideration for the research community to consider, however, is the distribution of research findings. Both the citation of and publication in open sources are ethical considerations in the 21st century. Open resources are available to access, especially digitally, without payment (Tackett et al., 2021). Providing free, public, digital access (open access) to research has been identified as a form of redistributive justice (Farrow, 2016; Lambert, 2018) because it enables access to knowledge by populations who are non-privileged and otherwise under-represented in the readership of research disseminated through profit-oriented journal or newspaper subscriptions (i.e., paywalls).

Researchers, educators, and practitioners have identified paywalls as unjust when information is "electronically copied and transferred around the world at almost no cost, we have a greater ethical obligation than ever before to increase the reach of opportunity ... give answers, and exchange ideas" (Caswell et al., 2008, p.7). In the context of mental health, healthcare, and public health, maximizing the distribution of information about research, treatments, and self-care to patients or clients is an additional ethical consideration especially when outreach to underserviced and low-income populations may ensure more widespread readership and adoption of public health recommendations (Madhok et al., 2018). Ultimately, citations to and publications in open access resources support dissemination to underserviced populations as well as under-resourced consumers, practitioners, leaders, and policy makers (Ashby, 2020; Madhok et al., 2018; Williams & Gregory, 2012). Hence, behavioral science researchers should consider using open access resources.

Concluding Remarks

Behavioral sciences research is produced and consumed rapidly and on a global scale as improvements in digital and public dissemination provides opportunities for individual access on personal devices, literally at our fingertips. The diverse and numerous consumers of behavioral science research rely on ethical and evidence-based research practices to inform their data-driven decision-making on a daily basis. For these reasons, it is imperative to produce research in an ethical manner as well as critically evaluate research that we consult. To this end, researchers should strive to collect the most reliable and valid data available by using sound instruments and methods. Once data are collected, secured, and analyzed, researchers continue their ethical practices by supporting their observations, statements of significance, and conclusions with defensible evidence. When disseminating the findings, authorship conventions within the discipline should follow the strictest guidelines to ensure fairness and equity among researchers. Finally, properly cited and widely distributed research advances the behavioral sciences by ensuring greater opportunity for research to be utilized, replicated, expanded upon, and disproven.

References

Addey, C., Maddox, B., & Zumbo, B. D. (2020). Assembled validity: Rethinking Kane's argument-based approach in the context of International Large-Scale Assessments(ILSAs). *Assessment in Education: Principles, Policy & Practice, 27*(6), 588–606.

American Psychological Association. (2019). *Publication manual of the American psychological association*. American Psychological Association.

Arias, V. B., Garrido, L. E., Jenaro, C., Martínez-Molina, A., & Arias, B. (2020). A little garbage in, lots of garbage out: Assessing the impact of careless responding in personality survey data. *Behavior Research Methods, 52*(6), 2489–2505.

Ashby, M. (2020). *Three quarters of new criminological knowledge is hidden from policy makers*. https://osf.io/preprints/socarxiv/wnq7h/

Caswell, T., Henson, S., Jensen, M., & Wiley, D. (2008). Open educational resources: Enabling universal education. *The International Review of Research in Open and Distance Learning, 9*(1), 1–11.

Cooke, S. J., Young, N., Donaldson, M. R., Nyboer, E. A., Roche, D. G., Madliger, C. L., Lennox, R. J., Chapman, J. M., Faulkes, Z., & Bennett, J. R. (2021). Ten strategies for avoiding and overcoming authorship conflicts in academic publishing. *FACETS, 6*, 1753–1770. https://scholarworks.utrgv.edu/cgi/viewcontent.cgi?article=1177&context=bio_fac

Dotson, B., McManus, K. P., Zhao, J. J., & Whittaker, P. (2011). Authorship and characteristics of articles in pharmacy journals: Changes over a 20-year interval. *Annals of Pharmacotherapy, 45*(3), 357–363.

Farrow, R. (2016). A framework for the ethics of open education. *Open Praxis, 8*(2), 93–109. https://files.eric.ed.gov/fulltext/EJ1103941.pdf

Frechtling, J., & Westat, J. S. (1997). User friendly handbook for mixed method evaluations. *National Science Foundation*. https://www.nsf.gov/pubs/1997/nsf97153/start.htm

García-Pérez, M. A. (2012). Statistical conclusion validity: Some common threats and simple remedies. *Frontiers in Psychology, 29.* https://doi.org/10.3389/fpsyg.2012.00325

Giuliano, T. A. (2019). Guiding undergraduates through the process of first authorship. *Frontiers in Psychology.* https://doi.org/10.3389/fpsyg.2019.00857

Hayes, A. F., & Coutts, J. J. (2020). Use omega rather than Cronbach's alpha for estimating reliability. *But....Communication Methods and Measures, 14*(1), 1–24.

Heale, R., & Twycross, A. (2015). Validity and reliability in quantitative studies. *Evidence-Based Nursing, 18*(3), 66–67.

Hester, N., Axt, J. R., Siemers, N., & Hehman, E. (2022). Evaluating validity properties of 25 race-related scales. *Behavior Research Methods,* 1–20.

HHS (2005). [1947]. *The Nuremberg Code.* U.S. Department of Human and Health Sciences. http://www.hhs.gov/ohrp/archive/nurcode.html

Ijzerman, H., Lewis, N. A., Jr., Przybylski, A. K., Weinstein, N., DeBruine, L., Ritchie, S. J., Vazire, S., Forscher, P. S., Morey, R. D., Ivory, J. D., & Anvari, F. (2020). Use caution when applying behavioural science to policy. *Nature Human Behaviour, 4*(11), 1092–1094. https://doi.org/10.1038/s41562-020-00990-w

Jabbehdari, S., & Walsh, J. P. (2017). Authorship norms and project structures in science. *Science, Technology, & Human Values, 42,* 872–900. https://doi.org/10.1177/0162243917697192

Johann, D. (2022). Perceptions of scientific authorship revisited: Country differences and the impact of perceived publication pressure. *Science and Engineering Ethics, 10.* https://doi.org/10.1007/s11948-021-00356-z

Kane, M. T. (2016). Explicating validity. *Assessment in Education: Principles, Policy & Practice, 23*(2), 198–211.

Koepsell, D. (2017). *Scientific integrity and research ethics: An approach from the ethos of science.* Springer.

Lambert, S. R. (2018). Changing our (dis) course: A distinctive social justice aligned definition of open education. *Journal of Learning for Development, 5*(3). https://jl4d.org/index.php/ejl4d/article/view/290

Lawrence, P. A. (2007). The mismeasurement of science. *Current Biology, 17,* 583–585.

LoBiondo-Wood, G., & Haber, J. (2021). *Methods and critical appraisal for evidence-based practice.* Elsevier.

Lortie, C. J., Aarssen, L. W., Budden, A. E., & Leimu, R. (2013). Do citations and impact factors relate to the real numbers in publications? A case study of citation rates, impact, and effect sizes in ecology and evolutionary biology. *Advanced Information and Knowledge Processing, 94,* 675–682. https://doi.org/10.1007/s11192-012-0822-6

Madhok, R., Frank, E., & Heller, R. (2018). Building public health capacity through online global learning. *Open Praxis, 10*(1), 91–97. https://www.learntechlib.org/p/182379/

Mahmoudi, M. (2019). Academic bullies leave no trace. *BioImpacts: BI, 9*(3), 129–130.

Miles, S., Renedo, A., & Marston, C. (2021). Reimagining authorship guidelines to promote equity in co-produced academic collaborations. *Global Public Health, 17*(10), 2547–2559. https://doi.org/10.1080/17441692.2021.1971277

Pruschak, G. (2021). What constitutes authorship? *Frontiers in Research Metrics and Analytics, 6,* 1–14. https://doi.org/10.3389/frma.2021.655350

Tackett, S., Torres, K. M., Arrastia, M. C., & Bradt, S. W. (2021). Breaching the paywall: Increasing access, recognition, and representation using open educational resources. In I. Jaafar & J. M. Pedersen (Eds), *Emerging realities and the future of technology in the classroom* (pp. 222–241). IGI Global. https://doi.org/10.4018/978-1-7998-6480-6.ch013

Teixeira da Silva, J. A., & Dobránszki, J. (2016). Multiple authorship in scientific manuscripts: Ethical challenges, ghost and guest/gift authorship, and the cultural/disciplinary perspective. *Science and Engineering Ethics, 22*(5), 1457–1472.

Watkins, M. W., & Pacheco, M. (2000). Interobserver agreement in behavioral research: Importance and calculation. *Journal of Behavioral Education, 10*(4), 205–212.

Wilhite, A., Fong, E. A., & Wilhite, S. (2019). The influence of editorial decisions and the academic network on self-citations and journal impact factors. *Research Policy, 48*(6), 1513–1522. https://doi.org/10.1016/j.respol.2019.03.003

Williams, J., & Gregory, B. (2012). Open education resources for interprofessional working. *British Journal of Midwifery, 20*(6), 436–439. https://doi.org/10.12968/bjom.2012.20.6.436

Zauner, H., Nogoy, N. A., Edmunds, S. C., Zhou, H., & Goodman, L. (2018). Editorial: We need to talk about authorship. *Giga Science, 7*(12). https://doi.org/10.1093/gigascience/giy122

Zhu, W. (2013). Reliability: What type, please. *Journal of Sport and Health Science, 2*(1), 62–64.

Kelly M. Torres is the department chair of the educational psychology and technology EdD program at The Chicago School. Her research interests are focused on international education, teacher certification programs, innovative technologies, and online learning.

Meagan C. Arrastía-Chisholm is an associate professor of educational psychology at Valdosta State University. At the graduate level, she teaches theories of learning and assessment for teachers, counselors, and other leaders. Dr. Arrastía-Chisholm's professional and research interests include parental separation, rural education, and college counseling.

Samantha Tackett serves as faculty with the Academic Center for Excellence (ACE) in the Division of Undergraduate Studies at Florida State University. Her professional and research interests include academic recovery, motivation, engagement, persistence, and resilience, and the academic experiences and retention of first-generation and other under-represented student populations within our educational systems.

Part II
Traditional Publication Preparation

Chapter 4
The Process of Scientific Writing: Developing a Research Question, Conducting a Literature Review, and Creating an Outline

Leif K. Albright

The process of scientific writing is quite straightforward if you recognize the formulas involved in developing each component of research. The critical aspect of writing is to plan everything to the best of your knowledge. This spans from your own writing scheduled to collaboration with colleagues. In the middle of somewhere is the need to ensure you have a research question worth studying and the development of a thorough literature review. This chapter covers the steps you can follow in your scientific writing journey specific to the content you plan to explore.

Creating a Research Question

As behavior science continues to branch out into new areas of practice so too does the research process. While a substantial amount of research involves interventions for individuals with disabilities, other areas of application have emerged, including business (Wilder et al., 2009), sports and fitness (Normand, 2008), and video game programming (Hopson, 2013). With these and other areas ripe for exploration, research possibilities are seemingly endless. But research is far more than simply the completion of an experiment. Inherent to any research study is the dissemination of information gleaned from that study. It is the process of identifying and organizing the empirical findings in a concise manner to justify relevance that often proves challenging, and in some ways more challenging than the experiment itself (Heard, 2016). The dissemination of those findings is typically done through the development of a scientific research paper. The process of developing a scientific paper can be considered as a series of steps performed in a not-so-linear fashion. However, the

L. K. Albright (✉)
Department of Special Education, Manhattanville College, Purchase, NY, USA
e-mail: leif.albright@mville.edu

© The Author(s), under exclusive license to Springer Nature Switzerland AG 2023   53
A. K. Griffith, T. C. Ré (eds.), *Disseminating Behavioral Research*,
https://doi.org/10.1007/978-3-031-47343-2_4

process is far from arbitrary, but rather should be seen as a dynamic work in progress until a conclusion has been met. What follows in the ensuing chapters are the general guidelines involved to successfully complete each component of a scientific research paper. To begin, a review of the paper's composition is necessary.

The canonical structure of the modern scientific paper is often referred to as IMRaD (Introduction, Methods, Results, Discussion) with each component serving its own unique purpose (Heard, 2016). While these components are clear and distinct, when brought together they are intended to tell a cohesive story. But, even before this IMRaD sequence can be initiated, the quintessential spark to the corresponding research experiment must commence, and that spark is the research question. This is where the true story begins. Before an introduction can be introduced, before a procedure can be described in a method, before any results or discussion of those results can be had, the reason for that study must be realized and coalesce into a cohesive purpose. As that purpose, a research question is a clear and concise statement that defines the problem or issue that a research study aims to investigate. It serves two primary functions: to narrow down a broad topic of interest into a specific area of study and sets the foundation and direction for the subsequent research study, guiding the selection of data collection methods, data analysis techniques, and the overall research design (Berger, 2015; Creswell, 2014). The development of a working research question that is relevant, decisive, and meaningful may be the most difficult part of the scientific writing process. In addition, it is also the part of the process that seemingly has the least amount of literature behind it guiding a path to its development (Doody & Bailey, 2016).

The first step involves choosing a topic of interest and to do this, it is important to cast the net wide starting with a broader area (Heard, 2016). Consider the general area of interest as the writer and/or to the wider research community. Which topics resonate as a student, as a clinician? A broad topic provides the writer with plenty of avenues and directions to explore. Even this step can be troublesome, however. Becoming acquainted with your local university's library search system (as well as other search systems) can also be beneficial at this stage as it will permit the user to conduct searches based on a whole host of criteria (e.g., keyword, title, author, range of years). This style of searching brings the writer in direct contact with the existing body of research. What is present and what is missing? These techniques are all designed to provide the writer with a base of interest but also to initiate the organization of thoughts as well as identify possible connections and relevant themes within the broad topic(s). It is likely that this initial search will yield a substantially high number of research studies. Typically, the broader the category the higher the number of results are returned. For example, a search through Ebscohost (a common search system used in many academic institutions) with the word "aggression" in the title produced over 13,000 results. If an area of interest does not present a high number of results, it is suggested to expand your search systems. If a limited number of returned results continue to be presented despite searching through several systems, it might mean that that area simply has not been explored yet or it might represent an area that has limited potential.

Following the initial broad area search, Farrugia et al. (2010) suggest a preliminary revision of the returned list of results. The two primary goals of this step are to review the existing literature surrounding those searched topics as well as to begin the identification of areas missing within the research. It is often through this process that the broad areas of research are narrowed down. Furthermore, this process of narrowing down topics often requires multiple iterations. While the search for the word "aggression" in the title resulted in over 13,000 results, the search for "aggression" and "children" in the title reduced that list of results to just over 1100. When the search criteria were expanded to include "aggression", "children" and "autism", the returned list of results was further reduced to 22 research articles. It is not uncommon to conduct concurrent searches across multiple broad areas as an initial way to begin isolating a topic.

Once the general topic has been isolated, the next step includes a series of additional searches aimed at narrowing down the search to a specific topic. At this stage, the writer should have the area of interest that will ultimately become the target of the future study, but the specific question may still be vague. From these searches, not only will the existing literature of a particular topic become apparent, but the areas of deficit will become more apparent as well. These are referred to as the gaps in the existing literature. These gaps offer potential areas of exploration, and as such gap-spotting is the most common strategy used by researchers. Gap-spotting refers to the active identification of limitations and/or overlooked areas within a particular area of study as well as identifying questions that potentially extend the findings of current existing literature. These are the limitations and future areas of research suggestions often cited by the experimenters themselves in published literature.

Sandberg and Alvesson (2011) identified three basic versions of gap-spotting: confusion, neglect and application. The focus of confusion spotting is to locate contradiction within the literature of a topic. Previous research has supported one perspective; however, opposing views have been empirically validated. The primary application of this mode of developing research questions is to search for competing explanations in the existing literature (Sandberg & Alvesson, 2011). Neglect spotting represents the most common form of gap-spotting whereby the focus is to identify a topic or area where limited research has been conducted. This can include areas that have been under-researched, overlooked entirely, or that have a lack of empirical support. The third mode is referred to as application spotting, and under this style searches are conducted for a shortage of a particular perspective and/or generalization within the literature. Under this style, researchers are attempting to locate areas where the literature can be extended to. This may include different populations, settings, or behaviors.

Gap-spotting is generally accepted as the most common way of identifying research questions; however, not all gaps provide acceptable areas to explore. That new area must be different enough from the previous literature while still connected by its conceptual roots. With this in mind, Sandberg and Alvesson (2011) suggest an alternative to gap-spotting known as problematization. Problematization refers to an approach whereby a research question is derived through challenging and scrutinizing the current trends of a particular area of research. If the consensus of a topic moves in a specific direction, problematization would lead to a research question that challenges that stance. A central goal under this method is to attempt to disrupt the continuation and reproduction of an established line of research, and specifically the perspective that that line perpetuates. While gap-spotting is aimed at identifying various gaps in the research, that method is not directly focused on challenging the assumptions underlying that particular line. Conversely, problematization is predicated on disputing the norm. Just as there are differing degrees of gap-spotting, so too does problematization vary: from questioning minor assumptions to challenging an entire theoretical paradigm. Bold but necessary in any field of science. When trends are no longer challenged, progress can be limited. As such problematization has the opportunity to produce new and exciting departures from existing lines of research.

A third option exists for identifying potential research questions; one not based on either existing gaps or mainstream challenges, but rather on clinical necessity. Lipowski (2008) suggests a practice-based method. With this strategy, the researchers use their clinical experience as the primary motivation to guide the development of new research. The practice-based method is largely dependent on the unique characteristics of the primary care setting, as well as the relationship between patient and professional. The goal of most practice-based research is to foster effective and lasting change. Although it may be difficult to locate a socially significant and sound study, once one is targeted it has the potential to affect direct change. In any case, whether through research gaps or applied practice, the ending result of this step is the development of a potential or several potential research questions.

At this stage the writer has conducted several increasingly refined literature searches; first to generate a broad area of interest, then to narrow down that broad area to a specific focus, and finally to identify a potential or several potential research questions. However, not all questions are worth pursuing. The researcher may generate a series of interesting hypothetical questions, but only certain questions should be followed up. Hulley et al. (2007) suggested the use of the FINER criteria when determining the soundness of a potential research question. Consider the (F) feasibility of the study. Will the proposed study have access to adequate participants, be guided by those with adequate technical expertise, and will it be affordable in time and money? The research question should be (I) interesting and intriguing to the research community while also proposing (N) novel extensions of previous literature. At all times, the question should propose an (E) ethical study that is amenable to an institutional review board. Finally, a good research question is (R) relevant to scientific knowledge and future research. The FINER criteria outline the relevant aspects of the question in general, but when it comes to the specific elements needed for the study Richardson et al. (1995) details the PICOT framework. Under this format one is to take into consideration the (P) population of interest, the (I) intervention being studied, the (C) comparison group or what is the intervention being compared to, the (O) outcome of interest, and finally the (T) time frame over which the study will be conducted.

Collectively, the FINER criteria and the PICOT framework aid in constructing a sound and specific research question, which ultimately aids in the protocol development of the subsequent study itself. When the population of interest, intervention, and desired outcomes are clearly outlined, it allows the researcher to identify appropriate measurement tools, which in turn permits more valid, reliable, and accurate measures. The better defined the population of interest, the more stringent the inclusion and exclusion criteria can be allowing for a more accurate interpretation and subsequent generalization of the research findings. Similarly, a precisely defined intervention decreases bias and increases the internal validity of the study. Conversely, a poorly defined research question may result in the poor choice of a research design, potentially leading to a misrepresentation of the subsequent results.

The development of the research question is a dynamic and evolving process that often involves frequent revision (Maxwell, 2013). As more literature is reviewed more information is gained, and that progression leads to further revisions and refinement to a potential research question. Without devoting appropriate resources to developing that question, the quality of the study and subsequent results may be compromised. Therefore, it is imperative during the initial stages of any research study, to formulate a research question that is both clinically relevant and answerable (Farrugia et al., 2010).

Conducting Literature Reviews

Once the research question has been developed the next step in the scientific writing process is to conduct a comprehensive literature review. The structure and function of this review differs from the earlier searches conducted while creating the research question. During that earlier process, searches were conducted to ascertain gaps in existing areas of research. However now, the focus of the comprehensive literature review is to conduct an in-depth analysis on the existing literature of a chosen topic (Galvan & Galvan, 2017). This may result in the review of new seminal studies and/or extension of the previous analysis conducted on the studies reviewed when developing the research question. In either case, the purpose of the comprehensive literature review is to extend the analysis somewhat deeper by extracting more specific details from each study and then to inform the researcher on the development of each subsequent component in the IMRaD sequence.

Organization is key to the development of a comprehensive literature review. As more articles are targeted and reviewed, vital information from each study will be extracted. A centralized place such as a table or spreadsheet will allow the writer to organize information in a single place across all studies, allowing for a better perspective to view similarities and differences (Galvan & Galvan, 2017). With the research question now front and center, a comprehensive search can be conducted through relevant academic articles, books, and other sources of information on the particular topic. It is likely that some of those sources may have already been gathered through previous searches conducted to develop the chosen research question, but often additional sources are necessary to augment the literature already collected. Locating and reviewing the troves of literature can be streamlined through the use of relevant academic databases (Galvan & Galvan, 2017). Search parameters can target keywords, populations, treatments, and publication year. This will help the writer retrieve the most relevant and current articles to use in the review.

As the relevant research articles are identified, a thorough read of each article will need to be conducted distilling key information such as study purpose, participants, dependent and independent variables, generalization and maintenance, results, and limitations (Galvan & Galvan, 2017). Extracting and reorganizing the key information from the chosen articles into a central system enables the writer to identify patterns across the literature. This can include those studies that focused on certain features of a population such as age and/or diagnoses, similar or different measurement systems, behaviors, and treatment variations. In addition, this permits the writer to view which studies shared similar results and which did not; which filled in the previous research gaps and which gaps are still left unexplored, presumably opening the door for the purpose of the current study.

As the information from the literature is centralized and analyzed, the writer can begin to synthesize the details into a cohesive composition surrounding the question (Galvan & Galvan, 2017). What establishes a comprehensive literature review as a synthesis rather than a manuscript segmented by several distinct research studies, is the aggregation of that key information. How many participants took part across the studies reviewed? What behaviors functioned as the dependent variables and how were they collectively measured? Across all the studies what interventions were used? How were they related to each other? Ultimately what were the collective results? This will typically require the writer to reanalyze the results within and across the reviewed studies. However once completed, the writer will be able to provide a thorough and critical analysis of the existing literature.

The final stage is to create the actual comprehensive literature review using the data derived from the synthesized analysis. The literature review should be structured and organized in a way that is clear and easy to follow. The arrangement of the manuscript follows the traditional IMRaD structure with an introduction that provides an overview of the research question and the rationale for the review, a method section that describes the search strategy and selection criteria, a results section that summarizes the key findings of the analysis, and a discussion section that interprets the findings and identifies gaps in the research. Some additional tips for creating a quality literature review include: use clear and concise language to describe the research question and the methods used to select and analyze the studies, use tables, graphs, and other visual aids to present the data in a clear and concise manner, provide a critical evaluation of the quality and relevance of the studies included in the review, highlight areas where further research is needed and identify potential directions for future investigation, and finally be objective and avoid bias in your interpretation of the data (Galvan & Galvan, 2017). In conclusion, creating a scientific literature review requires a systematic and comprehensive approach that involves defining the research question, conducting a comprehensive search for relevant studies, screening and selecting studies, extracting data, analyzing the data, and writing the review. By following these steps and tips, researchers can produce high-quality literature reviews that provide a critical analysis of the existing research and identify areas for future investigation.

Outlining Your Paper

Once the comprehensive literature review has been completed, the next step is to create an outline. An outline is an ordered list of topics or points that summarizes the projected content within the main sections and subsections of the intended paper (Heard, 2016). While it may be tempting to dive directly into the body of the paper, constructing an outline permits the writer the ability to adhere to a formal narrative structure expected in a scientific paper.

The outline process begins by identifying the main sections of the paper, including Abstract, Introduction, Methods, Results, and Discussion (Heard, 2016). Each section can be identified with its own unique value (e.g., roman numerals, letters, numbers) differentiating main sections from subsections. The Abstract section can be further broken down into background or aim, methods, key findings, and conclusions or significance. Next is Introduction and this can include additional subheadings to organize the narrative flow such as why the topic is important, what is already known about the topic and what information is missing, and finally the research objective or purpose (Heard, 2016). Then comes the Methods where the subheadings will highlight the procedural blueprint of the study such as participants and settings (where the inclusion/exclusion criteria for participation will be described), experimental design, dependent and independent variables, and procedures for generalization and maintenance. The Results main section will vary depending on the format of the study and will likely be filled out following the completion of the study. However, placeholders can be created based on chosen protocols described in the Methods. If multiple procedures will be conducted throughout the duration of the study (e.g., functional analyses, treatment conditions, maintenance), then a subheading for each procedural result should be created (Heard, 2016). Finally, is the Discussion with subheadings that may relate to the questions or points raised in the Introduction as well as considerations pertaining to sources of data variability. This will also be where the writers address any potential limitations.

After the framework of the outline is complete, it can now be elaborated by inserting actual verbiage into the subheadings. For example, in the Introduction, the subheading delineating why the topic is important can now be replaced with a topic sentence that will spell out some of those important benefits. Each subsequent bullet within that subheading can then serve as supporting sentences providing specific details related to the topic sentence (Heard, 2016). Turning to the next subheading regarding what is known and what information is missing; the writer would follow the same system described above where the first bullet would function as the topic sentence with each subsequent bullet providing additional details. However, in this section, the writer can apply the information gathered during the comprehensive literature review. The final subheading under the Introduction section outlines the specific research objective. Again, through the work conducted during the literature review, research gaps would have been identified, thus opening the door to the objective of the current project. The same process would be applied to each subsequent heading and subheading, adding more text until all of the relevant details are included. By starting with a detailed outline, the IMRaD structure will flow far easier, and a well-organized scientific paper can be written that makes the case that the research is meaningful and justifiable.

References

Berger, R. (2015). Now I see it, now I don't: Researcher's position and reflexivity in qualitative research. *Qualitative Research, 15*(2), 219–234. https://doi.org/10.1177/1468794112468475

Creswell, J. W. (2014). *Educational research: Planning, conducting, and evaluating quantitative and qualitative research* (5th ed.). Pearson Education.

Doody, O., & Bailey, M. E. (2016). Setting a research question, aim, and objective. *Nurse Researcher, 23*(4) https://journals.rcni.com/doi/pdfplus/10.7748/nr.23.4.19.s5

Farrugia, P., Petrisor, B. A., Farrokhyar, F., & Bhandari, M. (2010). Practical tips for surgical research: Research questions, hypotheses and objectives. *Canadian Journal of Surgery. Journal canadien de chirurgie, 53*(4), 278–281.

Galvan, J. L., & Galvan, M. C. (2017). *Writing Literature Reviews: A guide for students of the social and behavioral sciences* (7th ed.). Routledge.

Heard, S. (2016). *The scientist's guide to writing: How to write more easily and effectively throughout your scientific career*. Princeton University Press.

Hopson, J. (2013). *A behavioral approach to fun*. Invited address at the Second Education Conference of the Association for Behavior Analysis International, Chicago, IL. https://www.abainternational.org/events/education.aspx

Hulley, S. B., Cummings, S. R., Browner, W. S., Grady, D. G., & Newman, T. B. (2007). *Designing Clinical Research* (3rd ed.). Lippincott Williams and Wilkins.

Lipowski, E. E. (2008). Developing great research questions. *American Journal of Health-System Pharmacy, 65*(17), 1667–1670. https://academic.oup.com/ajhp/article-abstract/65/17/1667/5128061

Maxwell, J. A. (2013). *Qualitative Research Design: An Interactive approach* (3rd ed.). Sage.

Normand, M. P. (2008). Increasing physical activity through self-monitoring, goal setting, and feedback. *Behavioral Interventions: Theory & Practice in Residential & Community-Based Clinical Programs, 23*(4), 227–236.

Richardson, W. S., Wilson, M. C., Nishikawa, J., & Hayward, R. S. A. (Eds.). (1995). The well-built clinical question: a key to evidence-based decisions. *ACP Journal Club, 123*(3), A12. https://doi.org/10.7326/acpjc-1995-123-3-a12

Sandberg, J., & Alvesson, M. (2011). Ways of constructing research questions: Gap-spotting or problematization? *Organization, 18*(1), 23–44. https://doi.org/10.1177/1350508410372151

Wilder, D. A., Austin, J., & Casella, S. (2009). Applying behavior analysis in organizations: Organizational behavior management. *Psychological Services, 6*(3), 202–211.

Leif K. Albright, Ph.D., BCBA-D is an Advanced Research Project Instructor in the Applied Behavior Analysis Program at The Chicago School of Professional Psychology. He is also an assistant professor in the Applied Behavior Analysis Program in the Department of Special Education at Manhattanville College. His research interests include stimulus equivalence and stimulus transfer of function, improving learning outcomes and efficiency, function-based behavior interventions, and behavioral interventions to childhood disorders.

Chapter 5
Writing the Introduction

Amanda Mahoney, Katherine Davis, and Shannon Martinez

The Purpose of the Introduction

A good introduction carries several functions. It grabs the reader's attention, provides the background or context to the paper, summarizes key information, and leads logically into the stated purpose. It might be helpful to apply this to a personal example. Imagine you are at a social event and are asked about your professional background. You might begin your personal story by talking about your values or why your area of work is important to you, then move into specific events that afforded you opportunities to advance professionally, and finally talk about your current work and future goals. This reflection lets the person know why you are in the field, how you go to where you are today, and what you aim to do next. An introduction to a research study is similar in that it lets the reader know why you embarked on the study, what has been done on the topic in the past, and what you have elected to do as the next step. More specifically, a well-written introduction will:

A. Mahoney (✉)
Behavior Analysis Department, College of Graduate and Professional Studies
at The Chicago School, Chicago, IL, USA
e-mail: amahoney@thechicagoschool.edu

K. Davis
Cornerstone Therapies, Huntington, CA, USA
e-mail: katie.davis@cornerstonetherapies.net

S. Martinez
ABA Services, Firefly Therapy Clinic, Greenville, SC, USA
e-mail: shannonm@fireflytherapyclinic.com

A. K. Griffith, T. C. Ré (eds.), *Disseminating Behavioral Research*,
https://doi.org/10.1007/978-3-031-47343-2_5

Evoke Interest from the Intended Audience

To target the motivations of an audience you must first decide which audiences you hope to reach. For example, if you conduct a behavior analytic study with general education teachers, do you plan to disseminate this article to behavior analysts, teachers, or administrators? The audience will, in part, determine how you situate the context and significance of your study. Or it might influence the type or level of technical phrasing you use. Sometimes you might have multiple audiences or a broad audience and will need to think about how to reach everyone. This can be somewhat challenging to do in a concise and cohesive manner and will likely require that you read broadly and cite broadly. An example from the literature is presented in the pop out "Choosing Your Audience" below (see Fig. 5.1). The important thing to keep in mind is that you will more effectively disseminate your ideas by tailoring your context, problem statement, and background to the motivations of the group you are targeting.

Provide a Clear Rationale for the Research Question and Methodology

In addition to supporting a specific research question, the introduction addresses things like "why this question," "why now," "why this theoretical approach," and "why this methodology." If you cannot answer these questions you should return to the literature, consult your co-authors, or obtain more experience before sitting down to write this section. We will expand on this in the next section.

Help the Reader Understand the Study's Outcomes

The information you include in the introduction should provide background and context that helps the reader understand the importance of the results in the context specific to the study. This means you do not need to include every detail of every study. For example, many studies are conducted to try to address limitations of prior works. If you plan to use a different research design to control for some potential confounds of prior studies then your introduction will likely need to discuss the research designs used in the past. On the other hand, if your study plans to extend previous studies by evaluating maintenance or generalization you might not need to describe their research designs.

Researchers often write an introduction while developing the research proposal and later simply "plug" that introduction into their final research report of, for instance, a thesis or dissertation. This is poor practice. Introductions of theses differ from those of dissertations, and both differ pretty drastically from the introduction of a journal publication. Moreover, the introduction for a thesis, dissertation, or

APOPO is an organization that uses behavior analytic principles to train rats in scent detection tasks, including tuberculosis detection from human sputum samples. The examples below show the variation in presenting these principles to those in the behavioral sciences and those in the epidemiology.

Example A: Targeting Readers of *The Psychological Record*
(From Mahoney, A., Weetjens, B., Cox, C., Jubitana, M., Kazwala, R., Mfinanga, G. S., Durgin, A., Poling, A. (2012). Giant African pouched rats as detectors of tuberculosis in human sputum: Comparison of two techniques for sputum presentation. *The Psychological Record, 63*. 583-594.)

"Although the goal of applied behavior analysts typically is to improve human behavior, altering animal behavior to benefit participating animals or to benefit humans is also a legitimate part of the discipline (Edwards & Poling, 2011). In Tanzania a humanitarian organization called Anti-Persoonsmijnen Ontmijnende Product Ontwikkeling (APOPO) uses operant discrimination techniques to train giant African pouched rats to detect landmines and deploys the rats in Mozambique and elsewhere (Poling, Weetjens, Cox, Beyene, et al., 2010). Similar techniques also are used to train the rats to detect Mycobacterium tuberculosis by sniffing human sputum (Poling et al., 2011). Mycobacterium tuberculosis (MTB) causes tuberculosis (TB), a bacterial disease that typically affects the lungs and is a significant public health concern in resource-poor countries. Recent studies have demonstrated the rats' value for the second-line screening of sputum samples initially evaluated through microscopy (Mahoney et al., 2011; Mahoney et al., 2012; Poling, Weetjens, Cox, Mgode, et al., 2010; Weetjens, Mgode, Davis, Cox, & Beyene, 2009). For example, in 2009 and 2010, the rats screened more than 20,000 patients that had been evaluated by microscopy technicians at Direct Observation of Treatment–Short Course (DOTS) centers, which routinely screen for and treat TB in Tanzania, and increased new case detections by 44% (Poling, Weetjens, Cox, Mgode, et al., 2010) and 42.8% (Mahoney et al., 2011), respectively. Given that TB is a debilitating and often fatal disease and that each person infected with TB typically infects 10 to 15 other people each year (World Health Organization, 2012), these are clinically significant findings."

> Context is the altering of animal behavior for benefit.

> Problem stated is public health.

Example B: Targeting Readers of *Tuberculosis Research and Treatment*
(From Mahoney, A. M., Weetjens, B., Cox, C., Beyene, N., Reither, K., Makingi, G., Jubitana, M., Kazwala, R., Mfinanga, G. S., Kahwa, A., Durgin, A., and Poling, A. (2012). Pouched rats' detection of tuberculosis in human sputum: Comparison to culturing and polymerase chain reaction. *Tuberculosis Research and Treatment*, doi:10.1155/2012/716989.)

"A major hurdle in combating tuberculosis (TB) is diagnosing the disease in resource-poor countries. Sputum smear microscopy, the technique typically used, is relatively slow and characteristically has high specificity but low sensitivity [1, 2]; therefore, the international medical community has prioritized developing a quick, accurate, and affordable alternative diagnostic. In an attempt to develop one, researchers recently have investigated the use of scent-detecting pouched rats (*Cricetomys gambianus*) as a TB diagnostic. An initial proof of principle investigation [3] revealed that pouched rats trained through operant conditioning procedures could detect TB in human sputum, and three subsequent studies, involving a total of over 20,000 patients, showed that using the rats in second-line screening of sputum samples initially screened by smear microscopy at direct observation of treatment—short course (DOTS) centers in Tanzania increased new case detections by 31.4% [4], 44% [5], and 42.8% [6]."

> Context is tuberculosis diagnostics.

> Problem stated is the lack of a suitable diagnostic tool.

Fig. 5.1 Writing to your audience

publication should address what happened in the study, which often differs in important ways from what was planned at the outset of the study. One way to think about this is to consider the story you want to tell about the results that were obtained. The introduction plays an important role in providing the framework for that story by presenting issues that are going to come up again in the method and results. To give one extreme example, imagine that just as you were ready to begin collecting data in the classroom, a worldwide pandemic suddenly shut down all nearby schools. You forge on after receiving ethical approval by collecting data via telehealth. Even though your initial introduction might not have mentioned telehealth at all, this is an important component to your study that would certainly need to be woven in the introduction to put it in the appropriate context. A less extreme example would be that you found interesting outcomes in your maintenance probes and decided to continue probing for an extended period. It would be appropriate to highlight the frequency and outcomes of prior studies' maintenance probes in your introduction. But note that any time you make ad hoc modifications to your study you should be transparent about this in the paper by clearly stating your original plan, what you modified, when you made the decision, and why you made the change.

The Anatomy of the Introduction

You might recognize that the functions described in the previous section correspond to three main parts of the introduction: a rationale or significance statement, a literature review, and a purpose statement. These parts all work together to bring the reader to an understanding of what you hope to accomplish and why. There are many ways to present this information in a logical or coherent manner. Ledford and Gast (2018, pp. 59–60) provided a non-exhaustive list of six models for organizing the introduction: accumulating evidence, contrasting opinions, historical perspectives, deficits in knowledge about a practice, discrepant knowledge, and expanded applications. Whichever organizational system you choose, your introduction should at minimum include a description of the problem or issue, a literature review, and a summary that leads into a well-defined purpose. We describe guidelines for each component below.

Background, Context, and/or Social Significance

Most writers begin their introduction by describing the problem, providing context for the topic, or giving some background into why the topic is important. The topic is broader than the context of your study and this is the first step in funneling down to the purpose of your research. One way to establish your foundation is to ask yourself the following questions:

- Why is this research important?
- Who could benefit from this research?
- If this research were not conducted, who would be affected and in what ways?
- What do we currently not know or understand that this research will tell us?
- Why is now the right time for this research to be conducted?
- Why is my field of study well-suited to conduct this research?

In short, research should be of applied significance (if applied research) or of importance to some body of systematic knowledge (if basic research) or both (if translational research). Your goal as a researcher is to engage in the ongoing development of science and produce generalizable information. If you are writing a research paper and cannot tie your study to ongoing research in a meaningful way, stop writing and return to formulating your question. This section of your introduction should:

Be Clear and Concise

If the context or problem cannot be explained within a few sentences (or in some cases a couple paragraphs) it is probably not a well-formulated problem and stands a weaker chance of generating well-formulated solutions. This does not mean you need to abandon the topic, although it might mean you need to spend more time understanding your subject matter. Alternatively, you might think of several reasons the research is important and several populations who stand to benefit. But if you are thinking about this too broadly or emphatically (*Everyone will benefit! This study will totally change our practices!*) it may be necessary to consider what can feasibly be accomplished in a single study. While you might spend a sentence or two on longer-term outcomes, it is most critical that you state a practical and clear statement of significance.

Be Grounded in Evidence

Rather than simply telling the reader your topic is important, back up your assertions with data and evidence. The engagement-generating tactic of "pulling on heartstrings" can be compelling but should be avoided in academic writing in favor of logical, objective, and empirically derived statements. If you do not have evidence that the problem exists or the topic is important, stop writing and return to investigating the topic. This evidence might be found outside of your immediate field of study. To give an example, imagine you are conducting a study with the aim of improving adherence to an occupational safety program using a behavior analytic intervention. It would be appropriate to provide statistics on things like incidence of injuries resulting from the safety violation and costs typically incurred by the organization. Because the purpose of research is to produce generalizable information, you would present industry- or country-wide trends in your introduction and save the description of the problem at your research site for the method section. In other cases the evidence might be drawn from a small subset of studies. For instance, if you are comparing two self-management procedures for healthy eating, your problem statement might be the stated limitations of one of these procedures in terms of efficacy, cost, time, or social acceptability. In yet other cases your problem statement might not be data driven. For example, if you are conducting a study to improve compassionate and person-centered care, your problem statement might draw from humanistic sources that are rooted in ethical perspectives.

Generate Possible Avenues for Research

Your problem statement should allude to broad interest in a solvable problem. This is logical if you recall that your research aim is to produce generalizable knowledge (not just solutions for your site or company) that contributes to an ongoing body of work. The absence of information, such as gaps in the research, is solvable by collecting relevant data. The muddied outcomes of previous research are solvable through innovative experimental design. The lack of clarity around active treatment variables is solvable by conducting a component analysis. You get the idea. These considerations will allow you to connect the problem to your literature review, which will present theory, empirical evidence, historical trends, and/or informed opinion that lead to your proposed study.

Have a Clear Conceptual Framework

Your study is essentially an exploration of relationships among variables. Your conceptual framework is the model you apply to explain conceptually why those relationships might emerge. For much of the research conducted by behavior analysts, the conceptual framework will be based on operant and respondent conditioning principles. On a molecular level, the conceptual framework is a speculatory endeavor regarding potential moderating and mediating variables. Before we get too muddled by confusing language, let us look at an example. Imagine you are conducting a study on the effects of the teacher's classroom management on student behavior with the aim being to lessen teacher perception of burnout. Your conceptual framework might position the teacher–student relationship as a mediating variable to teacher burnout, meaning you assume the intervention will work only insofar as it improves that relationship. You might also expect teacher perception of self-efficacy to moderate this relationship whereby teachers with higher self-efficacy have better student outcomes after the classroom management intervention. Alternatively, you might expect the classroom management intervention to improve student behavior and reduce teacher burnout only if it involves timely, consistent, and predictable reinforcers for the desired student behaviors and the mitigation of conditions that cause teachers to report burnout, irrespective of whether the teacher–student relationship improves or the level of self-efficacy of the teacher. The importance of mediating and moderating variables is that, rather than simply describing a simple relationship between variables, they help explain the results and allow for better predictions in real-world circumstances. As you consider your conceptual framework, remember it should reflect your field of study and be grounded in empirical evidence. Use the prompts in Fig. 5.2 to help you to develop your problem statement.

Writing the Problem Statement Exercise
Prepare to write your problem statement by concisely answering the following questions (skip any that do not pertain to your research): 1. Why is this research important? _____ 2. Who could benefit from this research? _____ 3. If this research were not conducted, who would be affected and in what ways? _____ 4. What do we currently not know or understand that this research will tell us? _____ 5. Why is now the right time for this research to be conducted (considering both why it is the next logical question in a line of research as well as sociocultural factors)? _____ 6. Why is my field of study well-suited to conduct this research? _____ See the table *Conventions in Academic Writing* and practice using the frames next to Problem Statement by replacing the text in the brackets with phrasing that applies to your research. Once you have done so, write your brief problem statement here: _____ _____ _____

Fig. 5.2 Writing the problem statement exercise

Literature Review (the Body of the Introduction)

The literature review is a summary with intentionality. This means the review does not simply describe characteristics of studies related to your topic but is written with an awareness of critical issues the reader must understand in order to (a) evaluate the need for the study within an ongoing series of works and (b) evaluate the internal, external, and social validity (if applied research) of your study as you designed and implemented it. We use the term "evaluate" to highlight the importance of the literature review in establishing the reader's insight. It is not enough to simply tell the reader what to conclude; a good writer provides context and reasoning to convince the reader. On the other hand, it is not your role to bring the reader to the same level of understanding you have or to provide a full bibliography of past research.

Let us consider an example: say the studies in your review were largely conducted with college students and you determine more studies must be done to improve understanding of the external validity of the intervention (i.e. conduct the study with people who are not in college). In this scenario one way you might move away from *telling the reader* and toward *giving insight* is to describe characteristics of the college setting—or characteristics of college students—that support the intervention but are absent for same-aged adults who are not enrolled in college or adults of different ages, citing examples. Or, you might present data on the poor generality of interventions from college settings to non-college settings.

A well-written literature review:

Does Not "Stack" Articles

A strong literature review requires a synthesis of your knowledge and resources into a cohesive research argument, rather than simply listing or copying your bibliography into the body of your introduction. When organizing the outline you should question how each resource fits and where it will have a significant impact in your introduction. Consider the example of a team of lawyers preparing for an upcoming trial. The team must devise their strategy and argumentation based upon legal precedent (i.e. court decisions that inform current cases). It would do no good, and very likely harm their case, to simply present each previous court decision and the characteristics of the case in turn. The judge (read: your reader) might interject and ask "why are you telling me this?" The lawyers could avoid this embarrassing scenario by presenting their arguments or facts logically while citing earlier court cases (read: earlier research) for support. Put succinctly: state, then cite. Essentially, you should aim to build a case for your research in a systematic and organized way.

This guideline is easily understood through an example. Imagine you are writing an article about a very new technology and there are only a few earlier articles exploring the technology with your population of interest. You could simply describe the problem this technology aims to solve and then summarize each previous study in turn. Then, you could simply state the purpose of your study and move on to the method section. The problem with this approach is that the reader will get to your purpose statement with so many details that do not pertain to your study that they might feel confused or even misled. Your individual abstracts have not provided the foundation for describing a knowledge gap, controversy, or logical extension of those studies. We are pointing this out as a problem and you might not feel clear on how to fix it. We will address that in the final section of this chapter.

Organizes Points Logically and Clarifies the Relevance of Each Point

You might look at your references and wonder how to decide whether they fit in your introduction and where. One way to draw such conclusions is to consider the function each reference serves within your introduction. Table 5.1 provides some example questions to help get you started. We will expand on this and explain the difference between broad, tailored, and pinpointed information in a bit.

Considers Multiple Sides of the Research Argument

A natural aim of research is to replace outdated or ineffective strategies, yet it is not uncommon for conflict to arise when this happens. The conflict could be among researchers or could be an internal conflict of a single researcher. In fact, that researcher could be you. Researchers, being human, approach their own work and the work of others with biases that may show up in their writing. The writer might, for instance, unequally represent two sides of an argument, or they might diminish the success of an intervention that came before their own work. In some cases, these biases can become so strong that they create challenges that must be navigated, like tensions that arise during peer review or siloing researchers from one another. Failing to give counterarguments an evaluative analysis can also have detrimental effects on the populations the research is supposed to help. This can occur if one's own biases have caused them to deemphasize economic, sociocultural, or pragmatic variables that might render a treatment more or less effective. That said, equal representation of ideas is not always warranted; you should consider its relevance, your aims, the audience, and your allotted space. It is, however, a good practice to become aware of counterarguments and their argumentative strength. You might not include this information in your final paper but, at minimum, you will understand what your approach aims to replace.

Table 5.1 Organizing references by function

Organizing references by function
Does this resource provide general knowledge about my topic (broad information)?
Does this resource inform my general argument (tailored information)?
Am I using the theory or procedures of this resource in my research (tailored information)?
Does this resource tie in directly to my purpose (pinpointed information)?
Am I replicating important parts of the study (pinpointed information)?

Purpose Statement

For research studies, the purpose statement is mostly simply stated as "the effects of X on Y" with X being the independent variable and Y being the dependent variable. A well-written purpose statement will make the method more digestible by describing the major components of the study. In addition to the independent and dependent variables this may include the population, experimental design, or setting. Many, if not most, studies have multiple purposes. A good purpose statement:

Extends a Body of Research

Hopefully by now this point is clear. Your purpose statement can only be written after you have dived deep into the literature to understand how past researchers have tried to address the problem and have determined your specific study has not yet been conducted. Purpose statements describing a direct or systematic replication often reference the study being replicated.

Is Accurate

The purpose statement should describe aims that were achieved. If the study was amended and some original aim was unable to be achieved, this should be explained next to the purpose statement, so the reader does not approach the next sections with undue expectations. Attend carefully to the verbs you use in your purpose statement. If you say your purpose was to "analyze the effects of" some intervention on behavior this suggests you will do more than simply summarize the literature in this area. It may be similarly misleading to state the purpose is to "review the literature in order to quantify the effectiveness of" some intervention if you did not calculate effect sizes or otherwise quantify effectiveness.

Is Doable

This means the purpose should be within the researcher's methodological wheelhouse and require resources at the researcher's disposal. Resources include things like expertise, time, money, mentorship, and access to participant pools. In some fields it is common to rely on assistance from a statistician, methodologist, programmer, or other professional for certain components of the study. Very few people can do it all! However, if you are an undergraduate or graduate student you should note that programs have varying levels of tolerance for inviting outside expertise into your study. Consult your advisor or committee chair if you are unsure of what is acceptable in your program.

Use the prompts in Fig. 5.3 to guide the development of your purpose statement.

Exercise
Practice writing your purpose statement by concisely stating what the study will do, what independent variable will be evaluated, what dependent variable it will affect, and with which population.

1. What is the general approach (e.g., create, evaluate, compare)?

   _____

2. What is the independent variable of interest?

   _____

3. What is the dependent variable (behavior or phenomenon) of interest?

   _____

4. What population does it affect?

   _____

Write your completed purpose statement here:

The present study aims

_____

_____

Fig. 5.3 Practice writing your purpose statement

Additional Components

Depending on your topic's technicality, complexity, and intended audience you may or may not choose to include the following in your introduction:

1. Key terms
2. Overview of the paper's structure
3. Synopsis of the method (if research paper)
4. Explaining reasons for author's interest in the topic.

Organizing and Writing the Introduction

In this section, we provide guidelines for constructing the body of your introduction. As you become more confident in writing academic papers you will develop your own preferences and style, but we strongly recommend an approach that looks something like plan, outline, write, revise, edit, obtain peer review, revise, and edit. Continue this recursive writing process until the introduction is accurate, complete, follows grammar and formatting guidelines, and flows well. As we have covered, introductions to research proposals often begin with general statements about the topic, then provide a scan or analysis of past research, and end with a discussion and justification for the current project. The information starts broadly applicable and

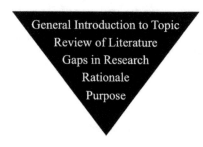

General Introduction to Topic
Review of Literature
Gaps in Research
Rationale
Purpose

Fig. 5.4 Introduction information funnel

Table 5.2 Structuring the introduction

Structuring the introduction	
A Very Basic Outline	Interpretation
Problem	What you are trying to solve
Research topic	Your approach to solving the problem
Scope of research	What has been done; outcomes and limitations
Gaps in research/limitations	What is still unknown/what to improve now
Purpose of current study	Your specific research question(s)

gradually becomes more applicable only to the current study. This is represented by the inverted triangle below (see Fig. 5.4).

You should begin with a plan on how to frame your research argument followed by an outline or model to organize your approach. In Table 5.2, "Structuring the Introduction" we provide some basic strategies for starting your outline. In practice, your outline might end up multiple pages long. It just depends upon the complexity of your topic. It might be helpful to remind yourself that the purpose of the outline is to help ensure that your introduction is logical and goal focused.

You might look at this outline and feel confused about how to organize certain sections and how much to write about those topics. This is where your research plan comes in. Unless you are conducting a very simple study that is based upon a relatively small body of work, you will probably need to make some decisions about how each article fits into your paper. Additional information may be interesting but have the unintended effect of being distracting or confusing. Cutting out information can be difficult, especially if you have spent a lot of time on reading and understanding these studies, but doing so judiciously will help you draw a streamlined connection from the problem to the purpose.

Another way to say this is that the review should be intentional. The writer provides information only as it pertains to the goal of helping the reader understand the context, significance, and delimitations of the proposed study. By the time the reader gets to the purpose statement, they should be able to wager a good guess on what the current study aims to do. Some common goals are to present a conceptual issue, describe a problem or controversy, or lay out empirical evidence. In all cases, the literature review is a foundation for and justification for your ideas. Identifying your goals for this section can help you present information in a more concise and effective way. We recommend you take a moment to complete the Goal Setting exercise in Fig. 5.5 before moving on.

Goal Setting Exercise
Think of your study or a study that you would like to complete. In one sentence, state what you hope to test or demonstrate. Then, list three goals (or concepts) of your literature review section that are appropriate for your topic.
Topic:
_____
_____
Goal 1:
_____
Goal 2:
_____
Goal 3:
_____
Example: On the topic of training scent detection dogs to identify a new drug, we might have the following goals: 1) Overview what the dogs do and how they are trained, 2) Describe the new drug and the importance of detecting it in public settings, 3) Compare and contrast trainings developed for other drugs, focusing on what makes this drug a special challenge

Fig. 5.5 Goal setting exercise

Once you understand your goals and intentions it should be easier to start sorting information into the important stuff you must include, the fringe stuff that might have a place in your argumentation, and the irrelevant stuff. The breadth of information covered in a literature review can seem broad and overwhelming, but starting to think of information as hierarchical or nested can help you to develop an organizational structure. This is conveyed in Fig. 5.6.

It is important to organize the information in a way that makes sense for your research plan and argument. Let us imagine you are comparing Intervention A to Intervention B. Depending on your argument, you may present relevant works for Intervention A followed by relevant works for Intervention B or present them together while focusing on issues like effectiveness and generality. Sometimes you will think you have a good organizational plan but then find that it does not work out as you intended. It is okay to be flexible with your organizational plan and make changes as needed. If you are flexible and patient with yourself and the writing process you will find it much more enjoyable.

Typically writers lay out information starting with the broader, more general, topics and principles and then narrow down the review by introducing more specific aspects of the topic until they unveil the specific problem or need. You can narrow down by starting with areas of general understanding, followed by areas with strong empirical demonstration or general agreement, and leading into areas of weaker empirical demonstration or disagreement, and then specific gaps or discrepancies that point to a need for your investigation. Another way to think of this is starting with information that is broadly applicable about your topic, then moving to tailored

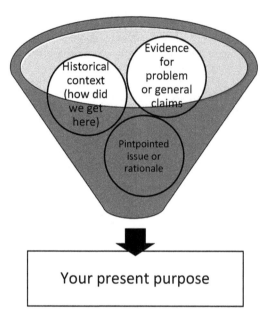

Fig. 5.6 Organizing your introduction

information that the reader should know to understand the context of your study, and then moving to pinpointed information that the reader must know to understand your specific purpose.

Broadly applicable information is information that applies to all or nearly all studies in your area of investigation. It is usually commonly known or easily uncovered information about the topic. It includes views that are typically accepted or believed about the topic. This can touch on information that you assume your reader already knows or understands about the topic. If there is a common perspective about your topic, introduce that first, before moving into new or little-known perspectives. The Summarizing Broad Knowledge exercise (see Fig. 5.7) should help you get started with writing about your study's background, context, and significance.

After introducing your broadly applicable information, you can present *tailored information* that your reader should know before you get to the specific needs or dilemma. Tailored information can include key terms, general research findings, gaps in knowledge, controversies, or conflicting viewpoints. As you outline this section, consider the implications of the findings, controversies, research gaps, or conceptual perspectives. In other words, consider what these points convey to the reader and how it directs their expectations for your study's purpose and methodology. It is also useful to self-audit occasionally to make sure you are presenting all critical information and not just cherry-picking evidence because of things like publication recency, bias toward popular authors, or incidental exposure.

Once you have led the reader through a broad understanding of the topic and then tailored their understanding to your approach, you can introduce *pinpointed information* on the problem or need. Be sure to discuss specific research approaches,

Summarizing Broad Knowledge Exercise

Now that you have your topic and goals for your introduction, list five broadly applicable things the reader should know about the empirical foundation of your research area. Write these in the logical order in which they should be introduced. List citations for each point.
 	
Concept 1: _____
 	
    Citation 1: _____ Citation 2: _____
 	
Concept 2: _____
 	
    Citation 1: _____ Citation 2: _____
 	
Concept 3: _____
 	
    Citation 1: _____ Citation 2: _____
 	
Concept 4: _____
 	
    Citation 1: _____ Citation 2: _____
 	
Concept 5: _____
 	
    Citation 1: _____ Citation 2: _____
 	
Example: On the topic of evaluating stimulus equivalence to teach derived manding we might have the following concepts: 1) children with autism who have learning delays often experience communication benefits from behavior analytic interventions (DeSouza et al., 2017), 2) stimulus equivalence is the emergence of stimulus-stimulus relations typically established by match-to-sample procedures (Sidman, 1994), 3) stimulus equivalence was first explored to teach children with learning delays to read (Sidman, 1971; Sidman & Cressan, 1973), 4) stimulus equivalence is recognized as an important foundation in complex language (Critchfield, 2018), and 5) derived mands, tacts, and intraverbals have been observed following stimulus equivalence training in children with autism (Belisle et al., 2020; McClay et al., 2013)

Fig. 5.7 Summarizing broad knowledge

findings, and limitations and lead the reader to the main concerns that guide your study's purpose. This information justifies your specific research question, method, population, dependent variables, and/or procedures. The Tailoring and Pinpointing exercise below (see Fig. 5.8) should help with generating some main ideas to support your study's rationale.

The literature review requires a writing style that is concise, clear, relatively unbiased, and logical. This is called academic prose. It is important to keep in mind that the purpose of academic writing is to clearly convey information and ideas, rather than to impress the reader with fancy language or complicated sentence structures. Many writers believe they must use inflated or embellished writing, such as writing "we would be remiss if we failed to mention the researchers utilized..." rather than stating more succinctly that "the researcher used..." Another common practice is writing in a passive voice with static—rather than active—verbs, such as writing "the stimuli were presented by the teacher" rather than "the teacher presented the stimuli." Using clear and concise language, active voice, and specific verbs can help your reader understand your ideas more easily. Additionally, avoiding bias and being logical in your presentation can help build trust with your reader and increase the effectiveness of your argument. The conventions presented in the table Conventions in Academic Writing (see Table 5.3) can be helpful guidelines, but remember to adapt your writing style to your specific aims and audience.

Chapter Summary

For your convenience, we have organized some general strategies with Dos and Don'ts into Table 5.4. Three key ideas for writing the introduction that we hope you took away from this chapter are to be intentional, or start with a plan on what you want the reader to know and organize your ideas to get there, progressively narrow down your topic, and funnel this information into a logical and clear purpose statement.

A Note on Style and Structure

You should recognize that, because writing an introduction is such a complex task, the structure and style of your introduction might vary depending on whether you are reporting a research study, brief report, conceptual paper, or systematic literature review. You might also find yourself deviating from our guidelines as you work toward specific aims or develop your personal style. Because personal style can negatively influence effective prose, we recommend continually seeking feedback and returning to this chapter now and again. An excellent practice is to have multiple seasoned colleagues read and critique your writing. Now that you understand that (a) introductions are complex and cannot be boiled down to a specific formula and (b) your personal style should not take priority over effective writing, you are ready to move on to the main material.

Tailoring and Pinpointing Exercise

List 2-4 concepts, views, or main points about the controversy, research gap, or dilemma you are addressing. This should be information tailored to your study. Write these in the logical order in which they should be introduced. Then describe the pinpointed problem that will lead to your purpose statement.

Concept 1: _____

    Citation 1: _____ Citation 2: _____

    Citation 3: _____ Citation 4: _____

Concept 2: _____

    Citation 1: _____ Citation 2: _____

    Citation 3: _____ Citation 4: _____

Concept 3: _____

    Citation 1: _____ Citation 2: _____

    Citation 3: _____ Citation 4: _____

Concept 4: _____

    Citation 1: _____ Citation 2: _____

    Citation 3: _____ Citation 4: _____

Pinpointed problem that will lead to your purpose statement:

    _____

    _____

    Citation 1: _____ Citation 2: _____

Fig. 5.8 Tailoring information for your study

Table 5.3 Conventions in Academic Writing

Conventions in Academic Writing (Something to Help You Get Started)		
Component	Purpose	Sentence Starters
Problem Statement	Establish the importance of the topic for society, the discipline, or the area of research	[Social skills] are a fundamental component of… [Telehealth] is quickly becoming [a key instrument in]… In recent years, [Behavior Analysis has focused heavily on]…
	Establish the topic as a problem	Along with [this growth in the field] comes greater pressure on… Of particular concern in [serving adult populations] is… Following [a traumatic brain injury], [patients] are at an increased risk of…
	Identify gaps in knowledge	Despite evidence of [the effects of mindfulness on burnout], it remains unclear whether… These recent developments have refreshed the debate over [whether behavior analysts should]… While the importance of [social validity] has been well-established, there is a paucity of research evaluating…
Literature Review	Describe the historical trends	Over the past few decades, there has been a growing interest in... Research on [topic] dates back to [time period], with early studies focusing on... A seminal study by [author] in [year] paved the way for subsequent research on... Historically, behavior analysis has primarily focused on [topic], but recent studies have expanded this focus to include...
	State what is established or currently known	Previous research has demonstrated that... Studies have consistently shown that... Researchers have established that... The current understanding of... is based on previous research indicating that...
	Use transition statements between topics and paragraphs	"Having established the historical context and previous research in this area, it is important to now focus on..." "While previous research has provided important insights into this topic, there are still gaps in our understanding, which this study aims to address by..." "Building on the previous literature, this study seeks to..." "However, there are limitations to the current literature, which this study aims to overcome by..." "In light of the existing research, this study takes a novel approach by..." "While previous studies have primarily focused on X, this study expands on the literature by examining Y..." "The next logical step in the literature would be to explore the implications of X for Y, which this study seeks to do by..."

(continued)

Table 5.3 (continued)

Conventions in Academic Writing (Something to Help You Get Started)

Component	Purpose	Sentence Starters
	Detail individual investigations	In their study, [author] investigated... Using a single-subject design, [author] examined... [Author] conducted a series of experiments to explore... Previous research by [author] has demonstrated that... In a recent study, [author] explored the effects of... [Author] investigated the impact of [variable] on [dependent variable] using a quasi-experimental design. In an effort to replicate previous findings, [author] conducted a systematic replication study. [Author] sought to address a gap in the literature by investigating... Using an alternating treatments design, [author] compared the effectiveness of two interventions... [Author] used a multiple baseline design to assess the effects of [variable] on [dependent variable].
	Synthesize investigations	Taken together, these studies suggest that... A synthesis of the literature indicates that... Overall, the findings from these studies suggest that... These studies collectively demonstrate that... In combination, the results of these studies suggest that... An analysis of the literature reveals that... These investigations point to the conclusion that... A common theme emerging from these studies is... The literature consistently demonstrates that... When considered as a whole, these studies highlight...
Purpose Statement	Summarize the literature review	Overall, the literature indicates... In summary, the studies reviewed... Taken together, the findings of these studies... In conclusion, the literature provides... Based on the review of the literature, it is clear that... Overall, the literature supports the need for further investigation into... In brief, the literature reviewed suggests that... The collective results of the studies reviewed suggest that... In essence, the literature reviewed highlights...
	State the purpose of the current investigation	The purpose of this study is to... The primary aim of this research is to... In this study, we seek to... This research project is designed to investigate... The goal of this study is to examine... The aim of this research is to determine... The primary objective of this study is to assess... This study aims to explore... The purpose of this research is to contribute to our understanding of... The overarching objective of this study is to...

(continued)

Table 5.3 (continued)

Conventions in Academic Writing (Something to Help You Get Started)

Component	Purpose	Sentence Starters
	Overview the method (optional)	The present study utilized a [research design] to investigate... A [research method] was employed to assess... Participants were recruited using [recruitment method] and assigned to [condition/group] using [assignment method]. The intervention was implemented using [procedure], which involved... Data were collected using [data collection method], which allowed for the measurement of... The study was conducted in [setting/context] to ensure ecological validity. A single-subject design was used to investigate the effects of... The study employed a multi-component intervention, which included... The study utilized a between-subjects design, with participants randomly assigned to [condition/group]. The study was conducted in multiple phases to assess the effects of...

Table 5.4 Introduction Dos and Don'ts

Strategies	Dos	Don'ts
1. Be intentional	Determine your goals for each section and paragraph of your introduction (e.g., present a conceptual issue, discuss a problem or controversy, lay our empirical evidence)	Arbitrarily state the method and findings of each study without relating them back to your section goals and topic
	Use an outline to lay out the order of studies that you will discuss and the point that each one will make or support	Introduce studies without first explaining what they show or support or how they relate to other studies
	Introduce topics in a logical order	Describe studies without also summarizing the implications of findings and adding a logical transition to the next study
2. Progressively enlighten your reader Nice-to-Know	It is okay to present evidence of a problem or conceptual issue that is related to your study but is not required to understand your study. Information like this can be useful if it helps establish cohesive bonds across publications.	Present unnecessary information or overload the reader with facts and details about past studies that are irrelevant to your work.

(continued)

Table 5.4 (continued)

Strategies	Dos	Don'ts
Should-Know	Tailor the details of your introduction to your outlet. For example, assume if you are submitting to a behavior analytic journal your audience will have basic foundational knowledge.	Assume the reader has more than basic foundational knowledge. Explain technical terms and concepts even if they are already described in the research you cite.
Must-Know	Present all relevant information the reader needs to understand the problem, your research aims, and your approach to fulfilling your study's purpose	Give hasty or overly simplified descriptions of previous research that would be misleading
3. Get to the Point	Keep your purpose statement clear and concise Take note of current events and societal concerns when pointing out discrepancies and needs while being sensitive to the impact your descriptions could have on the reader	
4. General Strategy	Use transition links to connect paragraphs for time, cause-effect, addition, and contrast links Logically introduce each piece of information Look at similar peer-reviewed articles for examples to follow Cite frequently but sensibly including definitions, clarifications, and implications Clarify your assumptions, particularly when discussing sensitive or ill-defined topics Use an interesting compelling style and tone	Include conflicting perspectives and contradictions in research findings in a single paragraph; DO separate these into separate paragraphs so each can be given due diligence Include irrelevant information that distracts from your point (even if it is interesting) Use models that are poorly written, in sketchy outlets, outdated, or relevant only in that they support your ideas Cite the same article after multiple contiguous sentences; DO rearrange phrasing to make clear the ideas are all related to that source Assume that you speak for any one group of people, even if you identify as that specific population Exaggerate the implications of your issue by catastrophizing possible outcomes; DO cite the literature with factual outcomes

References

*Article Referenced for Illustrative Purposes

*Belisle, J., Stanley, C. R., Schmick, A., Dixon, M. R., Alholail, A., Galliford, M. E., & Ellenberger, L. (2020). Establishing arbitrary comparative relations and referential transformations of stimulus function in individuals with autism. *Journal of Applied Behavior Analysis, 53*, 938–955. https://doi.org/10.1002/jaba.655

*Critchfield, T. S., Barnes-Holmes, D., & Dougher, M. J. (2018). What Sidman did--historical and contemporary significance of research on derived stimulus relations. *Perspectives on Behavior Science, 41*, 9–32. https://doi.org/10.1007/s40614-018-0154-9

*DeSouza, A. A., Akers, J. S., & Fisher, W. W. (2017). Empirical application of Skinner's verbal behavior to interventions for children with autism: A review. *The Analysis of Verbal Behavior, 33*, 229–259. https://doi.org/10.1007/s40616-017-0093-7

Ledford, J. R., & Gast, D. L. (Eds.). (2018). *Single case research methodology* (pp. 59–60). Routledge. https://doi.org/10.4324/9781315150666

*Mahoney, A. M., Weetjens, B., Cox, C., Beyene, N., Reither, K., Makingi, G., Jubitana, M., Kazwala, R., Mfinanga, G. S., Kahwa, A., Durgin, A., & Poling, A. (2012a). Pouched rats' detection of tuberculosis in human sputum: Comparison to culturing and polymerase chain reaction. *Tuberculosis Research and Treatment*. https://doi.org/10.1155/2012/716989

*Mahoney, A., Weetjens, B., Cox, C., Jubitana, M., Kazwala, R., Mfinanga, G. S., Durgin, A., & Poling, A. (2012b). Giant African pouched rats as detectors of tuberculosis in human sputum: Comparison of two techniques for sputum presentation. *The Psychological Record, 63*, 583–594. https://doi.org/10.11133/j.tpr.2013.63.1.002

*McLay, L. K., Sutherland, D., Church, J., & Tyler-Merrick, G. (2013). The formation of equivalence classes in individuals with autism spectrum disorder: A review of the literature. *Research in Autism Spectrum Disorders, 7*, 418–431. https://doi.org/10.1016/j.rasd.2012.11.002

*Sidman, M. (1994). *Equivalence relations and behavior: A research story*. Authors Cooperative.

*Sidman, M. (1971). Reading and auditory-visual equivalences. *Journal of Speech and Hearing Research, 14*, 5–13.

*Sidman, M., & Cresson, O., Jr. (1973). Reading and crossmodal transfer of stimulus equivalences in severe retardation. *American Journal of Mental Deficiency, 77*, 515–523.

Dr. Amanda Mahoney received her PhD in psychology from Western Michigan University and is currently associate professor of behavior analysis at The Chicago School. She has published dozens of peer-reviewed articles in behavior analytic and non-behavior analytic journals and is past action editor of Behavior Analysis: Research and Practice.

Dr. Katherine Davis received her PhD in applied behavior analysis from The Chicago School and is a Board-Certified Behavior Analyst-Doctoral. She is the clinical director of a pediatric therapy practice in Southern California and has 14 years of experience working with individuals with developmental disabilities, ADHD, ODD, and ASD. Her research interests include acceptance and commitment therapy (ACT), derived relational responding, and rule governed behavior.

Dr. Shannon Martinez has a PhD in applied behavior analysis from The Chicago School. She has over a decade of experience using ABA with children with autism and other disabilities, including two of her own children who were diagnosed with ASD. Shannon is a Board-Certified Behavior Analyst-Doctoral, she is the clinical director of ABA Services for a children's clinic in South Carolina, and an adjunct faculty for Simmons University. Shannon's work has been published in Behavior Analysis in Practice, and her research interests include cultural competency, and staff and parent training.

Chapter 6
Writing the Methods of a Manuscript

Chrystal Jansz Rieken

The publication manual of the American Psychological Association describes journal article reporting standards (JARS) across research designs (APA, 2020). Within the JARS, the APA explains that the standards for the abstract and introduction of a paper share many common features across designs, whereas the methods section requires standards specific to the research type. In this chapter, we will review how to develop critical features of the methods section for behavioral research.

Behavioral researchers present conclusions about whether an intervention (i.e., independent variable) resulted in changes in a target behavior (i.e., dependent variable). It is often thought that the methods section is merely presented to tell the reader what was done, without a corresponding understanding of how the methods directly relate to the other sections of the manuscript (i.e., interpretation of findings). An equally important purpose of the methods is to allow the reader to independently evaluate the research that was conducted. The methods section contains all information against which the results, and interpretation of results (i.e., conclusions), are evaluated (Cooper et al., 2020). Therefore, the researcher must provide the reader sufficient detail about what was done to answer the research question, how it was done, why it was done (i.e., justify the process), and how the results were analyzed. In doing so, the reader can independently evaluate the methods, and their validity, related to reported outcomes and explanation of those outcomes.

The way the methods are written should establish that experimental selections made by the researches was based on and informed by previous literature. Rationales for the selected methods (e.g., why a measurement tool or research design was used) are needed to establish that evidence-base for the reader. Just as research questions

C. J. Rieken (✉)

Behavior Analysis Department, College of Graduate and Professional Studies at The Chicago School, Chicago, IL, USA

e-mail: cjansz@thechicagoschool.edu

A. K. Griffith, T. C. Ré (eds.), *Disseminating Behavioral Research*,
https://doi.org/10.1007/978-3-031-47343-2_6

are born from prior research, so too are the methods. Doing so continues the scientific process of implementing evidence-based strategies in research.

Behavioral research literature is intended to have applied impact and guide clinical practice. Clinicians consuming literature to inform treatment decisions for individual clients use information in the methods section to assess similarity and fit-of-methods for their client. As such, information reported in the methods should provide details that allow the clinician to evaluate the context of the method for applicability to their setting. These details also allow the clinician to interpret generality of findings.

Finally, researchers should provide sufficient detail to allow for replication and extension of the methods. Replication of methods that produce the same outcomes establishes validity of the independent variables under the same conditions. Extension of methods also lends to validity, but further adds to generality of procedures to novel conditions (e.g., participant groups, settings), as well as refinements to increase social validity (e.g., less time consuming, costly; Carter & Wheeler, 2019).

Participants

In the introduction section of the paper, the researcher has already made the case to the reader about why the population under study was, in fact, in need of studying, along with the current state of knowledge about that population with regard to the variables to be investigated. Based on that review, the reader should already be able to anticipate who the participants were before reaching the methods section. There should be a direct connection between information presented about the targeted population in the introduction and those selected for participation in the study.

In the methods section of the manuscript, authors explain who the participants were and how they were selected. This information is very important for establishing external validity as it allows the reader to assess applicability and likelihood of achieving similar outcomes, as well as to make comparisons across studies. This usually begins with noting the total number of participants who completed the experimental phases. In certain instances, attrition numbers are relevant to report; however, in behavioral research, this is less common. After reporting the sample size, recruitment and sampling methods are described. In behavioral research, recruitment is often achieved through convenience sampling (e.g., referred and recruited through a clinic), where participants were already accessible or known to the researchers. Next, selection is described through the description inclusion and exclusion criteria. Depending on the sampling method, researchers set specific parameters for inclusion into a study. These could include demographic characteristics (e.g., age range), conditions (e.g., diagnoses), performance (e.g., score on a pre-assessment) or behaviors (e.g., can use a keyboard) that make a participant eligible for inclusion. Exclusion criteria can also help define the sample (e.g., receiving >5 hours of treatment per week). Inclusion and exclusion criteria should be informed by the research questions and purpose of the study. Statements about consent and assent, where applicable, should be included.

Descriptive information about individual participants, emphasizing those characteristics that are relevant to the research question and dependent variables (e.g., age, adaptive test scores, information describing abilities, treatments and medications received during participation). Participants can also include secondary participants such as procedures where caregivers implemented the independent variable. If their participation is experimental in nature, their information should be included. In the example provided, this might include caregiver education achieved, age, number of children in the home, etc.

Care for the protection of privacy and anonymity should be taken. For example, physical locations can be referred to by region (e.g., mid-West) instead of city, treatment or center names should be omitted, and pseudonyms can be assigned if needed.

For example:

> Three female participants were included: Jena, Veronica, and Margie. Participants were 27, 32, and 30 years old, respectively, and self-identified as White. All participants were typically developing adults and held sales positions at the company hosting the study. For recruitment, all company employees were sent an e-mail with a study flyer. Those interested were advised to contact the first author, schedule an appointment, and review informed consent. Jena reported that she casually engaged in routine exercise about five times a month. Her exercise routine included cardiovascular exercises, but not running, jogging, or other treadmill exercise. Veronica and Margie engaged in exercise more often, on average two times per week. Both reported including running and treadmill exercise during their routine exercise routine. During the study, participants reported not engaging in any treadmill exercise outside of the study sessions. For each session, participants were properly dressed in exercise attire (e.g., form-fitting clothing, shorts, jogging pants, and athletic shoes) and were able to safely engage in cardiovascular activity (e.g., walking, jogging, or running) on a treadmill according to a self-report measure and a prescreener (Rosado et al., 2021).

Group Assignment and Matching

Behavioral research using group conditions should include a description of the groups and how they were assigned. In some cases, random assignment of all participants who met inclusion criteria is used. The method for random assignment should be described to show that each participant had equal chance of being assigned to any group. In other cases, an added step to achieve further homogeneity of groups is completed. Here, participants are compared based on relevant criteria (e.g., age, gender) and then divided in a way that balances representation of those variables across groups. For example, in the assignment description below, participants were all college students enrolled in a specific course at the same time. Assignment to experimental groups was randomly conducted based on that criteria alone. A benefit of this assignment method was that it assigned participants under naturally occurring processes; the researchers did not add any steps to the existing process. In applied research, this adds validity to the methods. However, when random assignment without balancing occurs, experimental groups can end up looking very different, which can affect outcomes. In the referred study, the authors noted that it could be the case that, as a natural artifact of random assignment, students in one group had completed more coursework on the topic than those in the other group, thereby possibly influencing their assignment scores. Where balancing of groups is not possible, it is suggested that researchers still report on this in the manuscript. This can be done by looking at participant demographic information and describing the groups, noting any areas of discrepancy (e.g., mean age in one group being much higher than the other). Implications of that should be further evaluated in the discussion section.

For example:

> There were two sections of the course, taught by two different instructors: teaching as usual (control; $N = 26$) and IT (experimental; $N = 22$). Students were electronically assigned to one of the two sections when registering for the course using the university's online registration system. Sections were then randomly assigned to instructors by that same registration system. It was then decided by the researchers, who were also the instructors, that the instructor who had taught using IT in face-to-face classes would teach the experimental (IT) group, whereas the other instructor would teach the course as usual to the other section (Jansz Rieken et al., 2018).

Setting

This section should include information about the location of the experimental sessions, as well as contextual information that could have or did affect implementation of the independent variable or participant behavior. Setting information lends to interpretation of the validity and probability of a reader obtaining the same outcomes, as well as information allowing for comparisons across studies. Consider, for example, two researchers conducting separate studies examining the effects of an intervention used to encourage play in young children. Researcher 1 conducts her study on the playground with the latest toys on the market. Researcher 2 conducts her study in a small office at a local university with toys the participants' caregivers brought from home. A reader comparing these studies notices that the results in Researcher 1's study were better than Researcher 2's, despite using a very similar procedure. Comparing the results within the context of the differing settings (i.e., playground vs. office), the reader can hypothesize that the setting may have impacted the behavior of the participant, leading to different outcomes. Using their knowledge of behavioral principles, the reader might conclude that following Researcher 2's method of starting in the office, while more controlled, would likely require the additional steps of planned generalization to the more natural setting. Researcher 1's method showed that starting in the controlled setting was not necessary as a first phase of the intervention. The applied implications of this should not be missed. Ethical application of research procedures in behavioral practices is driven by the goal to achieve maximum benefit for the client with the fewest resources used (e.g., their time).

As mentioned, information in the setting section of a manuscript will differ depending on the type of setting used. Research conducted in laboratory settings will mimic natural settings the least. These settings are often void of anything or anyone that is not directly needed or related to the study. In this sense, experimental control is at its highest while generality of outcomes is lowest. Settings for applied behavioral research are often active treatment settings or settings created to mimic the natural environment. While there are fewer manipulations to reduce confounding influences, these settings include contextual variables that influence participant behavior in the natural setting. This feature increase generality of findings. Finally, research conducted in the natural setting offers the highest degree of generality but lowest degree of control. Regardless of setting type, the researcher should describe the setting with sufficient detail for the reader to evaluate degree of control, or lack thereof, thereby influencing interpretations of results. This can include room dimensions, equipment and furniture in the immediate setting, presence of others, common interruptions, or distractions, etc. Information that could identify participants (e.g., name of the city, school) should be avoided.

For example:

> All sessions took place in the participants' designated classrooms after school hours to reduce the likelihood of peer distraction and extraneous variables. The classrooms contained a desk for each student, a teacher's desk, multiple bookshelves with academic and leisure activities, and two play corners containing mats, yoga balls, and a computer. A desk was placed in front of the two-way mirror for all sessions. This was to minimize distractions and signal a different expectation than the typical classroom activities. The therapist sat next to the student, and all materials were placed on the students' desks within arm's reach. Data were collected by the therapist via video recordings following each session. The video camera was placed within 3 ft. of the desk and diagram to sufficiently measure accuracy (Quigley et al., 2018, p.317).

Materials

This section should include everything that was used to select participants, implement the independent variable, and collect data about the dependent variable. The apparatus used to collect data about the dependent variable should be informed by the dimensions of the dependent variable itself. In this section, the reader requires detailed information about the apparatus used for data collection to evaluate the validity of measurement choices. For example, if the research question specified the purpose of the study was to lower gambling behavior and the DV was operationally defined as hours spent at a casino, using a money counter to measure winnings would not be a valid measurement tool as total winnings would not represent data about hours spent at the casino. Alternatively, if the participant often forgot to start a timer when entering the casino, or the batteries quickly ran low, self-report data based on the timer would not be a reliable measurement tool.

In addition to validity and reliably of data collection materials used, scientist-practitioners also rely on information about the complexity of data collection methods to assess feasibility of those methods in applied settings. For example, in an analogue research setting, the research team might have access to several research assistants or sophisticated recording technologies that are not available in clinical settings. Descriptive information here allows clinicians interested in implementing the procedures to best adapt data collection methods to their resources.

If published materials were used (e.g., an IQ assessment to determine eligibility), the researcher should efficiently describe the tool (i.e., its purpose or intended use), and provide evidence of the appropriateness of the tool for the study. In a journal article, this is often accomplished by referring directly to recent or seminal publications where the tool was validated or used effectively for similar purposes. This can be done by referencing those studies for the reader. The purpose for including the tool should be clear, including how data obtained from the tool were used in the study. If modifications were made, these steps should be described, along with the process for validating those modifications.

If the methods include materials created by the researchers (e.g., an assessment, data collection system, social validity survey), the researcher should describe the development of the tool. This can include the literature review process initially used to inform tool development, processes involving subject matter expert review and feedback, piloting, testing, and calibration of instruments, and the systematic steps taken to revise the tool at each step. Finally, materials include any instruments used the implement the independent variable. Depending on the specifications of the journal, photos can be used to depict study materials.

For example:

> Equipment included a ProForm ZT4 treadmill, a Polar H7 Bluetooth Heart Rate Sensor & Fitness Tracker, an Alcatel OneTouch Pixi 7 Tablet to display and record heart rate data from the sensor and fitness tracker, and a speaker for music. Hand towels and water were provided for each participant. The necessary data recording materials (e.g., data sheet and a pen or pencil) were present as well. A video camera was used to record all experimental sessions for the sake of interobserver and procedural reliability. Lastly, two social validity questionnaires were used, the Physical Activity Enjoyment Scale (Teques et al., 2020), and a questionnaire developed specifically for this study (Rosado et al., 2021).

Another example:

> Each student had a visual cue on their desk to denote the items they chose to earn and DRL criteria. The visual cue was a laminated piece of paper with a blank space to write what the student wanted to earn and what would happen if all students in the group met their individual goal. Below these statements were smiling face images representing the student's DRL criteria for reinforcement, if at least one smiling face image was visible, the student was still below the pre-determined criteria. At the end of the row, there was one frowning face image and if marked out indicated the student had exceeded his goal (Ré et al., 2023).

Dependent Variables

The purpose of this section is to describe and define the behavior under study. The purpose of the research question in behavioral research is to determine if a target behavior (i.e., dependent variable, the function of) is in fact dependent on the independent variable as presented in the study (Cooper et al., 2020). When the effect of an independent variable on the dependent variable is reproduced under the same conditions (e.g., participant profiles, setting), validity of findings increases. When the effect of the independent variable on the dependent variable is reproduced under *similar* conditions, but not the same, conditions, generality increases. Therefore, it is crucial that the target behavior be described in a way that allows other researchers to measure the behavior in the same way.

In addition to replication, a complete description allows researchers to reliably measure behavior within their own study. This is particularly true when more than one person is collecting measurement data. This, in turn, provides the reader with necessary information to evaluate validity of measurement methods and, therefore, resulting outcomes. If the reader does not have clear picture of what the target behavior was or how it was measured, confidence decreases and everything that follows is doubted.

Most common in behavioral research are topography-based definitions. This includes dimensions of the behavior that are available to an observer without further assessment (e.g., how it looks or sounds). Researchers should include detail about the dependent variable such that the reader gains a clear understanding of what was, and was not, targeted and measured. This is achieved with a carefully written operational definition describing the observable dimensions of the unit under study (e.g., force, magnitude, duration, frequency).

For example:

> *Vocal disruption* was defined as any audible utterance that occurred without permission by the teacher, excluding any type of signaled choral responding. An example of audible utterance with permission by the teacher included the student raising their hand and waiting to speak until they were called upon or responding after being called upon by the teacher (Ré et al., 2023)

The dependent variable is, of course, chosen before preparation of the manuscript and selected for study based on the importance of findings to the field. Though the behavior is defined for measurement according to its form, it is selected based on social validity. As such, a class of behaviors that produce similar outcomes (i.e., function) can be the unit of study. For example, there any many behaviors someone can engage in to procrastinate from studying for an exam (e.g., watching TV, texting friends, sleeping, eating). If the purpose of a study is to reduce procrastination, the researchers might measure all things the participant does that leads to a delay in reading their textbook. Here, the function (i.e., delay studying) is what determines if a behavior was counted (i.e., measured), not its form. In those cases, researchers have the added responsibility to document the function, and process of determining function, of behaviors of differing topographies included in data analysis.

We have focused on observable and researcher-measured dependent variables thus far however it is possible to study behaviors that are not accessible to the researcher. These can include behaviors that occur in private settings or the occurrence of which would be influenced by an observer. For example, sexual, hygiene medication administration, and sleep behavior. Likewise, covert behavior (e.g., thoughts) can be studied with the input of participants. When those behaviors are under study, similar to reporting training provided to research assistants, researchers should report how participants were trained to reliably report (e.g., collect data) and collect data about their own behavior.

Measurement

In this section of a journal article, researchers describe *how* data were collected. That is, the procedures followed for data collection using the tools described in the Materials section are explained. This section is important for replication, but also allows the reader needed information to interpret quality and validity of results. Authors should keep in mind that results can only be "presented and interpreted…in terms of what was measured, and the observation and recording procedures used" (Cooper et al., 2020, p.161). Therefore, what is presented in the measurement section sets the stage for what can, and cannot, be reported as results.

Measurement decisions are directly informed by the research questions and dependent variable(s); therefore, the description of measurement should follow and align with descriptions of the dependent variable(s) and research design(s). For example, in a study examining the effects of an intervention on gambling behavior, and the dependent variable was named as the number of times the participant used a VLT, measurement might be written as, "every time any part of participant's hand contacted the VLT lever and pulled downward, the observer pressed the counter one time. Observers counted a new occurrence when the participant's hand left contact and made contact again. Observers did not count an occurrence of contact without pulling downward". Alternatively, is time spent in the casino was collected, the researchers could then not report on the effect of the independent variable on the number of times the participant used a VLT.

The description in this section of the manuscript should include the name and description of the of data collection system used to measure participant behavior during each phase of the study (e.g., trial-by-trail, per opportunity, interval recording). If established measurement methods were used, the research may refer to the reader to those studies where the method was previously employed and validated. If calculations or conversions were used, such as percentages, provide the calculation formula used.

An important point in this section includes how those collecting data were instructed and trained. This should include data about reliability of scoring across data collectors (i.e., inter−/intra-rater/observer reliability/agreement; IOA), and steps that were taken to align scoring (e.g., changes to the data sheets, clarifying operational definitions, revising instrumentation). Kratochwill et al. (2012) have advised that for a study to be considered as evidence-based, "each outcome variable must be measured systematically over time by more than one assessor. Interobserver agreement (for the dependent variable) must be documented on the basis of an accepted psychometric measure of agreement" (p. 28). Without this information, the reader cannot assess the validity of the results.

For example:

> Exact count-per-interval interobserver agreement (IOA; Cooper et al., 2020) was used to assess measurement reliability for participant-initiated changes in intensity. A second observer was trained via a live online meeting platform. During training, the experimenter read and explained the definition of the dependent variable. Next, the experimenter and the second observer independently recorded data from the session video. Then, the experimenter compared the recorded data and reviewed any discrepancies with the second observer. This continued until agreement was achieved to at least 90%. The level of IOA was calculated for 36% of the total sessions included in the study; seven baseline sessions and seven heartrate feedback sessions. The level of agreement between the two observers was 92%, with a range between 82% and 100% (Rosado et al., 2021).

Experimental Design and Procedure

It is common for journals with a focus on behavioral research to prompt authors to combine the description of the experimental design and procedures because of the closely related information they provide readers (see instructions for authors before submitting your manuscript to a specific journal). That is, the manner in which the authors applied the experimental design is captured through their account of the procedures while the description of procedures allows the reader to evaluate the applicability and accuracy of the research design used to evaluate the effects of the procedures on the dependent variable.

When describing the experimental design, authors should name the design(s) and provide reference to literature that further describes and validates its robustness for identifying a functional relationship from like-research (i.e., evidence-based). Providing reference to other literature allows the reader to access additional information about the design, which also serves as rationale for its selection in the study. Cooper et al. (2020) describe the infinite number of experimental designs pointing out that, "because an experimenter's design includes careful selection and consideration of each component [of the study] (i.e., subject, setting, behavior, etc.), not counting the direct replication of experiments, one could say that there are as many experimental designs as there are experiments" (p.161). Here, the authors are highlighting that the research design is chosen and driven by the research question and specific parameters of the study variables needed to answer the question. Therefore, though it must meet the requirement to demonstrate a functional relationship where one exists, the research design can be unique to the study. Therefore, it is important that the authors not only state and describe the design but also provide the reader with a statement about why that specific design was chosen.

For example:

An ABABAB reversal design was implemented for the current study. In a classroom setting, a reversal design can demonstrate a functional relationship with the introduction and
removal of the proposed treatment package across repeated introductions. The reversal
design allowed the investigator to analyze the true level of behavior change (Cooper et al.,
2007) by directly comparing the rate of responding in baseline and treatment conditions,
allowing for a clear functional relation to be demonstrated. In this study, baseline consisted
of the procedures regularly implemented in the classroom and the treatment condition
included the addition of a full session, signaled DRL, with concurrent independent and
interdependent group contingencies (Ré et al., 2023)

Moving into the description of procedures, it is common to begin with a general
statement of the number and timing of experimental sessions. For example,
"Baseline and intervention sessions were conducted one to three times per day, 1 to
5 days per week, for individual participants. On days when multiple sessions were
conducted, a minimum of 15 min between sessions was required" (Schroeder et al.,
2023, p.186).

Next, provide the reader with a detailed description of what was done in each
phase or condition of the study, in chronological order, including any pre-training or
testing that occurred before experimental phases began. This can include information regarding instructions that were given to participants, how the researcher
responded to participant behavior, who implemented the phase, measurement timing, and any other components of the experimental manipulation. Where difference
or discrepancy in procedures across participants occurred, authors should describe
those differences.

Those learning to prepare a manuscript are often taught that the procedures
should be written in a way that allows the reader to replicate how the study was
conducted. While this is true and important, the details of this section accomplish
other means, such as determining ecological validity and procedural fidelity, equally
important to the scientific and consumption process. "Ecological validity refers to
how closely an experiment aligns with real-world phenomena. In applied behavioral
research, ecological validity may guide decisions about experimental settings, stimuli, people, and other design features" (Fahmie et al., 2023, p.302). "Procedural
fidelity is the extent to which procedures were implemented as designed or described.
Implementing   interventions…frequently   involves   topographically   complex
responses and conditional discriminations, actions that are both difficult to perform
correctly and to measure accurately" (Essig et al., 2023, p.83). Reporting procedural
fidelity as well as IOA data for procedural fidelity measurement is necessary. Note
that the example is provided in this section of the chapter as it applies to the understanding of the procedure; however, reporting standards for certain journals require
that procedural fidelity processes and data be reported under within the measurement section.

For example:

Trial-by-trial IOA (Cooper et al., 2020) was used to evaluate procedural fidelity. A data
sheet with task-analyzed steps was used, and each step was considered as one trial. Each
data sheet contained three steps, the first and third reported on if the participant engaged in

appropriate treadmill warm up and cool down, and the second step which reported if the participant navigated the treadmill at their leisure. The second observer was trained in the same manner for trial-by-trial IOA as for measurement reliability. Procedural IOA was calculated for 36% of all sessions; seven baseline sessions, and seven heartrate feedback sessions. The level of agreement between the two observers was 100% (Rosado et al., 2021).

Summary

In this chapter, we have reviewed the critical components of the methods section of a manuscript. We have discussed the importance of the methods section, to provide the reader all information needed to interpret the validity and reliability of results and implications provided by the researchers. Information in the methods accomplishes more than a step-by-step explanation of what was done. If study outcomes are favorable, the methods become the treatments that make significant and positive impacts in the lives of others.

References

American Psychological Association. (2020). *Publication manual of the American Psychological Association 2020: The official guide to APA style* (7th ed.). American Psychological Association.

Carter, S. L. & Wheeler, J. J. (2019). The *social validity manual: Subjective evaluation of interventions* (2nd ed.). Elsevier Academic Press.

Cooper, J. O., Heron, T. E., & Heward, W. L. (2007). *Applied behavior analysis* (2nd ed.). Upper Saddle River, NJ:Pearson Prentice Hall.

Cooper, J. O., Heron, T. E., & Heward, W. L. (2020). *Applied behavior analysis* (3rd ed.). Pearson Education, Inc.

Essig, L., Rotta, K., & Poling, A. (2023). Interobserver agreement and procedural fidelity: An odd asymmetry. *Journal of Applied Behavior Analysis, 56*, 78–85. https://doi.org/10.1002/jaba.961

Fahmie, T. A., Rodriguez, N. M., Luczynski, K. C., Rahaman, J. A., Charles, B. M., & Zangrillo, A. N. (2023). Toward an explicit technology of ecological validity. *Journal of Applied Behavior Analysis, 56*, 302–322. https://doi.org/10.1002/jaba.972

Kallet, R. H. (2004). How to write a method section of a research paper. *Respiratory Care, 49*, 1229–1232. https://web.archive.org/web/20190728022714id_/http://rc.rcjournal.com:80/content/respcare/49/10/1229.full.pdf

Kratochwill, T. R., Hitchcock, J. H., Horner, R. H., Levin, J. R., Odom, S. L., Rindskopf, D. M., & Shadish, W. R. (2012). Single-case intervention research design standards. *Remedial and Special Education, 34*, https://doi.org/10.1177/0741932512452794

Quigley, J., Griffith, A. K., & Kates-McElrath, K. (2018). A comparison of modeling, prompting, and a multi-component intervention for teaching play skills to children with developmental disabilities. *Behavior Analysis in Practice, 11*, 315–326. https://doi.org/10.1007/s40617-018-0225-0

Ré, T. C., Jansz Rieken, C., Brandt, J. A., Pacitto, J., & Yepez, J. (2023). Differential reinforcement of low frequency behavior as an interdependent group contingency for children diagnosed with Autism Spectrum Disorder. *Journal of Behavioral Education*. https://doi.org/10.1007/s10864-023-09512-w

Rieken, C. J., Dotson, W. H., Carter, S. L., & Griffith, A. K. (2018). An evaluation of interteaching in an asynchronous online graduate-level behavior analysis course. *Teaching of Psychology, 45,* 264–269. https://doi.org/10.1177/0098628318779275

Rosado, C. M., Jansz Rieken, C., & Spear, J. (2021). The effects of heart rate feedback on physical activity during treadmill exercise. *Behavior Analysis: Research and Practice, 21,* 209–218. https://doi.org/10.1037/bar0000223

Schroeder, C., Ragotzy, S., & Poling, A. (2023). Young adults with intellectual and other developmental disabilities acquire vocational skills with video prompting. *Journal of Applied Behavior Analysis, 56,* 181–200. https://doi.org/10.1002/jaba.963

Dr. Chrystal Jansz Rieken began her research training in Applied Behavior Analysis (ABA) at the University of Manitoba in 2000 under the supervision of Dr. G. Martin. She holds a postgraduate certificate in ABA and Advanced B.A. from the University of Manitoba, Behavioral Sciences Diploma from St. Lawrence College, M.A. in Disability Studies with specialization in ABA from Brock University, and Ph.D. in Special Education with specialization in ABA from Texas Tech University. She has over 23 years of experience as a professor, researcher, and clinician in behavior analysis in Canada and The United States. Her research interests include verbal behavior, behavior assessment, evidence-based instruction in higher education, psychotropic medication interventions in ASD, ethics in research, and the role of trauma in behavior analytic assessment and treatment. She and her students have presented their work at regional, national, and international conferences. Dr. Jansz Rieken is credentialed as a Board-Certified Behavior Analyst, Licensed Behavior Analyst, and International Behavior Analyst. She is a Master Trainer for The Road to Recovery. She currently works as assistant professor and Program Chair in Department of Behavior Analysis in the College of Graduate and Professional Studies at The Chicago School.

Chapter 7
Reporting Results for a Behavior-Science Audience

Andrew R. Craig, Megan A. Boyle, Sean W. Smith, and William E. Sullivan

Every component of a manuscript is critical for effective scientific dissemination. That said, the Results section may be of particular importance. It is the section wherein authors have the opportunity to showcase the outcomes from their research and to communicate key relations between their independent and dependent variables. Indeed, without clear and compelling data display accompanied by appropriate analyses, an author is unlikely to sway a scientific audience. Without a well-structured Results section, a study's outcomes are just anecdotes. Though anecdotes have a place in science, they are not sufficiently rigorous sources of data from which to develop an evidence base (Limb, 2011).

Given the central role of the Results section in communicating science, one may feel intimidated by the process of writing this section. To be transparent, authors are faced with myriad questions when structuring their Results. Which data are the most important ones to communicate to readers? How should they be analyzed? How should they be graphically displayed? And what steps can be taken to maintain high ethical standards throughout the process? But writing a Results section does not need to be a daunting task. A small amount of organization can turn a proverbial mountain into a molehill. Our purpose in writing this chapter is to provide researchers with some general guidelines to follow when writing up their Results that may help them organize their efforts.

A. R. Craig (✉) · S. W. Smith · W. E. Sullivan
Golisano Center for Special Needs, SUNY Upstate Medical University, Syracuse, NY, USA
e-mail: smithse@upstate.edu; sullivaw@upstate.edu

M. A. Boyle
Upstate Caring Partners, Utica, NY, USA
e-mail: megan.boyle@upstatecp.org

© The Author(s), under exclusive license to Springer Nature Switzerland AG 2023
A. K. Griffith, T. C. Ré (eds.), *Disseminating Behavioral Research*,
https://doi.org/10.1007/978-3-031-47343-2_7

We are writing this chapter from the perspective of behavioral scientists who wish to disseminate their research outcomes to other behavioral scientists. Accordingly, contents of the chapter will focus on topics that are particularly relevant to the behavioral sciences, such as single-case research designs, visual analysis, and observational data collection. Nevertheless, many of the considerations that we describe are sufficiently general across scientific domains and will benefit readers from all disciplines.

Selecting Data to Display

The amount of data that an author collects when conducting a study can be staggering. Think of all of the assessments that may precede a treatment analysis, or the various training phases that one may conduct to help subjects or participants acquire a new behavior before a more formal analysis. There is limited space in a manuscript, which often means authors will be unable to display all the data they collected during their research. Selecting which data to display is a critical part of writing the Results section. The onus is on the researcher to make a compelling case about how their research fits among existing research and how it extends current knowledge, and the researcher's data provide all the evidence supporting their claims. In this way, the authors must be careful to display the data that clearly convey the outcomes of the most relevant procedures they used for answering their research question(s). In this section, we provide general rules for selecting the data that are most relevant to the claims the authors make.

To demonstrate these guidelines, we will often refer to Zangrillo et al. (2016) as a case example. As a brief overview, Zangrillo et al. used a functional analysis to identify that the dangerous behavior of two children was maintained by escape from instructions. Then, across two different conditions, Zangrillo et al. conducted reinforcement schedule thinning with chained schedules of reinforcement by gradually increasing the number of instructions the participants completed before obtaining reinforcement. In the escape-only condition, participants obtained escape from demands as a reinforcer for completing instructions. In the escape-to-tangibles condition, participants received access to preferred tangible items in addition to escape from demands as reinforcers for completing instructions. We use Zangrillo et al. as a case example because they conducted multiple assessments and collected data on a variety of dependent variables, thereby demonstrating what an author should consider when selecting what to include in their results section.

Using the Supporting Information Section

As a general note for selecting data to display, authors should be aware that most journals publish articles online, and these online publications typically permit inclusion of an additional section for an article. Although the additional section is not included with the rest of the article nor is it included in the print version of the journal, readers can typically access the additional section through the journal's online portal. Different journals may refer to this supplementary, online-only section of an article by slightly different names (e.g., Supporting Information, Additional Information, Appendices). This section frequently serves as an additional way for authors to share their data. Unlike other sections of the manuscript, publishers often do not set limits on the size of their online-only sections, which can allow authors to provide all the data they are interested in sharing with their readers. The authors simply need to add one sentence to their manuscript to let readers know that the additional data are available and where to find them (e.g., "Please see Supporting Information for these data").

We advocate that authors make extensive use of these supplemental sections. They may increase the transparency of authors' research and help other researchers build upon the work of others. Throughout this section, whenever we suggest against including data, we do not mean to imply that the data should be excluded from the manuscript entirely. The data could (and, in most cases, probably should) be included in the section of the manuscript that may appear online only. Additionally, given the wide availability of the internet, we suggest that authors should opt for providing additional data in these sections instead of saying that the corresponding author will provide the additional data upon request. The latter practice may produce barriers to access that are circumvented by supplying data online: Authors may become difficult to track down if they move institutions, they may lose access to the data in question, or they may inadvertently miss requests for information.

Dependent Variables: Primary and Secondary

In any manuscript that reports outcomes from an experiment, it is necessary to report the data related to the dependent variables defined in the Methods section of the manuscript. Often, dependent variables may be divided into two general categories: primary dependent variables and secondary dependent variables. As their name implies, primary dependent variables are the variables of primary interest to the author of the manuscript. Researchers often describe these variables in the manuscript's "purpose statement," which frequently appears in the last paragraph of the introduction, and in the first paragraph of the Discussion section. When researchers collect and report data about multiple dependent variables, they sometimes distinguish the primary dependent variable(s) and other dependent variables in the Methods section. Researchers should always report data about the primary independent variables in the text of the manuscript and provide a graphic depiction of these data to demonstrate how these data relate to other variables. In so doing, researchers clearly communicate that these dependent variables are the most important aspect of the research and provide as much evidence as possible to support their claims about how these variables relate to the independent variable(s).

Deciding whether to include data on secondary dependent variables is often more nuanced. Below, we outline some considerations for deciding which data on secondary dependent variables may be important to include in the body of the Results section. One consideration is whether presenting data on additional variables will take up substantially more space in the manuscript. If the authors can display additional data without using more space in the manuscript, the authors are justified in including the data. Space is an important consideration for at least three reasons. First, journal editors often have an eye on reducing the length of manuscripts when possible. Printing additional pages in a physical journal is expensive, so they may suggest removing additional analyses that they consider superfluous. Second, readers may become overwhelmed if too many variables are analyzed. They may lose the forest for the trees, so to speak. Finally, some article classifications like short reports explicitly limit the length of manuscripts, so authors may need to be particularly mindful of their analyses in these cases. A useful example of how authors may show more data without substantially increasing the amount of space you use in a manuscript is by displaying multiple data paths on a single figure. For example, Figures 2 and 3 in Zangrillo et al. (2016) displayed data for three dependent variables (i.e., dangerous behavior, functional communication responses [FCRs], and compliance) in each graph.

A second consideration is the relevance of the secondary variable to clinical practice or the extant literature. If the additional variable has important implications for clinical practice or research, then the authors should attempt to display data pertaining to this variable. For example, Zangrillo et al. (2016) were most concerned with decreasing dangerous behavior when applying their treatment. It was, however, also important for them to show whether the intervention improved compliance with instructions because an intervention that reduces dangerous behavior and increases compliance could be used to help the participant gain new skills more effectively than an intervention that reduces dangerous behavior but does not increase compliance.

A third consideration is whether data on the secondary variable provide useful additional information. If the additional data provide novel information compared to the data on the primary variable, then the authors are justified in including the additional data in their manuscript. For example, Zangrillo et al. (2016) displayed data on dangerous behavior, FCRs, and compliance because it could have been the case that the intervention had an effect on some, but not all, of these variables. Displaying data for each variable increases the information the manuscript provides overall. It also increases the diversity of reasons readers may wish to consume a researcher's work. For example, the Zangrillo et al. study described above may be of interest to practitioners who are interested in reducing dangerous behavior, increasing communication, increasing compliance, or any combination of these goals.

If the secondary data in question do not show an identifiable relation among variables, it is often reasonable to omit them from the main body of the manuscript because it is unclear what information they convey. It could be the case that the variables are truly unrelated, but it could also be the case that the variables are related in a way that was not made clear by the experiment's procedures or the researcher's data analysis. After all, absence of evidence is not evidence of absence when it comes to relations between variables. For this reason, it is best to focus on the clearer relations and show data for those relations. Data that may not show functional relations can typically be discussed by the authors briefly and the data can be displayed in the supplemental, online-only section of a manuscript.

Sometimes, it is also a good idea to depict data for the same dependent variable in more than one way. For example, Zangrillo et al. (2016) depicted the percentage of instructions completed with compliance on multiple graphs, but they also depicted the cumulative number of compliant responses across sessions on a separate graph. Importantly, they included this separate graph because displaying cumulative compliant responses conveyed new information that could not be gleaned easily from the other graphs. Specifically, the cumulative graph more clearly showed that one intervention increased the rate of compliant responses to a greater extent than the other intervention. This example highlights why displaying additional data that provide novel information is encouraged. If, however, displaying additional data (or the same data in a different format) does not reveal any new relations among variables, then the authors should likely exclude them from the main body of their manuscript.

Selecting Data Based on the Methods

As another general guideline for determining which data to include in the Results section, authors should prioritize displaying data from assessments based on how closely the assessment relates to the overall purpose of the manuscript. Assessments that directly test the main hypothesis of the research can be thought of as primary assessments, and authors should always display data from these assessments. Assessments that do not directly test the main hypothesis of the research can be considered secondary assessments. Whether to include outcomes from secondary assessments is more ambiguous.

Although a secondary assessment may not directly test the main hypothesis, the results of secondary assessments may dramatically affect the way one interprets results from the primary assessment. Unfortunately, as noted above, constraints on manuscript length may preclude authors from including data from all secondary assessments, so they often need to choose which secondary assessments to include and exclude. As a general guideline, authors should prioritize displaying data from the secondary assessments that are more likely to affect interpretation of the outcomes from the primary assessment in the main body of their manuscript. Deciding which procedures are more likely to have affected outcomes may be quite nuanced, so we will provide some additional guidelines to consider when making these decisions.

One consideration is whether the procedures were used to include or exclude certain participants from analysis. For example, Zangrillo et al. (2016) were interested in evaluating the effects of their intervention on the behavior of participants with dangerous behavior maintained by escape from instructions. For this reason, it was important for Zangrillo et al. to include data from their functional analyses to demonstrate that participants met their inclusion criteria (i.e., escape-maintained dangerous behavior). Similarly, if it is possible that participant characteristics may significantly impact the results of an experiment and the authors conducted an assessment to evaluate appropriateness for the study, the author should likely include the data from this assessment in their Results section.

A second consideration is whether the procedures were used to inform the independent variable. One common example of a secondary assessment being used to inform an independent variable is conducting a preference assessment to inform an intervention that compares the effect of high- and low-preferred tangible reinforcers on behavior. In this scenario, the validity of the independent variable relies on the outcomes of a secondary assessment, so the authors should present the data from the secondary assessment. On the one hand, for example, a participant who shows a large difference in responding between their most and least preferred stimuli during a preference assessment might show large differences in response rates when those stimuli are used in a subsequent reinforcement procedure. On the other hand, a participant who shows small differences in responding during the preference assessment might show small differences in response rates when those stimuli are used in a subsequent reinforcement procedure. Thus, displaying data from the secondary assessment (i.e., the preference assessment) may help explain the results obtained during the primary assessment (i.e., the reinforcement procedure).

Sometimes secondary assessments may be used to inform assessments, but it may be less likely that the results would have a profound effect on the primary assessment. For example, Zangrillo et al. (2016) conducted a preference assessment to inform the stimuli they used in their functional analyses. For them, the preference assessments did not directly inform the independent variable and there was a relatively limited possibility that the results of this assessment would drastically affect the results of their primary assessment. For this reason, Zangrillo et al. (2016) appropriately omitted these data from their Results section to save space in their manuscript to display data more pertinent to the purpose of their manuscript.

A third consideration is the amount of research validating the procedures used in the secondary assessment. If an assessment has a lot of empirical support, there is a greater chance that readers would be familiar with the assessment and have greater confidence in the conclusions that the authors may derive from the data obtained during the assessment. This is another reason supporting the exclusion of preference-assessment data in Zangrillo et al. (2016). They used a well-supported preference assessment procedure (i.e., paired-stimulus preference assessment; Fisher et al., 1992), which provided further justification for excluding data from the assessment in the body of their manuscript. If, however, authors of a manuscript use a novel set of procedures, it is best practice to display those data so readers may evaluate the outcomes from the unique procedures.

Cherry-Picking Data: Choosing Data Based on (Dis)Confirmation of Hypotheses

During the process of selecting the data to display, researchers should avoid letting their biases (explicit or implicit) influence their decisions. Often research is hypothesis driven, so it may be tempting for researchers to choose to display data that confirm their hypothesis and omit data that may shed doubt on their hypothesis. Ethical research practices are paramount—researchers must remember that their data may influence future research and clinical practice. Choosing to display data based on whether it confirms or disconfirms a hypothesis can mislead others, potentially causing researchers to waste resources continuing an unproductive line of research or leading clinicians to try interventions that might not work as well as the data suggest they do. Thus, it is of the utmost importance that researchers are honest and transparent when choosing which data they display.

As a general guideline, researchers should not make decisions about including or omitting data based on the outcome they represent. The guidelines for selecting data we described in the previous sections are based on how pertinent the dependent variables and the assessments are for answering the experimental question. Researchers should apply these guidelines whether or not the data support their hypothesis. Further, if a researcher decides to include data on a dependent variable or from a certain assessment, they should typically report all the data without omitting specific data points. The only exceptions to this rule may be when the researcher is aware of confounds that may have affected the collected data. Given that this text is written for early career researchers and extensive discussion would be needed to cover this murky topic, we will suggest a conservative approach to working with data that may have been affected by uncontrolled extraneous variables. Authors may consider including all of the data in the manuscript, explaining why and how certain data may have been affected by confounds, and providing interpretations of the overall set of data while including and explaining the potentially confounded data.

It is also worth reiterating that authors should make abundant use of supplemental, online-only sections to increase transparency in reporting their results. Even if the authors decide to exclude certain data from the main body of the manuscript, they should consider including the additional data in a supplementary online section of the publication because access to these data may be valuable for other researchers and clinicians.

Selecting an Analysis Strategy

After deciding which data to include in a manuscript, researchers next need to settle on an appropriate analysis strategy. The data-analysis strategy will depend on at least two factors. First, specifics of the research design will guide researchers to a constellation of analysis methods that may be appropriate for a specific project. For example, single-case research designs applied to a treatment that produces a large effect size may obviate the need for inferential statistical analysis of a study's outcomes to draw conclusions—visual analysis may suffice. Group-design or large-n research may require inferential statistics to draw conclusions from the resulting data because it may be difficult to draw firm conclusions based solely on descriptive statistics like means and standard deviations. The specific research question under study will further delimit the classes of analyses that are applicable.

Second, the strategy may depend on the researcher's target audience. Graduate training in behavior analysis emphasizes single-case design logic and visual analysis. Therefore, articles written for an audience of behavior analysts may place particular emphasis on visual analysis. Training in other related fields with which behavior analysts interface such as education, medicine, or neuroscience may place particular emphasis on statistical analysis as a means of data communication. Authors of articles written for such audiences may wish to incorporate statistical analysis to increase the ease with which audience members are able to interpret behavioral outcomes.

A Note on Diversity of Analyses

Our statements above may seem to imply that visual analysis, alone, should be applied to data from single-case research designs and that statistical analysis, alone, should be applied to data from group designs. To the contrary, we argue that both visual and statistical analyses have places in both single-case and group-design research. Single-case research benefits from the inclusion of inferential statistics in that inferential statistics may (a) provide a useful second opinion to visual analysis when treatment effects are not particularly clear, (b) increase the visibility of experiments that use single-case research designs to audiences who are more comfortable with statistical analysis than visual analysis, and (c) increase the likelihood that data from single-case research designs will be included in meta-analyses (see Craig & Fisher, 2019; Fisher & Lerman, 2014). Group-design research benefits from inclusion of careful and ongoing visual analysis throughout the course of an evaluation because such analyses begin to address some of the well-founded criticisms of statistical inference (Branch, 1999; Perone, 1999). For example, visual analysis places emphasis on behavior of the individual rather than population parameters and helps to prevent place responsibility on the part of the scientist to establish experimental control over study outcomes.

Frequentist statistics, the type of statistical analysis used most frequently in social sciences like psychology, were developed to make inferences about phenomena at the level of the population based on observations of a small subset of members from that population. "Student's" *t*-test (Student, 1908), for example, is used to compare mean differences on an outcome between two groups, and the inference about group differences is based on assumed characteristics of the distribution of scores at the level of the population. Accordingly, methods that follow from this tradition often are inappropriate for single-case or small-*n* research designs because the sample sizes often are too small to make meaningful inferences about outcomes at the level of the population.

Fortunately, development of analysis strategies for small-*n* and single-case research designs is an active area of research in statistics (for relevant reviews, see Kratochwill & Levin, 2014; Lobo et al., 2017; Shadish, 2014b). For example, researchers have developed measures of effect size that may be used to summarize the magnitude of treatment effects from single-case analyses (e.g., Parker et al., 2011; Swan & Pustejovsky, 2018), and methods like Bayesian analysis and multilevel modeling may allow for statistical hypothesis testing with few data sets (e.g., Borckardt et al., 2013). Indeed, special issues of several journals that publish research using single-case designs, such as the *Journal of School Psychology* (Shadish, 2014a) and the *Journal of the Experimental Analysis of Behavior* (Young, 2019), have been dedicated to these topics. We encourage readers to explore these analysis strategies.

Guidelines for Reporting Analysis Outcomes

Style

Whatever a researcher's data-analysis plan looks like, there are a few general guidelines we suggest when reporting the results of their analyses. Given that many of the journals in which behavior analysts publish follow the style guidelines of the *Publication Manual of the American Psychological Association* (the *Manual*; APA, 2020), we suggest that authors become acquainted with the specific style rules outlined in the *Manual*. "APA style" is rather specific and offers recommendations on a host of specifics that pertain to the Results section, including guidance on reporting descriptive and inferential statistics, syntax, and section formatting. Note, too, that the APA frequently updates the *Manual* and, when they do, formatting recommendations tend to change slightly. It is important for authors to ensure that they format their manuscript based on the most up-to-date version of the *Manual*.

Organization

Because behavior-analytic data are time series, it is important for authors to consider chronology when reporting the outcomes from their analyses. They should start from the beginning and work their way forward in time to the end of the data set. For example, it would not make much sense to report outcomes from a treatment analysis before describing what behavior looked like under a preceding set of baseline observations.

If working with a few participants' or subjects' worth of data, authors may wish to report analyses for each individual subject/participant separately. Doing so capitalizes on the strengths of single-case design logic and facilitates within-subject comparison of data between phases of an experimental analysis. If working with many participants' or subjects' worth of data, we recommend that authors consider presenting outcomes from aggregated data so long as those data are representative of outcomes at the level of individual participants/subjects. Readers of a manuscript may be overwhelmed if confronted with dozens of individual data sets, each of which receives its own analysis in the Results.

Above, we introduced a little bit of subjectivity, which may make scientists uneasy. What does "representative of outcomes at the level of individual participants/subject" mean? Who makes that judgment? If the answers to those questions seem murky to you, don't worry. They are murky to us, too. For these reasons, we recommend including individual-subject data along with aggregated data whenever space permits. We direct readers to a few representative examples of this practice from our own work (see Craig & Shahan, 2016; Craig et al., 2017a, b, 2019). In each, we studied rats' behavior, and the experiment used a group design to answer specific questions about relapse. Our primary data analyses focused on behavior at the group level, but we also presented and discussed data from individual subjects in conjunction with the group-based analyses. In the preceding sections of this chapter, we recommended that authors consider including data in the supplementary online-only section of a publication for the sake of transparency. If space does not permit inclusion of data from all subjects/participants in the Results section of the manuscript, authors may consider including individuals' data in the online-only section.

Reporting Data Characteristics

When reporting results from visual-analysis based strategies, authors should focus on changes in relevant data characteristics across phases of the experiment. These include the level of the data, its variability, and any trend that may be present (e.g., Kazdin, 2011). It is difficult to interpret changes in any one of these characteristics across phases without reference to the others. For example, imagine that you arrange an intervention that aims to increase the level at which academic behavior occurs. A student's mean rate of task engagement might increase between the baseline and treatment phase, but if a therapeutic trend were present during baseline, it might be difficult to draw conclusions about the efficacy of the arranged intervention. Moreover, presenting measures of central tendency (means or medians) of data aggregated across a phase is insufficient to effectively communicate a study's outcomes in the absence of information about the spread or variability of the data. The same is true for outcomes from group-design research. Reporting measures of central tendency without corresponding measures of spread may at the best leave readers unsure of authors' outcomes. At worst, it may be misleading.

Displaying Results

After selecting an analysis strategy, researchers need to decide how to present results in such a way that readers are able to consume them. Often, data display and data analysis go hand in hand. Researchers who use visual analysis do so by evaluating data that are displayed visually in the form of line or bar graphs. Researchers who use statistical measures do so by evaluating values of certain statistics, usually displayed as text in tables. To conduct these analyses, the data need to be displayed in a way that allows for detection of (a) the magnitude of effects and, often, (b) the extent to which researchers achieved experimental control (i.e., internal validity). Behavior analysts use a variety of methods to display their data, and they favor different types of display in different situations.

In general, and as described above, it is best to include only the figures and tables necessary to effectively and completely present a study's outcomes. Again, concision in data presentation may help readers focus on the most relevant data on which the authors base their conclusions and prevent readers from becoming fatigued by data consumption. Further, many journals produce paper copies of their publications, so minimizing figures may be economically advantageous, as well. Revisit the section above on selecting data to display for considerations relevant to determining which data to represent graphically in the Results section. In the sections that follow, we will describe different methods for graphically displaying data and some conventions that may apply to behavior analysts who intend to develop such graphics.

Types of Data Displays

Line Graphs

Researchers use line graphs when they display changes in behavior that occur over time. A line graph displays data points associated with values of dependent variables along the y-axis, plotted per unit of time (e.g., sessions, minutes, days) on the x-axis. For example, a researcher might evaluate rates of dangerous behavior during multiple conditions of a functional analysis. One way to display these data would be to plot rates of behavior in each session, with different data paths representing each condition (see Fig. 7.1 for an example, taken from Kunnavatana et al., 2018). Plotting data in a line graph allows the reader to evaluate session-by-session changes in the dependent variable.

Line graphs are especially well suited for within-subject designs, which are characterized, in part, by repeated measures of behavior for each participant. Line graphs are popular in behavior analysis because, as described above, behavior-analytic data most often are time-series data. Displaying repeated measures of behavior allows

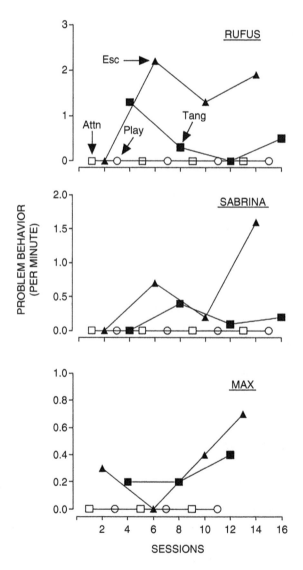

Fig. 7.1 Line graphs displaying results of functional analyses, taken from Kunnavatana et al. (2018)

researchers to evaluate the effectiveness of their intervention by examining level, trend, and variability in the data across phases or conditions and the extent to which behavior has reached a steady state (Sidman, 1960). If desired behavior change is not occurring or if behavior is unpredictably variable, researchers may then modify aspects of their contingencies to exert greater control over behavior and produce desired behavior change. Applied behavior analysts often use within-subject designs (Johnston & Pennypacker, 2009; Kazdin, 2011), and thus display their data with line graphs when they are interested in evaluating behavioral changes that occur over time.

Bar Graphs

Researchers typically use bar graphs to display aggregated levels of behavior in a particular phase or condition. A bar graph displays bars that are oriented vertically or horizontally and usually represent the mean or median of some continuous behavioral outcome. Moreover, these bars are plotted per level of a variable that is often categorical (e.g., group, phase). For example, a researcher might conduct a stimulus preference assessment to evaluate preferences for different toys where the categorical variable would be "stimulus" and each "toy" would represent a different level of that variable. One way to display data from such a preference assessment is to plot the percentage of trials with selections of each toy (see Fig. 7.2 for an example, taken from Hoffmann et al., 2017). Plotting data in an aggregated manner allows the reader to quickly determine the relative preference of each item without the need to inspect each individual data point that contributes to the aggregated mean or median.

Behavioral researchers often display results of specific assessments with bar graphs, including stimulus preference assessments (Fisher et al., 1992; Roane et al., 1998), competing-stimulus assessments (Piazza et al., 1998), trial-based functional analyses (Bloom et al., 2013), and the performance diagnostic checklist (Austin, 2000; Carr et al., 2013), among others. These assessments entail presenting items or arranging reinforcement contingencies to determine preference, the extent to which items compete with target behavior, and behavioral function, respectively. It is useful to display these results in a way that allows for easy comparison across stimuli or functions. A notable drawback of bar graphs is that they typically do not allow for analyzing changes in behavior across trials or sessions. To circumvent this limitation, researchers might first evaluate trial-by-trial/session-by-session data to identify variability across time prior to displaying data on a bar graph to ensure that aggregated data reflect behavior at a steady state (e.g., LeJeune et al., 2019).

Combination Bar and Line Graphs

Researchers may construct displays that contain elements of both bar and line graphs (e.g., Boyle et al., 2021; Coffey et al., 2021; Saini et al., 2016). For example, a researcher might evaluate the extent to which an intervention affects dangerous behavior and engagement with items, and they may wish to determine whether dangerous

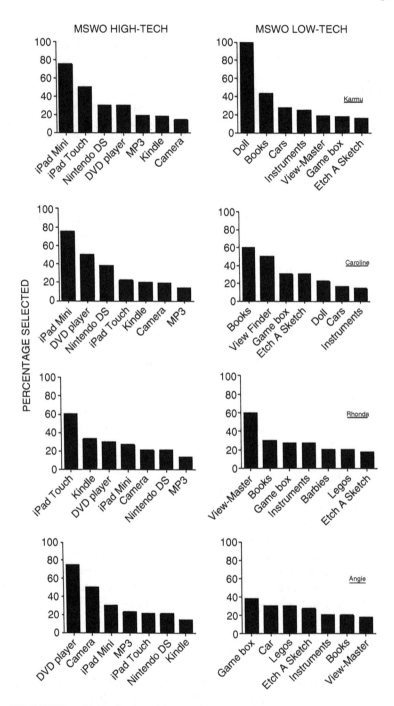

Fig. 7.2 MSWO multiple stimulus without replacement. Bar graph displaying results of preference assessments, taken from Hoffmann et al. (2017). Each row shows data for a participant. The first column shows results for high-technology stimuli and the second column shows results for low-technology stimuli

behavior covaries with engagement. One way to accomplish this task would be to plot dangerous behavior in the same panel as engagement, with dangerous behavior plotted as a line and engagement plotted as bars (see Fig. 7.3, taken from Saini et al., 2016).

Researchers may plot data in both lines and bars on the same panel in a graph in the interest of space (see the section titled "Dependent Variables: Primary and

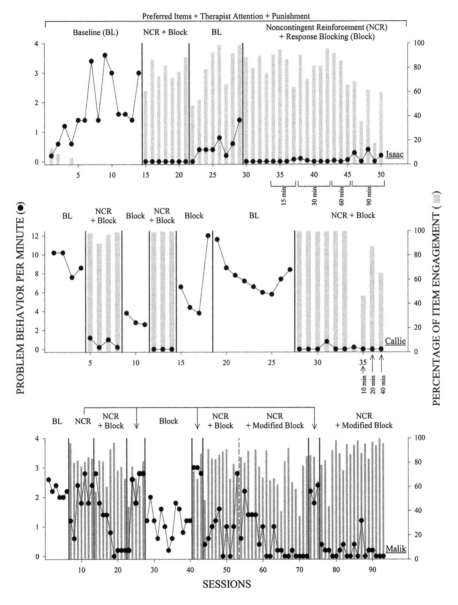

Fig. 7.3 BL baseline, NCR noncontingent reinforcement. A combination line and bar graph displaying results of a treatment analysis for three participants, taken from Saini et al. (2016)

Secondary" above), in that two panels of a figure can be combined into one. Researchers may also combine bar and line data into one panel if they are evaluating the extent to which different dependent variables covary. One consideration with plotting bars and lines on the same panel of a graph is that there is often the need for double *y*-axes—a *y*-axis that corresponds to the bars and a *y*-axis that corresponds to the lines (as in Fig. 7.3). Double *y*-axes may be cumbersome for readers to consume, as they need to first match each data path to its relevant axis before evaluating the data. Researchers should assist readers by stating in the figure caption the axis to which each data set corresponds.

Scatterplots

Researchers use scatterplots when they evaluate the relation between different variables, values of which are associated with the *x*- and *y*-axes. Unlike line graphs, which display changes in a dependent variable (*y*-axis) over time and experimental conditions that change across time (*x*-axis), scatterplots display data according to the values of two variables to identify the nature of the relation between the two (e.g., Briggs et al., 2018; Shahan & Greer, 2021). For example, a researcher might evaluate the nature of the relation between resurgence (a form of behavioral relapse) and decreases in alternative reinforcement rates. One way to do this would be to plot data in terms of the values of each variable (e.g., see Fig. 7.4 from Shahan & Greer, 2021). Plotting data within a scatterplot also facilitates additional analyses that quantify the relation between variables.

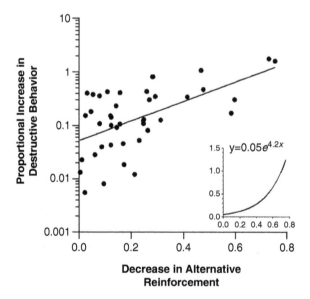

Fig. 7.4 Scatterplot displaying destructive behavior as a function of the decrease in alternative reinforcement, taken from Shahan and Greer (2021)

Tables

Although behavioral researchers typically prefer to display data in graphical formats because doing so facilitates visual analysis, there are some situations in which tables may be more appropriate. A general rule is that tables are useful when large amounts of text are necessary to situate or explain the data or when no numbers are being presented at all. In addition, when conducting comparative analyses, researchers might also present key outcomes across procedures in tables to facilitate efficient comparisons (e.g., Curtis et al., 2020; Fisher et al., 2016; Slaton et al., 2017). For example, a researcher might compare outcomes of several functional analysis variations in terms of functions of behavior. In addition to presenting line graphs of individual participants' results, researchers might present the outcomes of each assessment type in a table (see Table 7.1, taken from Fisher et al., 2016).

It is also common for researchers to present results of literature reviews in tables when displaying prevalence of procedural variables or outcomes (e.g., Boyle & Adamson, 2017; Slaton & Hanley, 2018). These outcomes could often be presented in bar graphs, but doing so would take up considerably more space, and it is likely faster for a reader to consume data displayed in a single table compared to reviewing several bar graphs. Finally, when researchers present large numbers of statistics, they often do so in tables instead of in narratives within the text (e.g., Lambert et al., 2014; Muething et al., 2021). Aligning numbers in rows and columns in a table allows readers to compare values across conditions more efficiently than when the same data are presented within the text.

Table 7.1 Comparative Results of the Open-Ended Interview, Structured Observations, IISCA, and Traditional FA

Participant	Open-ended interview	Structured observation	IISCA	Traditional FA
Alan	**Attention,** tangible, escape	**Attention,** tangible, escape	Differentiated, without individual or interaction effects	Tangible, escape
Allie	**Attention,** tangible, **escape**	**Attention,** tangible, **escape**	Differentiated, without individual or interaction effects	Tangible
Cameron	Tangible, **escape**	Tangible or tangible and **escape**	Differentiated, without individual or interaction effects	Tangible
Sylvia	**Attention, tangible, escape**	No problem behavior observed	No problem behavior observed	No problem behavior observed
Tina	**Attention,** tangible, **escape**	*No problem behavior observed*	Differentiated, without individual or interaction effects	Tangible

Note. Functionally relevant stimuli identified during the open-ended interview and structured observation are presented in regular typeface, irrelevant stimuli are in boldface type, and missed functions are in italics. *IISCA* interview informed synthesized contingency analysis. Table displaying results of four functional assessment procedures across five participants, taken from Fisher et al. (2016)

Graphing Conventions and Additional Considerations

After a researcher decides on the type of data display, they need to construct the display in a way that accurately conveys the study's findings. Journals often have specific requirements for figures and tables or follow guidelines described by relevant professional organizations (e.g., the *Manual*). We encourage researchers to review the websites of the journals to which they are submitting and follow their guidelines.

In addition, a variety of resources exist to guide researchers in developing graphical displays (e.g., Cooper et al., 2020; Johnston & Pennypacker, 2009; Mitteer et al., 2018; Tufte, 2001). Below, we will review the elements we consider most impactful that are also mentioned across multiple sources. For readers who are interested in a comprehensive guide to best practices in data display (not specific to behavioral research), we recommend Tufte (2001). Finally, when authors are in doubt, "above all else show the data" (Tufte, 2001, p. 92), even if this means including the data as "Supporting Information."

General Conventions

Internal validity refers to the extent to which a researcher has ruled out the influence of extraneous variables as explanations for or causes of behavior change. Behavioral researchers use a variety of experimental designs to minimize threats to internal validity (Kazdin, 2011), and we prefer data displays that allow for the detection of experimental control. Such methods for display allow readers to interpret data not only for change in level, trend, and variability, but also for the presence or absence of experimental control.

Use of Ink

Researchers should strive to use ink to display "data-information" (Tufte, 2001, p. 93). In other words, ink should generally be used to display important information only. Inasmuch, figures should not include grid marks or other uninformative components like boarders—they would use unnecessary ink. Gravitation toward minimizing the use of ink also helps to explain why we favor thin axes and data-path lines as well as relatively small data points. Similarly, authors should omit redundant or "non-data" features that use ink. For example, if one data path on a line graph displays "percent correct" derived from a matching-to-sample task, it would be unnecessary to include a second data path showing "percent incorrect". That information can be deduced from the "percent correct" data path and would thus waste ink.

Axis Considerations

Scaling of axes refers to the range of values they contain (e.g., 1–100 vs. 1–10). Researchers should use care when scaling their axes (Mitteer et al., 2018), as using different y-axis ranges can affect the way the researchers and their readers interpret data. For example, Fig. 7.5, taken from Dart and Radley (2017), shows the same data displayed on graphs with different y-axis ranges. Using a large range may compress data or mask variability (top panel). Conversely, using a smaller axis range may make changes in data look more pronounced (bottom panel).

Tic marks refer to the small lines that denote values on each axis. We recommend that researchers use the minimum number of tic marks possible to facilitate reasonable consumption of data (Mitteer et al., 2018). Further, we recommend that authors ensure equal spacing and numbers of tic marks on x- and y-axes when possible. This is an aesthetic recommendation only, and we are not aware of any effects on visual analysis of different numbers or spacing of tic marks. Though research on that topic would be informative!

When multiple panels are presented in the same figure (e.g., Fig. 7.1), authors should consider whether the y-axis ranges should be consistent or whether they can vary. If they choose to vary y-axis lengths for whatever reason, we encourage authors to state that this is the case in the figure caption and in the body of the Results section to assist readers in visual inspection (e.g., "Note that y-axis ranges differ across panels"). We also recommend that researchers take care to align panels of graphs that are presented within the same figure (Mitteer et al., 2018). Researchers should also consider the relative lengths of their axes. Others have suggested that the y-axis be shorter than the x-axis, with recommended ratios ranging from 5:8 and 3:4 (Cooper et al., 2020; Johnston & Pennypacker, 2009; Katzenberg, 1975; Tufte, 2001).

Generally, applied journals favor arithmetic (i.e., equal-interval, linear) axes over logarithmic (ratio or proportional) axes. Equally spaced values on arithmetic axes increase by a constant absolute amount (e.g., intervals of 5; 0, 5, 10, 15, etc.). All figures in this chapter except the large figure in Fig. 7.4 are plotted on arithmetic axes. Conversely, equally spaced logarithmic axes increase by a proportional amount (e.g., 1 $\log_{10}$ unit = 10, 2 $\log_{10}$ units = 100, 3 $\log_{10}$ units = 1000). Plotting data on logarithmic axes can facilitate visual inspection of data sets that contain values at extremes or data sets that are related in terms of proportional change; however, logarithmic axes can be more difficult for certain audiences to understand.

For figures in which it is nonsensical to have an x-axis value of 0 (e.g., when sessions are displayed on the x-axis), we recommend axes with no frame (Fig. 7.1). Non-framed axes also enable researchers to use the "floating 0" on the y-axis. Here, values of 0 are slightly elevated relative to the x-axis. Floating 0 axes are particularly helpful when some data points fall at 0 on the y-axis. With a floating 0, the data point is lifted off of the x-axis, which may increase the ease with which readers are able to consume the figure.

For most investigations, researchers need the ability to display zero instances of behavior. When data are displayed in terms of frequency, duration, or percent,

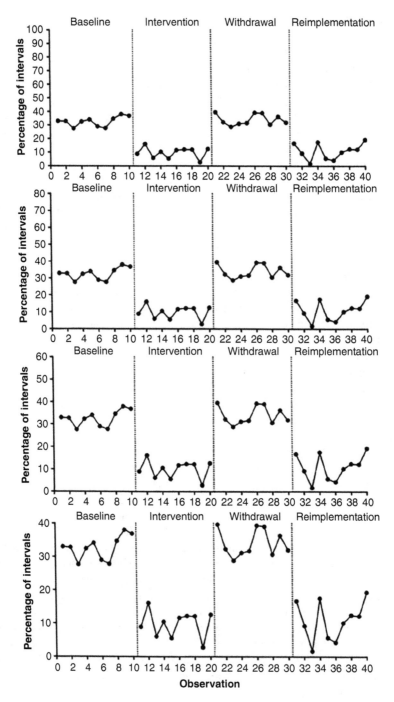

Fig. 7.5 The same data set plotted on differently scaled y-axes, taken from Dart and Radley (2017)

data plotted at $y = 0$ indicate that behavior did not occur. When behavior is scored in terms of latency, however, data plotted at $y = 0$ would indicate that behavior occurred at the same time as the relevant stimulus (e.g., the beginning of a session or the delivery of an instruction). Data points corresponding to higher y-axis values represent longer latencies to behavior. Thus, researchers plot "no occurrence" data on latency graphs by inserting either a dashed horizontal line or a "no response" area above the maximum possible latency value (see Figs. 7.6 and 7.7 for examples, taken from Traub and Vollmer (2019), and Jessel et al. (2018), respectively). Data points plotted on or above this line or in this area indicate that no response occurred.

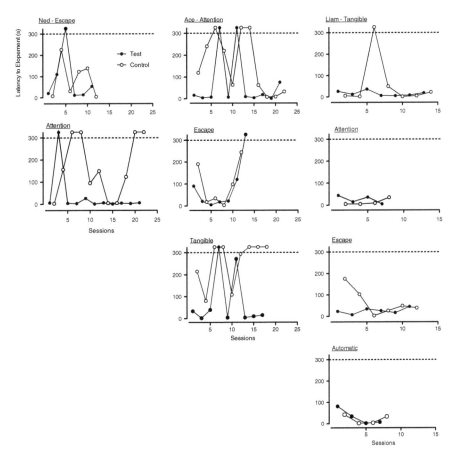

Fig. 7.6 Line graphs depicting latency to responding, taken from Traub and Vollmer (2019). Data points above the dashed horizontal line at $y = 300$ reflect that behavior did not occur

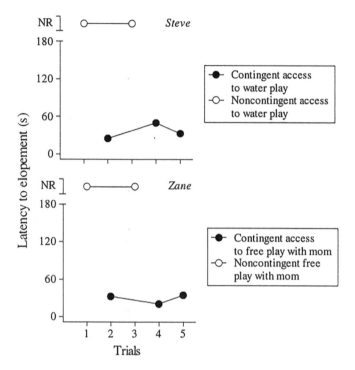

Fig. 7.7 NR no response. Line graphs depicting latency to responding, taken from Jessel et al. (2018). Data points within the NR region of the graph reflect that behavior did not occur

Data Paths and Labels

Within line graphs, behavioral researchers often prefer data-path labels to keys/legends. When using a data-path label, we recommend orienting arrows to data points (Fig. 7.1) instead of to data paths (the line between the data point), because the former does not require readers to follow the line to the nearest data point (Mitteer et al., 2018).

Software for Graphing

Formatting publication-ready graphs may seem like a daunting task, but there are a variety of software platforms available that enhance and simplify the process. We gravitate particularly strongly to platforms like GraphPad Prism (e.g., Mitteer et al., 2018), and Microsoft Excel (e.g., Lehardy et al., 2021), which provide substantial flexibility for users to create all of the graph types described above and several others to boot. In R, the ggplot2 package (Wickham, 2016) further enhances the base capabilities of R for data analysis and graphing. There are, however, dozens of platforms from which authors may choose. We encourage authors to try different platforms to identify which ones work best for them. Universities often have site licenses for graphing software like Prism and Excel. R is completely open source and free to use.

Integrity in Data Reporting

In behavior-analytic research, it is critical for researchers to demonstrate that changes in behavior were due to the systematic application of the independent variable. That is, having strong internal validity is necessary to demonstrate a believable functional relation between independent and dependent variables and to draw strong conclusions regarding the phenomenon under investigation. To do so, evidence needs to be provided that convinces others that the data accurately reflect valid and reliable measurement of the dependent variable and that the independent variable was implemented as prescribed. In other words, for the data and results to be considered trustworthy by the scientific community, they need to be produced through an accurate, reliable, and valid measurement system.

Accuracy, reliability, and validity are three distinct but related concepts. *Accuracy* refers to the extent to which data (i.e., observed values) reflect the actual dimension of the target behavior that occurred during the observation period (i.e., true value). Accuracy is not to be confused with the concept of *reliability*, which refers to the degree to which the measurement system produces consistent data. For example, an observer may record the wrong dimension of the target behavior, rendering inaccurate data, but they may do so consistently and thus reliably. Although accuracy of data collection is not a necessary condition for reliability of data collection, unreliable data would raise concerns about the accuracy of the data and indicate that the measurement system needs to be recalibrated (e.g., by adjusting operational definitions or retraining observers; Poling et al., 1995). *Validity* refers to the extent to which the appropriate dimension of the target behavior is being measured accurately and reliably during the time and place relevant to the analysis and is not an artifact of the measurement system itself. Thus, a valid measurement system produces data that consistently reflect the actual occurrence of the target behavior, under the relevant circumstances for the target behavior's observation, throughout the analysis.

Beyond the validity of the measurement system itself, it also is important to demonstrate that changes in the dependent variable were due to the application of the independent variable and not an artifact of the measurement system or some other confounding variable. Within behavior-analytic research, the consistency and accuracy with which the independent variable is applied often is referred to as procedural fidelity. Without knowing the fidelity with which the independent variable was applied in an analysis, it is difficult, if not impossible, to determine whether the independent variable was truly responsible for changes in the dependent variable (Cook et al., 1979; Kazdin, 2011; Peterson et al., 1982). Appropriately, several authors have highlighted the importance of measuring and reporting on procedural fidelity to strengthen the internal validity of behavior-analytic research (e.g., Brand et al., 2019; DiGennaro Reed & Codding, 2014; Hagermoser Sanetti & Kratochwill, 2014; Van Houten et al., 1988).

Given the importance of reliability and procedural fidelity data for behavior-analytic research, we provide a deep dive into both of these topics in the following sections. Although these data are frequently reported in the Method section of a manuscript (see Chap. 7), they are intimately linked to the results of the study. Thus, considering them in this chapter seems appropriate. We will offer guidance on reporting such data in published work as they relate to the Results section of a manuscript. Moreover, we will discuss measures of social validity in applied research and how to report such data in a manuscript.

Data Reliability

How data are collected in behavior-analytic research will determine the ways in which data reliability is conveyed in a manuscript. In the basic laboratory, data often are gathered through automated computer systems (e.g., MedPC®). This type of data collection has the obvious benefit of minimizing human error. That is not to say, however, that automated systems are free from error. These systems should be frequently tested for accuracy and recalibrated as necessary. Researchers' methods for checking and recalibrating automated data collection systems are not often reported in the Method section, but we strongly encourage authors to report the procedures. Outcomes from those checks could then be reported within the Results section.

In applied settings, behavior is most often measured through direct observation. As with any human-run system, error and biases are possible. To account for these potential measurement errors, and to help convince audiences that data reflect the actual occurrence of the target behavior being measured, applied researchers collect data on interobserver agreement (IOA). Obtaining scores of IOA is common in both research and practice (Hartmann, 1977) and refers to the extent that two independent observers agree on the occurrence of a target behavior. The purpose of reporting IOA is to convince others that the data were recorded consistently and were a function of the participant's behavior rather than the observer themselves. Additionally, IOA may be used to determine if the target behavior's operational definition and data collection system are sufficient to capture the relevant dimension of the target behavior and to detect observer drift over time. As noted above, data reliability does not directly correspond to data accuracy, but reliability often is used as a proxy for accuracy because one can never *really* be sure whether data collection was accurate. By demonstrating that behavior was measured reliably, the results of a study are more believable.

There are many ways data on IOA can be collected, calculated, and reported. The purpose of this chapter is not to provide a summary of the relative strengths and weaknesses of each method for obtaining and calculating IOA, as this has been described extensively elsewhere (e.g., Cooper et al., 2007; Kazdin, 2011). Rather, our aim here is to provide general guidance on reporting IOA that would convey that reliable data collection has occurred. To do so, reporting on the frequency with which IOA data are collected and the degree of agreement is needed. Generally, more frequent checks on IOA within each phase or condition of the study will increase others' confidence in the data. It has been suggested that 25% to 30% of sessions across conditions or phases should have checks on IOA (Bailey & Burch, 2002; Poling et al., 1995; Kahng et al., 2021). Regarding the degree of agreement, a general guideline is that IOA scores at or above 80% would convey a high degree of agreement (Kahng et al., 2021; Johnston & Pennypacker, 1993).

Typically, IOA scores are aggregated across sessions to report a mean level of agreement with the range of the scores (e.g., $M = XX\%$, range X% to X%). At times, researchers will further aggregate IOA to report mean level of agreement for all topographies of behavior and across the entire analysis. By aggregating IOA scores, low IOA for one topography of behavior or in a specific condition may be masked by high IOA scores obtained elsewhere. This is not to say that reporting IOA for the entire analysis or across topographies of behavior is always inappropriate—we simply suggest that more frequent reports of IOA across specific topographies of behavior, conditions, or phases provides more convincing evidence of reliability.

The way in which IOA is calculated is also necessary to report in a manuscript, as the calculation method will influence the degree of agreement with some methods being more conservative than others. For example, *total agreement IOA* is calculated by comparing two observers' measurement of a target behavior across an entire session and dividing the smaller measurement by the larger measurement and multiplying by 100% to yield a percent agreement. This is the simplest index of IOA and is rather imprecise in that it does not account for the time at which the target behavior was scored. That is, one observer may record a single occurrence of the target behavior during the first 10 s of the observation period, whereas the second observer may score one occurrence of the target behavior during the final seconds of the session. In this instance, 100% IOA would be obtained from a total agreement calculation even though the observers scored two separate occurrences of the target behavior. In contrast, an *interval-agreement* calculation divides the session into smaller intervals (e.g., every 10 s of the session) and examines agreement between observers during each interval separately before aggregating scores over intervals within the session. This method for calculating IOA provides a more rigorous estimate of IOA that accounts for the time at which the target behavior occurred during the session. Regardless of the calculation method, researchers would then calculate the average percent agreement across sessions within a condition, phase, or analysis and report the mean percent agreement with a range of scores. It is generally recommended to use more conservative estimates of IOA like interval-agreement because they will increase others' confidence in the reliability of the data to a greater extent than less rigorous methods like total agreement.

Procedural Fidelity

Although calculating and reporting IOA is common in behavior analysis and required for studies that use observational data-collection methods, measurement and reporting of procedural fidelity is less common and not a requirement for publication (Vollmer et al., 2008). A recent review by Han et al. (2022) examined the percentage of studies that reported procedural-fidelity data published in *Journal of Applied Behavior Analysis (JABA)* between 1980 and 2020. Of the studies reviewed, 25% stated that procedural fidelity was assessed, 24% collected procedural fidelity data, and 23% reported those data in the manuscript. It should also be noted that an increasing trend in the reporting of procedural-fidelity data was observed over time, with 50% of articles reporting procedural-fidelity data in 2020. Nonetheless, reporting on procedural fidelity is important for convincing readers that a study is internally valid (e.g., Van Houten et al., 1988). Without such measures, erroneous conclusions may be drawn from a study's results (Gresham et al., 1993).

Within the basic laboratory, automated systems often are used to deliver the independent variable (e.g., providing reinforcement, presentation of study-related stimulus changes). By using automated systems, the likelihood of human error is minimized. However, errors may still occur (e.g., pellet dispenser jams, a light bulb used to illuminate the chamber burns out) and should be reported within the manuscript. Reporting such errors allows the audience to interpret the data accordingly. Moreover, we recommend that researchers collect data on the implementation of the independent variable, when possible, and report those data in the Results section. To illustrate, suppose a reinforcer-rate manipulation is the independent variable of a study. In this scenario, data should be collected on the rate of reinforcement across conditions or phases, and the mean rates with ranges or standard deviations should be reported across conditions or phases, relative to the programmed rates of reinforcement. We also recommend that these data be presented in a table or graphically displayed on a time-series figure like a line graph (see above) to aid in interpretation.

The importance of reporting data on procedural fidelity is underscored in applied work wherein humans often deliver the independent variable. For example, a treatment that is person-implemented and requires multiple intervention components may be considered at high-risk for integrity errors (Falakfarsa et al., 2022; Han et al., 2022; Mcintyre et al., 2007; Peterson et al., 1982). In such cases, it would be particularly important to report on procedural fidelity as errors may affect the outcomes of the study and the reader's interpretation of the data. Typically, procedural fidelity is calculated as a percentage of opportunities in which the procedure was implemented correctly (Vollmer et al., 2008) and reported as a mean with a range of scores. If there are multiple intervention components (e.g., reinforcement for functional communication; extinction for dangerous behavior), fidelity often is reported as an aggregated mean with a range encompassing all components. Although including an aggregate measure of procedural fidelity is helpful because it increases others' confidence that the treatment was responsible for behavior change, reporting procedural fidelity for each individual component is more conservative. In the applied context, procedural fidelity is particularly relevant as some types of fidelity errors may be differentially detrimental to behavior (e.g., St. Peter Pipkin et al., 2010).

Although reporting procedural fidelity in behavior-analytic research has been recommended (e.g., Vollmer et al., 2008), there are no hard-and-fast rules regarding the frequency with which fidelity should be checked, the "acceptable" degree of fidelity, or whether IOA is needed when taking fidelity measures. In general, more frequent checks, higher levels of fidelity, and the inclusion of IOA increase others' confidence in the effect of the independent variable on the dependent variable. Thus, we recommend that authors embrace a more conservative approach to collecting and reporting these data.

Social Validity

In 1978, Montrose Wolf published a seminal paper on the topic of social validity in applied behavior analysis. Social validity, from a behavior-analytic perspective, refers to the extent in which outcomes of a study hold value to the consumer or society at large (Schwartz & Baer, 1991). From the consumer's perspective, a socially valid study would produce findings that are relevant to their functioning in everyday life, describe interventions that are acceptable and feasible to implement, and produce clinically significant changes in behavior (Kazdin, 2011). Wolf (1978) suggested that, for applied behavior analysis to appeal to the mainstream public and be perceived as a benevolent form of treatment, some measure of social acceptability is needed. Later, when Baer et al. (1987) provided an update on the dimensions of applied behavior analysis (i.e., that it be applied, behavioral, analytic, technological, conceptual, effective, and generalizable), they too noted that measures of social validity in behavior-analytic work are necessary to uphold the key *applied* dimension of the field. Despite the dramatic growth of the field, the inclusion of social-validity measures in behavior-analytic research remains sparse.

Kennedy (1992) evaluated the assessment and reporting of social validity in *JABA* from 1968 to 1990 and in *Behavior Modification* from 1977 to 1990. Kennedy found that the percentage of articles reporting social validity increased over time but only about 20% of articles reported such data throughout the late 1980s. Carr et al. (1999) updated this work by examining prevalence of social-validity data reported in *JABA* through 1998 and found that approximately 25% of articles published in the 1990s reported some measure of social validity. More recently, Ferguson et al. (2019) examined trends in reporting social validity in *JABA* from 1999 to 2016 and found that only 12% of articles reported measures of social validity. Taken together, these findings suggest that measures of social validity are not commonly reported in behavior-analytic research, even though the topic has been highlighted as an area of need in our field (e.g., Baer et al., 1987; Hanley, 2010; Schwartz & Baer, 1991; Wolf, 1978).

Social validity may be assessed by obtaining consumers' perspectives on treatment goals, treatment procedures, and treatment effects (Wolf, 1978). This information may be gathered with questionnaires or rating scales, or by conducting preference assessments. Hanley (2010) suggested that measures of social validity are especially important and should be reported when (a) two treatments are equally effective for an individual and have similar reported efficacy within the literature, (b) a more effective treatment relies on aversive control, (c) the more effective treatment is less preferred by the consumer, or (d) the necessity of an intervention component is unknown. When reporting these outcomes within a Results section, the type of measure that was used dictates how the data should be displayed. Open-ended questionnaires require authors to summarize the consumers' responses to convey their perspective on the aspect of social validity being assessed. If rating scales or standardized questionnaires are implemented, the specific quantitative score should be reported along with the associated qualitative descriptor. Our purpose in writing this section is not to describe each method of obtaining social validity but instead to focus on the circumstances under which including such a measure would be recommended. We encourage readers to consider collecting and reporting social validity data with any form of applied work so that the field of applied behavior analysis is better able to understand the extent to which it is living up to the "applied" dimension by which it is defined.

Conclusions

Data are the doers of science. They provide basic scientists insights into the processes that make the world work, and they also allow applied scientists and practitioners to evaluate the effects of interventions on socially relevant problems. What's more, healthy science depends on the effective dissemination of data between scientists. It is how we generate collective knowledge. Indeed, it is difficult to imagine the snail's pace at which science and technology would progress in the absence of efficient communication of research outcomes between scientists.

In this chapter, we provided general guidelines that authors may find helpful when effectively communicating the outcomes of their study in the Results section. On the one hand, some of these guidelines were fairly standard (e.g., being transparent in data reporting, using analysis strategies that fit with the experiment conducted, using graphing conventions that allow the data to shine, and reporting IOA for data collected for direct observation). Following these guidelines will reduce barriers to publication, as they are more-or-less required by many of the major behavior-analytic journals for a study to be considered for publication.

On the other hand, some of our guidelines were aspirational in nature (e.g., including data in online-only supplemental materials, reporting both visual and statistical analyses of a study's outcomes, using graphics to fully flesh out the outcomes from an experiment, and reporting procedural-fidelity and social-validity data). We hope that readers of this chapter see the value in our aspirational suggestions. Science ought to be as transparent as possible to all stakeholders in the enterprise. A properly written Results section ensures that an author's science meets this standard.

References

American Psychological Association. (2020). *Publication manual of the American Psychological Association 2020: The official guide to APA style* (7th ed.). American Psychological Association.

Austin, J. (2000). Performance analysis and performance diagnostics. In J. Austin & J. E. Carr (Eds.), *Handbook of applied behavior analysis* (pp. 321–349). Context Press.

Baer, D. M., Wolf, M. M., & Risley, T. R. (1987). Some still-current dimensions of applied behavior analysis. *Journal of Applied Behavior Analysis, 20*(4), 313–327. https://doi.org/10.1901/jaba.1987.20-313

Bailey, J. S., & Burch, M. R. (2002). *Research methods in applied behavior analysis*. Routledge.

Boyle, M. A., & Adamson, R. M. (2017). Systematic review of functional analysis and treatment of elopement (2000–2015). *Journal of Applied Behavior Analysis, 10*(4), 375–385. https://doi.org/10.1007/s40617-017-0191-y

Boyle, M. A., Bacon, M. T., Sharp, D. S., Mills, N. D., & Janota, T. A. (2021). Incorporating an activity schedule during schedule thinning in treatment of problem behavior. *Behavioral Interventions, 36*(4), 1052–1064. https://doi.org/10.1002/bin.1813

Branch, M. N. (1999). Statistical inference in behavior analysis: Some things significance testing does and does not do. *The Behavior Analyst, 22*, 87–92. https://doi.org/10.1007/BF03391984

Brand, D., Henley, A. J., DiGennaro Reed, F. D., Gray, E., & Crabbs, B. (2019). A review of published studies involving parametric manipulations of treatment integrity. *Journal of Behavioral Education, 28*(1), 1–26. https://doi.org/10.1007/s10864-018-09311-8

Briggs, A. M., Akers, J. S., Greer, B. D., Fisher, W. W., & Retzlaff, B. J. (2018). Systematic changes in preference for schedule-thinning arrangements as a function of relative reinforcement density. *Behavior Modification, 42*(2), 472–497. https://doi.org/10.1177/0145445517742883

Brockardt, J. J., Nash, M. R., Balliet, W., Galloway, S., & Madan, A. (2013). Time-series statistical analysis of single-case data. In G. J. Madden, W. V. Dube, T. D. Hackenberg, G. P. Hanley, & K. A. Lattal (Eds.), *APA handbook of behavior analysis, Vol. 1. Methods and principles* (pp. 251–266). American Psychological Association. https://doi.org/10.1037/13937-003

Carr, J. E., Austin, J. L., Britton, L. N., Kellum, K. K., & Bailey, J. S. (1999). An assessment of social validity trends in applied behavior analysis. *Behavioral Interventions, 14*(4), 223–231. https://doi.org/10.1002/(SICI)1099-078X(199910/12)14:4<223::AID-BIN37>3.0.CO;2-Y

Carr, J. E., Wilder, D. A., Majdalany, L., & Mathisen, D. (2013). An assessment-based solution to a human-service employee performance problem. *Behavior Analysis in Practice, 6*(1), 16–32. https://doi.org/10.1007/BF03391789

Coffey, A. L., Shawler, L. A., Jessel, J., Bain, T., Nye, M., & Dorsey, M. F. (2021). Generality of the practical functional assessment and skill-based treatment among individuals with autism and mental health disorders. *Behavioral Interventions, 36*(1), 298–314. https://doi.org/10.1002/bin.1755

Cook, T. D., Campbell, D. T., & Day, A. (1979). *Quasi-experimentation: Design & analysis issues for field settings* (Vol. 351). Houghton Mifflin.

Cooper, J. O., Heron, T. E., & Heward, W. L. (2020). *Applied behavior analysis* (3rd ed.). Pearson Education, Inc.

Craig, A. R., & Fisher, W. W. (2019). Randomization tests as alternative analysis methods for behavior-analytic data. *Journal of the Experimental Analysis of Behavior, 111*(2), 309–328. https://doi.org/10.1002/jeab.500

Craig, A. R., & Shahan, T. A. (2016). Behavioral momentum theory fails to account for the effects of reinforcement rate on resurgence. *Journal of the Experimental Analysis of Behavior, 105*(3), 375–392. https://doi.org/10.1002/jeab.207

Craig, A. R., Browning, K. O., Nall, R. W., Marshall, C. M., & Shahan, T. A. (2017a). Resurgence and alternative-reinforcer magnitude. *Journal of the Experimental Analysis of Behavior, 107*(2), 218–233. https://doi.org/10.1002/jeab.245

Craig, A. R., Browning, K. O., & Shahan, T. A. (2017b). Stimuli previously associated with reinforcement mitigate resurgence. *Journal of the Experimental Analysis of Behavior, 108*(2), 139–150. https://doi.org/10.1002/jeab.278

Craig, A. R., Sullivan, W. E., & Roane, H. S. (2019). Further evaluation of a nonsequential approach to studying operant renewal. *Journal of the Experimental Analysis of Behavior, 112*(2), 210–233. https://doi.org/10.1002/jeab.546

Dart, E. H., & Radley, K. C. (2017). The impact of ordinate scaling on the visual analysis of single-case data. *Journal of School Psychology, 63*, 105–118. https://psycnet.apa.org/doi/10.1016/j.jsp.2017.03.008

DiGennaro Reed, F. D., & Codding, R. S. (2014). Advancements in procedural fidelity assessment and intervention: Introduction to the special issue. *Journal of Behavioral Education, 23*(1), 1–18. https://doi.org/10.1007/s10864-013-9191-3

Falakfarsa, G., Brand, D., Jones, L., Godinez, E. S., Richardson, D. C., Hanson, R. J., Velazquez, S. D., & Wills, C. (2022). Treatment integrity reporting in behavior analysis in practice 2008–2019. *Behavior Analysis in Practice, 15*, 443–453. https://doi.org/10.1007/s40617-021-00573-9

Ferguson, J. L., Cihon, J. H., Leaf, J. B., Van Meter, S. M., McEachin, J., & Leaf, R. (2019). Assessment of social validity trends in the journal of applied behavior analysis. *European Journal of Behavior Analysis, 20*(1), 146–157. https://doi.org/10.1080/15021149.2018.1534771

Fisher, W. W., & Lerman, D. C. (2014). It has been said that, "There are three degrees of falsehood: Lies, damn lies, and statistics". *Journal of School Psychology, 52*(2), 243–248. https://doi.org/10.1016/j.jsp.2014.01.001

Fisher, W., Piazza, C. C., Bowman, L. G., Hagopian, L. P., Owens, J. C., & Slevin, I. (1992). A comparison of two approaches for identifying reinforcers for persons with severe and profound disabilities. *Journal of Applied Behavior Analysis, 25*(2), 491–498. https://doi.org/10.1901/jaba.1992.25-491

Gresham, F. M., Gansle, K. A., & Noell, G. H. (1993). Treatment integrity in applied behavior analysis with children. *Journal of Applied Behavior Analysis, 26*(2), 257–263. https://doi.org/10.1901/jaba.1993.26-257

Hagermoser Sanetti, L. M., & Kratochwill, T. R. (2014). *Treatment integrity: A foundation for evidence-based practice in applied psychology.* American Psychological Association.

Han, J. B., Bergmann, S., Brand, D., Wallace, M. D., St Peter, C. C., Feng, J., & Long, B. P. (2022). Trends in reporting procedural integrity: A comparison. *Behavior Analysis in Practice*, 1–11. https://doi.org/10.1007/s40617-022-00741-5

Hanley, G. P. (2010). Toward effective and preferred programming a case for the objective measurement of social validity with recipients of behavior-change programs. *Behavior Analysis in Practice, 3*(1), 13–21. https://doi.org/10.1007/BF03391754

Hartmann, D. P. (1977). Considerations in the choice of interobserver reliability estimates. *Journal of Applied Behavior Analysis, 10*(1), 103–116. https://doi.org/10.1901/jaba.1977.10-103

Hoffmann, A. N., Samaha, A. L., Bloom, S. E., & Boyle, M. A. (2017). Preference and reinforcer efficacy of high- and low-tech items: A comparison of item type and duration of access. *Journal of Applied Behavior Analysis, 50*(2), 222–237. https://doi.org/10.1002/jaba.383

Jessel, J., Ingvarsson, E. T., Metras, R., Whipple, R., Kirk, H., & Solsbery, L. (2018). Treatment of elopement following a latency-based interview-informed, synthesized contingency analysis. *Behavioral Interventions, 33*(3), 271–283. https://doi.org/10.1002/bin.1525

Johnston, J. M., & Pennypacker, H. S., Jr. (2009). *Strategies and tactics of behavioral research* (3rd ed.). Routledge/Taylor & Francis Group.

Kahng, S., Ingvarsson, E. T., Quigg, A. M., Seckinger, K. E., Teichman, H. M., & Clay, C. (2021). Defining and measuring behavior. In W. W. Fisher, C. C. Piazza, & H. S. Roane (Eds.), *Handbook of applied behavior analysis* (2nd ed.). The Guilford Press.

Katzenberg, A. C. (1975). *How to draw graphs*. R.R. Donnelley & Sons Company.

Kazdin, A. E. (2011). *Single-case research designs: Methods for clinical and applied settings* (2nd ed.). Oxford University Press.

Kennedy, C. H. (1992). Trends in the measurement of social validity. *The Behavior Analyst, 15*, 147–156. https://doi.org/10.1007/BF03392597

Kratochwill, T. R., & Levin, J. R. (2014). Single-case intervention research: Methodological and statistical advances. *American Psychological Association*. https://doi.org/10.1037/14376-000

Kunnavatana, S. S., Bloom, S. E., Samaha, A. L., Slocum, T. A., & Clay, C. J. (2018). Manipulating parameters of reinforcement to reduce problem behavior without extinction. *Journal of Applied Behavior Analysis, 51*(2), 283–302. https://doi.org/10.1002/jaba.443

Lambert, J. M., Bloom, S. E., Clay, C. J., Kunnavatana, S. S., & Collins, S. D. (2014). Training residential staff and supervisors to conduct traditional functional analyses. *Research in Developmental Disabilities, 35*(7), 1757–1765. https://doi.org/10.1016/j.ridd.2014.02.014

Lehardy, R. K., Luczynski, K. C., Hood, S. A., & McKeown, C. A. (2021). Remote teaching of publication-quality, single-case graphs in Microsoft excel. *Journal of Applied Behavior Analysis, 54*, 1265–1280. https://doi.org/10.1002/jaba.805

LeJeune, L. M., Lambert, J. M., Lemons, C. J., Mottern, R. E., & Wisniewski, B. T. (2019). Teacher-conducted trial-based functional analysis and treatment of multiply controlled challenging behavior. *Behavior Analysis: Research and Practice, 19*(3), 241–246. https://doi.org/10.1037/bar000012

Limb, C. J. (2011). The need for evidence in an anecdotal world. *Trends in Hearing, 15*, 3–4. https://doi.org/10.1177/1084713811425751

Lobo, M. A., Moeyaert, M., Cunha, A. B., & Babik, I. (2017). Single-case design, analysis, and quality assessment for intervention research. *Journal of Neurologic Physical Therapy, 41*, 187–197. https://doi.org/10.1097/NPT.0000000000000187

McIntyre, L. L., Gresham, F. M., DiGennaro, F. D., & Reed, D. D. (2007). Treatment integrity of school-based interventions with children in the journal of applied behavior analysis 1991–2005. *Journal of Applied Behavior Analysis, 40*, 659–672. https://doi.org/10.1901/jaba.2007.659-672

Mitteer, D. R., Greer, B. D., Fisher, W. W., & Cohrs, V. L. (2018). Teaching behavior technicians to create publication-quality, single-case design graphs in GraphPad Prism 7. *Journal of Applied Behavior Analysis, 51*(4), 998–1010. https://doi.org/10.1002/jaba.483

Muething, C., Pavlov, A., Call, N., Ringdahl, J., & Gillespie, S. (2021). Prevalence of resurgence during thinning of multiple schedules of reinforcement following functional communication training. *Journal of Applied Behavior Analysis, 54*(2), 813–823.

Parker, R. I., Vannest, K. J., & Davis, J. L. (2011). Effect size in single-case research: A review of nine nonoverlap techniques. *Behavior Modification, 35*, 303–322. https://doi.org/10.1177/0145445511399147

Perone, M. (1999). Statistical inference in behavior analysis: Experimental control is better. *The Behavior Analyst, 22*, 109–116. https://doi.org/10.1007/BF03391988

Peterson, L., Homer, A. L., & Wonderlich, S. A. (1982). The integrity of independent variables in behavior analysis. *Journal of Applied Behavior Analysis, 15*, 477–492. https://doi.org/10.1901/jaba.1982.15-477

Piazza, C. C., Fisher, W. W., Hanley, G. P., LeBlanc, L. A., Worsdell, A. S., Lindauer, S. E., & Keeney, K. M. (1998). Treatment of pica through multiple analyses of its reinforcing functions. *Journal of Applied Behavior Analysis, 31*(2), 165–189. https://doi.org/10.1901/jaba.1998.31-165

Poling, A., Methot, L. L., & LeSage, M. G. (1995). *Fundamentals of behavior analytic research*. Plenum Press.

Roane, H. S., Vollmer, T. R., Ringdahl, J. E., & Marcus, B. A. (1998). Evaluation of a brief stimulus preference assessment. *Journal of Applied Behavior Analysis, 31*(4), 605–620. https://doi.org/10.1901/jaba.1998.31-605

Saini, V., Greer, B. D., Fisher, W. W., Lichtblau, K. R., DeSouza, A. A., & Mitteer, D. R. (2016). Individual and combined effects of noncontingent reinforcement and response blocking on automatically reinforced problem behavior. *Journal of Applied Behavior Analysis, 49*(3), 693–698. https://doi.org/10.1002/jaba.306

Schwartz, I. S., & Baer, D. M. (1991). Social validity assessments: Is current practice state of the art? *Journal of Applied Behavior Analysis, 24*, 189–204. https://doi.org/10.1901/jaba.1991.24-189

Shadish, W. R. (2014a). Analysis and meta-analysis of single-case designs: An introduction. *Journal of School Psychology, 52*, 109–122. https://doi.org/10.1016/j.jsp.2013.11.009

Shadish, W. R. (2014b). Statistical analyses of single-case designs: The shape of things to come. *Current Directions in Psychological Science, 23*, 139–146. https://doi.org/10.1177/0963721414524773

Shahan, T. A., & Greer, B. D. (2021). Destructive behavior increases as a function of reductions in alternative reinforcement during schedule thinning: A retrospective quantitative analysis. *Journal of the Experimental Analysis of Behavior, 116*(2), 243–248. https://doi.org/10.1002/jeab.708

Sidman, M. (1960). *Tactics of scientific research: Evaluating experimental data in psychology.* Basic Books.

Slaton, J. D., & Hanley, G. P. (2018). Nature and scope of synthesis in functional analysis and treatment of problem behavior. *Journal of Applied Behavior Analysis, 51*(4), 942–973. https://doi.org/10.1002/jaba.498

Slaton, J. D., Hanley, G. P., & Raftery, K. J. (2017). Interview-informed functional analyses: A comparison of synthesized and isolated components. *Journal of Applied Behavior Analysis, 50*(2), 252–277. https://doi.org/10.1002/jaba.384

St. Peter Pipkin, C., Vollmer, T. R., & Sloman, K. N. (2010). Effects of treatment integrity failures during differential reinforcement of alternative behavior: A translational model. *Journal of Applied Behavior Analysis, 43*, 47–70. https://doi.org/10.1901/jaba.2010.43-47

Student. (1908). The probable error of a mean. *Biometrika, 6*, 1–25. https://doi.org/10.23078/2331554

Swan, D. M., & Pustejovsky, J. E. (2018). A gradual effects model for single-case designs. *Multivariate Behavioral Research, 53*, 574–593. https://doi.org/10.1080/00273171.2018.1466681

Traub, M. R., & Vollmer, T. R. (2019). Response latency as a measure of behavior in the assessment of elopement. *Journal of Applied Behavior Analysis, 52*(2), 422–438. https://doi.org/10.1002/jaba.541

Tufte, E. R. (2001). *The visual display of quantitative information* (2nd ed.). Graphics Press LLC.

Van Houten, R., Axelrod, S., Bailey, J. S., Favell, J. E., Foxx, R. M., Iwata, B. A., & Lovaas, O. I. (1988). The right to effective behavioral treatment. *Journal of Applied Behavior Analysis, 21*, 381–384. https://doi.org/10.1901/jaba.1988.21-381

Vollmer, T. R., Sloman, K. N., & St Peter Pipkin, C. (2008). Practical implications of data reliability and treatment integrity monitoring. *Behavior Analysis in Practice, 1*, 4–11. https://doi.org/10.1007/BF03391722

Wickham, H. (2016). *ggplot2: Elegant graphics for data analysis.* Springer-Verlag. https://ggplot2.tidyverse.org

Wolf, M. M. (1978). Social validity: The case for subjective measurement or how applied behavior analysis is finding its heart 1. *Journal of Applied Behavior Analysis, 11*, 203–214. https://doi.org/10.1901/jaba.1978.11-203

Young, M. E. (2019). Modern statistical practices in the experimental analysis of behavior: An introduction to the special issue. *Journal of the Experimental Analysis of Behavior, 111*, 149–154. https://doi.org/10.1002/jeab.511

Andrew R. Craig, PhD, is an assistant professor of Pediatrics, Behavior Analysis Studies, and Neuroscience and Physiology; director for research in the Golisano Center for Special Needs; and chair of the Behavior Analysis Studies Program at SUNY Upstate Medical University. Dr. Craig is a recipient of several awards, including the B. F. Skinner Foundation New Researcher Award from Division 25 of the American Psychological Association and the Joseph V. Brady Significant Research Contribution Award from the Society for the Experimental Analysis of Behavior. He is an associate editor of the *Journal of the Experimental Analysis of Behavior* and *Behavior Analysis: Research and Practice*, a guest associate editor for the *Journal of Applied Behavior Analysis*, and an ad hoc editor or reviewer for several other journals that publish research in behavior analysis and neuroscience. He also serves in leadership positions in regional and national behavior-analytic organizations, including Division 25 of the American Psychological Association and the Society for the Quantitative Analyses of Behavior.

Megan A. Boyle, PhD, is the director of Applied Research at Upstate Caring Partners, where she guides applied and clinically driven research to improve the lives of students and residents with intellectual and developmental disabilities and the staff who serve them. She previously served as assistant and associate professor at Missouri State University. Megan specializes in the assessment and treatment of severe behavior of individuals with autism, and her research focuses on elopement, behavioral contrast, refining methods of functional analysis, functional communication training, and schedule thinning, and evaluating aspects of practical functional assessment and skill-based treatment. Her work has been published in peer-reviewed journals and she serves as an ad hoc reviewer and guest associate editor for behavior-analytic journals.

Sean W. Smith, PhD, is an assistant professor of Pediatrics and Behavior Analysis Studies at SUNY Upstate Medical University. Sean's research has won the Tony Nevin Award from the *Society for the Quantitative Analysis for Behavior*. Sean serves on the board of editors for the *Journal of Applied Behavior Analysis* and as an ad hoc reviewer for several other journals that publish behavior analytic research. Sean has published numerous behavior analytic journal articles and book chapters.

William E. Sullivan, PhD, is director of outpatient behavioral services at the Golisano Center for Special Needs and assistant professor of Pediatrics and Behavior Analysis Studies at SUNY Upstate Medical University. He currently serves on the board of editors for the *Journal of Behavioral Education* and *Behavior Analysis: Research and Practice* and has served as Guest Associate Editor for *Behavioral Development, Behavior Analysis in Practice*, and the *Journal of Applied Behavior Analysis*. He has published numerous research articles and book chapters on the assessment and treatment of severe behavior displayed by individuals with intellectual and developmental disabilities.

Chapter 8
Discussion Section

Tara Fahmie, Stephanie Hood, and Javid Rahaman

The overarching goal of the discussion section is to move beyond the presentation of study findings to examine, interpret, and qualify the results for the reader (American Psychological Association, 2020). Goodson (2017) describes the discussion section as a space for authors to pose questions such as, "Are we moving in the appropriate direction? Should the field continue pursuing this line of inquiry? And are we being ethical in our approach to this topic?". This chapter will guide you in developing and writing the discussion section of your manuscript by providing tips on writing style and structure, reviewing examples and non-examples, and arranging your position among related research.

Writing Style and Structure of a Discussion Section

After introducing your study, detailing your method, and summarizing your results, you tie it all together in one final section. Think of the discussion section as a mirrored reflection of the introduction section. It begins with a restatement of your purpose, positions your study among the research you previously cited, draws conclusions that balance your study's strengths and limitations, and closes with the broader implications of your work. There is considerable flexibility in the ordering of these components of the discussion section, but you should generally aim for a triangular shape (Fig. 8.1), that begins narrowly and widens in scope as you move

T. Fahmie (✉) · J. Rahaman
Severe Behavior Department, University of Nebraska Medical Center, Omaha, NE, USA
e-mail: tfahmie@unmc.edu; javid.rahaman@unmc.edu

S. Hood
Psychology Department, Marquette University, Milwaukee, WI, USA
e-mail: stephanie.hood@marquette.edu

© The Author(s), under exclusive license to Springer Nature Switzerland AG 2023   131
A. K. Griffith, T. C. Ré (eds.), *Disseminating Behavioral Research*,
https://doi.org/10.1007/978-3-031-47343-2_8

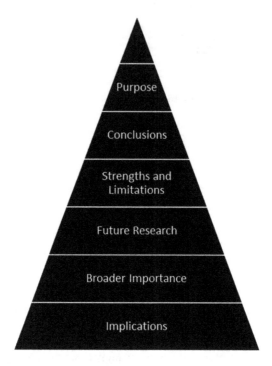

Fig. 8.1 General structure of the discussion section

Table 8.1 Writing style tips

Writing style tips
1. Consider your audience.
2. Provide justifiable commentary.

down. The final sentence of the discussion, perhaps the most difficult to craft, should bring the reader back to the initial statements of importance made in the opening sentences of your introduction.

Because the discussion section is less technical than the method and results section, it can be a place for you to infuse your personal writing style. However, word choice matters as much in the discussion section as in any other section of your manuscript. Two important tips to consider while drafting the discussion section are highlighted in Table 8.1.

The first is to consider your audience. For example, you may adapt your writing style to communicate to other behavior analytic researchers or clinicians, researchers or clinicians outside of behavior analysis, caregivers (e.g., parents, teachers), or the general public. Audience will also vary depending on the outlet of your submission. Many behavior analytic researchers write for other behavior analytic researchers, as the primary goal of their work is to build on the corpus of research in the field. However, many of these same researchers have a secondary goal of directly impacting behavior analytic practice; thus, writing to a broader audience (e.g., clinicians, caregivers) in the discussion section is generally advised. One way to accomplish a style compatible with reaching a broader audience is to orally discuss your study widely and often (e.g., Zoellner, 1969). It does not help to contain discussion of your work to your research lab meetings because your homogenous audience (other lab members, mentor) will be less likely to provide the feedback necessary to broaden the scope of your thinking and writing. Instead, talk about your research to clinicians outside of your lab, your family, and your friends. If you can present your study as a research poster in outlets outside of behavior analysis (e.g., *American Psychological Association* conference), do so. Embrace the challenge of seeing and hearing various perspectives of your work (the more critical, the better for your writing!). Working through the struggle of describing your work in lay terms to audiences outside of your field will refine your verbal behavior. Hearing diverse interpretations or critiques of your work will broaden your perspective and help you pinpoint areas for revision. That is, you are often intimately knowledgeable about the topic of your research and have viewed the same data for months or sometimes years; thus, you may not "see" diverse interpretations, points of ambiguity, or novel insights on your own. When interacting with others regarding your work, take notes that will serve as writing prompts for your discussion section.

The second tip in Table 8.1 is to provide justifiable commentary. That is, all components of the discussion section must be justified by the method and results of your study. Your word choice, sentence structure, and style should never imply conclusions that transcend the limits of your study outcomes. An example and non-example is found in Table 8.2. Consider that you just concluded a study assessing preschoolers' preference for contingent and noncontingent teacher attention. Your study included a dozen preschoolers located at one preschool in the northeast of the United States. All participants of your study preferred contingent to noncontingent teacher attention and you are ready to write your discussion. Although your results are compelling, in that you replicated the outcome across 12 participants, there are important limits to the generality of your findings that should not be overlooked in the construction of your discussion section. In the non-example in Table 8.2, your conclusion about the study implies that contingent reinforcement (generally) is preferred by preschoolers (generally), without acknowledgement that your outcomes were not replicated across other reinforcer classes (e.g., negative reinforcement), other sources of attention (e.g., peer attention), or other settings (e.g., other cultures). In the example in Table 8.2, slight changes to the tense of your sentence (e.g., "prefer" → "preferred"), sentence structure (e.g., "Preschool-aged children *in our study*"), and specificity (e.g., "reinforcement" → "teacher attention") shifts the sentence to one that is justified by the study you conducted.

Table 8.2 Non-example and example of justifiable commentary

Non-example and example of justifiable commentary
Non-example: This study shows that preschool children prefer contingent to noncontingent reinforcement. (Note how the use of present tense, word choice, and sentence structure imply a finding that has broad generality)
Example: Preschool children in our study preferred contingent to noncontingent teacher attention. (Note how the use of past tense, word choice, and sentence structure do not imply generality of the statement)

Ensuring that you are data- and fact-driven in your discussion section should not be interpreted as the need to excessively hedge your conclusions. With reference to the hypothetical study described above, an example of excessive hedging is "The results of this study *may show* that it is *possible* that children *might prefer* contingent to noncontingent reinforcement *sometimes*." Here, the words in italics are intended to give pause to the reader and prevent them from jumping to unjustified conclusions. But the hedging is excessive in that it is occurring multiple times in a single sentence; ultimately, this degree of hedging is unnecessary when you can simply reword the sentence as shown in the example in Table 8.2. The appropriate use of hedging should be reserved for assertions beyond the direct outcome of the study or current body of research (scientific interpretations).

Components of the Discussion Section

Next, we describe various components of the discussion section in more detail. Each component is intentionally labeled in active voice (e.g., "Refresh the Reader") to signal that your writing should be guided by audience impact (i.e., function), and not by a standard structure. There are multiple ways to accomplish the functions described, and perhaps unlike other sections of the manuscript, there is considerable variability in the structure of the discussion section across publications. Variability will be imposed by the journal outlet, the purpose of the study (e.g., efficacy vs. effectiveness; Ghaemmaghami et al., 2021), outcomes of the study (e.g., aligned with past research vs. divergent from past research), and the intended audience, to name a few.

Refresh the Reader

The first purpose of the discussion section is to refresh the reader on what you did and what you found. Typically, this begins with a reminder of the purpose(s) of your study. Although this reminder may seem redundant to you, trust that the reader will welcome it. The purpose may be stated as clearly as it was in the introduction (i.e., "the purpose of the study was…") or may be indirectly referenced in a brief summary of results. Table 8.3 provides several samples of the final paragraph of the introduction and the first paragraph of the discussion to highlight this alignment. Let us walk through the first example of the writing of Hanley et al. (2014). In this study, the authors' stated purpose (introduction section) was to "demonstrate the utility of the model in an outpatient clinic…by implementing, generalizing, and socially validating the treatments…." Each of these features of the purpose (implementation, generalization, and social validity) are recalled in the first paragraph of the authors' discussion section. First, the authors described the implementation of their model by stating "The problem behavior of three children…was effectively

Table 8.3 Samples of the final paragraph of the introduction compared to the opening paragraph of the discussion in published studies

	Last paragraph of introduction	First paragraph of discussion
Hanley et al. (2014)	"Our purpose was to demonstrate the utility of the model in an outpatient clinic with the first three families who attended the clinic by implementing, generalizing, and socially validating the treatments designed from the results of the interview-informed analyses. Single-subject designs demonstrated the influence of the separate treatment components that were progressively synthesized to produce socially valid outcomes for participating families." (p. 17)	"The problem behavior of three children with autism was effectively eliminated and multiple important social skills were acquired when behavioral interventions were developed from an abbreviated functional assessment process and then gradually brought to scale in an outpatient clinic. The effective treatments were then implemented by the parents of the children in their homes and during the conditions initially reported as evoking severe problem behavior. Despite the length of the consultation process, all parents reported that the consultation was very helpful and that they were satisfied with the process and the amount of improvement in their child's problem behavior." (p. 30)
Greer et al. (2016)	"The purpose of current study was to use a methodology similar to that described by Tarbox et al. (2004) and Simon and Thompson (2006) to evaluate the combined and sequential effects of the training procedures used in an early childhood education center. We conducted an add-in component analysis to evaluate the effects of placing children in underwear, arranging a dense schedule of sits on the toilet, and programming differential reinforcement on the acquisition of toileting skills in children. We specifically targeted increases in urinary eliminations in the toilet, decreases in urinary accidents, and increases in independent requests to sit on the toilet." (p. 71)	"We evaluated the combined and sequential effects of three recommended toilet-training procedures on levels of accidents, appropriate eliminations, and self-initiations. When these three training components were combined, we observed clear improvements in toileting performance for two of the six children, including the only child (Aaron) with autism. At least two of found clear improvements in performance for two of five children (a 40% success rate)." (p. 80)
Hood et al. (2017)	"We aimed to extend previous literature by improving greeting and conversation skills during unscripted interactions with two teenagers and a child with an ASD without an associated intellectual impairment. We taught several skills in the context of the same conversation to approximate a typical conversation. We assessed stimulus generalization of performance across several unfamiliar conversation partners and maintenance of performance over a 1- or 4-month period. We also assessed the participants' and parents' social acceptability of the teaching." (p. 462)	"We identified deficits in conversations and greetings exhibited by three individuals via a broad assessment composed of direct and indirect measures. Based on the results, we taught multiple skills that led to generalization across conversation partners and settings as well as maintenance over time. Participants and their parents were satisfied with the improvements in performance. These outcomes of robust acquisition, demonstration of generalization and maintenance, and high acceptability scores indicate that individualized treatments with methods similar to this study may help individuals with an ASD become more successful in greeting and conversing with unfamiliar adults." (pp. 481–482)

eliminated…when behavioral interventions were…brought to scale in an outpatient clinic." Next, the authors commented on the generality of their model by stating, "The effective treatments were then implemented by the parents…in their homes." Finally, the authors commented on the social validity of their model by stating "…all parents reported that the consultation was very helpful…" (p. 30).

In sum, the first paragraph of your discussion should be close in scope to the purpose and outcomes of your study (i.e., the top tip of the triangle in Fig. 8.1). However, your word choice will likely be broader than that found in the method and results sections due to the relatively limited space (one paragraph) used to summarize details contained in those sections. Therefore, the first paragraph is *not* the place to discuss the minutia of your data or thought-provoking details of your findings. These points will be made later in your discussion. If your outcomes were surprising and you did not meet the original purpose of your study, it is helpful to clearly state this in your first paragraph as well. You will have space later in your discussion to hypothesize potential reasons for the surprising results.

Provide a Summary and Interpretation of Your Outcomes

The goal of the discussion section is to not only highlight the most important outcomes or findings but also to provide an interpretation of those outcomes to the reader. The interpretation will guide the reader to consider the importance, relevance, implications, and applications of the obtained results. The reader is not likely to be as knowledgeable about the subject area as you are, so it is important to write with maximal clarity and transparency. In essence, you are having a conversation with your reader about the current findings among other published findings.

Thus, you should first summarize the overall (general) conclusions that can be directly derived from your data, noting any participant deviations if they exist. When you are referencing a particular outcome, you may refer the reader back to the table or figure by number to provide maximal clarity. Sometimes, your interpretations of the data will extend beyond the original questions you set out to answer. In these cases, you should provide a scholarly foundation for your claim and not rely too heavily on speculation or anecdote. The scholarly foundation may be based in published research, a conceptual analysis, or a secondary analysis of existing data from your study. However, if your interpretations must remain speculative, describe them as such and call for future research in the area. For example, in a study of various functional analysis (FA) patterns, Virues-Ortega et al. (2022; p. 507) stated:

> Additionally, the proposed function of various suppressive components of an FA (e.g., punishment in the attention condition) remains speculative, as our procedures did not attempt to confirm the necessity of the contingency versus the mere presence of the stimulus (Thompson & Iwata, 2005). Future research in this area should consider additional phases

of the component analysis that enable a firmer conclusion about the function of the stimulus events. Whereas some patterns (e.g., attention lowest and everything else elevated) would suggest the necessity of the contingency, these patterns were not always observed in our retrospective analysis. Thus, in light of the patterns revealed in Study 1, our a priori hypotheses about the function of stimuli in the FA should be explored more carefully.

Perhaps most importantly, interpretations of your data should always be described in terms of basic behavioral processes. When all authors have linked their study findings to the same conceptual framework, the science benefits from progression and cohesion (Baer et al., 1968).

Sometimes, the obtained outcomes differ from the hypothesized outcomes guiding the study's experimental design and approach. At these times, researchers may modify the procedures to seek further understanding of the variability (Sidman, 1960) or to increase experimental control. For example, in a study comparing an ABA approach with a modified sequential oral sensory (M-SOS) approach using a multiple baseline across foods design, Peterson et al. (2016) wrote:

> One potentially important finding was that we observed treatment generalization for two of the three children who participated in M-SOS (James and Jerry) when we subsequently implemented ABA. When we implemented ABA for one target food, they began to accept the other two target foods in the absence of treatment. We did not observe a similar pattern of treatment generalization for children who received only ABA. To evaluate whether previous exposure to the target foods during M-SOS played a role in treatment generalization, we conducted ABA treatment with James using three foods that we never presented during M-SOS or ABA. We did not observe treatment generalization with the three novel target foods. One possible explanation for this finding is that exposure to the target foods during M-SOS produced a desensitization effect that was observable only when we implemented ABA with one of the foods. This explanation is tentative, given that we conducted the treatment generalization assessment with only one participant. Nevertheless, this finding is potentially important for several reasons. Although ABA was highly effective, one criticism of ABA is that some children eat only when treatment is present and not when it is absent. Therefore, methods to increase the likelihood of more age typical eating (i.e., eating without treatment) are needed. Second, many investigators have advocated for alternatives or adjuncts to nonremoval of the spoon (Seubert, Fryling, Wallace, Jiminez, & Meier, 2014). If this treatment generalization finding is robust, then implementation of M-SOS before ABA would reduce the number of applications of nonremoval of the spoon needed to achieve treatment effectiveness and may be associated with sustained eating in the absence of ABA treatment for some children. More research is needed to replicate this finding.

This passage exemplifies several recommendations worth pointing out; the authors (a) used a neutral tone and balanced evaluation of results; (b) directed the reader to relevant results; (c) included a clear description of the observed limitation (namely, lack of experimental control when generalization occurred across food types) with accompanying secondary analyses to increase confidence in the interpretation; and (d) provided a clear signal of the importance of their interpretations and need for future research.

Table 8.4 provides several "Dos" and "Don'ts" when interpreting study outcomes in your study in the discussion section.

Table 8.4 Dos and Don'ts of outcome interpretation

Dos	Don'ts
Cite relevant research to support your interpretation of the outcome	Go beyond your data in your interpretation of the outcomes
Directly reference what figure or tables you are describing	Make statements of generality without support
Include secondary analyses that increase the confidence in your conceptual interpretations	Provide excessive anecdotes without empirical foundation
Be clear about the extent to which the outcomes you summarize are consistent across all participants	Reference results that are difficult to find in the "Results" section
Describe potential boundary conditions or variables that may influence the variability in obtained outcomes	

Position Your Study Among Related Research

Next, you should highlight the convergence and divergence of your data with other published findings. That is, position your study's outcomes among those already available to the reader. Questions this section of your discussion should answer include: What other research exists on the behavioral processes validated by your study? If divergence is noted, what conceptual systems may explain the divergence?

The strategy of aligning your findings with behavioral processes is particularly useful when you have obtained findings that are unique from previous literature. Two examples are shown in Table 8.5, and the first will be described as an illustration. In the study by Heal and Hanley (2011), the researchers found that a teaching strategy (embedded teaching) that has a robust research basis was neither effective nor preferred by their child participant relative to child-led or teacher-directed learning. The authors provided a hypothesis on the conceptual basis for this finding, in that embedded prompts may have served as punishment. In the discussion of their results, the authors positioned their study among published research on embedded teaching, noted procedural variations that may have accounted for the divergent findings, and rooted their work in the conceptual foundations of verbal behavior described by Skinner (1957). The authors also called for future research related to the unanswered questions uncovered by their study. In the final sentences of the excerpt in Table 8.5, Heal and Hanley clearly described the gap that remained with respect to the broader research basis for their study and outlined the next logical step in research in this area.

Great discussion sections will give the reader confidence that the authors have a clear vision of the position of their study among related research and of the conceptual foundations underlying their obtained data. For newer researchers, we recommend developing tables or figures (for personal use, and not included in the manuscript) to help clarify this vision before you embark on the writing process. Time investment in these front-end processes will pay off greatly in the editorial process.

Table 8.5 Examples describing unique findings in the discussion section

Examples describing unique findings	
Heal and Hanley (2011)	"Embedded teaching methods have varied across and within studies with respect to the timing of the delivery of embedded prompts and the consequences provided for correct responding (e.g., Schepis et al., 2001; Tate et al., 2005). In the context of teaching language skills, the procedural variability can be directly related to the specific learning objective. The verbal behavior conceptual system (Skinner, 1957) may be useful for understanding the important differences in the manner in which embedded teaching is implemented. When teaching a mand (e.g., requesting; i.e., verbal behavior largely under the control of a specific establishing operation and reinforced by a related and specific consequence), embedded prompts are delivered prior to item access and the consequence for correct responding is access to the requested item. In contrast, when teaching a tact (e.g., color identification; i.e., verbal behavior under the control of a discriminative stimulus and reinforced with a nonspecific and generalized reinforcer) embedded prompts are often delivered following access to items and the consequence for correct responding is praise (Fox & Hanline, 1993; Tate et al., 2005). In the current study, the learning objective was tacting colors and animals, and the procedures arranged in our Strategy 2 were consistent with recommended embedded teaching procedures (Grisham Brown et al., 2002). Therefore, the type of verbal operant taught may be a moderator of the observed effects. In other words, the ineffectiveness of Strategy 2 and the avoidance of this strategy by Ali and the children in Heal et al. (2009) may occur only when tacts are taught with these procedures. Thus, researchers should evaluate whether similar relations are found when mands are taught with embedded procedures. Meanwhile, it seems important to conduct embedded teaching of tacts under mand-like conditions (see Hart & Risley, 1975, for these language elaboration procedures)." (pp. 129–131)
Lerman and Iwata (1996)	"Although these results appear to contradict those of a number of studies in which the PREE has been clearly demonstrated, the results are consistent with those of basic studies using within- rather than between subjects designs (e.g., Adams et al., 1982; Flora & Pavlik, 1990). Factors that are responsible for conflicting outcomes among basic studies are still relatively unclear. However, results of studies using within-subject designs may be particularly vulnerable to confounding by sequence or interaction effects. Research findings on the PREE may also be equivocal because resistance has been defined and measured in a variety of ways. In most basic studies, resistance to extinction has been based on response rates, total number of responses, or amount of time to meet an extinction criterion. In general, these studies demonstrated greater resistance to extinction following INT schedules than CRF schedules. Others have attempted to adjust for the differences in responding associated with the different baseline conditions by calculating the rate of change in responding during extinction or the proportion-of-baseline response rates (cf. Nevin, 1988). Results of these studies indicated that CRF schedules were associated with greater resistance to extinction than were INT schedules. The current study provides further data showing that reinforcement schedules can produce apparently different outcomes solely as a function of the measure used to reflect resistance. When traditional measures of resistance (e.g., response rate, number of responses) were examined, a PREE was obtained with 2 subjects (Sue and Harold), whereas a reversed PREE was obtained with just 1 subject (Brandon). These findings suggest that the relationship between reinforcement schedules and responding during extinction is more complex than that depicted in many texts and articles on application." (pp. 166–167)

Table 8.6 Limitation descriptions

	Type of limitation	Example
Cortez et al. (2022)	Imposes interpretive boundaries	"One limitation of this study is that we did not implement within-subject replications (i.e., we only taught one set of stimuli to mastery in each condition), and neither did previous studies on the topic except for Matter et al. (2020). Within-subject replications would strengthen experimental control by ensuring that the optimal procedure is identified for each participant. This is especially important because there were small differences in efficiency (i.e., trials to criterion) between conditions, which could be attributed to uncontrolled variables or confounds inherent to the adapted alternating treatments design (e.g., unequal difficulty, multiple treatment interference, and history)." (p. 261)
Erath et al. (2021)	Sets up a clear direction for future research	"One limitation was that we did not collect data on the time spent creating the training video because the training video was an adaptation of content created for previous trainings conducted in a group-based format. As such, we are unable to provide a supplemental cost–benefit analysis on the total amount of time needed to create the training materials. When replicating and extending these findings, future researchers should collect data to allow for a cost–benefit analysis to determine organizational return-on-investment" (p. 1262)

Recognize Limitations and Propose Future Directions

No study is without its limitations, and the most important limitations should be revealed to the reader in the discussion section. This should not be a list of *all* the potential limitations, but only the most relevant. Relevant limitations will be those that impact study interpretation and pose next steps in research (see top two rows of Table 8.6). It is important to outline both the relevant limitations and the impact they should have on the reader. That is, you should not assume readers will understand the degree to which the limitation matters to them as a researcher, clinician, or otherwise without it being explicitly stated. Begin by selecting the most important limitations to discuss. The most important limitations will be those directly related to the internal validity of your study (e.g., design, measures, independent variables) and that affect your interpretations of the data. Keep in mind that there is typically a rationale for each decision you made in the study, and often, a limitation will be offset by a solution to another problem you could have encountered. Consider a basic formula for describing your limitations proposed by Goodson (2017) and summarized in Table 8.7: (a) state the problem or limitation, (b) describe the potential affect on the results of the study, (c) propose solutions employed within the study or in future studies, and (d) remind the readers of the relevant strengths of the study. The readers will remember what they read last, so it is important to end with the strengths and merits of the study (see bottom row of Table 8.7).

Try not to fall into the trap of identifying false limitations, such as citing a small participant sample as a limitation of a single-subject design study (unless, of course,

Table 8.7 Basic formula for limitations

Basic formula for limitations
(a) Important limitation faced
(b) How the limitation may have affected your results
(c) The solution you employed or the solution a future researcher could employ
(d) Strength of the study

the purpose of your study was better aligned with a group design). After all, a collection of studies using single-subject design, as opposed to a single study, is required to demonstrate generality across populations (Walker & Carr, 2021). As another example, much applied research occurs under tightly controlled conditions and may be relatively weak in ecological validity (i.e., conditions representative of everyday life); this may be cited as a limitation insofar as your conclusions are intended to inform the everyday environment. But it should not be cited as a limitation if your study is primarily aimed at demonstrating efficacy under controlled conditions (Fahmie et al., 2023). Also, keep in mind that one study cannot answer *all* relevant questions; thus, although it is reasonable to cite omitted study features as a limitation (see example in Table 8.6 by Erath et al., 2021), do not rely on this mechanism to the exclusion of calling out important limitations that affect your conclusions. Instead, use this as a mechanism to promote future studies on the topic (see example in Table 8.6 by Erath et al.).

If you intend for your study to inform clinical practice, there are likely several limitations you may draw related to the feasibility or scalability of the intervention. Thus, unless your study is conducted as an effectiveness evaluation (which considers cost, ecological validity, feasibility, accessibility, etc.), do not assume or imply that it *can* directly inform clinical practice. Doing so will require you to raise many limitations and may detract from otherwise helpful conclusions. Instead, detail the ways in which your study should be extended to inform clinical work. This might include conducting the study under more natural conditions, minimizing costs of the research, improving social validity of the outcomes, etc.

One rule of thumb is to call attention to any limitations that an editorial reviewer is likely to raise prior to them having the opportunity to do so. Keep in mind that a reviewer will not be able to distinguish a researcher who does not recognize the limitations of their work from a researcher who is attempting to hide the limitations of their work. Either option is not a good reflection of your abilities as a scientist. Thus, write to anticipate editorial reviews by calling out your own limitations. If you have not previously received editorial reviews, consider reaching out to your mentors to ask for opportunities to complete reviews. Serving as a reviewer typically gives you access to several critical opinions (i.e., other reviewers, editor) of the same manuscript and can sharpen your critique of your own work. Relatedly, sometimes it is helpful to tell the reader what the data *do not* show. Consider, for example, a study by Goldberg et al. (2017; p. 891) that examined the reinforcing value of stimuli within social and non-social contexts. In the discussion section, the authors stated:

It is important to note that any conclusion drawn from this study cannot be generalized toward understanding the extent to which boys with and without HFA [high-functioning autism] actually 'enjoy' engaging in activities with their mother (compared to alone), as this study did not specifically measure the equality/extent to which participants actually engaged with their mothers during the post-session access to social activities.

Strong discussions will have directions for future research integrated throughout the description of limitations. Provide sufficient detail so that readers can understand the next research steps and their rationale. Remember that the reader is likely less familiar with the topic than you are, so do not assume they will understand your recommendations without accompanying rationale. Table 8.8 summarizes components of helpful research recommendations and Table 8.9 provides some examples. The example by Athens and Vollmer (2010; Table 8.9, top row) will be used for illustrative purposes. First, the authors reminded the reader that the study was limited to one type of concurrent schedule. Next, the authors clearly and concisely suggested a future study involving naturalistic observation and a variety of reinforcement parameters. Last, the authors answered "why" this recommendation mattered by mentioning concerns with acceptability and integrity of clinical application of their research outcomes.

Table 8.8 Future research recommendations

Future research recommendations
(a) Connect each limitation to a future research question
(b) Clearly and concisely state the next step in research inquiry
(c) Describe necessary procedural nuances
(d) Provide rationale for your suggestions. Answer the question "Why pursue this future research?" related to conceptual, procedural, or applied implications

Table 8.9 Examples of describing future research in the discussion section

Examples of describing future research	
Athens and Vollmer (2010)	"These experiments included concurrent schedules of VI 20-s reinforcement for problem and appropriate behavior. Future research may involve similar analyses using concurrent-schedules arrangements based on naturalistic observations. The extent to which relative response allocation is similar under descriptive and experimental arrangements may suggest values of reinforcement parameters that may increase both the acceptability and integrity of treatment implementation by caregivers." (p. 586)
Jones and St. Peter (2022)	"The use of probabilistic errors contributed a notable limitation to our study: Some participants may have had insufficient exposure to the errors to affect responding. For example, because P3 never engaged in target responding during reduced-integrity FT phases, this participant experienced only omission errors during phases that nominally included combined errors (see Supporting Materials for data on obtained integrity values per participant). To permit interpretation of findings in the context of obtained integrity errors, researchers should report integrity values for all components of their intervention rather than reporting integrity solely as an aggregate value. Reporting only an aggregate would conceal the differences in error types and possible sources of behavioral control (Cook et al., 2015)." (p. 1121)

Provide Take Home Points

"Take home points" (THPs) contain information you want your reader to retain after they have finished reading your publication. THPs are helpful to include at the conclusion of your discussion and should bring your readers back to the central themes of your manuscript (bottom of the triangle in Fig. 8.1). Table 8.10 provides questions to ask yourself when developing your THPs. It is acceptable for THPs to reiterate important statements made throughout your discussion, but THPs should not be another summary of your study; instead, they should leave the readers with an understanding of how your study impacts the broader conceptualization, experimentation, and practice of behavior analysis. At times, it is helpful to communicate the impact of your study in bulleted format in contrast to typical writing conventions. Some publication outlets, like *Behavior Analysis in Practice,* have formats that require bulleted THPs at the end of the discussion section (see examples in Table 8.11). You should refer to the author's guidelines for submission when considering different stylistic approaches to writing your manuscript.

You may frame your THPs to evoke various effects on the reader, including (a) cautionary messages, (b) responses to criticism, (c) calls to action, and (d) celebratory comments. Table 8.12 provides an example of each effect. To illustrate, Iwata et al. (2013) provided a cautionary message regarding the utility of the Functional Analysis Screening Tool (FAST) for determining behavioral function by stating "Therefore, we reemphasize the fact that the FAST is not an approximation to an FA of problem behavior; it is simply one way to gather information during an interview." In another example regarding contingency management (CM) research, Dallery et al. (2020) stated "Higgins et al. (2019) recently made a strong argument that although CM is efficacious, it is underutilized in clinical care for addictions in general. Technology-based CM may be one way to increase its use and impact on individual and population health" after discussing the contributions of technology-based CM interventions. This is a "response to criticism" example because it identifies a novel pathway to increase the use of CM interventions in clinical care.

Table 8.10 Questions your take home points can answer

Questions your take home points can answer
1. What do you want the reader to remember from your study?
2. Why should your outcomes matter to the reader?
3. How does your study impact the conceptualization, experimentation, and practice of behavior analysis?
4. How does your study affect other scientific and clinical practices outside of behavior analysis?

Table 8.11 Examples of bulleted take home points

Examples of bulleted take home points	
Pence et al. (2019)	"Implications for Practice • Individuals with ASD and their families may be at risk for interventions that lack empirical evidence. • Behavior analysts are ethically obligated to rely on the scientific method and make judgements based on that method. • Behavior analysts should use data to determine if interventions are therapeutic. • Behavior analysts should use experimental designs to evaluate if an intervention is beneficial, has no effect, or is countertherapeutic." (p. 636)
Ausenhus and Higgins (2019)	"Implications for Practice • Remote real-time feedback is an efficient procedure to train staff. • Exposure to one instance of feedback can improve performance. • A box plot display allows for analysis of trainee progress on specific components. • Trained skills can generalize to actual consumers and preference assessments with edibles." (p. 647)
Brand et al. (2020)	"Implications for Practice • The personal privacy of individuals with disabilities receiving long-term services is an important issue for survey respondents. • The secure and private storage of data captured by technology is extremely important when providing services using technology. • Technology may appear less invasive if clients and their families and caregivers have the opportunity to meet remote staff either remotely or in person. • The acceptability of technology-based service models may increase by addressing concerns regarding privacy." (p. 20)

Table 8.12 Big picture descriptions

	Effect on the reader	Example
Iwata et al. (2013)	Cautionary message	"A distinct danger in formalizing the role of verbal report in the assessment of behavior is its adoption for reasons other than those intended regardless of what the data show because verbal reports are easily obtained. Therefore, we reemphasize the fact that the FAST is not an approximation to an FA of problem behavior; it is simply one way to gather information during an interview. Nevertheless, because the clinical interview is a common context for posing all sorts of questions about behavior, efforts to improve its consistency may be helpful." (p. 283)

(continued)

Table 8.12 (continued)

	Effect on the reader	Example
Dallery et al. (2021)	Response to criticism	"Since the first use of information technology to deliver CM (Dallery & Glenn, 2005), technological advances have expanded the geographical reach of CM from local to nationwide (Dallery et al., 2017), permitted detection of smoking and alcohol using mobile phones (for a review see Dallery et al., 2019), and allowed automation of all aspects of technology-based CM (i.e., smoking monitoring, reinforcer delivery, user authentication; Kendzor et al., 2020). Higgins et al. (2019) recently made a strong argument that although CM is efficacious, it is underutilized in clinical care for addictions in general. Technology-based CM may be one way to increase its use and impact on individual and population health. The present study adds to the growing literature indicating that mobile phone-based CM is efficacious and acceptable in promoting smoking cessation." (p. 50)
Sivaraman and Fahmie (2020)	Calls to action	"Despite limited research on necessary and sufficient modifications, cultural and linguistic considerations should be made and documented carefully to provide a baseline upon which such research can be conducted in the future. Subsequently, researchers may recruit participants from a region where the need for treatment has been established (e.g., using pilot surveys, advertisements, meetings with existing practitioners of allied fields). It is possible that obtaining the most robust measures of behavior change may not be feasible at first, but embracing less robust measures lays the groundwork for exploring culturally sensitive interventions in a more rigorous manner. Thus, we hope this study serves as a small step in a movement toward the type of international dissemination that our field has desired for decades." (pp. 858–859)
Dogan et al. (2017)	Celebration	"Services for children with autism remain difficult for many families to access or afford. The simple nature of the BST method increases the likelihood that social skills training could be implemented in the home, group clinical settings, and school settings. It also has proven to be an efficient approach to teaching skills within a short period of time. Moreover, the simple and straightforward language used in the BST handout should allow for it to be easily understood by nonexperts and translated into a wide range of languages to reach larger populations." (pp. 816–817)

References

Adams, J. F., Nemeth, R. V., & Pavlik, W. B. (1982). Between-and within-subjects PRE with sucrose incentives. *Bulletin of the Psychonomic Society, 20*(5), 261–262. https://doi.org/10.3758/BF03334834

American Psychological Association. (2020). *Publication manual of the American Psychological Association 2020: The official guide to APA style* (7th ed.). American Psychological Association.

Athens, E. S., & Vollmer, T. R. (2010). An investigation of differential reinforcement of alternative behavior without extinction. *Journal of Applied Behavior Analysis, 43*(4), 569–589. https://doi.org/10.1901/jaba.2010.43-569

Ausenhus, J. A., & Higgins, W. J. (2019). An evaluation of real-time feedback delivered via tele-health: Training staff to conduct preference assessments. *Behavior Analysis in Practice, 12*(3), 643–648. https://doi.org/10.1007/s40617-018-00326-1

Baer, D. M., Wolf, M. M., & Risley, T. R. (1968). Some current dimensions of applied behavior analysis. *Journal of Applied Behavior Analysis, 1*(1), 91. https://doi.org/10.1901/jaba.1968.1-91

Brand, D., DiGennaro Reed, F. D., Morley, M. D., Erath, T. G., & Novak, M. D. (2020). A survey assessing privacy concerns of smart-home services provided to individuals with disabilities. *Behavior Analysis in Practice, 13*(1), 11–21. https://doi.org/10.1007/s40617-018-00329-y

Cortez, M. D., da Silva, L. F., Cengher, M., Mazzoca, R. H., & Miguel, C. F. (2022). Teaching a small foreign language vocabulary to children using tact and listener instruction with a prompt delay. *Journal of Applied Behavior Analysis, 55*(1), 249–263. https://doi.org/10.1002/jaba.885

Cook, J. E., Subramaniam, S., Brunson, L.Y., Larson, N. A., Poe, S. G., & St. Peter, C. C. (2015). Global measures of treatment integrity may mask important errors in discrete-trial training. *Behavior Analysis in Practice, 8*(1), 37–47. https://doi.org/10.1007/s40617-014-0039-7

Dallery, J., & Glenn, I. M. (2005). Effects of an internet-based voucher reinforcement program for smoking abstinence: A feasibility study. *Journal of Applied Behavior Analysis, 38*(3), 349–357. https://doi.org/10.1901/jaba.2005.150-04

Dallery, J., Raiff, B. R., Kim, S. J., Marsch, L. A., Stitzer, M., & Grabinski, M. J. (2017). Nationwide access to an internet-based contingency management intervention to promote smoking cessation: A randomized controlled trial. *Addiction, 112*(5), 875–883. https://doi.org/10.1111/add.13715

Dallery, J., Raiff, B. R., Grabinski, M. J., & Marsch, L. A. (2019). Technology-based contingency management in the treatment of substance-use disorders. *Perspectives on Behavior Science.* https://doi.org/10.1007/s40614-019-00214-1

Dallery, J., Stinson, L., Bolívar, H., Modave, F., Salloum, R. G., Viramontes, T. M., & Rohilla, P. (2021). mMotiv8: A smartphone-based contingency management intervention to promote smoking cessation. *Journal of Applied Behavior Analysis, 54*(1), 38–53. https://doi.org/10.1002/jaba.800

Dogan, R. K., King, M. L., Fischetti, A. T., Lake, C. M., Mathews, T. L., & Warzak, W. J. (2017). Parent-implemented behavioral skills training of social skills. *Journal of Applied Behavior Analysis, 50*(4), 805–818. https://doi.org/10.1002/jaba.411

Erath, T. G., DiGennaro Reed, F. D., & Blackman, A. L. (2021). Training human service staff to implement behavioral skills training using a video-based intervention. *Journal of Applied Behavior Analysis, 54*(3), 1251–1264. https://doi.org/10.1002/jaba.827

Fahmie, T. A., Rodriguez, N. M., Luczynski, K. C., Rahaman, J. A., Charles, B. M., & Zangrillo, A. N. (2023). Toward an explicit technology of ecological validity. *Journal of Applied Behavior Analysis, 56*(2), 302–322. https://doi.org/10.1002/jaba.972

Flora, S. R., & Pavlik, W. B. (1990). Conventional and reversed partial reinforcement effects in human operant responding. *Bulletin of the Psychonomic Society, 28*(5), 429–432. https://doi.org/10.3758/BF03334059

Fox, L., & Hanline, M. F. (1993). A preliminary evaluation of learning within developmentally appropriate early childhood settings. *Topics in Early Childhood Special Education, 13*(3), 308–327. https://doi.org/10.1177/027112149301300308

Ghaemmaghami, M., Hanley, G. P., & Jessel, J. (2021). Functional communication training: From efficacy to effectiveness. *Journal of Applied Behavior Analysis, 54*(1), 122–143. https://doi.org/10.1002/jaba.762

Goldberg, M. C., Allman, M. J., Hagopian, L. P., Triggs, M. M., Frank-Crawford, M. A., Mostofsky, S. H., et al. (2017). Examining the reinforcing value of stimuli within social and non-social contexts in children with and without high-functioning autism. *Autism, 21*(7), 881–895. https://doi.org/10.1177/1362361316655035

Goodson, P. (2017). *Becoming an academic writer: 50 exercises for paced, productive, and powerful writing* (2nd ed.). Sage Publications Inc.

Greer, B. D., Neidert, P. L., & Dozier, C. L. (2016). A component analysis of toilet-training procedures recommended for young children. *Journal of Applied Behavior Analysis, 49*(1), 69–84. https://doi.org/10.1002/jaba.275

Grisham-Brown, J., Pretti-Frontczak, K., Hemmeter, M. L., & Ridgley, R. (2002). Teaching IEP goals an objectives: In the context of classroom routines and activities. *Young Exceptional Children, 6*(1), 18–27. https://doi.org/10.1177/109625060200600103

Hanley, G. P., Jin, C. S., Vanselow, N. R., & Hanratty, L. A. (2014). Producing meaningful improvements in problem behavior of children with autism via synthesized analyses and treatments. *Journal of Applied Behavior Analysis, 47*(1), 16–36. https://doi.org/10.1002/jaba.106

Hart, B., & Risley, T. R. (1975). Incidental teaching of language in the preschool. Journal of Applied Behavior Analysis, 8(4), 411–420. https://doi.org/10.1901/jaba.1975.8-411

Heal, N. A., Hanley, G. P., & Layer, S. A. (2009). An evaluation of the relative efficacy of and children's preferences for teaching strategies that differ in amount of teacher directedness. *Journal of Applied Behavior Analysis, 42*(1), 123–143. https://doi.org/10.1901/jaba.2009.42-123

Heal, N. A., & Hanley, G. P. (2011). Embedded prompting may function as embedded punishment: Detection of unexpected behavioral processes within a typical preschool teaching strategy. *Journal of Applied Behavior Analysis, 44*(1), 127–131. https://doi.org/10.1901/jaba.2011.44-127

Higgins, S. T., Kurti, A. N., & Davis, D. R. (2019). Voucher-based contingency management is efficacious but underutilized in treating addictions. *Perspectives on Behavior Science.* https://doi.org/10.1007/s40614-019-00216-z

Hood, S. A., Luczynski, K. C., & Mitteer, D. R. (2017). Toward meaningful outcomes in teaching conversation and greeting skills with individuals with autism spectrum disorder. *Journal of Applied Behavior Analysis, 50*(3), 459–486. https://doi.org/10.1002/jaba.388

Iwata, B. A., DeLeon, I. G., & Roscoe, E. M. (2013). Reliability and validity of the functional analysis screening tool. *Journal of Applied Behavior Analysis, 46*(1), 271–284. https://doi.org/10.1002/jaba.31

Jones, S. H., & St. Peter, C. C. (2022). Nominally acceptable integrity failures negatively affect interventions involving intermittent reinforcement. *Journal of Applied Behavior Analysis, 55*(4), 1109–1123. https://doi.org/10.1002/jaba.944

Kendzor, D. E., Businelle, M. S., Waring, J. J. C., Mathews, A. J., Geller, D. W., Barton, J. M., Alexander, A. C., Hébert, E. T., Ra, C. K., & Vidrine, D. J. (2020). Automated mobile delivery of financial incentives for smoking cessation among socioeconomically disadvantaged adults: Feasibility study. *JMIR MHealth and UHealth, 8*(4), e15960. https://doi.org/10.2196/15960

Lerman, D. C., & Iwata, B. A. (1996). Developing a technology for the use of operant extinction in clinical settings: An examination of basic and applied research. *Journal of Applied Behavior Analysis, 29*(3), 345–382. https://doi.org/10.1901/jaba.1996.29-345

Matter, A. L., Wiskow, K. M., & Donaldson, J. M. (2020). A comparison of methods to teach foreign-language targets to young children. *Journal of Applied Behavior Analysis, 53*(1), 147–166. https://doi.org/10.1002/jaba.545

Nevin, J. A. (1988). Behavioral momentum and the partial reinforcement effect. *Psychological Bulletin, 103*(1), 44–56. https://doi.org/10.1037/0033-2909.103.1.44

Pence, S. T., Wagoner, R., & St. Peter, C. C. (2019). Blue light covers increase stereotypy and decrease on-task behavior for students with autism. *Behavior Analysis in Practice, 12*, 632–636. https://doi.org/10.1007/s40617-018-00321-6

Peterson, K. M., Piazza, C. C., & Volkert, V. M. (2016). A comparison of a modified sequential oral sensory approach to an applied behavior-analytic approach in the treatment of food selectivity in children with autism spectrum disorder. *Journal of Applied Behavior Analysis, 49*(3), 485–511. https://doi.org/10.1002/jaba.332

Schepis, M. M., Reid, D. H., Ownbey, J., & Parsons, M. B. (2001). Training support staff to embed teaching within natural routines of young children with disabilities in an inclusive preschool. *Journal of Applied Behavior Analysis, 34*(3), 313–327. https://doi.org/10.1901/jaba.2001.34-313

Seubert, C., Fryling, M. J., Wallace, M. D., Jiminez, A. R., & Meier, A. E. (2014). Antecedent interventions for pediatric feeding problems. Journal of Applied Behavior Analysis, 47(2), 449–453. https://doi.org/10.1002/jaba.117

Simon, J. L., & Thompson, R. H. (2006). The effects of undergarment type on the urinary continence of toddlers. *Journal of Applied Behavior Analysis, 39*(3), 363–368. https://doi.org/10.1901/jaba.2006.124-05

Skinner, B. F. (1957). Verbal Behavior. *Appleton-Century-Crofts.* https://doi.org/10.1037/11256-000

Sidman, M. (1960). *Tactics of scientific research: Evaluating experimental data in psychology.* Cambridge Center for Behavioral.

Tate, T. L., Thompson, R. H., & McKerchar, P. M. (2005). Training teachers in an infant classroom to use embedded teaching strategies. *Education and Treatment of Children*, 206–221. https://www.jstor.org/stable/42899845

Tarbox, R. S., Williams, W. L., & Friman, P. C. (2004). Extended diaper wearing: Effects on continence in and out of the diaper. *Journal of Applied Behavior Analysis, 37*(1), 97–100. https://doi.org/10.1901/jaba.2004.37-97

Thompson, R. H., & Iwata, B. A. (2005). A review of reinforcement control procedures. *Journal of Applied Behavior Analysis, 38*(2), 257–278. https://doi.org/10.1901/jaba.2005.176-03

Sivaraman, M., & Fahmie, T. A. (2020). Evaluating the efficacy and social validity of a culturally adapted training program for parents and service providers in India. *Behavior Analysis in Practice, 13*(4), 849–861. https://doi.org/10.1007/s40617-020-00489-w

Virues-Ortega, J., Clayton, K., Pérez-Bustamante, A., Gaerlan, B. F. S., & Fahmie, T. A. (2022). Functional analysis patterns of automatic reinforcement: A review and component analysis of treatment effects. *Journal of Applied Behavior Analysis, 55*(2), 481–512. https://doi.org/10.1002/jaba.900

Walker, S. G., & Carr, J. E. (2021). Generality of findings from single-case designs: It's not all about the "N". *Behavior Analysis in Practice, 14*(4), 991–995. https://doi.org/10.1007/s40617-020-00547-3

Zoellner, R. (1969). Talk-write: A behavioral pedagogy for composition. *College English, 30*(4), 267–320. https://doi.org/10.2307/374179

Tara Fahmie, Ph.D., BCBA-D, is an associate professor at the University of Nebraska Medical Center's Munroe-Meyer Institute (MMI). Dr. Fahmie provides clinical oversight as the associate director of the severe behavior department of MMI; conducts research on the prevention, assessment, and treatment of severe destructive behavior; teaches courses; and mentors students and staff. Dr. Fahmie regularly engages in editorial work for journals in Applied Behavior Analysis.

Stephanie Hood, Ph.D., BCBA, is an assistant professor of psychology at Marquette University. Her primary research interests are related to determining the extent to which efficacious teaching procedures produce socially significant behavior change, effects transfer contexts and are longlasting, and expand the reach of behavior-analytic services. Dr. Hood's current work focuses on advanced social skills with children, adolescents, and adults.

Javid Rahaman, Ph.D., BCBA-D, is a postdoctoral fellow at the University of Nebraska Medical Center's Munroe-Meyer Institute. Dr. Rahaman has a wide range of applied and clinical experiences, from teaching social skills to promoting ecologically friendly driving behaviors. His current work aims to improve the generality and acceptability of behavior analytic interventions focused on preventing and treating severe problem behavior.

Chapter 9
Writing the Abstract

Kasey Bedard

An abstract is a brief, self-contained summary of your research or manuscript (Fowler, 2011). Typically, abstracts are situated at the very beginning of a published journal article and are meant to provide a preview of what you plan to present later in the document. Writing a good abstract is essential because it functions as the introduction to your work for potentially interested readers. The abstract's goal is to entice the reader to dive into your full manuscript by providing a clear, concise, and compelling introduction to your research. Abstracts are often used by researchers, professionals, and other interested readers to identify academic manuscripts and studies that have the potential to inform on a particular topic, whether the purpose is to provide information on specific experimental research, to provide a summary of literature, or to present an opinion or theory.

For many, the purpose of presenting academic research and other works for publication is to effectively disseminate meaningful information as a means of impacting future research and clinical practice. If the intention is to reach the largest audience, it is imperative that the reader's first introduction to the topic should be concise, compelling, and comprehensive. Writing a good abstract ensures not only that your reader is able to effectively find your article based on their interests and search terms, but also that they feel compelled to read your manuscript in full, and potentially to cite you as a source in future works. Because of the importance of the abstract to the dissemination process, it is essential to know a bit about how to write an abstract prior to doing it. This chapter will review the essential components and process of developing a strong abstract prior to submitting for publication.

K. Bedard (✉)
Behavior Analysis Department, College of Graduate and Professional Studies
at The Chicago School, Chicago, IL, USA
e-mail: kbedard1@thechicagoschool.edu

Abstract Purpose

The predominant purpose of the abstract is to assist readers in evaluating whether your article fits within their area of interest (Fowler, 2011). Oftentimes article titles give an incomplete picture, and readers, therefore, rely on the abstract as a preliminary measure to decide upon eliminating or including an article for full review. This is particularly important as articles are often not available for free, and the abstract helps the reader identify if your article is worth purchasing. A second purpose of the abstract is to ensure that your article is found when readers plug in relevant search terms. Including purposeful language and key words in your abstract increases the likelihood that your article will be found when potential readers search for associated topics, and, therefore, promotes dissemination.

Abstract Development

While the abstract is the first part of a manuscript that a reader reads, it should be the last part that an author writes (Fowler, 2011). It is imperative to finish writing your manuscript in full prior to developing your abstract as you will need to pull from the main components of your manuscript, including the discussion and conclusions, in order to write a fully informative abstract. Prior to writing your abstract, it may help to highlight or otherwise identify key sentences from your manuscript that can serve as a general indicator of the essential components that need to be included in the abstract (Fowler, 2011).

Length

The length of the abstract should typically be between 200 and 250 words. However, many journals have specific word requirements for abstracts, so it is worthwhile to check these requirements prior to completing the final revisions of your manuscript. It can often be difficult to summarize an entire, often lengthy manuscript in just a few words; however, highlighting or outlining key points prior to writing the abstract can help identify what is most impactful to include.

Components

Typically, the abstract is a brief outline of the main components of your manuscript, including the introduction, methods, results, and discussion (Fowler, 2011). Some journals may also request the inclusion of three to four key words to help readers find the article based on the main topics, findings, or population. As with the abstract length, it is important to check a journal's publication guidelines as some journals request specific abstract sections or require sections to be named in a specific manner to ensure consistency across published articles.

Introduction The introduction section of the abstract serves as a broad overview of the purpose of your manuscript. This section can be used to introduce your problem statement and associated research purpose. To write the introduction, use one or two sentences to first disclose the problem the article aims at resolving, or the gap in research that the manuscript aims to address. It is appropriate to include some references to the literature if doing so will assist in establishing problem or research gap. After introducing the problem, state how the content of the manuscript aims to solve that problem by introducing the purpose of the article.

Methods The method section of the abstract should briefly summarize the research design or data collection methods used within the manuscript. The description of the research methodology serves as the first opportunity for the reader to evaluate the credibility of your manuscript. Abstracts that include an unclear or vague description of the methods are less likely to be taken seriously by the scientific community and unlikely to be considered seriously for publication. It is important to include both a description of the methods used to carry out the research, and a description of the method of data collection. Manuscripts consisting of meta-analyses of data or systematic reviews of the literature should explain what methods were used to identify relevant articles and studies for inclusion, and what methods were used to complete secondary analyses of the data.

Results The results section of the abstract should clearly state the most salient findings of your manuscript. As the results are arguably the section of most interest to the reader, it can be helpful to air on the side of concision for other components of the abstract to allow for an additional sentence or two in the results section. In one to three sentences, clearly summarize the main findings of your manuscript. For manuscripts that include extensive findings across a variety of domains, broad statements categorizing the findings in each domain may be necessary to effectively cover the overall results, or authors may choose to just highlight the findings of highest importance or social significance.

Discussion The discussion section describes the main conclusions of the manuscript based on your findings. While your results statement should be an objective statement of your findings, your discussion may describe main takeaways or general applications of your findings. When writing the discussion, authors should consider one to two statements that best sum up what they would like the reader to take away from their manuscript, or what the manuscript adds to the body of research as a whole.

Keywords An article's keywords should efficiently indicate to the reader which topics are discussed in the manuscript. When choosing keywords, it is important to select words that will result in potentially interested readers finding the article. Keywords that are vague or indirectly related may results in your article failing to appear in related search queries. Keywords may be selected based on the topic of the research, intervention used, or the populations and settings involved.

Other Requirements Some journals may require you to include other sections in your abstract, such as ethical concerns, or conflicts of interest. Ethical concern sections include a brief statement of the inclusion of any ethically gray areas. If no ethical concerns are present, this section can include an assurance that the research conducted did not include any ethical concerns. The conflict of interest section should include a brief statement explaining if the researchers need to disclose any conflicts of interest, such as receiving funding from a party who could benefit from the outcome of the research. Due to the need for brevity in the abstract, these sections do not need to be included unless they are required by a journal or other publication source.

Pulling It All Together

It is important to think of the abstract as a stand-alone component of your manuscript, not an introduction. One of the most common misconceptions when writing an abstract is that it should introduce a topic to be elaborated on in the full manuscript. While this is partially true, you need to ensure that your abstract functions as a self-contained summary of your entire manuscript that is as compelling as the article itself. While an introduction serves to set the stage for further sections of an article, and to peak the reader's interest, an abstract should allow a reader to understand the entire scope of the manuscript and the main takeaways after reviewing the abstract alone. A good abstract is a succinct replica of the entire manuscript, with a clear summary of each of the article's components, that positively impacts the reader's ability to find the article in relevant searches.

This chapter sums up the main components of an abstract and how to develop them. In addition to the material included here, it is helpful to review abstracts written by other authors in journals targeted for publication prior to a manuscript's submission. As always, be sure to check a journal's requirements prior to completing a final submission.

Reference

Fowler, J. (2011). Writing for professional publication. Part 6: Writing the abstract. *British Journal of Nursing (Mark Allen Publishing), 20*(2), 120. https://doi.org/10.12968/bjon.2011.20.2.120

Kasey Bedard, PhD, BCBA-D   is a postdoctoral researcher at The Chicago School, and a practicing Board-Certified Behavior Analyst. Dr. Bedard's research focuses on developing behavior analytic interventions and support for individuals with Prader-Willi syndrome, a rare neurogenetic diagnosis. This includes the development and implementation of small-scale single-subject research, as well as large-scale randomized clinical trials to evaluate the feasibility and efficacy of various behavior-analytic interventions.

Part III
Submitting a Journal Article

Chapter 10
Selecting a Publishing Outlet

Jessica F. Juanico, Kylene Caquelin, Raena A. Quinnell,
and Ashley N. Romero

There are many benefits to publishing your research findings. First, publishing benefits other individuals such as practitioners, researchers, and educators. Researchers can identify new areas of study based on your outcomes and findings and, perhaps, conduct more rigorous evaluations based on your study's limitations (Dixon et al., 2015; Huston & Choi, 2017; Valentino, 2021; Wolery et al., 2018). Practitioners can identify new, innovative technology and procedures that could benefit the clients with whom they work and gain answers to clinical questions (e.g., Dixon et al., 2015; Huston & Choi, 2017; Valentino, 2021; Wolery et al., 2018). Educators can change their educational practices, implementing the most cutting-edge teaching technology and techniques, based on published literature (Wolery et al., 2018). Second, publishing directly benefits your field of study through dissemination of the science (Bailey & Burch, 2018; Valentino, 2021), while serving as a historical record, documenting important developments and driving your field in new directions as new research is published (Bailey & Burch, 2018). Finally, there are individual benefits to publishing such as career development in academia (i.e., publish and flourish or publish and perish; Huston & Choi, 2017), speaking at conferences, and presenting workshops (Bailey & Burch, 2018). Publishing may also serve as a reinforcer for scientific behavior (i.e., developing research ideas, conducting

J. F. Juanico (✉)
Department of Applied Behavioral Science, University of Kansas, Lawrence, KS, USA
e-mail: jjuanico@ku.edu

K. Caquelin
No Stone Unturned, Manhattan, KS, USA

R. A. Quinnell
Step Ahead ABA, Omaha, NE, USA

A. N. Romero
Little Leaves Behavioral Services, Weston, FL, USA
e-mail: ashley.romero@littleleaves.org

research, analyzing results, writing manuscript, submitting to a journal) for many individuals (Bailey & Burch, 2018; Valentino, 2021).

Given the many benefits to publishing, it is important to identify the most appropriate journal carefully and thoughtfully for your research (Bailey & Burch, 2018) as where you publish can have an impact on those who can access your research. Additionally, the publishing outlet could impact your field and professional recognition. Identification of the most appropriate journal is an important, early step of the writing process as manuscript requirements vary by journal, and these requirements should influence your writing (American Psychological Association [APA], 2020). Additionally, the reach and audience will also vary by journal (APA, 2020). Thus, selecting the best journal for your research will help you reach your intended audience and make the intended impact (Elsevier, 2020).

In this chapter, we will review how to identify appropriate journals for publishing your research. Specifically, we will review how to identify possible journals, along with variables to consider once you have identified possible journals to narrow down the number of journals as well as rank order the journals. We will discuss how we identified appropriate journals for a recent study we conducted in the Juanico Lab on a translational model of problem behavior (Caquelin, 2022). Finally, we have created a flowchart (Appendix A) that can be printed as a quick reference on selecting journals to publish your research.

Identifying Journals for Publishing

The first step to identifying journals for publishing your research is creating a list of possible journals in which you could publish your research. There are many ways to identify journals, including checking the references in your manuscript to determine where articles were most frequently published (Elsevier, 2020); consulting with others who recently published in the same area (Poling et al., 1995) or a librarian (Cooper Medical School of Rowan University [CMSRU], 2023); and consulting an online manuscript matching tool or search engine that identifies journals matching your research topic or area (APA, 2021). There are many online manuscript matching tools such as Jane: Journal/Author Name Estimator (The Biosemantics Group, 2007), JournalFinder (Elsevier, 2023), or Directory of Open Access Journals (Directory of Open Access Journals, 2023). These online manuscript matching tools are typically free of charge and often a great starting point (CMSRU, 2023), particularly when you are hoping to publish outside of your field.

However, online manuscript matching tools should not be solely relied upon when selecting journals as they have their limitations. For example, we conducted a search for a study we published in *Journal of Organizational Behavior Management* (i.e., Ruppel et al., 2023) through Jane (The Biosemantics Group, 2007) using the title of the manuscript. This study evaluated the use of remote rehearsal and feedback to train Registered Behavior Technicians to identify preferred items for children to use in skill acquisition programming. Prior to this search, we were considering five behavioral journals (i.e., *Journal of Organizational Behavior Management*, *Journal of Applied Behavior Analysis*, *Behavior Analysis in Practice*, *Journal of Behavioral Education*, and *Behavior Analysis: Research and Practice*) based on conversations with colleagues and previously published literature. Jane's search resulted in 37 possible journals, two of which overlapped with our identified list. Many non-related journals were suggested such as *Nurse Education Today* and *Journal of Surgical Education*. Interestingly, when we searched with the abstract, similar results were obtained. These searches highlight that online manuscript matching tools are not always accurate in identifying possible journals. Thus, using a combination of methods will be the best method for identifying journals rather than relying on one method.

Variables to Consider when Selecting a Journal

Once you have a list of possible journals, there are several variables to consider that may help you narrow down your list and rank order the remaining journals. These variables include goodness of fit and journal quality.

Goodness of Fit

Goodness of fit is perhaps the most important variable that should drive your decision. Goodness of fit refers to how well your research aligns with the journal's mission, aims, and scope and is often the primary factor of whether your manuscript will be considered for publication (APA, 2021). There are several considerations in identifying the goodness of fit. One variable to consider is the intended audience or who you would like your research to reach. The audience should influence your journal choice. For example, the audience for *Behavior Analysis in Practice* is "front-line service workers and their supervisors, scientist-practitioners, and school personnel" (Springer, 2022), whereas the audience for *Perspectives on Behavior Science* is "the community of behavior scientists" (Springer, 2023c). Although both are behavioral journals, the former publishes an array of types of papers (e.g., research articles, brief practices, discussion papers, tutorials) that will benefit practitioners, regardless of setting, whereas the latter publishes primarily reviews that are broad in nature that will interest basic, translational, or applied researchers.

The following questions may help you identify your audience. Are you hoping to disseminate your research to researchers, practitioners, educators, or other stakeholders? Do you want your research to have a regional, national, or international impact? Is your audience within your field or is it other stakeholders outside of your field such as other professionals that often collaborate with your field or caregivers? If a journal on your list targets a different audience than the one intended, you should remove the journal.

Once you have determined your audience, determine whether your research aligns with the journal's aims and scope as journals vary considerably from one another (APA, 2021) in relation to the topics addressed and required methodology (Poling et al., 1995). Access the journal's website to review their profile, mission, aims, scope, and author guidelines (Elsevier, 2020). Some journals publish exclusively in a specific area (e.g., *Journal of Organizational Behavior Management*; Taylor & Francis Online, 2022), some publish in specific populations (e.g., *Journal of Emotional and Behavioral Disorders*; Hammill Institute on Disabilities, 2023), whereas others publish research in a variety of areas (e.g., *Journal of Applied Behavior Analysis*; Wiley Online Library, 2022). For example, *Behavior and Social Issues* publishes papers on the "natural science of behavior to constructing cultures of social justice, human rights, and environmental sustainability" (Springer, 2023a), whereas *The Analysis of Verbal Behavior* publishes papers focusing on language from a behavioral perspective (Springer, 2023b).

Read articles from the journal to determine whether research on the same topic has been published (APA, 2021; Poling et al., 1995). Similarly, when publishing outside of your field, you might review the typical methodology published and how your research varies. For example, are group designs or single subject designs primarily published? The methodology matters and may affect the likelihood of publication if there are significant variations from the typical methodology published. For example, if you use single subject designs but want to publish in a journal that typically publishes group designs, you may need to consider adding additional analyses to your paper such as statistics that better communicate with the individuals reading the journal.

If you are unsure whether your research aligns with the journal, consider emailing the editor to determine goodness of fit (Poling et al., 1995). This is often referred to as a pre-submission inquiry. Although reaching out to the editor may seem intimidating, this is a welcomed and encouraged (and sometimes required) practice, particularly when you are usure your research is a good fit (Qureshi, 2019; Thomson, 2011); however, it is important that you read about the journal and understand it before reaching out. Qureshi (2019) suggested some dos and don'ts when submitting a pre-submission inquiry. Do understand the journal's scope and audience and determine whether there are pre-submission guidelines for the journal. When reaching out, address the editor directly with a personalized greeting. Your email should be brief and professional, include the title of your research and abstract, review the main findings and how they contribute to existing research in your field, and highlight how the research might be relevant to the journal's audience. Your email should not include your entire manuscript or provide too many details. Give the editor enough information to understand your paper and how it contributes to the literature such that they can quickly determine fit. Once you have drafted your email, send it to the editor and wait for a response. If the response is negative, you can remove the journal from your list. If the response is positive, consider the journal a viable option; however, a positive response from the editor does not guarantee your paper will be accepted. In fact, I had a student write a brief review on the use of functional analyses with animals. We submitted a pre-submission inquiry and received a positive response from the editor of the journal. Once the paper was sent to the associate editor for review, our paper was ultimately rejected as they did not feel there was enough literature to support a brief review.

If your research does not align with the journal's mission, scope, or aims, remove the journal from your list. At this point, your potential journal list should start to shrink as you have considered the goodness of fit of your research with each potential journal. You might consider rank ordering them based on goodness of fit. However, there are additional factors that can be considered to strengthen your rankings.

Journal Quality

Following goodness of fit, you should consider the quality of the journal. The quality of a journal can be assessed through different metrics. There are three different metrics that can be used to evaluate the impact of your work (Enago Academy, 2021). Journal-level metrics assess the impact of journals, article-level metrics assess the impact of an article, and author-level metrics allow you to assess the impact of an author. Typically, journal-level metrics are used as a guide to help identify journals in which to publish. Therefore, we will focus on journal-level metrics. Journal-level metrics allow you to understand the journal's reach, quality, and impact (Taylor & Francis Online, 2023d). Journal metrics are typically quantitative in nature and vary in how they measure the impact of a journal (University Library, 2023). Therefore, it is important to consider multiple metrics when reviewing journals to get a full, unbiased picture of the impact of each journal.

The original journal metric was the impact factor (John Hopkins Sheridan Libraries, 2023). The impact factor is a way to compare citation rates of journals (Garfield, 2006) as it assumes cited publications have had an impact on and contributed to the information in new publications (Abramo et al., 2019). Impact factors are often used in evaluations for academic promotion and by researchers to identify where to publish as research published in a journal with a higher impact factor will likely have a greater impact on your field (Scully & Lodge, 2005). The 2-year impact factor is calculated by dividing the number of citations of articles from the journal during the preceding 2 years by the total number of articles published in the journal during that time (Garfield, 2006; Valentino, 2021). For example, in 2020, a journal cited papers published in 2018 and 2019 1500 times. Between 2018 and 2019, the journal published 520 papers. The impact factor would be 2.88 (i.e., 1500/520 = 2.88), indicating that, on average, each of the articles published in that journal for the previous 2 years had been cited almost three times in the preceding 2 years. The impact factor can be used as a general guide to give a sense of the overall quality and significance of a journal, while accounting for the size of the journal and frequency of publications (Andersen et al., 2006). Typically, a journal's impact factor will be listed on their website (Valentino, 2021).

In addition to the 2-year impact factor, there are other journal-level metrics that can be considered such as the CiteScore, 5-year impact factor, immediacy index,

Eigenfactor® Score, SCImago Journal Rank, Source Normalized Impact per Paper, and h5 Index (Enago Academy, 2021; John Hopkins Sheridan Libraries, 2023). As mentioned above, each journal-metric is slightly different, so it is important to understand how the metric is calculated. For example, the 5-year impact factor is similar to the 2-year impact factor but takes into account 5 years. The Eigenfactor® Score is similar to the 5-year impact factor; however, it removes journal self-citations and adjusts for the specific discipline. Source Normalized Impact per Paper weights based on the number of citations within fields, so journals within fields with a smaller number of citations will have a higher score.

Although journal-level metrics allow an understanding of the journal's quality, there are inherent limitations with each metric. For example, the 2-year impact factor has many limitations and considerations (Bornmann et al., 2012; Garfield, 2006; Kurmis, 2003; Oh & Lim, 2009). Review articles tend to be cited more frequently than non-review articles (Kurmis, 2003). Therefore, a journal with a higher number of published review articles may have a higher impact factor, even if they do not publish new scientific material (Garfield, 2006). Another limitation is the inability of a journal impact factor to capture outside measures, such as the number of citations in a textbook or the clinical or political impact of an article (Oh & Lim, 2009), as the impact factor reflects citations from the journal. Similarly, impact factors are not normalized by discipline, so it can be difficult to compare impact factors across disciplines (University of Pittsburg Library System, 2023). It is recommended to compare impact factors within rather than across disciplines (Scully & Lodge, 2005; Sharma et al., 2014). Finally, the 2-year window was selected arbitrarily (Kurmis, 2003) and may not include substantial indicators of impact (Archambault & Larivière, 2009). If you are interested in learning more about journal-level metrics, there are many free, online resources that can be accessed (e.g., *Metrics Toolkit*, n.d.).

Some publishing companies also report on additional variables on their journals such as usage and acceptance rate. For example, Taylor & Francis Online (2023d) report on usage and acceptance. Usage refers to the number of times articles published in the journal are viewed or downloaded, allowing you to quickly understand the journal's reach. Acceptance refers to the percentage of papers accepted for publication. The acceptance rate is often considered a measure of quality. A journal with a small acceptance rate is often considered higher quality than a journal with a large acceptance rate. These additional variables can also be helpful in fully understanding the quality and reach of a journal. For example, the journal metrics for *International Studies of Management & Organization* as of March 27, 2023 was 62 k for usage and a 4% acceptance rate (Taylor & Francis Online, 2023b). These numbers suggest a large audience reach and the papers being published are high quality as few are accepted.

Another indicator of journal quality is the peer-review process. Many journals have a peer-review process (Valentino, 2021) in which researchers critically evaluate the quality of your work (Ali & Watson, 2016; Kumar, 2009; Rowland & Wine, 2015). The peer-review process may vary by journal but typically involves an editor receiving and reviewing the manuscript for goodness of fit, plagiarism, readability, and adherence to journal standards (Ali & Watson, 2016; Broome et al. 2010; Christenbery 2011; Lipworth et al. 2011). Once the editor completes their review, they may assign an assistant editor and two to three reviewers who critically evaluate the research and render publication decisions (e.g., reject, accept, needs revisions). The peer-review process is often referred to as a gold standard (Bordage & Caelleigh, 2001) as the peer-review process establishes additional confidence in the quality of published research (Jefferson et al., 2002; Kearney & Freda, 2005; Kumar, 2009; Manchikanti et al., 2015; Rowland & Wine, 2015). See Chap. 12 for more detailed information about the peer-review process.

Many journals also report metrics related to the speed of their peer-review process. Speed refers to how quickly your paper might go through different stages of the peer-review process such as the number of days from submission to first decision (i.e., whether your paper will be sent out for review), post-review decision (i.e., initial decision following initial peer review), online publication, or final acceptance. For example, the average speed from submission to first decision for *International Studies of Management & Organization* is 21 days (Taylor & Francis Online, 2023a). Although speed metrics are helpful in understanding how long your paper might be under review, it is important to remember that these are average or median figures. There are other factors that contribute to how quickly a paper goes through the peer-review process such as availability of reviewers and the volume of other submissions.

Although each journal metric has its limitations, these metrics may be used as a general guide to indicate the scientific or dissemination quality of a journal (Andersen et al., 2006); however, they should be considered in conjunction with other measures such as goodness of fit as journal metrics may lead you to inadvertently look over journals whose target audience would be better aligned with your research (Kurmis, 2003). For example, if you only look at the speed to final acceptance, you may miss the opportunity to publish in a journal with a greater reach or impact. Therefore, it is important to consider multiple journal metrics within the context of goodness of fit. At this point, you have likely removed journals for which your research did not fit. You might consider rank ordering the journals on your list using multiple journal metrics.

Other Variables to Consider

In addition to goodness of fit and quality, there are other variables you might consider in selecting a journal such as the cost to read articles and the cost to publish your research (APA, 2020). More traditional, subscription journals charge the reader a fee to access their published articles; however, there is typically no publishing fee (John Wiley & Sons, Inc., 2022). Readers could purchase a subscription to a journal or access to specific articles. For example, an individual subscription to the *Journal of Organizational Behavior Management* is $225 (Taylor & Francis Online, 2023b). To access a specific article such as Ruppel et al. (2023), a reader could pay $50 to download the article or $449.00 to purchase the issue. Both of these options allow the reader to download or print the purchased articles (Taylor & Francis Online, 2023c). These costs may be prohibitive to many readers, decreasing the likelihood of readers accessing articles in subscription journals and limiting the reach and visibility of your research. However, it is typically free for the author to submit their paper for the publication process (Wiley Online Library, 2022).

In contrast to subscription journals, some journals are fully open access or allow authors to publish an online, open access version of their paper (Björk & Solomon, 2012). Open access allows readers to access research in the absence of a fee. When publishing in an open-access journal, your research may be visible to more people. Thus, your paper may have a large impact and reach. Additionally, some funding sources such as the National Institutes of Health require that you publish in an open-access journal or repository (Björk & Solomon, 2012; Morrison et al. 2022). However, the cost to publish in an open-access journal may vary as there is a fee to submit or a flat rate charge for all processing (Wiley Online Library, 2022). This charge is often referred to as an article processing charge, which covers various fees such as production, marketing, and publishing (AKJournals, n.d.). In 2021, the average article processing charge for an article was $1626 (Morrison et al., 2022). In addition to the cost differences for readers and the author, open-access journals typically have a quicker submission-to-publication turnaround than subscription journals as journal articles are immediately published online once they are in their final form (APA, 2020).

Although there are differences in cost, visibility, and speed to publication of articles, articles published in subscription and open-access journals go through similar peer-review, production, and publishing processes. Additionally, both typically have reported journal-level metrics. Thus, when deciding between an open-access or paid journal, ensure you understand the policies and regulations that accompany a submission (Mudrak, 2022). Additionally, make sure to review the goodness of fit and quality of each journal. If you want to publish open access but the cost is prohibitive, consider publishing a version of your published article such as a pre-print in an open-access repository. An open-access repository is an online database that allows you to archive your work such that others can access it freely (Pinfield, 2005). However, ensure you understand the copyright agreement you signed with the journal as often there may be restrictions or an embargo period (Björk & Solomon, 2012).

Finally, beware of predatory journals. Predatory journals are pseudo-journals that profit from authors with no publishing services (e.g., editorial or peer review; Think. Check. Submit, 2023b), typically exploiting the open-access model (Beall & DuBois, 2016; Elmore & Weston, 2020). These journals most often unethically solicit articles for publication via email (APA, 2021). There are many characteristics that may suggest a journal is predatory such as informal solicitation, hidden publisher, hidden website, false advertisement of citation metric, atypical or quick submission-to-publication process, lack of rigorous evaluation or peer-review, lack of transparency related to fees, poor reputation, and lack of indexing in the database (APA, 2016; Elmore & Weston, 2020). Although it may be tempting to publish with a predatory journal given their false promises and a rush to publish your research, there are many negative consequences. Predatory journals undermine the scientific conversation given the fake peer review. Your research may be more difficult to find and less used by others as the journal will be of low quality. Finally, once you realize the journal is not legitimate, you might be scammed and completely lose your work (APA, 2021) as often these journals charge the author large fees to withdraw their work (Think. Check. Submit., 2023b). Therefore, it is important that authors identify and avoid publishing with predatory journals.

To identify predatory journals, look for evidence of indexing such as digital object identifiers (DOIs) associated with published articles and the journal's International Standard Serial Number (ISSN). DOIs and ISSNs typically demonstrate that journals have a clear publication process. Review research databases such as PsychINFO to determine whether the journal appears. Review articles published within the journal to determine the quality of included papers and whether there are any articles that appear "off-topic." Review the journal's website to determine whether there is a clear peer-review process and posted publishing fees. Look for inconsistencies that are common in phishing scams such as spelling mistakes and inconsistencies with country of origin and country code (Elmore & Weston, 2020). Consider using Think. Check. Submit's (2023a) checklist that contains many questions that can help you ensure the journal is trustworthy. Following your review, if you are unsure, contact a university library who can help determine whether the journal is predatory (APA, 2016).

Juanico Lab Example

My research lab recently conducted a translational study on the effects of fading schedules of noncontingent reinforcement in the treatment of problem behavior (Caquelin, 2022). Our goal was to disseminate the results of this study to researchers in behavior analysis such that more applied studies could be conducted. While attempting to create a list of possible journals, we reviewed the current translational problem behavior literature, spoke with several colleagues, and conducted a search in an online journal matching tool. First, my student and I noticed most studies published on translational models of problem behavior were published in *Journal of Applied Behavior Analysis* and *Journal of the Experimental Analysis of Behavior*. Second, during my student's thesis defense, we asked her committee members where they would recommend submitting her paper. Both committee members were active researchers in the assessment and treatment of problem behavior and both suggested *Journal of Applied Behavior Analysis* and *Journal of the Experimental Analysis of Behavior* as viable options to publish her study. Third, we ran a search in Jane (The Biosemantics Group, 2007; see Appendix B for the results of the search) using the title of the paper. The search in Jane resulted in 11 journal suggestions with their corresponding confidence, journal title, article influence, and relevant articles. Seven of the recommended articles seemed like possible fits based on our knowledge and experience of the journals and their aims and scope. Interestingly,

Table 10.1 Review of audiences, aims and scope, and fit

Journal	Audience	Aims and Scope	Fit?
BAP[a]	"… practitioners or consumers of behavior analysis"	"… service delivery in behavior analysis"	No
Behavior Modification	"… researchers, academics and practitioners in clinical psychology…"	"… applied behavior modification…"	No
Behavioural Processes		"… original research on animal behavior"	No
JABA[b]		"… experimental analysis of behavior to problems of social importance"	Yes
JEAB[c]		"… experiments relevant to the behavior of individual organisms"	Yes
Learning and Behavior		"… processes of learning and behavior [such as] sensation, perception, conditioning…"	No
PoBS[d]		Behavior analysis and behaviorism	No

[a]*Behavior Analysis in Practice (BAP)*
[b]*Journal of Applied Behavior Analysis (JABA)*
[c]*Journal of the Experimental Analysis of Behavior (JEAB)*
[d]*Perspectives on Behavior Science*

the top two recommended journals were *Journal of Applied Behavior Analysis* and *Journal of the Experimental Analysis of Behavior*.

From these searches and conversations, my student and I made a list of possible journals to submit her work, including *Journal of Applied Behavior Analysis, Journal of the Experimental Analysis of Behavior, Behavioural Processes, Behavior Analysis in Practice, Learning and Behavior, Perspectives on Behavior Science*, and *Behavior Modification*. Next, we reviewed the goodness of fit or how well our research aligned with the audience, as well as the aims and scope of each journal.

To review the audience, as well as aims and scope of each journal, we accessed each journal's website. Table 10.1 depicts the audience, aims and scope, and whether the journal was a match. During this review, we cut five journals, including *Behavioural Processes, Behavior Analysis in Practice*, and *Perspectives on Behavior Science* for various reasons. For example, *Behavioural Processes* focuses on animal research, and *Behavior Modification* publishes articles on applied behavior modification. Given the translational nature of the study, as well as our intended audience, we cut these journals from our list. Thus, there were two journals remaining on our list. Although the audiences were not directly stated, the *Journal of Applied Behavior Analysis* typically publishes more applied research, and the *Journal of Experimental Analysis of Behavior* publishes more basic research. Thus, we assumed more applied researchers would access our study in the former journal and more basic researchers would access our study in the latter journal. Given the translational nature of our study, we felt like our study would be a good fit for both journals.

Next, we reviewed the quality of *Journal of Applied Behavior Analysis* and *Journal of the Experimental Analysis of Behavior*. Table 10.2 depicts the

Table 10.2 Review of quality indicators

	JABAᵃ	JEABᵇ
Impact Factor (2021)	2.809	2.215
JCRᶜ (Psychology, Clinical)	81/132	
JCR (Behavioral Sciences)		41/53
JCR (Psychology, Biological)		8/14
JCR (Psychology, Experimental)		60/91
Peer Review	Double blind review	Double blind review
Open Access	$3140	$2940

ᵃ*Journal of Applied Behavior Analysis (JABA)*
ᵇ*Journal of the Experimental Analysis of Behavior (JEAB)*
ᶜ*Journal Citation Report*

journal-level metrics we were able to obtain for both journals. Specifically, we were able to access the 2-year impact factor, JCR, information about the peer-review process, and options for open access through the journals' websites (Wiley Online Library, 2023a, b). Based on these metrics, the *Journal of Applied Behavior Analysis* had a higher impact factor (2.809). The Journal Citation Reports were difficult to compare as the metrics were reported across different fields. Both journals had a double blind review and offered open access. The article processing charge fee was $3140 for *Journal of Applied Behavior Analysis* and $2940 for *Journal of the Experimental Analysis of Behavior*. Given our review of the quality metrics, we felt like both journals were good fits.

Given both journals were good fits for this study, my student and I decided that we would first submit to the *Journal of Applied Behavior Analysis*. If our paper was not accepted at the *Journal of Applied Behavior Analysis*, we would then submit to the *Journal of Experimental Analysis of Behavior*. Our paper is currently under review with the *Journal of Applied Behavior Analysis*. Hopefully, one of these journals will see our paper as a good fit and decide to publish it. However, if they do not, we will follow a similar process to identify other possible publishing outlets for this paper.

Conclusion

Given the importance of the dissemination of research, it is important to identify appropriate publishing outlets. Regardless of the journal, be attentive to all aspects before deciding to publish with them. Do your research. Know your study and your audience and how it aligns with identified journals. After evaluating goodness of fit, quality, and other variables, identify a short list of journals (e.g., three to five) in which you would want to publish your research (Huston & Choi, 2017). Rank order this short list based on the order in which you would want to publish. Once your manuscript is written following the journal's guidelines and formatting requirements, submit your paper and wait for a decision. Happy publishing!

Appendices

Appendix A: Selecting Journals Flowchart

Selecting Journals to Publish Your Research Flowchart

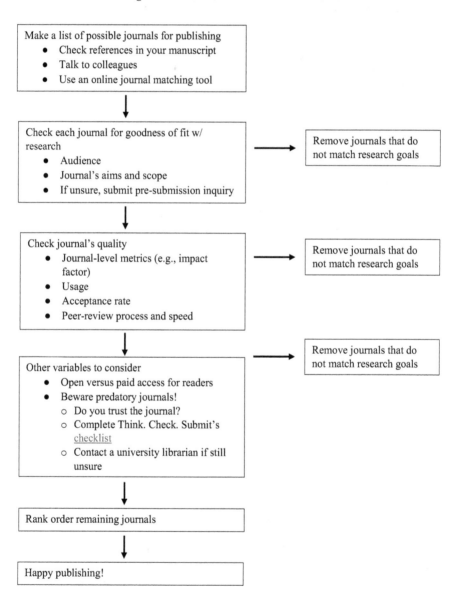

Appendix B: Example Jane Search

These journals have articles most similar to your input:
""The Effects of Fading Schedules of Noncontingent Reinforcement with and without Extinction&quo..."

Confidence	Journal	Article Influence ❷	Articles
	Journal of applied behavior analysis Medline-indexed	0.4	Show articles
	Journal of the experimental analysis of behavior Medline-indexed	0.7	Show articles
	Behavior analysis in practice PMC		Show articles
	Behavioural processes Medline-indexed	0.5	Show articles
	Learning & behavior Medline-indexed	0.6	Show articles
	Alcohol (Fayetteville, N.Y.) Medline-indexed	0.7	Show articles
	Appetite Medline-indexed	0.9	Show articles
	Journal of child psychology and psychiatry, and allied disciplines Medline-indexed	2.7	Show articles
	Perspectives on behavior science PMC		Show articles
	Behavior modification Medline-indexed	0.8	Show articles
	Journal of experimental psychology. Animal learning and cognition Medline-indexed		Show articles

Select all   Deselect all   Export citations

Click here to perform another search.

Copyright 2007, The Biosemantics Group. Research funded by NBIC. Created and maintained by Martijn Schuemie.
Hosting provided by the Observational Health Data Science and Informatics

References

Abramo, G., D'Angelo, C. A., & Felici, G. (2019). Predicting publication long-term impact through a combination of early citations and journal impact factor. *Journal of Informetrics, 13*(1), 32–49.

AKJournals. (n.d.). *Everything you need to know about article processing charges*. Akadémiai Kiadó. Retrieved December 27, 2022 from https://akjournals.com/page/article-processing-charge#:~:text=The%20article%20processing%20charge%20%28APC%29%2C%20or%20a%20publication,circulation%20among%20less%20influential%20scholars%2C%20institutions%2C%20and%20students

Ali, P. A., & Watson, R. (2016). Peer review and the publication process. *Nursing Open, 3*(4), 193–202. https://doi.org/10.1002/nop2.51

American Psychological Association. (2016). How to avoid predatory publishers. *Monitor on Psychology, 47*(4) https://www.apa.org/monitor/2016/04/predatory-publishers

American Psychological Association. (2020). *Publication manual of the American Psychological Association* (7th ed.). https://doi.org/10.1037/0000165-000

American Psychological Association. (2021). *Publishing in a scholarly journal: Part one, the publishing process*. Retrieved December 27, 2022 from https://www.apa.org/pubs/journals/resources/publishing-tips/publishing-process

Andersen, J., Belmont, J., & Cho, C. T. (2006). Journal impact factor in the era of expanding literature. *Journal of Microbiology Immunology and Infection, 39*(6), 436.

Archambault, É., & Larivière, V. (2009). History of the journal impact factor: Contingencies and consequences. *Scientometrics, 79*(3), 635–649.

Bailey, J. S., & Burch, M. R. (2018). *Research methods in applied behavior analysis*. Routledge.

Beall, J., & DuBois, J. M. (2016). Ethically speaking: Scholars beware. *Monitor on Psychology, 47*(4), 42. https://www.apa.org/monitor/2016/04/scholars

Björk, B. C., & Solomon, D. (2012). Open access versus subscription journals: A comparison of scientific impact. *BMC Medicine, 10*(73). https://doi.org/10.1186/1741-7015-10-73

Bordage, G., & Caelleigh, A. S. (2001). A tool for reviewers: Review criteria for research manuscripts. *Academic Medicine, 26*(9), 904–908. https://doi.org/10.1097/00001888-200109000-00013

Bornmann, L., Marx, W., Gasparyan, A. Y., & Kitas, G. D. (2012). Diversity, value and limitations of the journal impact factor and alternative metrics. *Rheumatology International, 32*(7), 1861–1867.

Broome, M., Dougherty, M. C., Freda, M. C., Kearney, M. H., & Baggs, J. G. (2010). Ethical concerns of nursing reviewers: An international survey. *Nursing Ethics, 17*(6), 741–748. https://doi.org/10.1177/0969733010379177

Caquelin, K. (2022). *The effects of fading schedules of noncontingent reinforcement with and without extinction* [Master's thesis, University of Kansas]. ProQuest Dissertations Publishing.

Christenbery, T. L. (2011). Manuscript peer review: A guide for advanced practice nurses. *Journal of the American Academy of Nurse Practitioners, 23*(1), 15–22. https://doi.org/10.1111/j.1745-7599.2010.00572.x

Cooper Medical School of Rowan University. (2023, February 20). *CMSRU pub hub.* https://rowanmed.libguides.com/pubhub/matching_manuscripts

Directory of Open Access Journals. (2023). *Directory of open access journals: Find open access journals & articles.* https://doaj.org/

Dixon, M. R., Reed, D. D., Smith, T., Belisle, J., & Jackson, R. E. (2015). Top 10 responses to the commentaries on Dixon, Reed, Smith et al. (2015). *Behavior Analysis in Practice, 8*, 165–169. https://doi.org/10.1007/s40617-015-0094-8

Elmore, S. A., & Weston, E. H. (2020). Predatory journals: What they are and how to avoid them. *Toxicologic Pathology, 48*(4), 607–610. https://doi.org/10.1177/0192623320920209

Elsevier. (2020). *How to get your research published… and then noticed.* Retrieved December 27, 2022 from https://www.elsevier.com/?a=91173

Elsevier. (2023). *Find journals.* https://journalfinder.elsevier.com/

Enago Academy. (2021, September 30). *Understanding research metrics: Journal-level, article-level, and author-level.* https://www.enago.com/academy/what-are-different-research-metrics/#:~:text=For%20example%2C%20we%20look%20at,level%2C%20and%20author%2Dlevel

Garfield, E. (2006). The history and meaning of the journal impact factor. *Journal of the American Medical Association, 295*(1), 90–93.

Hammill Institute on Disabilities. (2023). *Journal of Emotional and Behavioral Disorders.* Retrieved March 15, 2023 from https://journals.sagepub.com/home/ebx

Huston, P., & Choi, B. C. K. (2017). A guide to publishing scientific research in the health sciences. *CCDR, 43*(9), 169–175. https://doi.org/10.14745/ccdr.c43i09a01

Jefferson, T., Alderson, P., Wager, E., & Davidoff, F. (2002). Effects of editorial peer review: A systematic review. *Journal of the American Medical Association, 287*(21), 2784–2786. https://doi.org/10.1001/jama.287.21.2784

John Hopkins Sheridan Libraries. (2023). *Scholarly metrics.* Retrieved from https://guides.library.jhu.edu/metrics/journal-metrics

Kearney, M. H., & Freda, M. C. (2005). Nurse editors' views on the peer review process. *Research in Nursing & Health, 28*(6), 444–452. https://doi.org/10.1002/nur.20104

Kumar, M. A. (2009). A review of the review process: Manuscript peer-review in biomedical research. *Biology and Medicine, 1*(4), 240–242.

Kurmis, A. P. (2003). Understanding the limitations of the journal impact factor. *Journal of Bone and Joint Surgery, 85*(12), 2449–2454.

Lipworth, W. L., Kerridge, I. H., Carter, S. M., & Little, M. (2011). Journal peer review in context: A qualitative study of the social and subjective dimensions of manuscript review in biomedical publishing. *Social Science & Medicine, 72*(7), 1056–1063. https://doi.org/10.1016/j.socscimed.2011.02.002

Manchikanti, L., Kaye, A. D., Boswell, M. V., & Hirsch, J. A. (2015). Medical journal peer review: Process and bias. *Pain Physician Journal, 18*, E1–E14. https://doi.org/10.36076/ppj/2015.18.e1

Morrison, H., Borges, L., Zhao, X., Laurent Kakou, T., & Nataraj Shanbhoug, A. (2022). Change and growth in open access journal publishing and charging trends 2011–2021. *Journal of the Association for Information Science and Technology, 73*(12), 1793–1805. https://doi.org/10.1002/asi.24717

Mudrak, B. (2022). *Open access mandates: A new form of scholarly publishing.* AJE. Retrieved October 9, 2022, from https://www.aje.com/arc/open-access-changing-landscape/

Oh, H. C., & Lim, J. F. Y. (2009). Is the journal impact factor a valid indicator of scientific value? *Singapore Medical Journal, 50*(8), 749.

Pinfield, S. (2005). A mandate to self archive? The role of open access institutional repositories. *Serials, 18*(1) https://nottingham-repository.worktribe.com/output/1020014

Poling, A., Methot, L. L., & LeSage, M. G. (1995). *Fundamentals of behavior analytic research.* Plenum.

Qureshi, F. (2019, March). *How to write a presubmission inquiry: Dos and don'ts.* Editage Insights. https://www.editage.com/insights/how-to-write-a-presubmission-inquiry-dos-and-donts

Rowland, R., & Wine, B. (2015). Training the peer-review process: Perspectives from research, subject matter experts, and personal experience. *Academic Leadership Journal in Student Research, 3*, 1–7. https://doi.org/10.58809/NLHB2063

Ruppel, P. R., Juanico, J. F., & Johnson, K. D. (2023). The effects of remote instructions, rehearsal, and feedback on preference assessment implementation. *Journal of Organizational Behavior Management, 43*(1), 27–49. https://doi.org/10.1080/01608061.2022.2078455

Scully, C., & Lodge, H. (2005). Impact factors and their significance; overrated or misused? *British Dental Journal, 198*, 391–393. https://doi.org/10.1038/sj.bdj.4812185

Sharma, M., Sarin, A., Gupta, P., Sachdeva, S., & Desai, A. V. (2014). Journal impact factor: Its use, significance and limitations. *World Journal of Nuclear Medicine, 13*(2), 146. https://doi.org/10.4103/1450-1147.139151

Springer. (2022). *Behavior Analysis in Practice: Aims and scope.* Springer Nature. Retrieved December 27, 2022 from https://www.springer.com/journal/40617/aims-and-scope

Springer. (2023a). *Behavior and Social Issues.* Springer Nature. Retrieved March 17, 2023 from https://www.springer.com/journal/42822

Springer. (2023b). *The Analysis of Verbal Behavior: Aims and scope.* Springer Nature. Retrieved March 17, 2023 from https://www.springer.com/journal/40616/aims-and-scope

Springer. (2023c). *Perspectives on Behavior Science: Submission guidelines.* Springer Nature. Retrieved March 17, 2023 from https://www.springer.com/journal/40614/submission-guidelines

Taylor & Francis Online. (2022). *Journal of Organizational Behavior Management: Aims and scope.* Informa UK Limited. Retrieved December 27, 2022 from https://www.tandfonline.com/action/journalInformation?show=aimsScope&journalCode=worg20

Taylor & Francis Online. (2023a). *International Studies of Management & Organization.* Informa UK Limited. Retrieved March 27, 2023 from https://www.tandfonline.com/action/journalInformation?show=journalMetrics&journalCode=mimo20

Taylor & Francis Online. (2023b). *Journal of Organizational Behavior Management: Subscribe.* Informa UK Limited. Retrieved March 31, 2023 from https://www.tandfonline.com/pricing/journal/worg20

Taylor & Francis Online. (2023c). *The effects of remote instructions, rehearsal, and feedback on preference assessment implementation: Purchase options.* Informa UK Limited. Retrieved March 31, 2023 from https://www.tandfonline.com/doi/full/10.1080/01608061.2022.2078455

Taylor & Francis Online. (2023d). *Understanding journal metrics: Using data to choose a journal for submission.* Informa UK Limited. Retrieved March 27, 2023 from https://authorservices.taylorandfrancis.com/publishing-your-research/choosing-a-journal/journal-metrics/

The Biosemantics Group. (2007). *Jane: Journal/Author Name Estimator* [NAME]. https://jane.biosemantics.org/

Think. Check. Submit. (2023a). *Journals.* https://thinkchecksubmit.org/journals/

Think. Check. Submit. (2023b). *About predatory publishing*. https://thinkchecksubmit.org/resources/about-predatory-publishing/

Thomson, P. (2011, November). *Contacting journal editors; Six dos, a maybe and a don't*. https://patthomson.net/2011/11/25/contacting-journal-editors-six-dos-a-maybe-and-and-a-dont/

University Library. (2023). *Evaluating journals using journal metrics: Overview*. Walden University LLC. Retrieved March 27, 2023 from https://academicguides.waldenu.edu/library/journalmetrics

University of Pittsburgh Library System. (2023). *Research impact and metrics*. Retrieved from https://pitt.libguides.com/bibliometricIndicators/JournalMetrics

Valentino, A. L. (2021). *Applied behavior analysis research made easy: A handbook for practitioners conducting research post-certification*. New Harbinger Publications.

Wiley Online Library. (2022). *Journal of Applied Behavior Analysis: Article Publication Charges*. Wiley. Retrieved December 27, 2022 from https://onlinelibrary.wiley.com/page/journal/19383703/homepage/fundedaccess.html

Wiley Online Library. (2023a). *Journal of Applied Behavior Analysis: About this journal*. Wiley. Retrieved March 31, 2023 from https://onlinelibrary.wiley.com/journal/19383703

Wiley Online Library. (2023b). *Journal of the Experimental Analysis of Behavior: About this journal*. Wiley. Retrieved March 31, 2023 from https://onlinelibrary.wiley.com/journal/19383711

Wolery, M., Lane, K. L., & Common, E. A. (2018). Writing tasks: Literature reviews, research proposals, and final reports. In J. R. Ledford & D. L. Gast (Eds.), *Single case research methodology: Applications in special education and behavioral sciences* (3rd ed., pp. 43–76). https://doi.org/10.4324/9780203521892

Jessica F. Juanico is the assistant director and assistant professor of practice for the University of Kansas' online master's and certificate programs in Applied Behavior Analysis. She received a Bachelor of Arts in Psychology and Spanish from Auburn University in 2011, a Master of Arts in Applied Behavioral Science from the University of Kansas in 2014, and a doctorate in Behavioral Psychology from the University of Kansas in 2017. Jessica has served in numerous clinical positions and worked with a variety of populations including children with and without developmental disabilities, including autism, and adolescents with severe behavior disorders. She has conducted research in assessment and treatment of problem behavior, food selectivity, dog-safety skills, public speaking, and workplace victimization.

Kylene Caquelin is a Board Certified Behavior Analyst (BCBA) for No Stone Unturned in Manhattan, KS. She received a Bachelor of Science in Psychology from the University of Montana in 2012 and a Master of Arts in Applied Behavioral Science from the University of Kansas in 2022. Kylene has worked in the field of behavior analysis for the last 10 years, with a focus on parent training since receiving her BCBA. She has conducted research in the assessment and treatment of problem behavior.

Raena A. Quinnell works as a Registered Behavior Technician for Step Ahead ABA in Omaha, NE. She received a Bachelor of Science from South Dakota State University in Human Development and Family Studies and a Master of Arts in Applied Behavioral Science from the University of Kansas under the mentorship of Jessica Juanico. Raena has conducted research in the assessment and treatment of problem behavior.

Ashley N. Romero is a Supervising Behavior Analyst for Little Leaves Behavioral Services located in Weston, Florida. She received a Bachelor of Science in Psychology from the University of Florida in 2016, a Master of Arts in Applied Behavioral Science from the University of Kansas in 2018, and a doctorate in Behavioral Psychology from the University of Kansas in 2022. Ashley has worked within the field of behavior analysis for more than 10 years and across a variety of populations (i.e., toddlers with and without diagnoses, children with autism and related disabilities, adolescents with autism and related disabilities, and adults with autism and related intellectual and developmental disabilities) and across settings (i.e., schools, clinics, and homes). Additionally, she has conducted research in the areas of assessment and treatment of problem behaviors, skill acquisition of daily living (i.e., feeding and toileting), assessment of conditioned reinforcers (i.e., tokens), and functional communication.

Chapter 11
Manuscript Submission

Michelle A. Sereno and Julianne DiCocco

Gone are the days of printing and sending copies of a manuscript to a publisher via mail. Nearly all journals now rely exclusively on digital editorial management systems (Paltridge, 2020). The advent of online manuscript submission has arguably improved the process. Authors surveyed by Ware (2005) indicated experiencing digital submission as faster and more accessible than paper submission. Post-submission, authors can log into the editorial management system to check the status of submitted manuscripts, make revisions, and communicate with editorial staff. Other authors level criticisms against online submission systems, noting the time required to review submission instructions and to input material into fields as specified (Oh, 2020). This part of the process is presumably made more arduous by significant variations in manuscript requirements across journals, even among those of the same discipline (Jiang et al., 2019). Failure to attend to details for a given journal could mean immediate rejection of a manuscript (Welch, 2007), presumably necessitating resubmission (Oh, 2020). Fortunately, common errors in the submission process are easily avoidable with pre-planning, organization, and attention to detail.

In this chapter, we guide the reader step-by-step through preparing and submitting an academic manuscript for publication. We alert readers to common formatting and submission pitfalls that could result in manuscript rejection before review,

M. A. Sereno (✉)
Behavior Analysis Department, College of Graduate and Professional Studies, The Chicago School, Chicago, IL, USA
e-mail: msereno@ego.thechicagoschool.edu

J. DiCocco
Santa Clara County Office of Education, San Jose, CA, USA
e-mail: jdicocco@sccoe.org

© The Author(s), under exclusive license to Springer Nature Switzerland AG 2023   175
A. K. Griffith, T. C. Ré (eds.), *Disseminating Behavioral Research*,
https://doi.org/10.1007/978-3-031-47343-2_11

illustrated with examples from leading social sciences journals.[1] We propose strategies to facilitate error-free manuscript submission. We support recommendations with journal editor commentaries, peer-reviewed publications, and references to relevant sections of the *American Psychological Association (APA) Publication Manual* (7th ed.).[2]

Preparing for the Submission Process

Journal submission processes share many commonalities. Perhaps due in part to the commonalities, authors often miss the subtle differences in requirements between journals. Attending to specific requirements when submitting to a journal is crucial. Kapp and Albertyn (2008) surveyed 73 editors for major journals in South Africa regarding errors authors make when submitting to a journal. Nearly all responding editors (94%) noted frequent failure to follow submission rules, despite 74% of the associated journals providing author guidance on their journal page.

Orienting to the Process

Take time to become familiar with the journal's instructions for authors. Then, orient to the manuscript submission system. Note any information you will need to gather and forms you must prepare. Determine which formatting requirements apply to your paper and how manuscript components will be organized for submission. Some journals (e.g., *Journal of Contextual Behavioral Science*) offer a submission checklist to assist authors with the submission process. If a checklist is not provided, we strongly recommend creating your own. As you review the author instructions and submission portal, align your checklist with journal criteria.

Author Instructions Pages

Access instructions for submitting a manuscript through the journal's homepage. Look for an area on the page labeled as author instructions, guidelines for submission, or something similar. Alternatively, this information might be found via a tab

---

[1] Information is current as of the time this chapter was written but may change over time. We advise readers to reference journal pages for the most current information.

[2] There are four primary academic writing styles. Chicago/Turabian style is used in Business, History, and the Fine Arts. Journals targeting humanity, literature, and language use Modern Language Association (MLA) standards. Institute of Electrical and Electronics Engineers (IEEE) standards apply to publications focused on biotechnology and computing. Education and Social Science disciplines follow standards established by the American Psychological Association (APA).

or a menu. For the *Journal of Applied Behavior Analysis (JABA)*, author guidelines for submission are a drop-down menu option under the tab "contribute". Consider printing out author instructions for easy reference during the submission process. The *Journal of Contextual Behavioral Science* provides author instructions in .pdf format.

Journals offer various tools to assist authors through the submission process. The journal may provide a FAQ for authors. Video tutorials may be available (Johnson & Green, 2009). When reviewing instructions, follow any relevant links to additional information. For example, author instructions for *American Psychologist* include links to information specific to journal reporting standards and ethical standards and to forms that must accompany submissions. The scope and detail of the instructions for authors vary widely across journals. Note any aspects of the instructions that are unclear or ambiguous. Hartley and Cabanac (2017) caution attention to words like "appropriate" that might not sufficiently describe what is expected or allowed. When in doubt, contact the journal editorial staff for clarification.

Submission Portal

Access the journal submission portal via a clickable "Submit" link on the journal's homepage. The link will take you to a manuscript submission and publication system. Upon accessing the submission portal, you will be prompted through creating an account. Check your email for a registration verification link. Follow the email instructions to confirm registration. Save your username and password in a safe location. You will use this information when logging into the system to check manuscript status, manage revisions, and communicate with editorial staff. To facilitate interface and communication, add the editorial program site to your pop-up blocker exceptions and set permissions to allow emails from the system.

Two major online manuscript submission systems are *ScholarOne* (clarivate. com) and *Editorial Manager* (www.ariessys.com). ScholarOne hosts prestigious journals, including *Psychological Science, Behavior Modification, JABA,* and *Journal of the Experimental Analysis of Behavior (JEAB)*. Editorial Manager services all journals published by the American Psychological Association (APA) (e.g., *American Psychologist, Behavioral* and *Brain Sciences*). In addition, several flagship behavior analytic journals use Editorial Manager (e.g., *Analysis of Verbal Behavior, Perspectives on Behavioral Science, Behavior Analysis in Practice, The Psychological Record*). You may encounter other systems as well. For instance, *American Journal of Psychology* and *Journal for Advancing Sport Psychology in Research* use the *Scholastica* platform (https://scholasticahq.com).

Navigate through the submission portal to become familiar with the system format and workflow. Printable user's guides are available for ScholarOne (https:// clarivate.com/webofsciencegroup/wp-content/uploads/sites/2/dlm_ uploads/2019/10/ScholarOne-Manuscripts-Author-Guide.pdf) and for Editorial Manager (https://www.ariessys.com/wp-content/uploads/EM-Author-English.pdf). A web-based user's guide is available for Scholastica (https://help.scholasticahq.

com/article/72-author-guide). ScholarOne and Editorial Manager are largely similar in their author-related features (Kim et al., 2018). Procedures and requirements for submission do vary between the editorial management systems and within the systems across journals.

As you orient yourself to the journal home page and the manuscript submission system, continue to update your submission checklist. List all components of the submission in the order they will be included in the submission. Note whether each component will be uploaded as a document or entered into a field within the submission form. Highlight page limits and formatting requirements as they pertain to sections of your manuscript. Also, list any steps you intend to take before beginning the submission process (e.g., exploring data sharing options, running error checks). It is helpful, for instance, to identify what information will be needed and to collect these data before initiating the submission process.

Gathering Collateral Information

You will provide specific collateral data during the submission process. Where the system requires data before advancing to the next step, having information handy expedites submission. Collecting information ahead of time also helps to mitigate the impact of any related delays. For instance, you may experience delays in accessing information from other sources (e.g., co-authors, institutions). In gathering information, you may identify additional pre-submission tasks that could increase the likelihood of your manuscript ultimately being accepted for publication (e.g., registering the study protocol or data set). Begin collecting information now. You can use any delays in accessing information to attend to manuscript formatting.

Authorship

Take time before initiating your submission to clarify authorship and to collect information relevant to authorship. As the submitting author, you will provide names and contact information for all contributing authors. You will also identify each author's role in the study according to authorship conventions. Standards for establishing and validating author contributions vary across journals. Failure to adhere to authorship standards could result in submission rejection.

Named Authors

Each author named on your submission must be a significant contributor to the project. Named authors are those who have (1) contributed substantially to study design or acquisition, analysis, or interpretation of the data; (2) drafted or critically revised the manuscript; (3) given final approval for publication; and (4) agreed to be responsible and accountable for the accuracy and integrity of the work (ICMJE, n.d.). The Contributor Roles Taxonomy, or CRediT (https://credit.niso.org), can be used to identify contributors meeting criteria for authorship and to describe each author's contribution. Contributors who do not meet criteria for authorship should be acknowledged elsewhere. Be prepared to state and describe each named author's role in the study. Some journals (e.g., *Psychological Science*) publish this information in the article.

Order of Authors

Determine the order in which author names should appear on the paper. Authors are generally listed on the title page in order of the magnitude of their contribution to the project, with the person who conducted the primary research listed first. For works with co-authors, Teixeira da Silva (2021) suggests adding the designation co- before each equally contributing author. Alternatively, distinguish co-authors from other authors with bold typeface.

Author Information

For each author, be prepared to provide their preferred full name and highest degree earned. Some journals (e.g., *JABA, JEAB*) invite authors to include their preferred pronouns. Each author should provide you with an email address at which they will receive correspondence related to the submission. Additionally, you will need the name of each author's affiliation, the department they belong to, and the complete address of the institution. For authors in private practice, you will provide their geographic location.

Corresponding Author Identify one author to serve as the corresponding author. The corresponding author will manage all communication between the journal and all authors of the manuscript.

ORCID ID Collect each author's ORCID ID. The *Open Researcher and Contributor Identifier (ORCID)* ID is a 16-digit alphanumeric code unique to each researcher (https://orcid.org). An ORCID ID connects authors with their prior research and other biographic information. Some journals (e.g., *Behavior Modification* and *Behavioral and Brain Sciences*) require an ORCID ID for each contributing author. Other journals encourage an ORCID ID but do not require it. Authors who do not have an ORCID ID might consider registering for one before the manuscript is submitted.

Author Biographies Some journals request or require a biography for each named author. Biographies should highlight experience, credentials, and achievements related to the article topic. Attend to journal-specific word count limits, which may range from a maximum of 50 words to a maximum of 200 words per biography.

Study Registration

Gather information related to study pre-registration. Pre-registration is usually not mandatory, but it is encouraged. Pre-registration promotes rigor in experimental procedure and data analysis. Pre-registration also facilitates collaboration and replication (Johnson, 2005) and reduces the odds of duplication in research. If you pre-registered your study, confirm that you have included pre-registration information (site and registration number) in the methods section of your manuscript. Add this information to the author note on your title page (American Psychological Association, 2020, Section 3.9). You may also be asked to provide a pre-registration number within the submission form.

Registering your study prior to initiating research protocols is ideal. However, studies can be registered on clinicaltrials.gov at any time, even after the study has concluded (Clinicaltrials.gov). There are several sites on which to register a study. For example, Clinicaltrials.gov is a website that stores and allows access to information on various clinical studies. PROSPERO (https://www.crd.york.ac.uk/prospero/) is a site where an author can register a systematic review. If you did not pre-register your study or registered after the fact, indicate this in your cover letter.

Data Sharing

If your manuscript includes new data, confirm that the data sharing policy for your selected journal aligns with your project. Data sharing refers to providing other researchers with access to data resources. Data sharing policies promote transparency in research. Further, data sharing contributes to knowledge by facilitating replication and extension and empowering cross-disciplinary collaboration (Alter & Gonzalez, 2018). The FAIR Guiding Principles for scientific data management and stewardship (Wilkinson et al., 2016) call for research data to be findable, accessible, interoperable, and reusable (FAIR). Journals adopt data sharing policies in accordance. Find details on the FAIR data principles at Go Fair (https://www.go-fair.org/fair-principles/).

Levels of Data Sharing

Most journals subscribe to a hierarchy of data sharing requirements. For example, journals published by *Springer Nature* (https://www.springernature.com/gp/authors/research-data-policy/research-data-policy-types) apply one of four levels of data sharing: Type 1 policy encourages data sharing and citation, Type 2 encourages data sharing and evidence of data sharing, Type 3 encourages data sharing and requires a statement of data availability, and Type 4 requires evidence of data sharing and peer review. *Behavior Analysis in Practice*, *JABA*, and *The Psychological Record* are examples of journals that apply a Type 3 research data policy. Journals published by *Sage* follow a three-tier data sharing policy (https://us.sagepub.com/en-us/nam/research-data-sharing-policies). At Tier 1, data sharing, citing, and linking are encouraged. Tier 2 mandates data sharing, citing, and linking. At Tier 3, peer-reviewed data verification is required. The stringency of data sharing policies ranges across journals. Crosas et al. (2018) assessed public websites for 291 highly ranked social science journals. Across psychology journals reviewed, 60% posted a data sharing policy, with 22% of the policies requiring data sharing.

Considerations Related to Data Sharing

The often-personal characteristics of social science research topics may inhibit data sharing. Researchers express concerns that shared data might be used outside of intended parameters, or that data sharing might contribute to the reidentification of confidential information. Jeng et al. (2016) evaluated data sharing behavior using a profiling instrument. Of those profiled, 85% agreed that data sharing benefits collaboration in research. However, many were reluctant to share data.

Data Sharing with Qualitative Research Data sharing may be of particular concern for qualitative researchers. Qualitative data collection differs fundamentally from quantitative data collection (Tsai et al., 2016). Qualitative data are non-numerical data used to approximate or characterize information that is not easily counted. Qualitative data include focus group responses, direct observations or interviews, and audio or video recordings. The nature of qualitative data may increase the risk of reidentification (Tsai et al., 2016). Further, even with interview scripts and operationally defined coding procedures, there are concerns about fidelity in replication or analysis of qualitative data (Tsai et al., 2016).

Apprehensions notwithstanding, Tsai et al. (2016) suggests that data sharing might increase confidence in qualitative research. A small percentage of journals evaluated by Crosas et al. (2018) explicitly noted qualitative data in their data policies. Authors of qualitative studies might consider choosing such a journal. Journals with policies specific to qualitative data are more likely to support verifiable, reproducible, and safe qualitative data sharing (Crosas et al., 2018; Tsai et al., 2016).

Data Sharing and Study Approval

You should find the data sharing policy for a selected journal posted on, or accessible through, the author instructions pages. Confirm that the terms of your study approval align with the journal's data sharing policy. Data associated with a manuscript must be managed in accordance with the research protocol, the terms of the Institutional Review Board (IRB) approval, and the language of the informed consent (Meyer, 2018). Deviations may require that you request a change of protocol through the IRB.

In considering whether to share data and to what level, weigh potential risks to research participants as well as permissions granted. Ethical considerations will vary depending, in part, on whether participant consent forms address or omit the mention of data sharing (Meyer, 2018). If you determine that sharing your data in part or in full is not appropriate, state this in your Data Availability Statement (see below) and include a detailed rationale in your cover letter. Notably, most researchers profiled by Jeng et al. (2016) judged their research data wholly or mostly sharable. Only 5% said their data was not sharable. The authors found no significant difference in data sharing profiles across qualitative and quantitative researchers.

Data Repositories

If you have opted to post your study data to a data repository, include the name of the repository and the citation for your data set with your manuscript submission. A data repository is a sustainable virtual warehouse that maintains and distributes data used in scholarly work. Although journals do not typically require data sharing through a repository, it is strongly encouraged. Data repositories promote FAIR data sharing (Crosas et al., 2018). Repository-held data sets are assigned a DOI, making the data citable and discoverable. Further, data repositories curate data to ensure it is usable over time and across technological changes (Alter & Gonzalez, 2018).

If you have not posted your data to a repository, and doing so is within the parameters of your approval/consent, consider sharing your data to a data repository before submitting for publication. The National Institute of Health (sharing.nih.gov) offers guidelines on selecting an appropriate data repository. Consider long-term sustainability, confidentiality, curation, and quality assurance. Alter and Gonzalez (2018) recommends that authors use a domain-specific data repository. While general and institutional repositories have a broader range, domain-specific repositories focus on limited data and are more likely to offer curation. The Inter-university Consortium for Political and Social Research (ICPSR) is an example of a domain-specific repository. It hosts 21 specialized topic collections within the social and behavioral sciences (icpsr.umich.edu). Qualitative researchers might consider the Qualitative Data Repository (https://qdr.syr.edu/).

Formatting for Submission

Confirm that you have formatted your manuscript according to journal requirements. Editors endorse incorrect style and language as the category of author error most often noted in submitted manuscripts (Kapp & Albertyn, 2008). These errors are easily avoidable with close attention to detail. Review journal instructions carefully. While most social science journals advise authors to follow APA formatting guidelines, journal instructions do not always align with APA standards. Make notes on journal instructions pertaining to style and language in the corresponding sections of your checklist. Check for formatting resources provided by the journal. For example, some journals offer templates. Consider downloading a similar paper from the journal as a sample for reference (Hartley & Cabanac, 2017). Journal editors and editorial staff (Johnson & Green, 2009; Welch, 2007) alert authors to areas in which formatting errors are common. We discuss how to recognize and surmount those potential trouble spots below.

Type of Paper

Determine what type of manuscript you are submitting. The requirements and standards applied to a manuscript (i.e., formatting, components, standards for reporting or data sharing) can differ depending on the article type. As such, the submission portal may require you to select the category that best applies to your paper. Journals typically publish multiple article types, including original research, case studies, opinion papers, and editorials. To determine which category best suits your manuscript, check the journal's author instruction pages for category parameters and examples.

Word Counts and Page Limits

Confirm your manuscript complies with journal page or word count limits. Journals control the length of submissions by establishing such limits. Limits keep authors focused and concise and allow journals to maximize the number of papers they can include in an issue. Not attending to established limits is a primary reason for the immediate rejection of a manuscript (Welch, 2007). Journals vary in how word counts or page limits are applied.

Application of Word Count and Page Limits

Limitations may differ based on the type of paper you are submitting. For example, *Psychological Science* limits commentaries to 1000 words (including main text, notes, acknowledgments, and appendices) but accepts research articles of longer lengths. *Journal of Contextual Behavioral Science* accepts review articles of up to 10,000 words, but the journal caps empirical, conceptual, and practical application papers at 6000 words.

Check journal standards to determine which manuscript sections are included in word and page counts. A journal might apply limits to the body of the manuscript only. For example, *Psychological Methods* accepts manuscripts of 12,000 words, excluding references, tables, figures, and appendices. *American Psychologist,* on the other hand, includes the title page, abstract, references, tables, and figures in their 35 double-spaced page limit. The 6000-word limit imposed by the *Journal of Contextual Behavioral Science* includes the abstract but does not include references, tables, or figures.

Journals might differentially apply word count limits across sections of a manuscript. For example, *JABA*'s 3000-word limit applies only to the Introduction and Discussion sections of the manuscript. *Psychological Science* does not place a limit on the length of the Method or Results sections. However, the word count must not exceed 2000 across the Introduction, Discussion, footnotes, acknowledgments, and appendices. Some journals (*American Psychologist, Psychological Methods*) will make exceptions to page limits when the topic or the study format justifies additional pages (e.g., multiple studies or phases) and the article makes an exceptional contribution to the literature. *American Psychologist* requires that the author submit a request to the editor for additional page space prior to submission.

General Formatting Guidelines

Format your manuscript according to the standards indicated by the journal. When reviewing journal formatting standards, it is helpful to have a copy of the APA publication manual handy for reference. Be sure you are working with the most recent version (e.g., APA 7th Edition). As noted previously, there may be discrepancies between formatting instructions provided by a journal and APA standards. For example, the APA Publication Manual (2020) permits up to five levels of headings (Section 2.27), but *Analysis of Verbal Behavior* will accommodate no more than three heading levels. Discrepancies may also present when author instructions need to be updated. When in doubt, contact the journal to confirm formatting standards. Doing so could ultimately save you time.

Language and Tone

Confirm that your manuscript's language and tone align with journal requirements. The language standard for academic writing is English for Research Publication Purposes (ERPP). Applying standard language to academic writing promotes global dissemination of knowledge (Flowerdew, 2015). However, an ERPP standard may put international scholars at a distinct disadvantage. Journals can be inflexible in accepting variants of English (McKinley & Rose, 2018), presenting a bias against English speakers of other languages. Submission systems that rely on artificial intelligence may be exceptionally resistant to variations.

Format-free submission processes (Ganz et al., 2022) may benefit English speakers of other languages. In addition, as part of their commitment to Diversity, Equity, and Inclusion (DEI), many author instructions pages now include a link to access editing services specific to academic writing and English language editing. There is typically a cost for these services. However, authors may be eligible for a discount with some vendors. For instance, authors attempting to publish in an APA journal can access discounted editing services (https://www.apa.org/pubs/journals/resources/editing-services).

Diversity, Equity, and Inclusion in Language

Authors have a role in promoting DEI in academic publishing as well. Ensure you have written your manuscript in language that is inclusive and bias-free. For example, replace any gendered terms with gender-neutral variants (i.e., supplant she/he with they/them). The APA Publication Guide (2020) offers general and topic-specific guidelines for reducing bias in writing (Sections 5.1–5.10). DEI issues in academia perpetuate systemic oppression. Conversely, publications that promote bias-free and inclusive language benefit the scientific community by increasing contributions from otherwise underrepresented groups (Dewidar et al., 2022).

Text Formatting

Confirm that you have formatted text according to the requirements of the journal. Most journals require documents written in Microsoft Word (.doc or .docx). LaTeX (.tex) may be used if the manuscript includes mathematical content. Construct equations using software like MathType (https://www.wiris.com/en/mathtype/) or Equation Editor 3.0, a component included in some versions of Microsoft Word. Additional text formatting guidelines may specify font or font size (e.g., 10- or 12-point Times New Roman). Bolding and italics are typically acceptable for adding emphasis, but other text effects may not be permitted. Other specifications may include using the tab function to indent rather than the space bar and avoiding using field functions. Unless a journal states otherwise, the text should be double-spaced with standard margins of one inch on all sides. Maintain formatting design consistency across the document, including in tables and figures. Ensure that you have disabled macros and protections in Word.

Footnotes

Journals may have special instructions for authors using footnotes. Generally, footnotes are used to give additional information or to indicate copyright attributions. Not all journals allow footnoting. *JEAB*, for instance, permits footnoting only when they are essential. Journals that allow footnotes might specify how to include them (e.g., within the body of the manuscript, on a separate page). Authors submitting to *Psychological Methods* should add footnotes to the acknowledgments page.

Manuscript Components

Ensure your manuscript is clearly written and easy to follow. While many errors are amenable to correction during the review process, it is "vital" that authors submit a well-crafted, well-written manuscript (Bordage, 2001, p. 893). The *Journal Article Reporting Standards (JARS)* are guidelines for journal article content formulated by the APA (https://apastyle.apa.org/jars). JARS standards promote transparency and methodological integrity in research. There are JARS standards for quantitative, qualitative, and mixed methods studies. See the APA Style JARS website (https://apastyle.apa.org/jars) for in-depth information on the etiology and application of JARS. Chapter 3 of the APA Publication Manual (7th ed.) provides an overview of JARS. We discuss JARS here in terms of common formatting errors leading to manuscript rejection prior to review.

Title Page

The title of your article should concisely capture the theme of the paper and convey the study design and aim (Bordage, 2001; Johnson & Green, 2009). Prepare your title page according to APA standards and in line with journal specifications. Some journals may limit title length. JABA, for example, limits a title to 12 words or fewer. The running head, a shortened version of the article title, should be included at the top of the title page and all manuscript pages. See the APA Publication Guide (2020, Section 2.3).

Authors

List all study authors in order of their contribution to the project. Include each author's academic or non-academic affiliation (e.g., hospital, laboratory, other organization). For authors in private practice, state their geographic location.

Author Note

Organize the author note into paragraphs, each pertaining to a required information set (See APA Publication Manual, 2020, Section 2.7). The information included in the author's note varies across journals. We describe prevailing standards below.

Author Information For each author, provide full name, complete mailing address, email address, and ORCID ID (if applicable). Identify the corresponding author clearly. When requested, include each author's contribution to the study.

Disclosures State potential conflicts of interest or indicate that no conflicts exist. List funding sources and grant support. For each contributor, specify the nature of the support. Include grant numbers where applicable. Include study registration information if applicable. If study data are shared openly, include the citation for the data set.

Acknowledgments Acknowledge people who contributed to the study but did not meet criteria for authorship. Also include those who provided general support or technical assistance. Each acknowledgment should include the person or entity's name and their specific function or contribution. Clever (1997) advises authors to solicit consent from anyone they intend to name in the acknowledgments.

Abstract

Confirm your abstract meets the requirements for your selected journal. The purpose of the abstract is to provide a brief summary of the manuscript content. Some journals require structured abstracts, while others require an unstructured, paragraph-style abstract. The APA Publication Manual (2020, Section 3.3) describes JARS standards for abstracts. In general, abstracts should include background, purpose, research design and method, and conclusions (Hartley & Cabanac, 2017; Mosteller et al., 2004). Depending on the type of article, the abstract may also include information on the setting or population, the intervention, data analysis, and findings (Mosteller et al., 2004). A journal may specify additional required content. Most journals limit the length of the abstract to 150–250 words.

In some cases, journals require more than one abstract. *Behavioral and Brain Sciences*, for instance, asks for an abstract of 250 words or less and a shorter abstract of no more than 100 words. *Psychological Methods* requires a technical abstract at submission and a second non-technical, translational abstract with first revisions. Some journals offer authors the option to include a visual (Paltridge, 2020) or video abstract. Depending on the submission system, you will either upload the abstract as a separate document or cut and paste the abstract into a field within the submission form.

Keywords

Identify keywords or short phrases that represent your study or article according to journal parameters. Keywords are terms indicative of central topics, research themes, or discussion points in your manuscript. Publishers use these terms for indexing or cross-indexing your work. Some journals structure keywords, requiring the author to select a specific number of applicable words from a standard list. Alternatively, the author may be permitted to submit 3–10 words or short phrases of their choosing. Consider referencing a subject index when choosing keywords. APA, for example, offers a *Thesaurus of Psychological Index Terms* (www.apa.org). Johnson and Green (2009) caution against using terms taken from the common vernacular, which may convey meaning other than what a researcher intends.

During submission, you will either select keywords from a list of options or enter terms into a field within the submission form. Some journals require the author to submit keywords on the abstract or the title page. Check author instructions for other journal-specific requirements. For example, *JEAB* advises authors to list keywords in descending order of importance.

Introduction

Journals may reject manuscripts at submission if the introduction is too long or does not include clearly stated hypotheses (Johnson & Green, 2009). As per JARS, your introduction should frame your study by stating the importance of the problem and related implications. It should include a review of relevant literature, noting gaps to be addressed by your study. The introduction should conclude by stating the aim of the study and the research hypotheses. According to Johnson and Green (2009), three to four paragraphs should be sufficient to provide study context and related theories and to state the study aims and hypotheses.

Methods Section

Inadequacies in a manuscript's Methods section might also result in rejection before review. Common inadequacies include insufficient detail, inappropriate statistical analyses, and failure to note relevant approvals (Johnson & Green, 2009). Ensure your methods section provides sufficient information to facilitate study replication (See Jars, Method). Reference within the Methods section any supplementary materials that would support replication (e.g., extended scripts, surveys, visuals). Provide a clear, concise rationale for your chosen statistical approach. Consider consulting with a statistician as necessary. Include specific information related to study registration (i.e., registration number and the site registered with) and ethical approvals (e.g., IRB affiliation). Clearly state that research was conducted within the parameters of registered study protocols and ethical approvals.

Results Section

Common errors in the Results sections include unnecessary information or commentary (Johnson & Green, 2009) and incomplete reporting of statistical analyses (Giofrè et al., 2017; Johnson & Green, 2009). Reference JARS standards appropriate for your research design (i.e., quantitative, qualitative, mixed methods) to ensure your Results section includes all necessary components. Reserve commentary for the Discussion section. Review journal standards for reporting statistical findings. Failure to adhere to requirements will likely result in the rejection of your manuscript.

Standards for Reporting Statistical Findings

Confirm that you have reported findings according to journal standards. Many journals now require or strongly encourage authors to report new statistics (Giofrè et al., 2017). Increased standards include exact reporting of statistical findings. For example, when indicating statistical significance, a journal may require exact p values (e.g., $p < 0.0232$) rather than estimates ($p < 0.05$). Researchers should support p values with confidence intervals (e.g., 95% CI [3.27, 6.34]. Other features of new statistical reporting include indicating how the sample size was determined and what criteria were applied to include and exclude subjects from the sample. Researchers are also encouraged to conduct and report a meta-analysis of related results.

Typographical Errors in Statistical Reporting Typographical errors in reporting statistics may result in rejection prior to review. Some journals evaluate submissions using StatCheck (https://mbnuijten.com/statcheck/), an R program that assesses statistics for typographical errors. Manuscripts with errors will not progress to the review stage. *Psychological Science* recommends that authors run StatCheck or a similar program before submitting so that any typographical errors in statistics can be detected and corrected before review.

Tables and Figures

Tables and figures can enhance the readability and clarity of your manuscript. However, an unnecessary or poorly formatted table or figure could result in the rejection of your manuscript. Reference the Table Checklist (Section 7.20) and the Figure Checklist (Section 7.35) in APA Publication Manual (2020) for standards in formatting. Attend closely to journal-specific criteria for tables and figures as well.

Including Tables or Figures

Include a table or graph in your manuscript if the visual conveys the information more clearly and concisely than the text. If the information can be clearly presented in the text, *JABA* editors advise leaving it in the text. Reference any tables or figures in the body of the manuscript but avoid redundancy. Refrain from explaining in the text what you have depicted in the table or figure (Johnson & Green, 2009).

Formatting Tables and Figures

Journals habitually reject manuscripts that include figures with poor resolution, incorrect formatting, or missing legends or captions (Johnson & Green, 2009; Welch, 2007). Therefore, attend closely to formatting instructions for your selected journal. While text and style conventions for the manuscript body typically apply to tables and figures, there are likely to be exceptions.

Tables Create tables using the table function in Microsoft Word rather than importing a spreadsheet. Use borders or lines only where necessary for clarity. Do not use shading. Number your tables using sequential Arabic numerals. Cite tables within the text consistent with the numerical order of the table.

Figures Figures follow similar guidelines regarding numbering and sequential display within the text. Figures embedded into the text should be manipulatable. The journal may ask for editable files. When applicable, note which graphics program you used to create an image. Check journal policies on figure hue. Journals may publish figures in color online, but they typically print figures in black and white. Some journals allow authors to have a figure printed in color for a fee. *Psychological*

Methods, for example, charges the author $900 for an initial color image, with subsequent images printed in color at reduced rates. In lieu of color printing, Johnson and Green (2009) advise creating figures using symbols to maximize readability.

Confirm that your figures are of sufficient resolution for printing. Line art should generally be 900–1200 DPI, and images should be at least 300 DPI for color or 600 DPI for black and white. Journals may give instructions for specific types of figures. For example, *JABA* and *JEAB* specify criteria for line graphs, including standards for data points, axes, and lines. *Psychological Methods* specifies line weight based on the program used to create the image.

Submitting Tables and Figures

Determine requirements for submitting tables and figures. For example, some journals require authors to include tables and figures in the body of the manuscript, while others require authors to upload figures and tables as separate documents.

Tables and Figures in the Manuscript When including tables and figures in the manuscript, attend to directions for placement (e.g., within the text, after the references, on separate pages attached to the manuscript). Instructions for applying text components (i.e., title, notes, legend) to tables and figures also vary across journals. For instance, journals might instruct authors to embed text within a table or figure or to add associated text to the manuscript body.

Tables and Figures Uploaded as Separate Documents Alternatively, a journal may require authors to remove tables and figures from the manuscript and upload the items to the submission portal as individual documents. Ensure that you upload table bodies and figure images in the correct orientation. Determine how accompanying text is to be included. Tables and figures may be uploaded with accompanying text embedded. Alternatively, the portal may include a link for uploading the table body or figure with linked fields to add related text. You will also provide a section of text from the manuscript to orient the editor to table or figure placement within your main document.

Discussion Section

Your discussion should address whether your study results support your hypotheses. Include an interpretation of your results in light of the relevant literature, accounting for potential sources of bias. Remove any commentary not supported by your research or the related body of literature.

Addressing Limitations and Suggesting Future Directions

Scientists are ethically obligated to indicate any weaknesses in their research that might have influenced outcomes or conclusions. However, authors commonly err by failing to sufficiently consider and describe limitations (Johnson & Green, 2009). Ross and Bibler Zaidi (2019) provide a framework for considering study limitations. They recommend evaluating your study in terms of study design, data collection, data analyses, and threats to internal validity (e.g., attrition, maturation) and external validity (e.g., generalizability). For each potential limitation, describe contributing factors, explain the implications, and detail your efforts to minimize the effects of each limitation. When applicable, suggest alternative interpretations of and explanations for your results. All studies have limitations. Do not leave the task of identifying limitations to peer reviewers (Greener, 2018; Ross & Bibler Zaidi, 2019). Reviewers favor manuscripts that interpret results with regard for study limitations (Bordage, 2001; Ross & Bibler Zaidi, 2019). Doing so demonstrates rigor and transparency (Greener, 2018). A discussion of study limitations should segue into considerations for future research. Johnson and Green (2009) advise authors to go beyond stating the need for more research by offering considered strategies for extending research. For example, authors could suggest alternative approaches that might mitigate the effects of limitations in future studies.

In-text Citations and References

Review your document to verify that all in-text citations and references are correctly formatted and confirm agreement between in-text citations and the reference list. Proper citation is essential to research ethics and transparency. Nonetheless, editors endorse reference and citation mistakes as the second most noted category of author error (Kapp & Albertyn, 2008). Common mistakes include incorrect formatting, citing inappropriate references, and citing work that does not accurately support a statement in the text (Johnson & Green, 2009). Errors related to citations and references may result in your manuscript submission being rejected.

Confirming Citations and References

Use citations any time information is referenced from a previous text, including work previously published by a named author. For all in-text citations, include the source in your reference list. An exception is personal communications referenced in your text that readers cannot recover (e.g., emails, text messages, live speeches). See the APA Publication Manual (2020, Section 8.9) for details on citing and referencing personal communications. Include in your reference list only sources you have cited in your manuscript. Use the "find" feature in Microsoft Word's editing suite to reconcile in-text citations with the reference list. For each work, enter the primary author's name into the search box. Check the results to confirm that you have included all cited works in references and referenced all works cited in the text.

Ensure that works cited in your text match the associated statements. Avoid citing articles based solely on information gleaned from a review of the abstract. Before attributing content to another author, take time to read the article you intend to cite (Johnson & Green, 2009) and consider content within the context of the study. Limit your use of secondary or indirect citations (i.e., citing content found in one source but originally published in another). Access the original source when possible. If you cannot access the original source, cite the primary source in the text, add the phrase "as cited in," and cite the source where you found the information. Include the secondary source in your reference list (American Psychological Association, 2020, Section 8.6).

Formatting Citations and References

Verify that you have formatted in-text citations (American Psychological Association, 2020, Chapter 8) and references (American Psychological Association, 2020, Chapter 9) according to APA guidelines. Review journal-specific instructions for exceptions to standard guidelines. For example, the 7th edition permits authors to use shortened DOIs (American Psychological Association, 2020, Section 9.36), but some journals require full DOIs. Journals may give instructions specific to certain types of references. *The Psychological Record,* for instance, advises authors not to include references for works that are unpublished or in publication. A journal may also establish limits on the number of references an author can include in an article, although this practice is uncommon.

Plagiarism

Properly cite work that has influenced your manuscript to avoid the perception of plagiarism. Plagiarism is defined in the APA Publication Manual (2020, Section 8.2) as presenting material (text, theories, or images) created by another person as though it is your work. Increasingly, journals are using software such as Turnitin (https://www.turnitin.com) to verify the originality of submissions (Paltridge, 2020). Journals return manuscripts failing to meet standards of originality without review. There may be additional repercussions as well. Consider using anti-plagiarism software to evaluate your paper before submission.

Supplemental Materials

Supplemental materials are anything you have not included in the manuscript that would enrich understanding or facilitate replication of the study. Examples are extensions of manuscript content such as more detailed protocols, questionnaires or surveys, forms, and tables or figures too large to include in the manuscript. Supplemental material might also include enhancements such as audio or video clips, or simulations of models. Some journals promote submitting large data sets as supplementary material to encourage and facilitate data sharing (Crosas et al., 2018). Alter and Gonzalez (2018) encourage researchers to share data and program codes or scripts through a data repository rather than as supplementary material. Data repositories are likely to offer greater functionality and easier access. Include all supplemental materials with your initial submission. Refer to the supplementary material in the body of the manuscript and note it in your cover letter. For copyrighted materials, note the status of permissions for use as well (See Permission to Use Copyrighted Material later in this chapter).

Final Preparations for Submission

Deidentify Documents for Double-Blind (Masked) Review

Many journals routinely conduct double-blind reviews to minimize bias during the reviewing process. In a double-blind review, the editor conceals peer reviewer identities from authors and author identities from reviewers. You may be required to submit two copies of your complete manuscript, one blinded and one with the title page included. Alternatively, you may be instructed to submit a deidentified manuscript.

Deidentify your manuscript by removing author names and affiliations from the main document and all supplementary material. Ensure you save documents in a format that does not identify contributors. Check for indicators of authorship on data repository citations as well. Some journals advise against authors citing their previous work. Even in double-blind reviews, self-citation can increase the likelihood of author identification (Hill & Provost, 2003). See the APA Publication Manual (2020, Section 8.3) for instructions on concealing your previous work during the review process.

Blind reviews contribute to a bias-free publication process. Absent blind review, studies have shown reviewers are significantly more likely to select submissions from eminent authors or prestigious institutions (Okike et al., 2016; Tomkins et al., 2017). If your selected journal does not conduct blind reviews as a matter of procedure, consider requesting a blind review for your manuscript.

Organize Materials for Submission

Take time before submitting to organize your materials according to the submission process flow. Common submission errors include omitting a required element (Welch, 2007) and improperly sequencing documents (Johnson & Green, 2009). These oversights are avoidable with pre-planning and organization. Your submission checklist should list all components (e.g., manuscript, title page, supplemental materials) required for submission in the order specified by the journal. Make a note of how the submission portal will collect each component. For example, the abstract might be uploaded as a Word file or pasted into the submission form. Figures or tables may be submitted as part of your manuscript or as individual files.

For each component to be uploaded, save relevant content as a separate document. Check journal requirements related to naming conventions. *The Psychological Record*, for example, advises authors to save each figure as Fig plus the number (i.e., Fig1 for the first figure appearing in the manuscript). Confirm whether the journal permits spaces or special characters in file names. Note on your checklist how you named the document and the location to which you saved it. Follow journal instructions and submission prompts carefully to ensure you include all necessary documents in the submission, with documents uploaded to the correct links and in the correct order. Check off the listed components as you progress through the process.

Declarations and Attestations

Before finalizing a submission, authors must provide written declarations and attest to statements related to ethics, research reporting standards, and compliance with journal submission instructions. Declarations and attestations are included in the submission process to preserve the integrity of academic publications. Some are nearly universal (e.g., Disclosure Statement), while others are included at the journal's discretion. Whether a declaration or attestation applies to your submission may depend on the nature of your study. We review customary declarations and attestations below.

Disclosure Statement

Your submission must include a Disclosure Statement identifying any potential conflicts of interest directly or indirectly related to the paper seeking submission. Potential financial conflicts may include direct funding for the study, employment related to the funding, and other financial interests (e.g., holding company shares). If you received funding for your study, state how you used funding and whether the funder had a role in the research beyond funding. For research supported by grant funding, include information for the granting source and the grant number. Disclose potential non-financial conflicts as well (e.g., relationship to a member of the editorial board, institutional affiliations, academic associations). If you perceive no potential conflicts, indicate this in your Disclosure Statement.

The Disclosure Statement promotes objectivity, transparency, and ethical conduct. Failure to include a Disclosure Statement, or failure to include any potential conflicts in the Disclosure Statement, will likely result in rejection before review. Declaring a potential conflict does not necessarily mean that a conflict exists. Further, evidence of a potential conflict will not necessarily preclude your study from being published. Welch (2007) advises authors to demonstrate transparency by declaring any relationships that could be perceived as a conflict of interest and allowing readers to decide whether a conflict exists. Check the journal's author information pages for examples of Disclosure Statements. Note that journals published by APA also require authors to submit a Full Disclosure of Interests Form (https://www.apa.org/pubs/authors/disclosure-of-interests.pdf) with their manuscript.

Data Availability/Open Practices Statement

When submitting original research, include a Data Availability statement. Your statement should cover all data needed to interpret, replicate, and extend your research findings. Include in your statement where to find study data. Digitally sharable data are preferred (Giofrè et al., 2017). Cite your data set according to APA guidelines (10.9) and include a DOI or link for accessing the data set. Report any publicly available data you used to support the findings as well. If there are limitations on sharing your data, state the rationale (e.g., confidentially concerns, potential for harm to participants) and the conditions for accessing the data set (Alter & Gonzalez, 2018).

In some cases, authors may wish to request an embargo on data sharing (i.e., a period post-publication during which data cannot be shared) to allow for additional research activity (Alter & Gonzalez, 2018). Include this information in the Data Availability statement as well. If the paper did not include any original data, provide a statement declaring that data sharing is not applicable.

An Open Practices statement is an extension of the Data Availability statement that includes information on study registration. If your study was not carried out according to the pre-registration plan, note any changes to the initial plan in the Open Practices statement and indicate how you disclosed those changes. If you did not pre-register your study or if you registered after the fact, explain why. Examples of Data Availability and Open Practice statements are on most journal pages.

Compliance with Ethical Standards Statement

A Compliance with Ethical Standards statement might apply to your submission if you conducted your research with human or animal participants. State the ethics committees or Institutional Review Board (IRB) through which you obtained study approvals. Affirm that you conducted your study in accordance with approvals. If you feel your human subject data did not require IRB approval, include a statement to this effect and cite the rationale (Welch, 2007). State that researchers obtained informed consent or assent for participation from all human subjects. Consenting to participate in a study does not necessarily imply consent for data to be published or shared. Specify whether participants explicitly consented to the publication of study findings. The journal may require informed consent specific to publishing. If animals were involved in the study, include a statement regarding animal welfare.

Diversity and Inclusion Statement

The Diversity and Inclusion statement describes how the study demonstrates a commitment to diversity, equity, and inclusion (DEI). A study might demonstrate a commitment to DEI by drawing from multiple perspectives when formulating research questions and analyzing results. Authors should state how they endeavored to recruit a diverse participant group and how participant inclusion and exclusion criteria may have impacted representation within the sample (Dewidar et al., 2022). Consider the extent study results are likely to generalize beyond the participant group (Simons et al., 2017) and what might be done to extend generalizability to traditionally under-represented groups. In place of a formal statement, a journal might require authors to attest that DEI is addressed in their manuscript.

Statement of Relevance/Translational Abstract

A Statement of Relevance or Translational Abstract is a short paragraph (about 150 words) that describes the significance of the study findings beyond the associated area of research and ideally for the greater public. The Statement of Relevance is similar to an "elevator pitch," written in a manner that could solicit dialog with a layperson. For more information, reference the APA's *Guidance for Translational Abstracts and Public Significance Statements* (https://www.apa.org/pubs/journals/resources/translational-messages). Although this type of statement is not standard, some journals (e.g., *Psychological Science, American Psychologist*) require relevance to be communicated as a separate statement or within the body of the manuscript.

Constraints on Generality Statement

A Constraints on Generality (COG) statement clearly defines the target population for the study and describes how results may be limited to the specific participant group (Simons et al., 2017). The statement should address materials, procedures, and study context variables. Authors should suggest how methods could be varied to facilitate generalization without jeopardizing results. APA journals require a COG, as do select other journals.

Attest to Originality

Confirm that the manuscript has not previously been published and is not currently under review by another journal. Submitting a manuscript simultaneously to multiple journals is not ethical or acceptable. If your manuscript was previously submitted to and rejected by another journal, confirm whether you are required to formally withdraw your manuscript from consideration before submitting elsewhere. In your cover letter, disclose the previous submission and the outcome of the submission. Presenting a manuscript at a professional conference before submission or during the review process is typically permittable. Report any conference presentations in your cover letter. If your manuscript contains re-used material (e.g., portions of a study submitted elsewhere), also indicate this in your cover letter.

Manuscripts Containing Data from a Larger Study

More than one manuscript can be submitted from a large study, provided each is materially different. Feldman (2003) suggests your submission may not be considered a "new" study if you predominantly use the same sample or variables you used before. If your manuscript contains data from a more extensive study, state this in your cover letter. The *American Psychologist* submission instructions advise authors to clarify the relationship between their paper and others from the same study. Authors should describe any overlap in participants, measures, and analysis across papers. Describe the larger study and provide references to other study-related papers. State how the current manuscript adds value to the literature. Note that the journal may request copies of related manuscripts during the review.

Increasingly, journals are using software like Crossref (https://www.crossref.org) to verify the originality of submissions (Paltridge, 2020). Submissions failing to meet standards for new material are rejected prior to review. Therefore, applying such checks to your manuscript before a submission is advisable. Any potential overlap with previously published studies could be remedied before submission or addressed in your cover letter.

Author Agreement

Confirm that all named authors explicitly consent to submit the current version of the manuscript for publication in the selected journal. Depending on the journal, you may also have to attest that all named authors agree that they are authors (and by extension, they accept all associated responsibilities) and agree with their stated role in the project and their order on the title page. Some journals (e.g., *Journal of Applied Psychology*) require this information in the form of an Author Agreement. For the most part, the corresponding author signs attestations of authorship. Some journals may require signatures from all named authors.

Permission to Use Copyrighted Material

If your manuscript or supplemental resources include previously published text, tables, figures, or other materials, you must obtain permission from the copyright author(s). In your Permission to Use Copyrighted Materials statement, indicate which items you have acquired permission to use and how you have included proof of permission with your submission. If requested permissions are pending, include this information as well. Note any required permissions and the status of written permissions in your cover letter. Authors seeking publication in an APA journal must also submit a Permissions Alert Form (https://www.apa.org/pubs/authors/permissions-alert.pdf).

Other Declarations and Attestations

Journals may require other statements or declarations about ethical research and reporting standards. For example, *Psychological Science* requires authors to attest that all dependent and independent variables were included in the Methods section and that all excluded observations are noted and explained. Authors might also attest to compliance with submission instructions (e.g., deidentification of documents, adherence to page or word count limits, formatting conforms to APA standards).

Including Declarations and Attestations in Submission

Instructions for including declarations in the submission process vary across journals. Authors might post declarations into corresponding fields within the submission form. Journals may direct authors to include declarations on their title page, below the abstract, or as a separate page within the manuscript. In some cases, journals require the inclusion of declarations in more than one part of the submission (e.g., within the submission form and on the title page). Authors should include relevant declarations in their cover letter as well. Not all declarations or attestations will require a written response. Alternatively, you may be asked to attest to a set of bulleted statements by checking the associated box within the submission form.

In addition to declaration statements and other forms, journals published by the APA require authors to submit a *Certification of Compliance with APA Ethical Principles* form (https://www.apa.org/pubs/authors/ethics.pdf). This form addresses study approval, informed consent, care of animals, results reporting, authorship, and data sharing. All named authors are listed on the form, but only the corresponding author must sign it.

Suggesting and Excluding Reviewers

Authors may have the option to request that a particular peer reviewer be included or excluded from consideration for their manuscript. Excluding a reviewer might be beneficial if the reviewer is a competitor in the field or your viewpoints on the study topic are at odds. Communicate your request to the editor in the appropriate section of the submission form or within the cover letter. Provide a clear and concise rationale for your request. Alternatively, you may opt to suggest a specific reviewer for your work, especially if your research topic is not well-known or well-understood. If you suggest a reviewer, selecting someone active in the research community is advisable. Consider domestic and international candidates from all career levels. It is pertinent that the recommended reviewer is in no way affiliated with the named authors or with the work. Be clear and concise in your rationale for recommending the reviewer. Include information for contacting the recommended reviewer (e.g., name, institutional affiliation, and email address).

Editors are not required to use reviewers recommended by an author. However, if they do, it may help get your paper published. Kowalczuk et al. (2015) compared 800 reviewer reports for manuscripts submitted to medical journals. Reviewers suggested by authors were significantly more likely to recommend acceptance than reviewers selected by editors. Authors tend to recommend experts who are familiar with their study topic and recognize the importance of the study. Editors also seek reviewers with expertise relevant to the manuscript. However, experts chosen by the editor might be less interested in or even opposed to your specific paper's tenets (Schroter et al., 2006).

Cover Letters

A cover letter is the author's opportunity to summarize key aspects of their submission. Some journals require a cover letter. Even when not required, including a cover letter is highly advised (Welch, 2007). Use the cover letter to highlight how your study makes a fresh and meaningful contribution to the literature. The cover letter is also an opportunity to explain potential conflicts and issues of concern. See the APA Publication Manual (2020, Section 12.11) for guidance on what to include in a cover letter. Your selected journal may also stipulate statements or information to include. Sample cover letters are on the APA Style website (https://apastyle. apa.org).

Information to Include in a Cover Letter

Indicate the type of manuscript (e.g., case study, systematic review) you are submitting (Clever et al., 1997). State the title and list all named authors. Confirm that all named authors meet standards for authorship and agree to the journal's terms for publication. Provide contact information for the corresponding author. Some journals (e.g., *Behavior Modification*) require contact information for all named authors in the cover letter.

Describe the scientific value of your article and how it adds to the existing literature. Explain how your article aligns with the mission of the journal. Verify that all study tasks were conducted in accordance with ethical standards. Provide information on how this manuscript or any closely related material has been shared previously. For example, indicate if any part of this work has been submitted to this or other journals or shared on another platform (e.g., professional conference, Podcast). Inform the editor if your article is taken from a more extensive study and cite related manuscripts (Feldman, 2003).

Include the registration number or link for pre-registered studies. If you opted not to pre-register your study or registered after the fact, explain why. If your data are sharable, briefly state how data can be accessed (e.g., include the citation for your data set). List any supplementary materials. Inform the editor of the status of permissions for reproducing any copyrighted materials. Review any potential conflicts of interest. Identify funding sources (if applicable) and describe the funder's relationship to or role in the study. Include grant numbers. Explain any conflicts with required declarations and attestations. If you are asking to exclude or include specific peer reviewers, provide a rationale for your request. List any recommended reviewers with their full names and contact information.

Address your cover letter to the editor of the journal. It is usually sufficient for the corresponding author to sign the cover letter. Some journals require the signatures of all named authors. If the journal requires a cover letter, you will likely find a specified upload link within the submission form. Otherwise, include the cover letter in the optional or additional documents section.

Completing the Submission Process

Once you have collected all necessary information and confirmed that your manu-script is formatted to journal standards, you are ready to submit. Log into the system with your username and password. Select the "author" tab within the submission portal. The manuscript submission system will guide you through submitting infor-mation and uploading documents. Reference your checklist to ensure that one copy of each required document is included in the submission and uploaded in the correct order. Remember to save throughout.

Reviewing Your Proof

As a final step in the submission process, you may be given an opportunity to review a proof of your submission. The system will generate a .pdf document that includes all uploaded components of your manuscript in the order you submitted them. Cooper (2022) advises authors to review the proof carefully. Errors or omissions are easily corrected at this stage. Check for items you omitted from the submission or included more than once. Confirm manuscript components are ordered according to journal requirements. If you have forgotten to disable tracking in your document, a margin with editing notes will be evident. Return to the appropriate step in the sub-mission process for each error detected to make necessary adjustments or correc-tions. When editing a document, delete the file you initially submitted before uploading the edited version. Review the updated proof. Download the final version if the system allows it and save it for your records.

Confirming Receipt of Submission

After finalizing your submission, you should receive an automatically generated email confirming that your submission was received. The email will contain a link through which you can check the status of your submission. Contact the editor if you are still waiting to receive confirmation of your submission after three business days. Include the manuscript title and system-issued identifiers in all communica-tions (Johnson & Green, 2009). Ethical standards apply in the submission and pub-lication process as well. All correspondence between the author and the journal is confidential unless the parties have explicitly consented to share information.

Conclusion

For better or worse, the widespread adoption of digital editorial management systems has changed the manuscript submission process. Critics argue that rigidity within digital systems and variation across systems increase the likelihood of a manuscript being rejected prior to review. With proper preparation, authors are likely to find digital editorial management systems facilitate and streamline the manuscript submission process. Avoid common submission errors with pre-planning, organization, and attention to detail. Prepare by reviewing author resources specific to your selected journal and to the digital editorial system used by that journal. Use these resources to create a submission checklist. Note journal-specific formatting requirements and limitations on manuscript length. Confirm you have reported results consistent with journal standards (e.g., new statistics). Check journal guidelines for tables, figures, and supplementary materials. Ensure all required disclosures and attestations are included in your submission. Prepare a cover letter to convey essential information related to your submission. State your manuscript's unique contribution to the literature and highlight how it fits with the mission and values of the selected journal. Describe any potential conflicts or issues of concern.

Before initiating the digital editorial management process, review your submission requirements checklist. Verify that all elements of your submission are organized and according to author instructions. This will facilitate seamless submission and reduce the likelihood of immediate rejection related to missing or misfiled material. If the editorial management system generates a proof, take the time to review the proof before finalizing the submission. Errors are more easily addressed at this stage. If you encounter barriers to submission, do not be daunted! "To get to know, to discover, to publish (Arago, 1855) -this is the destiny of a scientist" (Mackay, 1977, p. 10).

References

Alter, G., & Gonzalez, R. (2018). Responsible practices for data sharing. *The American Psychologist, 73*(2), 146–156. https://doi.org/10.1037/amp0000258

American Psychological Association. (2020). *Publication manual of the American Psychological Association* (7th ed.). https://doi.org/10.1037/0000165-000

American Psychologist. (n.d.). https://www.apa.org/pubs/journals/amp

Analysis of Verbal Behavior. (n.d.). *Submission guidelines.* https://www.springer.com/journal/40616/submission-guidelines

Behavior Analysis in Practice. (n.d.). *Submission guidelines.* https://www.springer.com/journal/40617/submission-guidelines

Behavior Modification. (n.d.). *Submission guidelines.* https://journals.sagepub.com/author-instructions/BMO

Behavioral and Brain Sciences. (n.d.). *Author instructions.* https://www.cambridge.org/core/journals/behavioral-and-brain-sciences/information/author-instructions

Bordage, G. (2001). Reasons reviewers reject and accept manuscripts: The strengths and weaknesses in medical education reports. *Academic Medicine, 76*(9), 889–896.

Clever, L., Colaianni, L. A., Davidoff, F., Horton, R., & al, e. (1997). Uniform requirements for manuscripts submitted to biomedical journals. *The New England Journal of Medicine, 336*(4), 309–316. https://doi.org/10.1080/00313029700169515

Cooper, P. (2022). Proof before submission. *ECS Sensors Plus, 1*(3), 030001. https://doi.org/10.1149/2754-2726/ac865b

Crosas, M., Gautier, J., Karcher, S., Kirilova, D., Otalora, G., & Schwartz, A. (2018, March 30). *Data policies of highly-ranked social science journals.* https://doi.org/10.31235/osf.io/9h7ay

Dewidar, O., Elmestekawy, N., & Welch, V. (2022). Improving equity, diversity, and inclusion in academia. *Research Integrity and Peer Review, 7*(1), 1–4. https://doi.org/10.1186/s41073-022-00123-z

Ethical Principles of Psychologists and Code of Conduct. (2002). *American Psychologist, 57,* 1060–1073. https://doi.org/10.1037/0003-066X.57.12.1060

Feldman, D. C. (2003). When is a new submission "new"? *Journal of Management, 29*(2), 139–140.

Flowerdew, J. (2015). Some thoughts on English for Research Publication Purposes (ERPP) and related issues. *Language Teaching, 48*(2), 250–262. https://doi.org/10.1017/S0261444812000523

Ganz, P. A., Chen, R. C., & Boehm, A. L. (2022). Addressing diversity, equity, and inclusion at the JNCI journals. *Journal of the National Cancer Institute, 114*(9), 1207–1208. https://doi.org/10.1093/jnci/djac124

Giofrè, D., Cumming, G., Fresc, L., Boedker, I., & Tressoldi, P. (2017). The influence of journal submission guidelines on authors' reporting of statistics and use of open research practices. *PLoS One, 12*(4), e0175583–e0175583. https://doi.org/10.1371/journal.pone.0175583

Greener, S. (2018). Research limitations: The need for honesty and common sense. *Interactive Learning Environments, 26*(5), 567–568. https://doi.org/10.1080/10494820.2018.1486785

Hartley, J., & Cabanac, G. (2017). The delights, discomforts, and downright furies of the manuscript submission process. *Learned Publishing, 30*(2), 167–172. https://doi.org/10.1002/leap.1092

Hill, S., & Provost, F. (2003). The myth of the double-blind review? Author identification using only citations. *ACM SIGKDD Explorations Newsletter, 5*(2), 179–184. https://doi.org/10.1145/980972.981001

International Committee of Medical Journal Editors (ICMJE). (n.d.). *Defining the role of authors and contributors.* Retrieved March 20, 2023, from https://www.icmje.org/recommendations/browse/roles-and-responsibilities/defining-the-role-of-authors-and-contributors.html

Jeng, W., He, D., & Oh, J. S. (2016). Toward a conceptual framework for data sharing practices in social sciences: A profile approach. *Proceedings of the ASIST Annual Meeting, 53*(1), 1–10. https://doi.org/10.1002/pra2.2016.14505301037

Jiang, Y., Lerrigo, R., Ullah, A., Alagappan, M., Asch, S. M., Goodman, S. N., & Sinha, S. R. (2019). The high resource impact of reformatting requirements for scientific papers. *PLoS One, 14*(10), e0223976. https://doi.org/10.1371/journal.pone.0223976

Johnson, C. (2005). Transparency of research methods: Proud to be a naked emperor. *Journal of Manipulative and Physiological Therapeutics, 28*(6), 377–378. https://doi.org/10.1016/fjt2d2

Johnson, C., & Green, B. (2009). Submitting manuscripts to biomedical journals: Common errors and helpful solutions. *Journal of Manipulative and Physiological Therapeutics, 32*(1), 1–12. https://doi.org/10.1016/j.jmpt.2008.12.002

Journal of Applied Behavior Analysis. (n.d.). *Author guidelines.* https://onlinelibrary.wiley.com/page/journal/19383703/homepage/forauthors.html

Journal of Applied Psychology. (n.d.). https://www.apa.org/pubs/journals/apl

Journal of Contexual Behavioral Science. (n.d.). *Guide for authors.* https://www.elsevier.com/journals/journal-of-contextual-behavioral-science/2212-1447/guide-for-authors

Journal of the Experimental Analysis of Behavior. (n.d.). *Author guidelines*. https://onlinelibrary. wiley.com/page/journal/19383711/homepage/forauthors.html

Kapp, C., & Albertyn, R. (2008). Accepted or rejected: Editors' perspectives on common errors of authors. *Acta Academica, 40*(4), 270–288.

Kim, S., Choi, H., Kim, N., Chung, E., & Lee, J. Y. (2018). Comparative analysis of manuscript management systems for scholarly publishing. *Science Editing, 5*(2), 124–134. https://doi. org/10.6087/kcse.137

Kowalczuk, M. K., Dudbridge, F., Nanda, S., Harriman, S. L., Patel, J., & Moylan, E. C. (2015). Retrospective analysis of the quality of reports by author-suggested and non-author-suggested reviewers in journals operating on open or single-blind peer review models. *BMJ Open, 5*(9), e008707–e008707. https://doi.org/10.1136/bmjopen-2015-008707

Mackay, A. (1977). *The harvest of a quiet eye: A selection of scientific quotations*. Adam Hilger.

McKinley, J., & Rose, H. (2018). Conceptualizations of language errors, standards, norms and nativeness in English for research publication purposes: An analysis of journal submission guidelines. *Journal of Second Language Writing, 42*, 1–11. https://doi.org/10.1016/j. jslw.2018.07.003

Meyer, M. N. (2018). Practical tips for ethical data sharing. *Advances in Methods and Practices in Psychological Science, 1*(1), 131–144. https://doi.org/10.1177/2515245917746565

Mosteller, F., Nave, B., & Miech, E. J. (2004). Why we need a structured abstract in education research. *Educational Researcher, 33*(1), 29–34. https://doi.org/10.3102/0013189X033001029

Oh, H. (2020). A call for a more efficient submission process. *Publications, 8*(3), 40. https://doi. org/10.3390/publications8030040

Okike, K., Hug, K. T., Kocher, M. S., & Leopold, S. S. (2016). Single-blind vs double-blind peer review in the setting of author prestige. *JAMA: The Journal of the American Medical Association, 316*(12), 1315–1316. https://doi.org/10.1001/jama.2016.11014

Paltridge, B. (2020). Writing for academic journals in the digital era. *RELC Journal, 51*(1), 147–157. https://doi.org/10.1177/0033688219890359

Perspectives on Behavioral Science. (n.d.). *Submission guidelines*. https://www.springer.com/ journal/40614/submission-guidelines?gclid=Cj0KCQjwlPWgBhDHARIsAH2xdNeFgl6Sgen yuTyb8z96kohdj8RSvd6HyUr6f3rNP_PGDZZ0uBJDBFsaAn0wEALw_wcB

Psychological Methods. (n.d.). https://www.apa.org/pubs/journals/met

Psychological Science. (n.d.). *Submission guidelines*. https://journals.sagepub.com/ author-instructions/PSS

Ross, P. T., & Bibler Zaidi, N. L. (2019). Limited by our limitations. *Perspectives on Medical Education, 8*, 261–264. https://doi.org/10.1007/s40037-019-00530-x

Schroter, S., Tite, L., Hutchings, A., & Black, N. (2006). Differences in review quality and recommendations for publication between peer reviewers suggested by authors or by editors. *JAMA: The Journal of the American Medical Association, 295*(3), 314–317. https://doi.org/10.1001/ jama.295.3.314

Simons, D. J., Shoda, Y., & Lindsay, D. S. (2017). Constraints on Generality (COG): A proposed addition to all empirical papers. *Perspectives on Psychological Science, 12*(6), 1123–1128. https://doi.org/10.1177/1745691617708630

Teixeira da Silva, J. A. (2021). Multiple co-first authors, co-corresponding authors and co-supervisors: A synthesis of shared authorship credit. *Online Information Review, 45*(6), 1116–1130. https://doi.org/10.1108/OIR-06-2020-0219

The Psychological Record. (n.d.). *Submission guidelines*. https://www.springer.com/journal/40732/ submission-guidelines

Tomkins, A., Zhang, M., & Heavlin, W. D. (2017). Reviewer bias in single- versus double-blind peer review. *Proceedings of the National Academy of Sciences – PNAS, 114*(48), 12708–12713. https://doi.org/10.1073/pnas.1707323114

Tsai, A. C., Kohrt, B. A., Matthews, L. T., Betancourt, T. S., Lee, J. K., Papachristos, A. V., Weiser, S. D., &Dworkin, S. L. (2016). Promises and pitfalls of data sharing in qualitative research. *Social Science & Medicine, 169*, 191–198. https://doi.org/10.1016/j.socscimed.2016.08.004

Ware, M. (2005). Online submission and peer-review systems. *Learned Publishing, 18*(4), 245–250. https://doi.org/10.1087/095315105774648771

Welch, S. J. (2007). Avoiding common problems during online submission of manuscripts. *Chest, 131*(5), 1591–1594. https://doi.org/10.1378/chest.06-2906

Wilkinson, M., Dumontier, M., Aalbersberg, I., Appleton, G., Axton, M., Baak, A., Blomberg, N., Boiten, J., da Silva Santos, L., Bourne, P. E., Bouwman, J., Brookes, A. J., Clark, T., Crosas, M., Dillo, I., Dumon, O., Edmunds, S., Evelo, C. T., Finkers, R., et al. (2016). The FAIR guiding principles for scientific data management and stewardship. *Scientific Data, 3*, 160018. https://doi.org/10.1038/sdata.2016.18

Michelle A. Sereno, Ph.D., BCBA-D completed her Ph.D. in applied behavior analysis through the Chicago School of Professional Psychology. Dr. Sereno is passionate about applying ABA toward socially meaningful change for families experiencing abuse, trauma, and intimate partner violence (IPV). Her primary area of research is functional-contextual variables impacting victim-survivors of IPV, with a focus on problematic biases related to IPV evidenced by professionals.

Julianne DiCocco, Ph.D., BCBA-D completed her Ph.D. in applied behavior analysis through the Chicago School of Professional Psychology. Dr. DiCocco is an advocate and practitioner in public education, specifically working with at-promised youth and detained youth. Her research interests include mindfulness-based interventions, trauma-informed care, compassionate care, reducing recidivism for detained youth, and antecedent-based classroom behavioral interventions for problematic behavior.

Chapter 12
"Clearly Written by a Neophyte": Responding to Reviewer Feedback and Preparing Your Resubmission

Alexandra Hamilton, Jacqueline Huscroft-D'Angelo, and Sara W. Bharwani

Unlike MDs, PhDs have no Hippocratic Oath. There is no pledge to do no harm, and this oversight may be most apparent in reviewer feedback. Maybe words should not hurt, but "clearly written by a *neophyte*" was the only feedback I remember from my first attempt at publishing in a professional peer-reviewed journal. Ironically, I had to look up the word neophyte.

When it comes to professional writing no author can avoid being a neophyte. Moreover, if one intends to publish in peer-reviewed journals, no author can avoid learning to navigate the constructive, and sometimes not so constructive, feedback provided by our *blinded peers*. In this chapter, we will (1) pull back the curtain on reviewer feedback, revealing the strengths and limitations of the peer-review process, (2) describe what happens after you submit your manuscript for review for publication, (3) identify potential outcomes of your submission, (4) detail an approach for writing effective *response to reviewer letters*, and (5) provide a step-by-step process for resubmitting your manuscript. While we write this chapter from the collective perspective of three published authors across different career stages, each section includes individual experiences and insights we have learned along the way. Throughout, we share our lessons learned and conclude with concrete strategies for the next generation of behavioral researchers learning to navigate the professional writing process.

Before we discuss how to respond to peer reviews, it is important to understand the review process. As neophyte writers, we are typically taught very little about peer review or what happens after months, if not years, of effort are submitted into

A. Hamilton (✉) · J. Huscroft-D'Angelo
Oregon Research Institute, Springfield, OR, USA
e-mail: ahamilton@ori.org; jhuscroft@ori.org

S. W. Bharwani
University of Nebraska-Lincoln, Lincoln, NE, USA
e-mail: sara.bharwani@unl.edu

the ether. Looking back, I recall that after submission, I had assumed that my manuscript would quickly make it into the hands of my esteemed and experienced peers and that shortly I would receive notification that I had or had not written something that would make me a published author and contributor to the field.

Although my assumptions about the process were somewhat correct, with time I learned several lessons. First, while many journals aim to provide quick turnarounds, the process can take several months or even years, if multiple revisions are required. Occasionally, manuscripts are even lost in the submission queue, or overlooked due to editorial turnover. Typically, if you have not received feedback after three to four months (or the timeline outlined by the journal), an email query is warranted. A second lesson learned is that some peer reviewers are more skilled than others, and some are brand new to the peer review (and professional writing) process. Moreover, sometimes the reviewer knows little about the subject under review, and sometimes they are the researchers cited within. Finally, I learned that while most journals generally provide some guidelines as to what they expect from peer reviewers (and may have an internal scoring system for reviewers themselves that is only seen by the editorial board), there is no formal training on how to write a peer review, and no feedback is provided to the reviewers regarding the quality or efficacy of their feedback. As a result, while some reviewers provide clear and constructive feedback outlining limitations that should be addressed, others either provide limited constructive feedback and only approach your manuscript with a broad theoretical lens, or provide too much feedback critiquing every sentence, citation, and punctuation mark for readability, relevance, and APA style alignment. In short, reviewer feedback is opinion, not science.

Although incongruent feedback from reviewers can be frustrating, most reviewers will provide some helpful suggestions regarding how to strengthen your manuscript and the editor will often highlight the feedback across reviewers that will best increase your chances for acceptance for publication. As such, be open to the feedback and consider how you can edit your manuscript to improve both your current submission and your work moving forward. Your goal is not publication. Your goal is to ensure that your name is linked to quality work that will contribute to the field in a meaningful way.

What Happens After I Submit My Manuscript?

This section describes the events that occur after you submit your manuscript for review for publication. While journals may vary, the processes and timelines are relatively standardized within the field. Upon submission, we recommend that you look to see if the journal presents specific information that may help you determine when and how you should expect to receive feedback from the editor.

After you submit, you (and sometimes the coauthors) will receive an automated email from the journal's *editor* or *associate editors* verifying that your manuscript has been received. The editor and associate editors are typically either mid or late career, are considered experts in the journal's topic, and are typically nominated by their peers to serve in these roles. In most journals, it is a standard practice that the editor or associate editor will review the manuscript to ensure that it meets basic criteria (e.g., is complete and aligns with the journal submission requirements, aims, and scope) prior to sending it forward for review. If the manuscript does not meet basic criteria, the editor and/or associate editor will reject the manuscript (see "*desk rejection*" below) and will send a letter to the corresponding author informing them of this decision. Some journals also have the option of sending submissions to a different journal under the same publisher that may be in better alignment with the manuscript. However, if the manuscript is deemed appropriate to send forward for peer review, the editor will select one of the journal's associate editors (ideally an expert in the topic and methodology) to identify peer reviewers and complete the peer-review process.

Once an associate editor has been assigned, it is their job to identify, contact, and collect feedback from peer reviewers (typically two to three) who are familiar with the content area and available to provide a timely review. Peer reviewers are often identified via recommendations from the submitting authors, the journal's database of reviewers who are experts in the content area, or a search of the manuscript's cited authors. Although the goal is to quickly identify peer reviewers, this process can take several weeks and multiple emails to procure reviewers who are both willing and available. It is important to note that peer reviewers, associate editors, and editors are typically unpaid. Thus, although completing peer reviews has traditionally been viewed as an important part of "service" for the field, often other obligations are prioritized over review completion, which can delay the feedback process.

Peer reviewers are typically given three to six weeks to complete and return their review. When all reviews are submitted, the associate editor will consider the reviewers' comments and publication recommendations. The associate editor will also read the manuscript prior to writing the summary letter in which they will communicate a publication recommendation to the editor or make the final decision (depending on journal). This task is typically completed within two to four weeks after receiving all peer reviews. In behavioral journals, this complete process can take anywhere from three to nine months.

Possible Outcomes of Peer Review

After the review process is completed, the submitting author will receive an email from the editor or assistant editor with a subject line that typically includes the phrase "Decision on Manuscript." In addition to standard form letter information, the email will include an outcome decision (i.e., desk rejection, accept as is, rejection, accept with minor revisions, accept with major revisions, or revise and resubmit) and specific reviewer feedback. While the feedback is important for revising your manuscript, the outcome decision will help you determine your next steps towards publication.

Unfortunately, the quickest decisions generally come in the form of a desk rejection. A desk rejection, or desk reject, is when a manuscript is dismissed before being sent to reviewers. Desk rejections can happen for a variety of reasons such as misalignment between the manuscript and the journal's aims and scope, significant editorial errors (e.g., missing tables, poorly written), or methodological limitations. Most journals transparently share their aims and scope and provide specific information about what subjects the journal addresses, types of acceptable articles, and a description of the peer-review process. Articles may be rejected if they do not fit the journal's subject matter or if the submission does not align with the types of manuscripts accepted (e.g., a book review when the journal only accepts original, scientific manuscripts). Other reasons for desk rejections may include insufficient proofreading, significant errors in methodology, errant conclusions, or a lack of clarity. Below is an excerpt from a recent desk rejection (see Fig. 12.1). While the outcome was disappointing, we were heartened by the editor's kind comments and encouragement for us to seek publication elsewhere.

To avoid a desk rejection, we recommend authors familiarize themselves with the journal's aims and scope. If questions remain after reading the aims and scope, it is appropriate to contact the editor to determine if a subject matter or type of article aligns with the journal. Also, we recommend that you carefully proofread all parts of your manuscript (e.g., abstract, narrative, references, tables, figures) before sending it to a journal. If possible, have others review your work for grammatical errors, APA formatting, content, and coherency.

Dear Dr. Hope,

Thank you for submitting your manuscript for review for publication in the *Journal for Behavioral Research*. I have reviewed your manuscript and have decided to not move it forward. Although I see the value in what you are trying to do, I believe the current version of your manuscript isn't quite ready for peer review. Although I am sure that this decision is not one you were hoping to hear, I hope that you will find the feedback below helpful as you move forward with submission to a different journal.

In reviewing your manuscript, I offer the following:

- First, the front half of the manuscript does not align well to the second half. It is almost as if you are trying to cover too much in your literature review.
- Second, I would like to see more justification for your comparative case study approach. Why is that the best approach for your research questions?
- Third, your article reads a bit more like an evaluation report rather than an academic study. In particular, the fact that you have a recommendations section instead of a discussion at the end does not align with the style of this journal. It would be better to have a strong discussion where you contextualize your results in the wider academic literature.

Again, I know that a desk reject is a disappointing decision. I want to reiterate that I see the value in your study and encourage you to continue to revise this manuscript so that it can realize its full potential.

Fig. 12.1 Example editor response (excerpt) – desk reject

Desk rejects can occur within days of submission but may occur months after you submit. During this waiting period, you are not allowed to submit the same work to other journals as you typically will have made a commitment to the journal that your work is being shared exclusively with them.

If your manuscript avoids a desk rejection, you may receive an *"accept as is"* notification. This means the reviewers and the primary editor agree that your manuscript should be published, and no revisions are needed. In contrast, a manuscript might survive a desk rejection, but upon peer review, the manuscript is *rejected* by the journal. Although rejections can feel discouraging, a rejection from one journal does not necessarily mean that the manuscript should not be submitted for publication elsewhere. A rejection may just mean that the manuscript is not a good match for the journal. We recommend that you carefully consider the reviewers' comments to determine if your manuscript was rejected due to a mismatch to the journal's focus, an unearthing of a fatal flaw in the study, or to factors that can be addressed with revision. Unless the reviewers identify a fatal flaw, it is not uncommon to publish a manuscript that has been previously rejected. If a fatal flaw is identified, we encourage you to consider the feedback as an important lesson learned and use it to better guide your study design moving forward.

If the journal editor determines that your manuscript should be *accepted with minor revisions*, this indicates that your manuscript's acceptance is contingent on editing your paper to conform to their corrections. In a recent submission, we received this designation with feedback indicating that while the manuscript was well-written, it contained many colloquial American phrases that should be eliminated so the journal's international audience would have a higher likelihood of understanding the content in its entirety (see Fig. 12.2). Journals may differ on their protocols, but generally, the editor reviews your revised manuscript to ensure the changes were made and does not need to go back out for a second round of peer review.

This case study is well written and engaging to read, but it needs to be made applicable to more readers. Remember our readership is global and some readers will have English as an additional language. I don't think this will require a great deal of work, and the authors write so well that I have made very few notes on the manuscript; I think they will be able to apply these suggestions. [reviewer listed 7 items]

You will also need to give your finished case study a thorough proof-read – do not leave this to the automatic spell checker as there are some errors it won't pick up. Here's one: "...empathy is an important component. One never knows that is truly happening with another person..." I am sure that is not the impression you wished to convey!

I hope this long list of suggestions isn't too discouraging. I honestly don't think any of them will take much time to implement, and I do think that, overall, your case study is a really useful, warts-and-all account which will be of value to many readers.

Fig. 12.2 Example editor response (excerpt) – accept with minor revisions

Alternatively, you may learn that your article has been *accepted with major revisions*, which is still a positive outcome, although less commonly used across journals. This conditional acceptance is predicated upon making significant changes to your work, which will be outlined by the reviewers. Major revisions may include incomplete literature reviews, substantive data errors, the main components of the article being unclear, or the subject matter being too narrow for the readership. If you can adequately address the concerns of the reviewers, your article will be re-sent to peer review (to the same reviewers, if possible) for another round of examination. Typically, a manuscript does not go through more than two rounds of peer review, but some journals may require additional reviews if concerns regarding the revisions remain.

You may also receive notification that you can *revise and resubmit* your manuscript. This is one of the most common initial outcomes for many manuscript submissions, even among seasoned authors. A revise and resubmit means that the article has not been accepted for publication by the journal, but the editor will consider a revised version of the manuscript should you opt to address the reviewer and editor recommendations and resubmit for additional review. Revisions often involve a significant overhaul of the manuscript to address the editor's and reviewers' comments, and in some cases, the changes requested may not be feasible or may be misaligned with the intention of the study. Thus, dependent on the scope and type of edits requested, you may decide to pass on this option and submit the manuscript to a different journal. Regardless, it is generally beneficial to carefully consider the feedback provided by the peer reviewers and editor as there may be some suggestions you want to consider as you move forward in your pursuit of publication.

Responding to Peer Reviews

After you have carefully read your feedback and decision letter and have decided that it makes sense for you to proceed with a resubmission, it is time to make edits and craft an effective response to reviewer letter. As with writing a peer review, there are no set rules for responding to reviewer feedback. However, there are several strategies most authors use for successful resubmissions. Before you begin, we recommend that you first review and make note of the resubmission timeline. This timeline is the date provided by the editor on your decision letter that dictates when you need to have the edits completed and the manuscript resubmitted for further consideration. If you are the corresponding author, it is your responsibility to make sure that this deadline is met. If missed, you will be required to restart the submission process. If you believe you will be unable to meet the deadline, we recommend you email the corresponding editor to request an extension.

Step two is to read through the email from the editor and identify the *resubmission format*. Journals vary as to the required resubmission format and mode for documenting changes. Many journals require that you submit a new clean document and describe all edits made in the response to reviewer letter. However, other journals may prefer that you use track changes or highlighting to indicate edits made. It is important to be responsive to the journal's designated format as there is a possibility your resubmission could be returned if you fail to adhere, further delaying your publication timeline.

Once these initial steps are completed, you are ready to begin making decisions related to addressing reviewer feedback. In this process, you will want to reread the feedback provided by the reviewers and editor. As you reread, think about who may need to assist with the edits and the amount of time and effort needed to appropriately respond to the queries and concerns. For example, if there are multiple authors on the manuscript, will the edits require their input? If so, in which ways? If the reviewers identify significant concerns with the writing of the manuscript, will you need to identify an external source to assist with the writing mechanics? Similarly, begin to identify the edits that can be easily addressed, and those that will require more substantial time and effort. In some cases, there are edits that you are unable (or unwilling) to address given the scope of the manuscript or the available data. These factors are important to consider as you lay out your general response approach and anticipated timeline.

You will also need to notify other coauthors of the resubmission deadline, edit timeline, format for documenting edits, and task allocation. If coauthors will be responsible for responding to certain sections and need to prepare a response to reviewers, communicate this information and collaboratively identify a suitable timeline for completion. Clearly identify how documents need to be prepared (e.g., track changes, highlights, clean document with notes of specific edits for the response letter), what method you will use to work in a shared document (e.g., One Drive, Google Docs), and how you will label the most recent edits (we suggest using time and date) to ensure that conflicting documents are not created and that all authors are working on the most recent version.

After you identify who is needed for the response, your timeline, and how to proceed, it is time to begin to address the reviewer feedback. As a rule of thumb, it is best to address all feedback provided by each of the reviewers and the editor, if provided. You will also want to begin your response letter with a thank you to the editor and reviewers for their time and feedback and acknowledge how the feedback has assisted in improving the manuscript submitted for publication. Use headings and respond to feedback by reviewer so that it is clear which review you are responding to. We also recommend that you copy and paste each reviewer comment, suggestion, query, or concern into your letter and type out your response below. When appropriate, include the page number indicating where edits were made. Figure 12.3 provides an example of a response letter and the opening paragraph. Note that the author begins with a sentence of appreciation, identifies how the feedback was addressed, and concludes with future intentions.

Finally, as noted above, the feedback you receive from peer reviewers varies. Generally, the feedback is straightforward and easy to address. However, there are instances in which you may be irritated, offended, or confused by reviewer comments. Following are several examples of more challenging feedback, and suggested response recommendations:

Dear Dr. Smith,

Please accept the enclosed resubmission of the manuscript, "Parent Engagement in Special Education Programming", for review for possible publication in *Parents in Education*. We appreciate the opportunity to resubmit this manuscript and hope with this revision we are getting closer to a final decision. This letter explicitly outlines the changes that have been made and we have highlighted all edits in the resubmitted main document.

Reviewer(s)' Comments to Author:

Reviewer 1

Add a complete list of parent/child characteristics variables in Methods section. Also, the demographic variables are different for parents and for youth.
  - We appreciate this need for clarification. We have rewritten this section (see page 9, paragraph 2 and 3) to reflect that our intentions to gather both demographic items specific to parents and items specific to their child's special education status.

In the Methods, the author(s) note that they report relative risk ratios, however, the interpretation of the relative risk ratios needs an explanation for readers who may be unfamiliar with this approach.
  - We have added text to describe how relative risk ratios can be interpreted as a percent increase in probability (page 11).

Reviewer 2

Several references in the introduction are dated (e.g., Mouse et al., 2009; Carter, Smith, & Lorenzo, 2006).
  - We have revised the introduction to ensure that the references are more reflective of the recent literature on parent engagement (pages 2-5).

Page 4, line 51 – consider rewording from "not often" to say "this has rarely been…" to avoid the double negative.
  - We appreciate this feedback and have revised the sentence accordingly.

Page 6, paragraph beginning with "Given many parents of student with…" This sentence and the third one in this paragraph feel redundant from the preceding paragraphs. I suggest revising these sentences and merging the fourth sentence in this paragraph, which begins with "Similarly, … ", to reduce redundancy.
  - We have revised pages 6 and 7 as suggested to eliminate redundancy and more clearly streamline the introduction

Fig. 12.3 Example response letter (excerpt)

- Scenario A: The reviewer or editor requests content that is already provided in the manuscript (e.g., demographic information, IRB approval information). Recommended response: politely note the page number in which the information can be found in your response letter and/or edit slightly to add clarity. We often use the phrase, "additional narrative was added to clarify." Even if this is a bit of a stretch, we find that it more advantageous to provide an innocuous response than to offend the reviewer for their oversight. Recall, peer review is an unpaid task and oversights will occur.

- Scenario B: You strongly disagree with a reviewer's feedback (e.g., different theoretical approach). Recommended response: again, we recommend that you courteously address the reviewer concerns and acknowledge that there may be varying approaches that align. However, if you believe your approach is in better alignment with your study, we recommend you provide a concise rationale and supporting references (if appropriate) in your response letter.
- Scenario C: You are unable to address a reviewer's recommendation or query (e.g., data are unavailable to answer a query about the sample). Recommended response: in your response letter respectfully note why you are unable to address the query and acknowledge the contribution that that additional information would have provided. If appropriate, you may also want to address the limitation in the manuscript's "limitations" or "recommendations for future research" sections.
- Scenario D: Two or more reviewers provide contradictory recommendations that the editor has not addressed in the letter. Recommended response: reach out to the editor for clarity or direction.
- Scenario E: The reviewer provides unkind, but possibly true, feedback (e.g., this manuscript was clearly written by a neophyte). In this case, we strongly recommend that you (1) do not acknowledge the feedback at all in your response letter and (2) absolutely remember the feedback throughout your professional career and repurpose the observation as a snarky little title for a book chapter on the topic of responding to reviewer feedback in professional writing.

Resubmitting Your Revised Manuscript

Now that you have completed your revisions and response letter, it is time to resubmit your updated manuscript and supporting documents. I write this section as one who has been through the resubmission process more times that I can remember. However, while there have been many resubmissions throughout my career, my first experience was the most memorable. During my doctoral training one of my advisors forwarded me the editor email with the reviewer input and directions, "Please prepare this resubmission and send it back to me in two weeks." I stared at my computer thinking I have no idea what this even means. I was in the second semester of my doctoral program, and was not prepared for the revisions or the additional tasks that come with the resubmission process. This section provides a step-by-step tutorial of the resubmission process - something I wish would have been provided to me when I first began manuscript writing and journal submissions.

Initially, you will prepare a *revised cover letter* and response to reviewer letter. Indicate in the cover letter that the manuscript is a resubmission. The cover is different than the response to reviewer letter. The cover letter should be short and convey something along the lines of, "Please accept the enclosed revised manuscript, *Getting an Article Published* for review for possible publication in the Journal of Publishing in Behavioral Sciences. The manuscript reflects original work that has not been submitted nor published elsewhere. All authors agree to the submission of the manuscript to the Journal of Publishing in Behavioral Sciences. Please contact me if you have questions or need additional information. Thank you for consideration of our revised manuscript."

As described in section three, your response to reviewer letter should be clear, concise, and address all reviewer concerns. We also recommend writing the letter in a neutral tone. Once you have both letters prepared, be sure to label them accurately and place them in a resubmission folder.

Next, prepare the remaining *resubmission documents* (see Fig. 12.4). All revised documents should be properly labeled in your shared folder. In some cases, the journal will require uploading both the original manuscript submission and the revised version. We recommend clearly labeling the original and revised documents and note the document titles in your revised cover letter to the editor. If your documents are not easily discernable, this mistake could result in a new submission instead of a resubmit. Double check all documents before proceeding to the final steps.

Once you have prepared the required documents, it is time to upload and resubmit. To upload, you will need to access the electronic system used by the journal. We recommend that you keep your login information for each journal stored in an easily accessible document. Once you are in the submission portal, the process appears similar to the original submission, but you must select "start resubmission process" versus "start new submission". Once you have selected the option to resubmit, you will be directed through a series of steps. There will likely be many sections already completed based on the contents you submitted for the original submission. Carefully upload revised files to the portal and order your documents according to the preference of the journal.

Upon checking that all materials have been uploaded correctly, you will review the HTML and PDF submission *proofs* (see Fig. 12.5). This is a critical step in the resubmission process and is one of the final steps in the electronic system. Be sure that you review both the PDF and the HTML proofs. Many systems will not let you

> — Cover letter to the editor
> — Response to reviewer letter
> — Title page
> — Abstract page
> — Revised manuscript (prepared in accordance to journal/editor expectations)
> — References
> — Tables
> — Figures/figure legends
> — Charts/graphics
> — Acknowledgements (if applicable)
> — Author biographies (if applicable)

Fig. 12.4 Commonly required documents for resubmissions

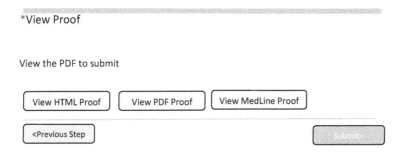

Fig. 12.5 Reviewing proofs

proceed until both have been viewed. Verify that all correct files were integrated into the combined document and read each proof carefully. Allow yourself enough time to go through the entire PDF and HTML documents to ensure there are no errors. If you do notice errors, this is your opportunity to make corrections. We strongly recommend taking your time with this stage of the resubmission.

Your final step in the process is to resubmit. You should receive a resubmission confirmation email from the editor within 30 min of submitting your revisions. We recommend that you inform your coauthors that the manuscript and associated materials have been resubmitted and forward all final copies. As a courtesy, you can also include the citation for your team members' curricula vitae.

Summary

The response to reviewer and article resubmission process requires organization, time, and attention to details. It is important to understand the entire resubmission process, including strategies for being responsive to peer reviews and writing effective letters to increase your likelihood for acceptance for publication. As there are no evidence-based approaches for manuscript resubmissions, the strategies presented in this chapter are based on our collective experiences and lessons learned. As such, we encourage you to submit manuscripts that have been carefully and thoroughly edited, select journals that align with your topic and type of submission, be open to and consider all feedback from reviewers as potentially relevant to your current and future submissions, show grace in your response letters and address all feedback systematically and respectfully, and take your time to carefully read and follow the resubmission process outlined by the journal. Although the peer-review process may not always result in helpful feedback or the outcome you desire, the intention is to strengthen the potential contribution of your manuscript to the field. If viewed in this light, even challenging feedback may provide valuable information you can use to hone your skills as you continue to develop as an author.

We conclude with a quick reference checklist to guide you through the process (see Fig. 12.6). Best of luck on your journey, be patient with the resubmission process, and happy writing!

Resubmission Checklist
☐ Identify resubmission date.
☐ Contact editor if the resubmission date is not attainable.
☐ Identify the resubmission format.
☐ Notify additional authors of resubmission timeline and format.
☐ Establish a plan for who will be responsible for completing identified sections of the resubmission.
☐ Gather and review all resubmission materials.
☐ Write a revised cover letter to the editor.
☐ Write a response to reviewer letter (include page numbers and specific revision information).
☐ Clearly label all revised materials.
☐ Access journal manuscript submission portal (e.g., Elsevier, Sage, Scholar One, Taylor & Francis, etc.).
☐ Upload all resubmission materials (double check accuracy).
☐ Download and preview submission HTML and PDF proofs.
☐ Make any necessary edits upon reviewing proofs.
☐ Submit revised manuscript and associated documents.
☐ Check for resubmission confirmation email.
☐ Communicate with team that the resubmission was successful and include a revised copy of the manuscript and associated documents.

Fig. 12.6 Resubmission checklist

Acknowledgements This work was supported by Grant number R324B160033 from the U.S. Department of Education, Institute for Education Science and Grant number U411C220201 from the U.S. Department of Education, Office of Elementary and Secondary Education. The statements in this chapter do not necessarily represent the views of the U.S. Department of Education.

Alexandra Hamilton, PhD, is a senior scientist at the Oregon Research Institute. She earned her MA in psychology and PhD in emotional and behavioral disorders at the University of Nebraska–Lincoln. Her work focuses on the development and evaluation of educational, social/emotional, and health literacy interventions for students with or at-risk for disabilities served across the continuum of care.

Jacqueline Huscroft-D'Angelo, PhD, is a research scientist at the Oregon Research Institute. Dr. Huscroft-D'Angelo's research focuses on developing and evaluating interventions to address the educational needs of students with or at-risk of emotional/behavioral disorders and those in out-of-home care settings. Her work focuses on improving educational outcomes and health literacy, parental involvement in school and understanding of special education, and professional development for educators working with these students. This includes exploration, development, efficacy, and program evaluation studies.

Sara W. Bharwani, EdD, is a postdoctoral research associate at the University of Nebraska–Lincoln and an assistant clinical professor in the department of medical humanities at Creighton University. She earned her MA in international relations and EdD in interdisciplinary leadership from Creighton University in Omaha, Nebraska. Her interests include child welfare, social determinants of health, and medical education.

Chapter 13
Now Your Manuscript Is Accepted… What's Next?

Yors Garcia, Amanda Muñoz-Martínez, Meredith Andrews, and Estefanía Junca

Historically, scientists have avoided publicizing their own work in favor of letting its merit speak (passively) for itself. Yet, even if a behavioral researcher publishes in a high-impact, esteemed journal, their scholarly work will have little to no effect if few people know about their article. The common strategy previously used by researchers to disseminate their work after publication consisted of presenting at national and international conferences, seminars, workshops, and in formal and informal meetings. However, in the past two decades, the scholarly communication landscape has changed with an increasing popularization of web-based technologies that go beyond print material, academic journals, and conference presentations (Ashcraft et al., 2020; McHugh & Barlow, 2010). These new communication technologies include but not limited to academic social networks, blogs, social media websites, personal websites, podcasts, and video clips (Hardman et al., 2020; Jordan, 2019). Some direct benefits of using web-based technologies are the quick dissemination of research and the broad scope of potential users such as clinicians, clients, researchers, and policy makers. These alternative channels of dissemination allow sharing of pre-prints (i.e., early views of accepted papers for publication) which provide the potential for implementation ahead of the final publication. They also allow sharing of post-prints, which provide an opportunity for receiving

Y. Garcia (✉) · E. Junca
Psychology Department, Pontificia Universidad Javeriana, Bogotá, Colombia
e-mail: yors.garcia01@javeriana.edu.co; estefania_juncaa@javeriana.edu.co

A. Muñoz-Martínez
Psychology Department, Universidad de los Andes, Bogotá, Colombia
e-mail: am.munozm@uniandes.edu.co

M. Andrews
Behavior Analysis Department, College of Graduate and Professional Studies,
The Chicago School, Chicago, IL, USA
e-mail: mandrews2@thechicagoschool.edu

© The Author(s), under exclusive license to Springer Nature Switzerland AG 2023   221
A. K. Griffith, T. C. Ré (eds.), *Disseminating Behavioral Research*,
https://doi.org/10.1007/978-3-031-47343-2_13

feedback on publications that are already accepted in academic journals (Brownson et al., 2018; Divecha et al., 2021).

An expanding movement known as *open science* contends that all research should be made publicly available to be transparent and reproducible (Chakravorty et al., 2022; Norris & O'Connor, 2019). The core elements of open science are open access, open data, open source, and open standards, which allow for the unrestricted dissemination of scientific discourse (Chakravorty et al., 2022). Citation counts, h-index, and journal impact factors are the most common metrics to estimate researchers' impact on their field or discipline. The open science movement brings new possibilities for behavioral researchers to measure their academic impact and promote their research beyond traditional dissemination strategies. In this new era of producing and disseminating academic work, scholarly communication does not end with a paper publication. Rather, publication is just the beginning of dissemination to broader audiences. Despite the rapid emergence of new web-based technologies and open science, there are few guidelines available to behavioral researchers to disseminate their work. The goal of this chapter, then, is to provide authors and behavioral researchers with a set of specific guidelines to disseminate their research after it has been published in an academic journal. In the following sections, we describe seven key strategies to promote scientific research after its publication: signing the contractual agreements, knowing your audiences, providing research summaries, identifying channels for dissemination, sharing your data, publicizing your research, and tracking your research paper.

Dissemination Strategies After Publication

Sign the Contractual Agreements

Receiving an email from a journal editor stating that your paper has been accepted for publication is one of the most rewarding moments in research activity. However, the publication process does not end there. Research articles published in academic journals are subject to copyrights and various licensing agreements. Thus, upon acceptance, as an author, you will have to sign an author agreement or copyright transfer agreement. This is a legal agreement, that can be negotiated between an author and the journal publisher, outlining exactly what you can and cannot do with your article once it is published (Yelamanchi et al., 2022). Although authors initially own all the copyrights to their work, many publishers require authors to transfer their rights before a research paper is published. Authors can and may lose the right to use and share their work depending on the type of agreement they sign. Therefore, before signing a licensing agreement, consider the potential uses you may want to make with your own work such as teaching, conference presentations, pre-prints, post-prints, institutional repository, personal website, subject archive (e.g., arXiv), or social network site (e.g., ResearchGate). In sum, when negotiating license agreements with publishers, authors and researchers should be cautious and aware of their rights to prevent unlawful use of their original work and avoid needless legal problems.

After you have completed the licensing agreement, then your paper goes into production for final checking, reformatting, and proofreading. Once those changes have been made by the journal's editorial office, you can decide to publish the paper as either open access or restricted access. *Open Access* means there are no financial, legal, or technical barriers in accessing published papers, while *restricted access,* or *pay-for-view,* allows access to a single research paper or full journal only after you have paid a fee. It is important to add that readers or researchers can access the article either through direct payment via the journal website or the library institution than can make the article available to its members. Remember, these types of access are agreed upon in the licensing agreement. Once the contractual agreements are signed, there are a few additional steps we recommend taking before you make your research public. The first is considering your target audiences.

Know Your Audiences

Identifying your target audiences does not end when writing your manuscript. Rather, it is an ongoing process. Knowing your audiences will play a role in determining which channels you use to disseminate your work and how you will present your research through those channels (Brownson et al., 2018). Consider the diverse populations who may be interested in your work. They are more than the obvious choice (e.g., policymakers, client groups, administrators, non-governmental organizations; Kelly et al., 2019; Ross-Hellauer et al., 2020). This is true now more than ever considering there is an initiative in the science community to increase the general populations' involvement in science (Bauer & Falade, 2014; Stilgoe et al., 2014).

Generally, there are two types of audiences. The *non-academic audience* consists of groups who can affect or be affected by your research. For example, parents, clients, employees, policymakers, etc. Ask yourself what they care about, how they might access your research, and what barriers they face in obtaining access (National Institute for Health and Care Research, 2019). Then, use a variety of dissemination strategies (such as those to follow) to reach and spark interest in the different groups.

The other main type of audience is the *academic audience* (e.g., behavior analysts, clinical psychologists, social workers, physicians). Disseminating your work to these groups requires different strategies than those you use with the non-academic audience. For instance, academic audiences are more likely to contact your paper directly, so choose the open access option for publication whenever possible. Open access has become one of the primary ways to increase research impact, expand visibility of your work, attract citations, and make science more inclusive (Chakravorty et al., 2022). Another efficient way to target this audience is to update your curriculum vitae (CV) with hyperlinks that lead interested groups to your publications (Divecha et al., 2021; Hardman et al., 2020).

Provide Research Summaries

After you have considered your audiences, provide summaries of your work that are tailored to your diverse groups and the various channels through which you plan to reach them. Your audiences are likely broad so write summaries that promote diversity and inclusion (Ross-Hellauer et al., 2020). For instance, consider whether your summaries are respectful of various cultural, ideological, and economical backgrounds (to name only a few).

Lay summaries are a powerful way to reach multiple populations, so use everyday language that anyone can understand (Hardman et al., 2020; Ross-Hellauer et al., 2020). Avoid jargon and give simple explanations of any technical language you must use. Keep your written explanations concise and use an active, first-person voice. For example, use phrases like "we agreed" rather than "it was agreed upon by the authors." Similarly, follow a logical order by presenting a broad overview of your topic then gradually add specifics. Consider that the logical order may not always follow the temporal order of your study.

In addition to your writing style, there are a few key elements to include in a summary. First, offer a rationale for your research. In other words, describe why your research is important. Second, provide the context and background for your work. What is and is not known about your area of study and what prompted you to conduct your research? Third, give a brief description of the methodology. This is important for your research to have a strong impact, especially with an academic audience. Fourth, describe the impact of your work. How is your contribution to science going to change society? Lastly, include a visual. Visuals go beyond a graph of your data. There are various forms of multimedia including video abstracts, slides, flowcharts, infographics, or art interpretations of your results (Hardman et al., 2020; Ross-Hellauer et al., 2020; Spicer, 2014). Get creative!

Identify Channels for Dissemination

The next steps in disseminating your research using web-based technologies are obtaining a researcher ID and finding the right social network for your work. A researcher ID consists of a permanent numerical code assigned to a researcher. Creating a researcher profile improves discoverability of your work, resolves name ambiguities across academic bibliographies and repositories, promotes networking and collaboration, and boosts research impact (Brownson et al., 2018; Craft, 2020). These identifiers stay with you throughout your career regardless of changes in name or affiliation. Some identifiers to help distinguish your publications are Open Researcher and Contributor ID (ORCID), ResearchID, Scopus Author ID, PubMed ID, Google Scholar ID, and arXiv ID (Craft, 2020).

ORCID is a widely accepted unique identifier for authors. It is a simple numerical identifier (e.g., 0000-0002-8868-0682) that can be used by editors, funding agencies, publishers, and institutions to reliably identify researchers (Bohannon & Doran, 2017). ResearcherID makes connections between you and your publications throughout the Web of Science ecosystem (e.g., Publons, InCites) and provides a useful information index within the global academic community. Scopus Author ID is an identifier automatically generated for you once your paper is indexed in the Scopus database. arXiv is an open access pre-print and post-print repository website that provides an arXiV ID and tracks authors as they submit research to this server for peer feedback and sharing. Similarly, PubMed ID and Google Scholar ID are identifiers associated with their respective research repositories (Singh et al., 2021).

Once you have obtained a unique researcher ID, consider how you will use web-based technologies to share your research summaries, data, and published papers. Some channels to promote your research can include brief presentations, webinars, or podcasts using video sharing websites such as YouTube® or Vimeo®. An important recommendation is to keep it short and add it to your Twitter®, Facebook®, or LinkedIn® accounts (see Klar et al., 2020; Smith, 2020 for additional recommendations). If you want to summarize and disseminate your work in other languages, Google Translate might be a good option (Hardman et al., 2020).

We also recommend that behavioral researchers and authors create an academic social network to share their scholarly work. These are similar to social networking sites but are designed for the academic community (Jordan, 2019). Two popular academic social networks are ResearchGate and Academia.edu, each with minor differences (see Manca, 2018). Both websites assist you in sharing your publications, connecting with colleagues, seeking new collaborations, obtaining statistics on peoples' engagement with your publications, and asking questions to researchers around the world who share your interests (Yan et al., 2021). As a reminder, be sure to check your copyright restrictions before sharing your work on any social networking site.

Share Your Data

Perhaps one of the most important ways to use web-based technologies for dissemination is to share your data. Data sharing involves complying with ethical principles and your contractual agreements. We recommend using the FAIR principles when making data available, namely, findability, accessibility, interoperability, and reusability (see Wilkinson et al., 2016 for more details).

Sharing your research data using social network sites aids in your work being accessible by wider audiences, making it easier for others to evaluate, validate, and replicate. In addition, it increases the likelihood your research will be cited and ensures long-term preservation of data for future researchers. Sharing your data does not start after the paper has been published. This process begins from the very moment you pre-register your study (Martone et al., 2018). In this section, however, we will show you some alternative strategies to share your data after your paper has been accepted for publication.

Data sharing and storage can also be accomplished using a *digital repository*. A digital repository is a mechanism for managing and storing digital content and can be service- or institutional-based. Service-based repositories preserve data outside of an institution's control which allows for flexibility and openness for other researchers, while institutional repositories limit open access, discovery, and reuse (Amorim et al., 2017). Researchers can also select a repository based on the type of architecture (e.g., storage location, maintenance costs), metadata (e.g., data validation/curation, data preservation schemas), and dissemination that involves repository facilitation for data visibility and reuse.

We recommend four popular repositories. Open Science Framework (OSF) is a digital platform built and maintained by the Center for Open Science, a nonprofit organization. OSF is a free, open-source, and long-term preservation digital repository that allows you to store records of your research (from planning to pre-prints), collaborate with other researchers through a project's research workflow documentation (posting activity dates), archive digital research materials, share pre-prints, and submit materials in any format and links them to third-party storage add-ons. OSF also stores data privately until you decide to make it public. Finally, OSF provides a hyperlink to the authors' profiles where social, employment, education, and other project information is available (Martone et al., 2018).

Figshare and Mendeley are two other open access digital repositories that focus exclusively on data preservation and have an integration feature with OSF. Both repositories have similar architecture to preserve datasets, images, and videos in any format. They also allow for *data embargo* (i.e., sharing data privately between researchers) and automatically create a *digital object identifier* (DOI) for citations. Dataset submissions vary between these two platforms. Mendeley only permits for direct datasets to be uploaded within the platform, whereas Figshare permits direct dataset submissions as well as integration with third-party repositories of source codes such as GitHub, GitLab, and BitBucket.

Dryad is another non-profit digital repository that specializes in long-term data preservation. However, there is a fee for submitting data into Dryad, except for researchers who have an institutional membership or are based in low- to middle-income countries. Dryad provides a "good data practices" guideline in which data presentation schemas are described. They also have a *data curation* team who ensures metadata and files meet validity and quality requirements. Dryad allows you to store data from any stage of the research's lifecycle. Authors can save other related works such as pre-prints, articles, supplemental information, and so forth in external servers. They can also track their data dissemination through a metrics section that provides information on views, downloads, and citations. Each of these four repositories allow you to track interest in your research paper by the professional and non-professional community.

Publicize Your Research

Thus far we have described considerations when signing contractual agreements, identification of target audiences and channels to reach them, and strategies for sharing your research summaries and data. The next step in disseminating your scholarly work is publicizing your paper. Publicizing your research means distributing complex scientific or technical information to academic and non-academic audiences. This is successfully done by creating a brand for yourself as a researcher and marketing your research (Ashcraft et al., 2020, Kreuter & Bernhardt, 2009; Ross-Hellauer et al., 2020). For instance, you may wish to build a website to advertise your publications and research interest or curate a consistent digital identity (e.g., ORCID ID, ResearchID, Google Scholar ID). Also, use personal and academic social networks (e.g., Facebook®, LinkedIn®, ResearchGate, Academica.edu) to share your research summaries, data, and papers. Getting your paper published is not enough. In fact, the most important work begins after your paper is accepted for publication. That is, spreading your findings across the globe.

Track Your Research Paper

One final step remains in the dissemination process, which is to check how much impact and interest your paper attracts. Tracking interest in your academic work is important because it allows you to learn which authors and institutions are using your work and how your work is being used. This can assist you in identifying similar research projects and future collaborators. Tracking your interest in your paper can also help you determine if your research findings are duplicated, confirmed, corrected, improved, or extended with different populations. In the following paragraphs, we present four of the most common web-based technologies to track interest in your paper, Altmetric, Plum Analytics, OurResearch, and ResearchGate (Ortega, 2018; Yang et al., 2021).

Altmetric is a web-based service that allows anyone to track, search, and measure online conversations about their research on an article-by-article basis. An alternative to this platform is Altmetric bookmarklet, which is a free browser plug-in that allows you to pull up Altmetric data on articles as you access them in your browser. An additional technology for tracking views and interest in your paper is Plum Analytics. This web-based service aids you in tracking the ways people interact with individual pieces of your research dissemination like research papers, conference proceedings, book chapters, and more. Lastly, OurResearch and ResearchGate are platforms that assist researchers in evaluating the effects of the products of their research, such as journal articles, blogs, datasets, and software.

Figure 13.1 displays a summary of the steps described in this chapter that an author or behavioral researcher may take after their paper has been published. Impactful research relies on more than publishing innovative ideas. It also depends

General steps after paper publication

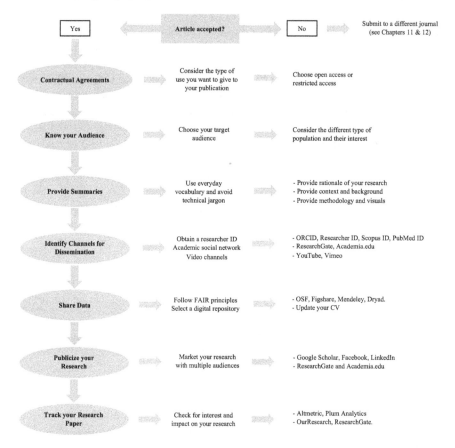

Fig. 13.1 General steps after paper publication

on effective disseminating to global audiences who may be interested in your work. Traditionally, researchers simply published their scholarly works and relied on citations to assess the impact and interest in their work. However, in recent years, we gained open science and web-based technologies that help make science accessible to academic and non-academic audiences alike.

Conclusions

The purpose of this chapter is to offer novel and seasoned behavioral researchers a set of guidelines and steps that will help them effectively share their academic work after publication. Just two decades ago researchers had a limited number of options to disseminate their academic work after publication. However, with the emergence of web-based technologies and the open science movement, scientists now have many alternatives in sharing their works with broader audiences. Data sharing, academic social networks, digital repositories, video sharing websites, podcasts, and personal websites are just some of those available alternatives. Passively waiting to see what happens with their scholarly work after publication is no longer a viable option. Successful dissemination requires researchers to actively engage their audiences with their work.

References

Amorim, R. C., Castro, J. A., Rocha da Silva, J., & Ribeiro, C. (2017). A comparison of research data management platforms: Architecture, flexible metadata, and interoperability. *Universal Access in the Information Society, 16*(4), 851–862. https://doi.org/10.1007/s10209-016-0475-y

Ashcraft, L. E., Quinn, D. A., & Brownson, R. C. (2020). Strategies for effective dissemination of research to United States policymakers: A systematic review. *Implementation Science, 15*(1), 1–17. https://doi.org/10.1186/s13012-020-01046-3

Bauer, M. W., & Falade, B. A. (2014). Public understanding of science: Survey research around the world. In M. Bucchi & B. Trench (Eds.), *Handbook of public communication of science and technology* (2nd ed., pp. 140–159). Routledge.

Bohannon, J., & Doran, K. (2017). Introducing ORCID. *Science, 356*(6339), 691–692. https://doi.org/10.1126/science.356.6339.691

Brownson, R. C., Eyler, A. A., Harris, J. K., Moore, J. B., & Tabak, R. G. (2018). Getting the word out: New approaches for disseminating public health science. *Journal of Public Health Management and Practice, 24*(2), 102–111. https://doi.org/10.1097/PHH.0000000000000673

Chakravorty, N., Sharma, C. S., Molla, K. A., & Pattanaik, J. K. (2022). Open science: Challenges, possible solutions and the way forward. *Proceedings of the Indian National Science Academy, 88*, 456–471. https://doi.org/10.1007/s43538-022-00104-2

Craft, A. R. (2020). Managing researcher identity: Tools for researchers and librarians. *Serials Review, 46*(1), 44–49. https://doi.org/10.1080/00987913.2020.1720897

Divecha, C. A., Tullu, M. S., & Karande, S. (2021). Published a research paper? What next?? *Journal of Postgraduate Medicine, 67*(4), 189–193. https://doi.org/10.4103/jpgm.jpgm_348_21

Hardman, T. C., Krentz, A. J., & Wierzbicki, A. S. (2020). Ten tips for promoting your research. *Cardiovascular Endocrinology & Metabolism, 9*(1), 30–35. https://doi.org/10.1097/XCE.0000000000000191

Jordan, K. (2019). From social networks to publishing platforms: A review of the history and scholarship of academic social network sites. *Frontiers in Digital Humanities.* https://doi.org/10.3389/fdigh.2019

Kelly, M. P., Martin, N., Dillenburger, K., Kelly, A. N., & Miller, M. M. (2019). Spreading the news: History, successes, challenges and the ethics of effective dissemination. *Behavior Analysis in Practice, 12*(2), 440–451. https://doi.org/10.1007/s40617-018-0238-8

Klar, S., Krupnikov, Y., Ryan, J. B., Searles, K., & Shmargad, Y. (2020). Using social media to promote academic research: Identifying the benefits of twitter for sharing academic work. *PloS One, 15*(4), e0229446. https://doi.org/10.1371/journal.pone.0229446

Kreuter, M. W., & Bernhardt, J. M. (2009). Reframing the dissemination challenge: A marketing and distribution perspective. *American Journal of Public Health, 99*(12), 2123–2127. https://doi.org/10.2105/AJPH.2008.155218

Manca, S. (2018). ResearchGate and Academia.edu as networked socio-technical systems for scholarly communication: A literature review. *Research in Learning Technology, 26*, 1–16. https://doi.org/10.25304/rlt.v26.2008

Martone, M. E., Garcia-Castro, A., & VandenBos, G. R. (2018). Data sharing in psychology. *American Psychologist, 73*(2), 111–125. https://doi.org/10.1037/amp0000242

McHugh, R. K., & Barlow, D. H. (2010). The dissemination and implementation of evidence-based psychological treatments: A review of current efforts. *American Psychologist, 65*(2), 73–84. https://doi.org/10.1037/a0018121

National Institute for Health and Care Research. (2019, January 1). *How to disseminate your research.* https://www.nihr.ac.uk/documents/how-to-disseminate-your-research/19951

Norris, E., & O'Connor, D. B. (2019). Science as behaviour: Using a behaviour change approach to increase uptake of open science. *Psychology & Health, 34*(12), 1397–1406. https://doi.org/1 0.1080/08870446.2019.1679373

Ortega, J. L. (2018). Reliability and accuracy of altmetric providers: A comparison among Altmetric.com, PlumX and Crossref Event Data. *Scientometrics, 116*(3), 2123–2138. https://doi.org/10.1007/s11192-018-2838-z

Ross-Hellauer, T., Tennant, J. P., Banelytė, V., Gorogh, E., Luzi, D., Kraker, P., Pisacane, L., Ruggieri, R., Sifacaki, E., & Vignoli, M. (2020). Ten simple rules for innovative dissemination of research. *PLOS Computational Biology, 16*(4), e1007704. https://doi.org/10.1371/journal.pcbi.1007704

Singh, V. K., Singh, P., Karmakar, M., Leta, J., & Mayr, P. (2021). The journal coverage of web of science, scopus and dimensions: A comparative analysis. *Scientometrics, 126*(6), 5113–5142. https://doi.org/10.1007/s11192-021-03948-5

Smith, A. A. (2020). Broadcasting ourselves: Opportunities for researchers to share their work through online video. *Frontiers in Environmental Science, 8*, 150. https://doi.org/10.3389/fenvs.2020.00150

Spicer, S. (2014). Exploring video abstracts in science journals: An overview and case study. *Journal of Librarianship and Scholarly Communication, 2*(2), eP1110. https://doi.org/10.7710/2162-3309.1110

Stilgoe, J., Lock, S. J., & Wilsdon, J. (2014). Why should we promote public engagement with science? *Public Understanding of Science, 23*(1), 4–15. https://doi.org/10.1177/0963662513518154

Wilkinson, M. D., Dumontier, M., Aalbersberg, I. J., Appleton, G., Axton, M., Baak, A., et al. (2016). The FAIR guiding principles for scientific data management and stewardship. *Scientific Data, 3*(1), 1–9. https://doi.org/10.1038/sdata.2016.18

Yan, W., Zhang, Y., Hu, T., & Kudva, S. (2021). How does scholarly use of academic social networking sites differ by academic discipline? A case study using ResearchGate. *Information Processing & Management, 58*(1), 102430. https://doi.org/10.1016/j.ipm.2020.102430

Yang, S., Zheng, M., Yu, Y., & Wolfram, D. (2021). Are Altmetric.com scores effective for research impact evaluation in the social sciences and humanities? *Journal of Informetrics, 15*(1), 101120. https://doi.org/10.1016/j.joi.2020.101120

Yelamanchi, R., Gupta, N., Goswami, B., & Durga, C. K. (2022). The basics of research article licensing. *Indian Journal of Surgery, 84*(1), 338–339. https://doi.org/10.1007/s12262-021-03166-6

Yors Garcia graduated from Southern Illinois University in 2011 with a Ph.D. in rehabilitation services with a specialization in behavior analysis. His previous professional experience includes adjunct and practicum supervisor in the Behavior Analysis program at the University of Nevada, Reno and associate professor at The Chicago School. Currently, he is associate professor at Pontificia Universidad Javeriana, Bogota, Colombia. He is the current president of the Culture & Diversity ABAI SIG and associate editor of The Psychological Record. His research interest includes acceptance and commitment training, derived relational responding, international supervision, bias, and racism.

Amanda Muñoz-Martínez received her Ph.D. in clinical psychology from the University of Nevada, Reno. Amanda is currently an assistant professor at the Universidad de Los Andes (Colombia). She has published several articles and book chapters. She is a certified functional analytic psychotherapy trainer and member of the FAP Certification, Policy, and Ethics Board. As a FAP trainer, she has facilitated several trainings for English- and Spanish-speakers to enhance interpersonal skills and create meaningful relationships. Her main research interest is optimizing and evaluating principle-based therapies for improving clients' and stakeholders' well-being, particularly, in Latin America.

Meredith Andrews is a doctoral-level Board Certified Behavior Analyst (BCBA-D) who started in the field in 2010. She is the Associate Director of Clinical Training at The Chicago School where she shapes the next generation of behavior analysts through evidence-based training and supervision. Her research interests include training/supervision, language and cognition, mindfulness, social justice, prosocial behavior, and ethics.

Estefanía Junca holds a master's degree in clinical psychology from the Pontificia Universidad Javeriana, Bogota, Colombia (PUJ). She works as a clinical psychologist at one of the lead psychiatric hospitals in Bogotá, Colombia. Besides the clinical realm, she is also a member of the social cognition research group at Universidad de Los Andes, where she recently published an investigation interested in quality of life in Huntington's disease and is currently participating in another study interested in social cognition in eating disorders.

Part IV
Getting Your Research Noticed

Chapter 14
Engaging in Conference Presentations to Support the Dissemination of Behavioral Research

Teresa Cardon

One venue that has been an established option for the dissemination of behavioral research is a conference presentation. Conferences are formal gatherings of professionals, often hosted by organizations focused on a particular area of focus, where research updates, instructional strategies, dissemination of new research, networking, etc., occur. Conferences often occur in a repeating cadence and can be held in person, virtually, or a combination of formats. Conference presentations are a common and practical tool for dissemination of research. Conference presentations can take several formats and often require the submission and acceptance of a proposal. This chapter will identify several factors that should be taken into consideration with regard to dissemination via conference presentations.

Determine the Why

To begin with, it is important to determine your why. Why do you want to share your work at a conference? Is it simply that your advisor or mentor told you to submit something to a particular conference? Does it happen to be the annual conference that you always attend, and presenting is a good next step? Are you worried about your research not being accepted into a journal so figured you would give a conference submission a whirl? Why is a conference presentation the correct venue for your work at this time?

While submitting to a conference is often considered a "rite of passage" and something that is commonly done, there are reasons why submitting a proposal and presenting at a conference can be a strategic step in advancing your work and the

T. Cardon (✉)
Department of Educational Psychology, University of North Texas, Denton, TX, USA
e-mail: teresa.cardon@unt.edu

© The Author(s), under exclusive license to Springer Nature Switzerland AG 2023
A. K. Griffith, T. C. Ré (eds.), *Disseminating Behavioral Research*,
https://doi.org/10.1007/978-3-031-47343-2_14

field of applied behavior analysis (ABA; Kranak et al., 2022). First, a conference presentation may be a good opportunity to present pilot data or test out a concept that you are considering researching more in depth (Ross-Hellauer et al., 2020). Some conferences accept proposals for research that is still in various phases of data collection and therefore the turnaround time from when you collect the data, to when you present at the conference can be much shorter than waiting several months or years for the traditional submission, review, and publication in a scholarly journal. More flexible submission requirements can be an excellent reason to choose a conference presentation as a dissemination option.

Second, conferences can be a good opportunity to test out a new concept or a topic that you are considering for research. A presentation may include hypothesis testing, systematic reviews, or proof of concept submissions that allow for researchers to share ideas with the audience and gauge their response. This flexibility can be helpful to inform research that may be heading in a unique direction, perhaps controversial, or even something potentially groundbreaking. In addition, conferences can be a great opportunity to showcase progress. Research is a time-consuming process and the timeline from conceptualization to publication in a peer-reviewed journal often takes years, if not decades (Rached et al., 2018). Presenting aspects of your research to demonstrate the progress you are making, the relevant findings, and the ongoing relevance of the research is an excellent "why" for a conference presentation.

Finally, conference presentations are a great venue to encourage collaboration and to solicit feedback from peers and colleagues. Sharing your research at a conference allows others with similar interests to find you and your work. As we will discuss later in the chapter, carefully choosing your title and describing your research in the presentation abstract is a critical component to supporting the dissemination of your behavioral research. When colleagues with similar interests attend your sessions, they have the opportunity to ask questions, propose counter arguments, offer critical insights and can provide you with the opportunity to analyze and think carefully about your work (Ross-Hellauer et al., 2020). In addition, sitting in a room, be it live or virtual, with colleagues who are clearly interested in your research can provide opportunities for collaboration. Soliciting feedback in areas of your work that you would like to examine further or areas that are presenting a particular challenge can be a huge benefit of conference presentations (Tripathy et al., 2017).

Determine the Who

Once you have a clear idea of why you want to present at a conference, it is important to determine who the appropriate audience is for your presentation (Ross-Hellauer et al., 2020). In general, conferences are often practitioner-based. In other words, a conference may be held for behavioral researchers by one of the major behavioral-based research groups such as the Association for Behavior Analysis

International (ABAI) or the Association of Professional Behavior Analysts (APBA). If the goal is to disseminate your work in the field of behavioral research to other behavioral scientists, then this type of practitioner-based conference can be an appropriate fit. Similarly, research that focuses on organizational behavior management may be an appropriate fit for the Organization Behavioral Management Network (OBM Network) annual conference.

If, on the other hand, you are interested in dissemination to a wider audience, then it is important to think more specifically about who will be attending particular conferences. Similar to behaviorally practitioner-based conferences, other disciplines hold regular events where clinicians can earn continuing education credit. If your research could be beneficial to share with a discipline outside of behavioral research (e.g., derived relational responding as it relates to communication at a speech-language pathologist conference), expands the reach of applied behavior analysis specifically, and behavioral research in general, to new fields (e.g., data collection strategies to support patients receiving dialysis at a nursing conference), or provides insights into a related field (e.g., tangible vs. intangible rewards as it relates to employee satisfaction at a business management conference), then presenting at a conference focused on a discipline outside of behavior may be a good fit.

Another conference consideration is a subject matter or topic-based conference. There are various conferences that highlight one topic where subject matter experts from different disciplines and professionals gather to share and update knowledge in the field. These types of conferences, sometimes referred to as symposiums, are often multidisciplinary or interprofessional in nature with attendees from a variety of professions (e.g., speech-language pathologists, occupational therapists, psychologists, medical professionals) all gathering to hear the latest updates in the field. For example, there are many conferences focused on autism spectrum disorder (e.g., International Meeting for Autism Research—IMFAR; Ohio Center for Autism and Low Incidence Conference—OCALIcon) where behavioral research is a welcome component. Similarly, the Society for Behavioral Medicine is another example of a conference where practitioners from a variety of professions (e.g., mental health professionals, behavior analysts, medical professionals, and health administration). If your work relates to a specific theme such as addiction, eating disorders, business management, developmental disabilities, traumatic brain injury, etc., then a topic-based conference may be a good fit for your presentation.

Determine the Where and When

While you think about who you want to share your research with, it is also necessary to think about the where and the when of dissemination. Most professional organizations, be they discipline-specific, or topic-based, have annual conferences set years in advance. You can search their websites to see when and where the conference will be held for the next several years. This can be helpful to consider as you plan your conference proposals and dissemination. Several questions worth considering with regard to where and when:

(1) Is the conference in a location I can travel to?
(2) Does the timing of the conference fit into my schedule?
(3) Do I have the necessary funds to travel to a particular conference?
(4) Is the timing of one conference better than another in terms of ongoing data collection or next steps in my career?
(5) Are there colleagues at this particular conference that will be beneficial to interact with?
(6) Is the conference virtual or in-person or hybrid? Is one format more beneficial than another?

In addition to thinking through the aforementioned questions, it is often helpful to think about the prestige of the conference you are considering submitting a proposal to (Taylor et al., 2006). Is there a specific conference that will be more relevant given the current stage of your research and career? For instance, are you an early career professional seeking to gain experience as a presenter and need to find a conference that has a high acceptance rate or are you an established academician looking to further solidify your work in the field at a prestigious conference?

Determine the What

Now that you have decided that a conference presentation may be a good fit, who your target audience is, and which conference you are focusing on, it is important to also consider the type of conference presentation you are interested in. While different conferences offer different formats, there are several presentation formats that are relatively common: poster sessions, seminars, and panel sessions.

A poster session typically consists of one or two presenters standing in front of their poster presentation in a large room with many other presenters and posters in the same room. Often posters are grouped by topic or some unifying theme. Traditionally, posters are printed on one large piece of paper or fabric with a template that displays their research in a visual format (e.g., Powerpoint slide). Posters often include the same elements that a manuscript would include, albeit a truncated version: title, author(s), introduction, method, results, discussion, and references. The size of the poster is predetermined by the conference venue, so be sure to check the poster requirements before printing your poster. Some conferences offer digital poster formats (e.g., iposter) where a roomful of digital monitors are present and authors stand by the digital monitor that displays their work in a variety of digital formats (Ross-Hellauer et al., 2020). Digital posters can be interactive, include audio, visual graphics, hyperlinks, etc. Virtual poster formats may include a traditional poster or a digital format. It is helpful to include a QR code and an email address where attendees can reach out with more questions, or simply for networking purposes. Virtual poster sessions may require a prerecorded description of the poster if the format is asynchronous or may include a live description with an opportunity for attendees to ask questions via chat or in the virtual room when synchronous. Whatever poster format is available, the goal of the poster is to provide an overview of your research with a brief insight into the introduction, methodology, results, and discussion, while allowing time for those interested in learning more to ask questions of the presenting authors.

A seminar session typically includes one or two authors presenting on a particular area of expertise, new research, pilot data, ongoing research updates, etc. Different conference venues offer a variety of seminar sessions, so be sure to consider what format may be the best for dissemination of your work. Often, seminar sessions are one- or two-hour presentations, but some conferences offer technical sessions that are shorter in length (i.e., 15–20 min) with the aim of being more singularly focused. Seminar sessions may be individual presentations based on individual submissions or may be combined with other submissions to create a seminar session based on a similar topic. Seminar sessions may also be presented by a group of presenters working to create a session based on a particular theme. Seminar sessions can take place virtually or in person, asynchronously or synchronously. Seminar sessions allow for more in depth descriptions of a topic, including specific details of research methods and results. Seminar sessions often include time for discussion, questions and answers, insights, feedback, and can be interactive or more didactic in nature (Ross-Hellauer et al., 2020). Seminars should have visual representation and often take the format of slides, video clips, graphs, figures, infographics, etc. Again, do not forget to include contact information and even a QR code, so attendees can engage with you and your research beyond the seminar and the conference.

A panel session is a specific type of seminar session where a group of researchers or presenters agree to each present a portion of the session around a focused topic. For example, a group of five or six presenters all researching feeding concerns in young children with Prader Willi Syndrome could present together as a panel at a conference. Panel sessions are a great way to disseminate your research by partnering with others involved in similar research, or someone who may be more established in the field, or potentially others who may be interested in partnering with you in the future. Panel sessions often include a quick slide presentation by each presenter (e.g., 7 min per presenter) and then time allowed for questions and discussion at the end of the session. In general, panel sessions are allotted more time than a seminar session given the number of presenters and interaction time with the audience. Panel sessions are great opportunities for students to get engaged in dissemination efforts with their mentors. Panel sessions are also a great way to disseminate your work at conferences that may be outside your discipline; as part of an interprofessional panel, for example. Similar to posters and seminar sessions, it is important to prepare presentation slides ahead of time with clear graphs and figures, infographics, working video and audio, etc. For panels, it is also critical to stay within the allotted time limits so as not to take time away from your colleagues on the panel or shortchange the question-and-answer time that allows for engagement with attendees. As always, be sure to include your contact information, website, affiliation, laboratory information, etc., for attendees.

Presentation Preparation

As mentioned, it is important to have well-prepared slides that include a variety of information including graphs, visual supports, and contact information, but there is so much more to think about in terms of presentation preparation. To begin with, choose your title very purposefully (Tripathy et al., 2017). Think about the key words that need to be included in your title that will indicate to attendees what your presentation will cover. Is there a specific type of intervention or procedure that helps your research stand out? Be sure it is included in the title. Have you used a novel assessment tool or an old standard assessment in a novel way? Again, be sure the title of your presentation offers enough information to catch an attendee's attention. Sometimes catchy acronyms can garner attention, just be sure you describe the acronym in the title or the abstract so that the topic of your presentation is clear and not left up to interpretation.

Conference programs often include the title of your presentation and an abstract (albeit sometimes a very condensed abstract). Consider the word count for your title, include key words, methodology, or results that can act as a "hook" to bring attention to your session. For example, if your research is focused on a unique methodology (e.g., Artificial Intelligence), highlight it in the title. Or if your work has something that sets it apart, be sure those aspects are highlighted in the title. For example, instead of stating "participants" in your title, you could highlight the unique nature of the "interprofessional participants" or "culturally diverse participants." Therefore, in addition to preparing a thoughtful title for your presentation, the abstract is a critical component of your conference proposal and presentation. Some conferences allow for video abstracts (Ross-Hellauer et al., 2020) where a high-quality video can garner a lot of attention and allows for a quick overview of your research and gives attendees an insight into your presentation style. While this digital abstract option is appearing more and more, particularly with online conferences, a well-written abstract with concise descriptions of your work is critical to encourage people to attend your presentation. Conference abstracts have word counts that often only allow for limited information to be included: a sentence for the introduction, a sentence or two for the method, etc. If the core of your presentation is focused on a new methodology, be sure to highlight that in your abstract. If you have pilot data that are unexpected and exciting, keep that as the focus. Again, think about the key elements of your presentation that you want to disseminate, remember the who, what, where, and why you have decided on a particular conference, then write your abstract with that focus in mind.

Now that you have your slides prepared, it is time to practice your presentation and focus on your presentation style (Teperek, 2020). If you feel confident in your presentation style, great! Now put that confidence to work, practice a few times by yourself, record yourself, watch it back (Tailab & Marsh, 2020), make the tweaks and adjustments you need to make, and then practice in front of several colleagues to collect their feedback. According to research, practice and preparation go a long way to increasing your awareness of your presentation style, confidence in the material, decrease nervousness, and support a well-prepared presentation (Seals, 2022; Tailab & Marsh, 2020). If you are less confident, or even downright scared of presenting in front of an audience, then practice and preparation are going to be important for you in a different way. There are numerous organizations (e.g., Toastmasters) and programs that can help you build your presentation skills. Many universities have supports in place to help students and junior faculty build their skillset as a presenter. Take advantage of professional development opportunities to improve your skills. Find a mentor or colleague who is willing to work with you, practice with you, and offer constructive feedback. Be sure you make time to practice, record yourself, and make adjustments long before the actual conference date arrives. Being prepared would not make all the nerves disappear, but being well prepared can go a long way in helping your presentation be a successful one.

Finally, it is helpful to upload your slides or handouts to the conference platform so that attendees (or those that could not attend your session but were still interested in your topic) can access information about your research (Teperek, 2020). One of the key components of dissemination is reach, so including information about your work in the form of slides or handouts on the conference website will allow fellow attendees to access your work long after the conference date has passed. Adding your conference slides to your own website, research platform (e.g., researchgate. com), university laboratory website, department website, etc., can also be a great way to promote your work and disseminate your findings. As your research, your network, and your presentation style starts to become more well known, an invitation to provide a keynote address at a conference may be just around the corner!

References

Kranak, M. P., Hall, H., & Jones, C. (2022). Excuse me, I'm speaking: Analysis of women's representation as keynote and invited speakers in behavior analysis. *Behavior Analysis in Practice*, 1–6.

Rached, G., Hobeika, C., Karam, E., Kourié, H. R., & Kattan, J. (2018). Urging medical students to publish: Advantages, disadvantages and new challenges. *Bulletin du Cancer, 105*(6), 626–628.

Ross-Hellauer, T., Tennant, J. P., Banelytė, V., Gorogh, E., Luzi, D., Kraker, P., et al. (2020). Ten simple rules for innovative dissemination of research. *PLoS Computational Biology, 16*(4), e1007704.

Seals, D. R. (2022). Talking the talk: Tips for effective oral presentations in biomedical research. *American Journal of Physiology-Regulatory, Integrative and Comparative Physiology, 323*(4), R496–R511.

Tailab, M., & Marsh, N. (2020). Use of self-assessment of video recording to raise students' awareness of development of their oral presentation skills. *Higher Education Studies, 10*(1).

Taylor, S., Abramowitz, J. S., McKay, D., Stewart, S. H., & Asmundson, G. J. G. (2006). Publish without perishing, part 2: More suggestions for students and new faculty. *The Behavior Therapist, 29*(2), 21.

Teperek M. (2020). How to make the most of an academic conference – A checklist for before, during and after the meeting. *Impact of Social Sciences Blog* [Internet]. March 16, 2018 [retrieved Dec 2022]. https://blogs.lse.ac.uk/impactofsocialsciences/2018/03/16/how-to-make-the-most-of-an-academic-conference-a-checklist-for-before-during-and-after-the-meeting/

Tripathy, J. P., Bhatnagar, A., Shewade, H. D., Kumar, A. M. V., Zachariah, R., & Harries, A. D. (2017). Ten tips to improve the visibility and dissemination of research for policy makers and practitioners. *Public Health Action, 7*(1), 10–14.

Dr. Teresa Cardon is a dually certified SLP and a BCBA-D and has worked with individuals with disabilities for over 25 years. Dr. Cardon is currently a Senior Lecturer at the University of North Texas. Her research interests include interprofessional practice, video modeling, autism in the media, and collaboration bias. Dr. Cardon serves on editorial boards for prominent journals, volunteers in various capacities for professional organizations, and enjoys supporting educators and clinicians who work with unique populations.

Chapter 15
Nontraditional Options for Dissemination

Diana Parry-Cruwys, Jacquelyn MacDonald, Robert Parry-Cruwys, and Matt Cicoria

There is an ongoing need for ways to connect board certified behavior analysts (BCBAs) to the literature, each other, and to our ethical standards. The recent exponential growth in our field (Behavior Analyst Certification Board [BACB], n.d.), the disparity in availability of in-person continuing education unit (CEU) offerings in varying parts of the USA, exacerbated following the pandemic, and the advances in online technology have changed the landscape for disseminating and consuming behavior analytic content in our field. In this chapter, we will review opportunities for connection and dissemination behavior analysts have through online sources, advantages, and disadvantages of engaging in these online spaces, and information that may be useful to behavior analysts looking to enter these spaces as disseminators themselves.

The field of behavior analysis represents a global community of professionals dedicated to the application of behavior analytic principles to address socially significant behavior. From the inception of the Board Certified Behavior Analysis

D. Parry-Cruwys (✉) · J. MacDonald
ABA Inside Track Podcast; Department of Applied Behavior Analysis, Regis College, Weston, MA, USA

Regis College, Department of Applied Behavior Analysis, Weston, MA, USA
e-mail: diana.parry-cruwys@regiscollege.edu; jacquelyn.macdonald@regiscollege.edu

R. Parry-Cruwys
ABA Inside Track Podcast; Department of Applied Behavior Analysis, Regis College, Weston, MA, USA

ABA Inside Track Podcast, Shrewsbury Public Schools, Shrewsbury, MA, USA

M. Cicoria
Behavioral Observations Podcast; Positive Behavioral Outcomes, LLC, Newbury, NH, USA
e-mail: matt@behavioralobservations.com

A. K. Griffith, T. C. Ré (eds.), *Disseminating Behavioral Research*,
https://doi.org/10.1007/978-3-031-47343-2_15

(BCBA) certification in 2000 (Johnston & Shook, 2001) to today, the growth of the field has steadily increased. As of the most recent data from 2023, 59,976 individuals were certified at the BCBA/BCBA-Doctoral level, 5580 at the BCaBA level, and 130,273 at the Registered Behavior Technician (RBT) level worldwide (BACB, n.d.). The number of newly certified behavior analysts, particularly at the BCBA-level, has significantly increased annually over the past 5 to 8 years. For example, in 2014 approximately 16,000 individuals held the BCBA credential (Deochand & Fuqua, 2016); that number has increased 375% to nearly 60,000 in the subsequent eight years (2014–2023). Over 50% of BCBAs working today received their BCBA certificate in the last 5 years (BACB, n.d.). This incredible growth in the number of BCBAs in such a short period of time poses unique challenges with regard to upholding the professional and ethical standards of the field, to fulfilling demand for quality continued education of certificants, and to ensuring field-wide dissemination of new ideas and research.

The technological changes that have occurred during the time period since the inception of the BACB have also been dramatic. The world is now always online, connected through social media, and able to access information through digital mechanisms in a way the year 2000 would not have predicted. Social media-based messaging can reach thousands of people in a matter of seconds. Behavior analytic groups on Facebook and Instagram freely share information, questions, web-based articles and journal articles, and opinions on a number of behavior analytic topics for their members, if not the online public, to see. Similarly, applied behavior analysis (ABA) personalities run websites and Twitter accounts for the purpose of sharing information and raising awareness regarding behavior analytic issues online. These changes in the accessibility of interaction between behavior analysts and others interested in behavior analysis across the world, and the ways in which behavior analysis is discussed and disseminated have dramatically changed in recent years, for both better and worse. It could be argued that the representation of our field in the social media realm shapes the cultural landscape of ABA as much as research publications. Those interested in consuming ABA services as parents or individuals, in learning about ABA as students, or in opposing ABA as critics are all more likely to encounter representations of ABA online rather than through published print media. This makes the social media footprint of ABA an important one, even if its impact on the field is not yet fully understood.

These recent changes in how behavior analysts interact with one another and access behavior analytic content are beginning to be documented. Kranak et al. (2022) surveyed 231 behavior analysts (169 BCBAs, 55 BCBA-Ds, and 7 BCaBAs) on their continuing education and media consumption practices. Respondents indicated they were very likely to receive their continuing education through online means, with webinars, virtual conferences, and virtual workshops representing the top three highest percentages of type of CEU obtained (23%, 19%, and 14%, respectively). Seventy to eighty percent of respondents also indicated they interact with online media sources of behavior analytic content, specifically social media posts, podcasts, and YouTube videos, although their opinion of those interactions varied by media type. Given these indications that the landscape of behavior analysis now includes a large online and social media component, several challenges arise in conjunction with the purported changes. The first challenge is the need to maintain professional rigor in the quickly growing online landscape. Given the near-exponential growth in the field, it remains critical that certified and licensed behavior analysts demonstrate required knowledge of the basic tenets of behavior analysis and compassionate, ethical application of that knowledge (Kelly et al., 2021). Additionally, the behavior analytic community must also consider the access to continued professional development opportunities for existing behavior analysts.

Following certification, all behavior analysts should be continuing their professional development including ongoing consumption of behavior analytic content (Briggs & Mitteer, 2022). We must consider how newly credentialed BCBAs will access this content, for both continuing education purposes and for remaining current with the literature. The increase in the number of recently certified and licensed behavior analysts in turn produces greater need for continuing education opportunities. This, combined with the disparity of access to in-person conferences in some regions and the normalization of interaction on remote digital platforms following the pandemic, has produced a greater reliance on online communities of behavior analysts to provide knowledge and to establish communities of practice to those newer, media-savvy analysts. As with most technological advancements, there are advantages and disadvantages in the use of social media to disseminate information about behavior analysis.

Advantages of Social Media

An advantage of having behavior analytic content available via varied online topographies is that information can be more easily accessed by many people. In Briggs and Mitteer's (2022) update on Carr and Briggs's (2010) recommendations for accessing scholarly literature, they note that reviews of the literature and peer-reviewed research can now be more easily accessed online. Specifically, Briggs and Mitteer point to accessibility of research via the BACB(R) portal, the collation of research and increased ease of searching articles via ResearchGate, the availability of online-first publications and Table of Contents notifications, the opportunities to learn about current research via podcasts and blogs, and the direct contribution to discussions of publications via social media as methods of accessing the literature that were not widely available at the time of the 2010 publication. As information provided through online sources can also be distributed more quickly than via traditional research publication avenues, practitioners and students may look here first for new information. The research to publication lag is well documented and long-standing; Boring (1937) found the lag from submission to publication in a psychological journal to range from 5 months to 21 months. Much more recently, Morris et al. (2011) infamously found the lag from research start to publication in health sciences translational research to be 17 years! Such a delay between research and dissemination of findings hinders the growth of a field and hamstrings practitioners who are looking to incorporate evidence-based research into practice (Kun, 2020). Online media outlets, such as virtual conventions and workshops, blogs, and open-source educational materials and videos, can help ease the dissemination lag and bridge the research to practice gap by providing a more instantaneous venue for researchers to share their ongoing work (Valentino & Juanico, 2020; Verhagen et al., 2013). However, these sources are not usually peer-reviewed, a consideration which will be discussed more below (see also Kranak et al., 2022).

Another advantage of our more connected world is the increased opportunity for practitioners to share information as well as to access it. Students of behavior analysis and professionals in the field alike can make and distribute behavior analytic-related content on multiple streaming platforms or via blogs and videos, as those in other fields have already discovered (e.g., Johannsson & Salek, 2020). Many social media channels and personalities promote new and current research, push the field to think critically about controversial or radical perspectives, and highlight marginalized voices in the field who may not have had the opportunity to be heard through mainstream, traditional outlets. Individuals in the field can also make their voices heard by responding to existing media posts and content. Calls for participation in survey research can be made easily on social media platforms and via email blasts, allowing behavior analytic researchers to learn much more quickly about the field's current opinions and practices (e.g., LeBlanc et al., 2020; Oliver et al., 2015; Sellers et al., 2019). These same avenues have also been used recently to petition for change with online opinion pieces (e.g., Kishbaugh et al., 2022, Vanderbilt Kennedy Center, 2022) serving as outlets to get time-sensitive and widely applicable position statements out quickly.

Communities of Practice

Communities on social media can be beneficial for practitioners, academics, and graduate students (e.g., Ajegbomogun & Oduwole, 2017; Donelan, 2016). While access to individuals and research for its own sake can support the continued dissemination and synthesis of information for behavior analysts, this access alone may not result in the adoption of techniques or opportunities to assess research-based findings in a practice context using the best available evidence. As behavior analysis stretches into additional fields (Friman et al., 1998; Normand & Kohn, 2013), many behavior analysts may function as a solo bastion of the science of behavior among multidisciplinary teams. When faced with environments in which daily focus may be on achieving client outcomes more than reflection on practice, access to research alone may not provide sufficient motivation to update practices, especially when colleagues may or may not pull from the same evidence-base. Social media groups and pages can produce networking opportunities in which clinicians and practitioners can find each other and learn about training protocols, research applications, supervision strategies, and collaboration opportunities. Such opportunities may provide a novel ground to actively develop meaningful communities of practice as a setting to both support ongoing dissemination and to advance the abilities of behavior analysts to synthesize disseminated information into more advanced treatments.

Based on the idea of situated learning in which knowledge acquisition, dissemination, and application serve as products of specific contexts and social interactions (Lave & Wenger, 1991), communities of practice developed as a practitioner-led initiative in which novice and senior-level service technicians gathered regularly to discuss on-the-job problems and their novel solutions. Through this informal gathering of troubleshooters, an increasingly organized system of professionals has spread from the technical to the business and medical fields. While some communities of practice are products of the larger organization, others may develop more organically in any setting where social interactions, common goals, and a shared skill repertoire meet (Li et al., 2009). As most communities of practice join together for varied periods of time with shifting goals and priorities, they are both simple to create across environments and flexible to the needs of their membership. Common activities of these groups may include research reviews, workshop-like presentations on frequently used procedures, shared exemplars of recent work, and social spaces for discussions and feedback on relevant topics in the field (Busch et al., 2020). While the exact requirements of what makes an effective community of practice vary wildly across disciplines and organizations, likely sources of strength in these groups include opportunities for social interaction, activities built around the sharing and creation of knowledge, a mix of expert- and novice-level professionals, and group facilitators (Li et al., 2009).

As behavior analysts may find themselves working in a variety of job roles, finding and/or creating communities of practice in person or online could be a socially and professionally rewarding opportunity. Such groups may increase the efficiency with which new technologies and evidence-based practices are disseminated and provide a safe and enjoyable setting to develop increased competence in these areas. For behavior analysts working in heterogeneous teams, communities of practice may allow for collaborative avenues to share behavioral research with other disciplines while opening a mutual sharing of practices and research relevant to group goals from these same disciplines. While research into the extent to which differing community of practice models may be more or less effective—data on the overall benefits from communities of practice in the medical and business worlds is somewhat mixed (Rammuthugala et al., 2011)—participation in these activities could provide opportunities to increase subject matter knowledge and fluency in the use of evidence-based techniques (Busch et al., 2020). When combined with the instantaneous access to communities collaborating across the Internet, such groups may provide guidance to mitigate some of the disadvantages of an always online world.

Disadvantages and Ethical Challenges of Social Media

Although the field of behavior analysis can use these nontraditional outlets for dissemination, the question still remains whether it is always beneficial to do so. Using social media platforms as a way to disseminate information may also come at a great cost for the field as well as for the clients served. Using social media in all of its forms requires much less response effort than searching through the literature or asking a colleague. In a survey of 212 behavior analysts and technicians reached via social media outlets, we found that 82% (173) used social media to access behavior analytic communities. Of those utilizing these communities, 47.8% (78) reported asking or following others' posts for ideas on addressing challenging behavior, and 37.4% (61) reported asking or following others' posts on addressing ethical issues (Parry-Cruwys et al., 2018b). These are some of the ethical dangers of social media highlighted in O'Leary et al. (2017). Since this time, social media has grown in its influence to require its own ethical standard, 5.10 Social Media Channels and websites (BACB, 2020). This standard highlights the need for behavior analysts to be knowledgeable about what is written on personal and private accounts on social media platforms to ensure confidentiality and consent from clients. In addition, 1.06 Maintaining Competence provides examples of appropriate professional development activities, such as supervision and mentorship. Rosenberg and Schwartz (2019) underline that the new guidelines move the focus from following a strict set of rules to using ethical best judgment to navigate complex situations, of which judicious use of social media for professional purposes certainly entails.

Even with our rigorous ethical code, violations still occur in our field. Britton et al. (2021) highlighted the most common violations reported to the BACB during 2016 and 2017. The most common violations included those around improper or inadequate supervision and acting with professionalism and integrity. Prior to the second version of the BACB supervision training (2018), supervisors were not trained on how to be effective supervisors. Supervision is very difficult in many areas of our field under the current standards of care including a large client caseload, a large volume of supervisees, and a requirement on billable time. Evidence-based practice suggests that behavior skills training (BST) should be used when teaching new skills (Parsons et al., 2013), however, it can be time consuming and difficult for supervisors to use for all skills and with integrity (Erath et al., 2020).

Since supervision is difficult, it is possible that inadequate and improper supervision have left behavior technicians at a loss for what to do with their clients (Sellers et al., 2019) and turning to the online community for support. O'Leary et al. (2017) provided an example of a behavior technician asking a question about a treatment implementation for a client and receiving many responses within a few short hours of posting. This short response time may increase the likelihood that a behavior technician may post on social media for answers on programming in the future. However, behavior analysts should be mindful when asking questions on social media as well as providing recommendations to posts on client programming. O'Leary and colleagues stress that there is no defined relationship between the asker and the answerer giving way to potential violations of the ethical code. Since the answerer does not know the client or relevant information about their needs, follow-up posts could unknowingly cause harm to the client. Additionally, since there is no contract in place between the two parties, the asker cannot follow up if issues arise. In order to mitigate this issue and to promote appropriate social media use, organizations and supervisors must establish systems where staff feel comfortable asking within the organization and to their specific supervisors. The presence of professional and supervisory relationships is the key to combat misuse of social media.

Another common violation discussed by Britton et al. (2021) was the failure to report and respond to the BACB within an appropriate time frame. Britton and colleagues suggested that it is possible that behavior analysts might not be clear on when and what to report. Continuing education credits typically do not focus on this specific question and thus instead of looking through the BACB newsletters, behavior analysts may go to social media for answers. Without specifically verifying the answer, behavior analysts may unknowingly be acting out of accordance with the guidelines set forth by the BACB due to social media. Dissemination in this way may lead to detrimental effects for the behavior analyst. Kelly et al. (2019) provide suggestions on how to ethically disseminate our field through social media platforms. These authors posit that dissemination efforts should focus on the area of expertise of the behavior analyst and always reference research related to the specific topic of discussion. Dissemination cannot be effective if it is not also ethical. Kelly et al. suggested strategies to effectively and ethically disseminate behavior analysis on social platforms. They recommended considering the cultural contexts and situations where behavior analysis is being disseminated and using simple language and appropriate verbal behavior so that the audience understands the message. Behavior analysts should plan to use dissemination to create a proactive instead of reactive message and, when doing so on social media, clearly establish online boundaries to protect confidential information and to avoid multiple relationships. While social media can be a great place to network with colleagues, as consumers of information themselves, behavior must think critically about the content viewed on social media platforms and verify the legitimacy of its message (Green, 2010; Kranak et al., 2022).

Dissemination Opportunities Via Social Media Platforms

As noted earlier, there are several types of media-based options for involvement and dissemination available to the behavior analytic community. The most common categories are (a) social media groups and personalities; (b) blogs, videos, and open education resources (OER) on the internet; and (c) podcasts. Senior analysts in our field have called for expansion of behavior analysis via different avenues and outlets (e.g., Heward et al., 2022; Morris, 2014); various social media platforms provide additional opportunities for wide dissemination that may reach varied audiences. Voices in these arenas can have far-reaching influence and the medium does not determine the quality (good or bad) of the content or its potential for use or misuse. An entity in any of these outlets could become a positive and influential voice within the field, or a detrimental and divisive one. Similarly, practitioners and students may find themselves viewing one of these entities as a meaningful community of practice for them and/or a source of professional development (Luo et al., 2020). The function of these groups for a practitioner may vary based on their needs; for example, the group may come to support and grow their professional identity, as a source of networking, or as a source of information (Prestridge, 2019). They may also come to find their involvement with some entities to negatively affect their overall self-perception and mental health, and should take steps to ameliorate those risks through education, self-assessment, and moderation of participation (Luo & Hancock, 2020).

On social media, several groups exist that practitioners and students of behavior analysis may be interested in participating in, from student study groups, to groups focused on teaching in public schools, to groups focused on a subspeciality of behavior analytic theory or practice, to special interest groups and conference pages. For practitioners looking to join a group in which they can actively participate by posting their own material and having others in the group respond to those posts, Facebook remains the most widely used and easily accessed option (via a Group, which can be public or private, or a Page). For practitioners looking to follow behavior analytic content creators and respond to content and posts presented by those creators, or become a creator themselves, Instagram, TikTok, Facebook, and Twitter are all currently available options. Dr. Amanda Kelly, who uses the social media name "BehaviorBabe," reviews tips on maintaining a professional web presence, including disclaimers, privacy considerations, rules of courtesy, and repair strategies (Cicoria, 2016). As mentioned previously, social media use comes with a series of recommendations for best practices in posting to avoid engaging in a variety of ethical pitfalls related to confidentiality and providing treatment recommendations to non-clients (O'Leary et al., 2017). Unfortunately, posts with potential violations of these ethical boundaries continue to occur (Parry-Cruwys et al., 2018a). Some larger groups on Facebook have over 10,000+ members, and oversight and moderation of posts for ethical gray areas may be beyond the capacity of the admins of the page.

That being said, the size of these groups indicate that many people in the world of behavior analysis at least tangentially participate in social media communities, which was supported by self-report as well (Kranak et al., 2022). However, survey participants' responses reported by Kranak et al. demonstrated skepticism regarding the quality or reliability of professional development information provided via social media posts, with about 20% viewing social media posts as a source of information positively and about 45% viewing them negatively. Due to their size (in terms of groups) or following (in terms of individual social media influencers), these entities remain powerful potential distributors of information and viewpoints, even if viewed by most with skepticism. Those who have had success in developing themselves as a behavior analytic social media presence usually follow the traditional advice on gaining traction as a social media influencer: find your voice and niche perspective; post, like, and comment often; engage and collaborate with other influencers; adapt to ongoing technologies; and engage followers in multiple ways (such as via an email newsletter, blog, or accounts across social media platforms) (The Daily BA, 2020; Vengapally, 2021). Specific to behavior analysis, many social media personalities commonly focus on the positive or reform-minded perspectives of our field, using language that is accessible and positively valenced, which may contribute to their acceptance and accessibility with larger swaths of the population (Critchfield et al., 2017).

Another category of media-based dissemination in behavior analysis is blogs, videos, and open education resources (OER). These may be supported via media platforms such as YouTube or TikTok, or exist as consumable or even downloadable content on personal websites. Several blogs and YouTube channels regularly post content written and curated by prominent behavior analysts in the field, providing information about current or historical behavior analytic events and research and their practical application. These sources, of course, are not peer reviewed, and many behavior analysts are rightfully skeptical, choosing not to believe everything they read on the Internet. Kranak et al. (2022) survey respondents were split almost evenly (20–25% of respondents) between viewing behavior analytic YouTube videos positively, negatively, or indifferently, with an additional 20% of the survey pool indicating they do not interact with YouTube videos. While not all OER is available via the internet, some resources are available in this way in the form of instructional manuals, introductory subject material overviews, and whole books, with the authors intentionally choosing to share their work for free (Howard, 2019). There are advantages for the field of behavior analysis in having OER available in this manner, including providing equal access to high-quality materials for behavior analysis students of all financial and racial backgrounds, both in terms of educational materials (Howard, 2019) and study materials (Pavone, 2018).

Since their entry into mainstream content channels in the mid-2000s (Hammersly, 2004), podcasts have become an increasingly preferred means of entertainment and education for a wide range of individuals worldwide (Grey, 2023). For behavior analysts, the instant delivery of actively chosen educational content to computers and smart devices combined with the ability to interact with hosts, guests, and other listeners creates an ersatz community of practice without the financial or temporal burden of similar information delivered at a conference or workshop. Podcast consumption allows for other benefits more likely to occur in the medium. Topics discussed on popular shows responsive to audience requests and/or shows with Black and Brown hosts may more closely reflect the needs and interests of their listenership, allowing for dissemination of more diverse research and voice (see Cirincione-Ulezi, 2020, for a discussion on reducing barriers to leadership in ABA). Research can be more swiftly reviewed, discussed, and analyzed in broader contexts, even including insights from the original authors (Peterson, 2021). The format and backgrounds of the show hosts can similarly promote a diversity of voice, areas of research interest, level of analysis, and means of further engagement. Searching for shows covering ABA and related fields (e.g., education, psychology, and business) behavior analysts have hundreds of additional options to individualize to their immediate learning needs. However, as with most new forms of dissemination, caution must be exercised as the low-barrier to entry for new podcasts may be both blessing and curse as behavior analysts must be aware of the expertise of the podcaster to avoid consuming inaccurate evidence. Additionally, as a new medium, many systems that support quality preparation and research in professional development or academic fields may not similarly exist for podcasts and could result in the swift termination of a given show and a wariness of new listeners to commit to ongoing subscribership.

Direct Recommendations for Disseminating Your Research on Podcasts

Over the last several years, podcasts have become one of the fastest-growing media sources (Grey, 2023; Edison Research, 2022). In yearly surveys of Americans 12 and over, Edison Research found that in 2022, 62% of respondents reported listening to a podcast in the last month (Edison Research, 2022). By way of comparison, when survey respondents were asked the same question in 2016 (when we started *Behavioral Observations* and *ABA Inside Track*), only 36% listened to a podcast in the previous 30 days. The digital research website Insider Intelligence predicts that by 2024, there will be almost 505 million podcast listeners worldwide, accounting for nearly one-fourth of all Internet use (Insider Intelligence, 2021).

In the same span of time, podcasts have become a popular medium in the ABA industry as well. Using the key words "Applied Behavior Analysis," a recent search in Spotify yielded over 60 ABA-related podcasts. These behaviorally oriented shows, especially interview-based podcasts, can be particularly helpful for researchers to share their work, mainly because long-form interview formats allow for extended discussions of a particular study or body of literature. Podcasts are not bound by the space limitations most scholarly journals have, and as such, authors can provide a broader context of their research endeavors, humanize the participants and investigators through sharing anecdotes, and more generally, encourage the audience to learn more about a given body of work.

Accordingly, becoming a guest on a podcast is worth considering as part of a comprehensive dissemination strategy. As podcasters of ABA content for over seven years, we share some recommendations for practice in serving as a guest on some best practices when pitching yourself for a guest appearance on an ABA-related podcast. First, if not a current listener to the show you are targeting, take some time to download and listen to several episodes to determine the themes and topics that are generally discussed and whether your topic is a match for that show's audience. For example, if sharing your recent publication of a translational study in *The Journal of the Experimental Analysis of Behavior*, your findings may be of less value to the listeners of a podcast that serves ABA professionals in public schools or a show that discusses behavior-analytic approaches to health and fitness. Alternatively, if you believe your findings to be relevant, spend some time thinking about a means to explain the value of your findings to the target audience. It is also helpful to spend some time reviewing the social media channels of your targeted podcasts, specifically the comments, to get a sense of what questions are on the mind of the listeners, and whether your contribution to the show can help with an answer. If you believe your knowledge base successfully meets these needs, an approach to a podcast host might consist of the following:

- An acknowledgement of how you learned about the show (i.e., whether you have been a long-time listener, or if you have recently discovered the show and have enjoyed specific episodes).

- A direct request to be considered as a guest.
- A rationale for why you would be a good fit for the show, stated in terms of how your information would benefit the audience. This may include a summary of your research.
- Some sample discussion points.
- One or two documents for further reading or discussion.

If your pitch turns out to be successful, it is worth spending some time planning how to make the most of your podcast experience. The first thing to consider is maximizing the audio quality on your side of the interview. This involves selecting a recording location where external sources of noise are minimized (e.g., avoid barking dogs, colleagues knocking on your office door, notifications popping up on an unsilenced phone, etc.). If you are using Wi-Fi to connect to the Internet, make sure you have a strong connection to your router. Though most modern computers ship with sufficient quality built-in microphones, testing your computer's audio quality with a friend or colleague in advance will confirm whether your current setup is sufficient or whether the purchase or borrowing of an external microphone may be in order. Fortunately, external microphones have continued to decrease in price and can be used for all online communications and calls. Your colleagues will appreciate it when it no longer sounds like you have called them from the bottom of a well.

While access to a podcast audience and audio quality will go a long way toward reaching a stage for dissemination, preparing what you will say on your host's platform will ensure that your message will be received well by listeners. With nearly 500 collective episodes recorded, some suggestions for making great podcast appearances:

- Prepare for the most common first question regarding sharing your background information. This is your chance to gain the full attention of the listener, so it is helpful to practice the answer to this question in advance. Listeners are very likely tuning in to learn about the show's content, so it is best to err on the side of brevity as well.
- Realize that most listeners to ABA-related podcasts are practitioners. If your primary activity is conducting research, you must connect to what your work means to the "everyday BCBA."
- Keep in mind that you are not delivering a lecture and resist the understandable urge to tell your entire research story in one answer. Create a conversational atmosphere by allowing for back and forth between you and the host.
- Tell stories to create a memorable podcast. If you have interesting anecdotes to share, let the host know in advance so they can occasion opportunities to tell them.
- Be open to sharing what you might have done differently, and/or how your research can be expanded upon.
- Remember to direct listeners to your platform whether a website, social media page, or other online property. Feel free to mention this more than once.

After you have concluded the recording, consider providing your host with materials for the episode's shownotes. In addition to social media and website links, include links to relevant research articles and other supplementary materials that listeners can use to further their learning. Finally, once the episode has been published, share the episode among your professional colleagues and social media networks. For guests who are affiliated with universities and colleges, we have seen institutions' public relations offices disseminate guests' podcast appearances on their platforms as well.

Concluding Remarks

Whether creating or consuming information related to behavior analysis, the genie of the online, always connected world is out of the bottle. While more data on the overall benefits of online versus in-person learning as well as the types of content most conducive to effective dissemination are needed, as the numbers in our field continue to grow and as younger generations of practitioners gain competence in a world of daily social media interaction and online group correspondence, we must view technology as our ally. During the 2020 worldwide lockdown, the use of technology provided for connections, learning, development, and collaboration in a way that would have been impossible less than a decade ago. Continued education of behavior analysts in identifying what does and does not constitute quality online information and maintaining ethical and professional boundaries on sites historically used for socialization alone will continue to be required with further research directed toward efficient means of including this work in fieldwork and supervision discussions and ongoing professional development. However, heeding a few caveats seems a small price to pay for the ability of behavior analysts to harness the near-instantaneous power of the online world to engage and learn with communities of practice, the literature, and leaders in the field.

References

Ajegbomogun, F. O., & Oduwole, O. K. (October 2017). Social media trends and collaborative learning for scholarly research among postgraduate students. Academic Conferences International Limited, 9–17.

Behavior Analyst Certification Board. (2018). *Supervision training curriculum outline (2.0).* Author.

Behavior Analyst Certification Board. (2020). *Ethics code for behavior analysts.* https://bacb.com/wp-content/ethics-code-for-behavior-analysts/.

Behavior Analyst Certification Board. (n.d.). *BACB certificant data.* Retrieved from https://www.bacb.com/BACB-certificant-data

Boring, E. G. (1937). The lag of publication in journals of psychology. *The American Journal of Psychology, 49*(1), 137–139. https://jstor.org/stable/1416069

Briggs, A. M., & Mitteer, D. R. (2022). Updated strategies for making regular contact with the scholarly literature. *Behavior Analysis in Practice, 15*, 541–552. https://doi.org/10.1007/s40617-021-00590-8

Britton, L. N., Crye, A. A., & Haymes, L. K. (2021). Cultivating the ethical repertoires of behavior analysts: Prevention of common violations. *Behavior Analysis in Practice, 14*, 534–548. https://doi.org/10.1007/s40617-020-00540-w

Busch, L., Zonneveld, K., Saini, V., Chartier, K., Leathen, N., Asaro, M., & Feltz, N. (2020). The more we get together: Communities of practice of behaviour analysts. *Canadian Journal of Behavioural Science, 52*(4), 277–284. https://doi.org/10.1037/cbs0000174

Carr, J. E., & Briggs, A. M. (2010). Strategies for making regular contact with the scholarly literature. *Behavior Analysis in Practice, 3*(2), 13–18. https://doi.org/10.1007/BF03391760

Cicoria, M. (Host). (2016, April 3). Amanda Kelly on licensure, social media practices, and more! (No. 4) [Audio podcast episode]. In *The Behavioral Observations Podcast.* https://behavioralobservations.com/session-4-amanda-kelly-licensure-social-media-practices/

Cirincione-Ulezi, N. (2020). Black women and barriers to leadership in ABA. *Behavior Analysis in Practice, 13*, 719–724. https://doi.org/10.1007/s40617-020-00444-9

Critchfield, T. S., Doepke, K. J., Epting, K., Becirevic, A., Reed, D. D., Fienup, D. M., et al. (2017). Normative emotional responses to behavior analysis jargon or how not to use words to win friends and influence people. *Behavior Analysis in Practice, 10*, 97–106. https://doi.org/10.1007/s40617-016-0161-9

Deochand, N., & Fuqua, R. W. (2016). BACB certification trends: State of the states (1999 to 2104). *Behavior Analysis in Practice, 9*, 243–252. https://doi.org/10.1007/s40617-016-0118-z

Donelan, H. (2016). Social media for professional development and networking opportunities in academia. *Journal of Further and Higher Education, 40*(5), 706–729. https://doi.org/10.1080/0309877x.2015.1014321

Edison Research (2022, March 23). The infinite dial 2022. *Edison Research.* https://www.edisonresearch.com/the-infinite-dial-2022/#:~:text=Seventy%2Dthree%20percent%20of%20the,by%2013%25%20year%20over%20year

Erath, T. G., DiGennaro Reed, F. D., Sundermeyer, H. W., Brand, D., Novak, M. D., Harbison, M. J., & Shears, R. (2020). Enhancing the training integrity of human service staff using pyramidal behavioral skills training. *Journal of Applied Behavior Analysis, 53*, 449–464. https://doi.org/10.1002/jaba.608

Friman, P. C., Hayes, S. C., & Wilson, K. G. (1998). Why behavior analysts should study emotion: The example of anxiety. *Journal of Applied Behavior Analysis, 31*, 137–156. https://doi.org/10.1901/jaba.1998.31-137

Green, G. (2010). Training practitioners to evaluate evidence about interventions. *European Journal of Behavior Analysis, 11*, 223–228. https://doi.org/10.1080/15021149.2010.11434346

Grey, C. (2023, January 5). Podcast statistics and industry trends 2023: Listens, gear, and more. *The Podcast Host.* https://www.thepodcasthost.com/listening/podcast-industry-stats/

Hammersly, B. (February 12, 2004). Audible revolution. *The Guardian.* http://www.theguardian.com/media/2004/feb/12/broadcasting.digitalmedia

Heward, W. L., Critchfield, T. S., Reed, D. D., Detrich, R., & Kimball, J. (2022). ABA from A to Z: Behavior science applied to 350 domains of socially significant behavior. *Perspectives on Behavior Science, 45*(2), 327–359. https://doi.org/10.1007/s40614-022-00336-z

Howard, V. J. (2019). Open education resources in behavior analysis. *Behavior Analysis in Practice, 12*, 839–853. https://doi.org/10.1007/s40617-019-00371-4

Insider Intelligence (2021, July 29). Podcast industry report: Market growth and advertising statistics in 2022. *Insider Intelligence.* https://www.insiderintelligence.com/insights/the-podcast-industry-report-statistics/

Johannsson, H., & Salek, T. (2020). Dissemination of medical publications on social media - is it the new standard? *Anaesthesia, 75*, 155–157. https://doi.org/10.1111/anae.14780

Johnston, J. M., & Shook, G. L. (2001). A national certification program for behavior analysts. *Behavioral Interventions, 16*, 77–85. https://doi.org/10.1002/bin.81

Kelly, M. P., Martin, N., Dillenburger, K., Kelly, A. N., & Miller, M. M. (2019). Spreading the news: History, successes, challenges and the ethics of effective dissemination. *Behavior Analysis in Practice, 12*, 440–451. https://doi.org/10.1007/s40617-018-0238-8

Kelly, E. M., Greeny, K., Rosenberg, N., & Schwartz, I. (2021). When rules are note enough: Developing principles to guide ethical conduct. *Behavior Analysis in Practice, 14*, 491–498. https://doi.org/10.1007/s40617-020-00515-x

Kishbaugh, A., Steinhauser, H. M. K., & Bird, F. L. (2022). *Rethinking non-compliance as a skill and promoting self-advocacy*. Autism Spectrum News. Retrieved from https://autismspectrum-news.org/rethinking-non-compliance-as-a-skill-and-promoting-self-advocacy/

Kranak, M. P., Andzik, N. R., & Falligant, J. M. (2022). Evaluating sources of continuing education and professional development used by behavior analysts. *Behavior Analysis in Practice*. https://doi.org/10.1007/s40617-022-00769-7

Kun, A. (2020). Time to acceptance of 3 days for papers about COVID-19. *Publications, 8*(30). https://doi.org/10.3390/publications8020030

Lave, J., & Wenger, E. (1991). Legitimate peripheral participation in communities of practice. In *Situated learning: Legitimate peripheral participation*. Cambridge University Press.

LeBlanc, L. A., Taylor, B. A., & Marchese, N. V. (2020). The training experiences of behavior analysts: Compassionate care and therapeutic relationships with caregivers. *Behavior Analysis in Practice, 13*, 387–393. https://doi.org/10.1007/s40617-019-00368-z

Li, L. C., Grimshaw, J. M., Nielsen, C., Judd, M., Coyte, P. C., & Graham, I. D. (2009). Use of communities of practice in business and health care sectors: A systematic review. *Implementation Science, 4*(27). https://doi.org/10.1186/1748-5908-4-27

Luo, M., & Hancock, J. T. (2020). Self-disclosure and social media: Motivations, mechanisms and psychological well-being. *Current Opinion in Psychology, 31*, 110–115. https://doi.org/10.1016/j.copsyc.2019.08-019

Luo, T., Freeman, C., & Stefaniak, J. (2020). 'Like, comment, and share' – professional development through social media in higher education: A systematic review. *Education Technology Research and Development, 68*, 1659–1683. https://doi.org/10.1007/s11423-020-09790-5

Morris, E. K. (2014). Stop preaching to the choir, publish outside the box: A discussion. *The Behavior Analyst, 37*, 87–94. https://doi.org/10.1007/s40614-014-0011-4

Morris, Z. S., Wooding, S., & Grant, J. (2011). The answer is 17 years, what is the question: Understanding time lags in translational research. *Journal of the Royal Society of Medicine, 104*, 510–520. https://doi.org/10.1258/jrsm.2011.110180

Normand, M. P., & Kohn, C. S. (2013). Don't wag the dog: Extending the reach of applied behavior analysis. *The Behavior Analyst, 36*, 109–122. https://doi.org/10.1007/BF03392294

O'Leary, P. N., Miller, M. M., Olive, M. L., & Kelly, A. N. (2017). Blurred lines: Ethical implications of social media for behavior analysts. *Behavior Analysis in Practice, 10*, 45–51. https://doi.org/10.1007/s40617-014-0033-0

Oliver, A. C., Pratt, L. A., & Normand, M. P. (2015). A survey of functional behavior assessment methods used by behavior analysts in practice. *Journal of Applied Behavior Analysis, 48*, 817–829. https://doi.org/10.1002/jaba.256

Parry-Cruwys, R., Parry-Cruwys, D., & MacDonald, J. (Hosts). (2018a, March 21). Ethics and social media (No. 51) [Audio podcast episode]. In *ABA Inside Track*. https://www.abainside-track.com/home/2018/3/21/episode-51-ethics-and-social-media

Parry-Cruwys, R., Parry-Cruwys, D., & MacDonald, J. (2018b, Oct 10–12). *Can you hear me now?* [Paper presentation.] Berkshire Association of Behavior Analysis and Therapy

Parsons, M. B., Rollyson, J. H., & Reid, D. H. (2013). Teaching practitioners to conduct behavioral skills training: A pyramidal approach for training multiple human service staff. *Behavior Analysis in Practice, 6*(2), 4–16. https://doi.org/10.1007/BF03391798

Pavone, M. (August 23, 2018). *Open educational resources: Why behavior analysts should care about OERs*. Connections Consulting Blog. Retrieved from https://connectionsconsulting.blogspot.com/2018/08/open-educational-resources-why-behavior.html

Peterson, S. M. (2021). Editor's note: Introducing BAPcast (behavior analysis in practice: The podcast). *Behavior Analysis in Practice, 14*, 293–294. https://doi.org/10.1007/s40617-021-00582-8

Prestridge, S. (2019). *Categorising teachers' use of social media for their professional learning: A self-generating professional learning paradigm.* Computers & Education. https://doi.org/10.1016/j.compedu.2018.11.003

Ranmuthugala, G., Plumb, J. J., Cunningham, F. C., Georgiou, A., Westbrook, J. I., & Braithwaite, J. (2011). How and why are communities of practice established in the healthcare sector? A systematic review of the literature. *BioMed Central Health Services Research, 11*(273) http://www.biomedcentral.com/1472-6963/11/273

Rosenberg, N. E., & Schwartz, I. S. (2019). Guidance or compliance: What makes an ethical behavior analyst? *Behavior Analysis in Practice, 12*, 473–482. https://doi.org/10.1007/s40617-018-00287-5

Sellers, T. P., Valentino, A. L., Landon, T. J., & Aiello, S. (2019). Board certified behavior analysts' supervisory practices of trainees: Survey results and recommendations. *Behavior Analysis in Practice, 12*, 536–546. https://doi.org/10.1007/s40617-019-00367-0

The Daily BA (June 24, 2020). *Seven tips for behavior analysts starting on social media* [video]. YouTube. https://www.youtube.com/watch?v=7fT5r9iTFUc

Valentino, A. L., & Juanico, J. F. (2020). Overcoming barriers to applied research: A guide for practitioners. *Behavior Analysis in Practice, 13*, 894–904. https://doi.org/10.1007/s40617-020-00479-y

Vanderbilt Kennedy Center (October 19, 2022). *TRIAD's response to ABAI's draft report/recommendations on CESS.* Retrieved from https://vkc.vumc.org/news/4059

Vengapally, M. (December 6, 2021). *How to quit your job and become a full-time social media influencer.* AllBusiness.com. Retrieved from https://www.forbes.com/sites/allbusiness/2021/12/06/how-to-quit-your-job-and-become-a-full-time-social-media-influencer

Verhagen, E., Bower, C., & Khan, K. M. (2013). How BJSM embraces the power of social media to disseminate research. *British Journal of Sports Medicine.* https://doi.org/10.1135/bjsports-2013-092780

Diana Parry-Cruwys, PhD, BCBA-D, is an Associate Professor of Applied Behavior Analysis at Regis College and one of the co-hosts of the behavior analytic podcast, *ABA Inside Track*. She has published and presented research on the topics of early intensive behavioral intervention, joint attention, fieldwork training, APA citation use, observational learning, and recycling behavior. She can be reached at diana.parry-cruwys@regiscollege.edu.

Jacquelyn MacDonald, PhD, BCBA-D is an Associate Professor and department chair of the Applied Behavior Analysis Programs at Regis College. She is the co-host of *ABA Inside Track*. She can be reached at jacquelyn.macdonald@regiscollege.edu.

Robert Parry-Cruwys, MSEd, BCBA, is a special education teacher and board certified behavior analyst who has worked in schools supporting learners with disabilities for almost 20 years. When no one came to his weekly journal club at the local coffee shop, he started producing and hosting the *ABA Inside Track* podcast to discuss research topics in ABA in 2016. Four million downloads later, he thinks he made the right choice. He can be reached at abainsidetrack@gmail.com.

Matt Cicoria is a Board Certified Behavior Analyst and consults in public school settings in New England. In 2016, he created *The Behavioral Observations Podcast*, which has been downloaded over four million times in over 100 countries. He can be reached at matt@behavioralobservations.com.

Chapter 16
Grey Literature

A. Delyla Ulm and Elizabeth Shaffer

One of the hallmarks of behavioral science is the methodical peer-review process that serves as a foundation for the dissemination of research, granting a trusted endorsement of validity and quality as published work; it functions as an element of professional practice and academic advancement, and as a tool in the process of scholarly publication (Lee et al., 2013)."Peer review signals to the body politic that the world of science and scholarship takes seriously its social responsibilities as a self-regulating, normatively driven community" (Lee et al., 2013). As a result, behavioral researchers and scholars traditionally disseminate their research through scholarly journals whose peer-review process, academic standing, and reputation promise the quality and originality trusted by the profession. A fulsome review of the scholarly publishing framework is beyond the scope of this chapter; however, of note for this discussion are the limitations of *only* adhering to a peer-review model for disseminating behavioral science.

Articles in peer-reviewed scholarly journals are written by researchers and experts in the field, reviewed and scrutinized by peers who are identified as experts in the same field, and are often affiliated with the academy and academic publishing models. This historically trusted model supports dissemination of evidence-based research and practice that is designed to uphold the integrity and trustworthiness of published peer-reviewed research in support of rigorous peer examination of reported findings, methods, and conclusions that are examined for their validity, quality, and originality. The peer-review process is not without its flaws and criticisms in areas such as its slowness, bias (e.g., prestige bias, nationality bias, gender

A. D. Ulm (✉)
Arizona State University, Tempe, AZ, USA
e-mail: delyla.ulm@asu.edu

E. Shaffer
University of British Columbia, Vancouver, BC, Canada
e-mail: elizabeth.shaffer@ubc.ca

bias, publication bias, etc.), and conservatism or stifling of innovation (e.g., Lee et al., 2013; Kelly et al., 2014; Murray et al., 2018; Walker et al., 2015) to name a few; however, peer review is currently the primary model of research dissemination supported in the majority of academic fields, including those in behavioral science. And while peer review is the predominant framework for research and scholarly dissemination, it is held to often "almost impossibly strict standards and routinely exposed to intense scrutiny by insiders and outsiders," with the "charge of bias" a threat to the "social legitimacy of peer review" (Lee et al., 2013). Some limitations of the peer-review process relevant to behavioral research include issues of access, timeliness, breadth, and equity.

While publication in peer-reviewed journals is often seen as the "gold standard" of academic research dissemination in the majority of fields, factors such as the high cost of institutional and/or individual journal subscription fees affect the ongoing availability of these journal articles, which are frequently limited to researchers associated with subscribing universities or organizations that make these journals available to their employees, or through professional association memberships. Students may also have access to peer-reviewed journals when enrolled in an educational program; however, they may lose this access once they have graduated and begin to practice. For other stakeholders, including the public and communities, access to peer-reviewed journals is extremely limited, both in practical means of access such as physical and/or digital access to content, as well as potential issues of comprehension and information accessibility. Scholarly journal articles are often written with an academic and/or professional audience in mind and as such are often formal in tone and contain discipline-specific jargon that may pose challenges to the nonprofessional/academic or lay person.

Increasingly, open access (OA) has been advocated as an alternative to the paid subscription model, removing the barrier of cost and rights restrictions from access to material, increasing dissemination of research findings in efforts to increase audience reach (Piwowar et al., 2018; Komarista, 2022). Traditionally, the cost of access has fallen to subscribers (i.e., readers); the OA model advocates removing cost and permission barriers to content in support of free and unrestricted access. Primarily focused on increasing access to peer-reviewed literature, OA is a set of principles that support free, digital, online access by moving away from a reader-funded model to one that relies on other funding sources such as authors and public funding (Kitchin et al., 2015). While OA is increasing in traction, cost barriers still exist for researchers/professionals keen to participate in the OA process and for users seeking to access peer-reviewed scholarly journal content.

In order to ensure the rigor that peer review affords, the peer-review journal model of dissemination can take months for research findings to reach the reader. This scholarly publication model requires editors to work with writers, reviewers, and publishers to ensure robust review and feedback processes that result in quality and trusted published works. Scholarly journals are also limited in the quantity of material they publish per issue and annually (although this can be increased with digital platforms) in order to sustain the peer-review model in publishing evidence-based studies. As discussed below, there are a number of alternate avenues for the dissemination and access of practical and evidence-based contributions from the behavioral science fields that fall outside of the scholarly publishing model.

As the academy continues the work of taking stalk of its shortcomings in areas of justice, equity, diversity, and inclusion (JEDI) as well as working to address gender and socioeconomic barriers, it becomes unambiguously clear that the implicit and explicit manner with which the gates are kept and maintained, and the boundaries of exclusion are drawn, permeate every aspect of the academy, including dissemination activities (Atkins et al., 2016; Saifuddin & Mette Jun Lykkegaard, 2016; Sigal 2009). Scholarship is beginning to examine the role of diversity, equity, and inclusion in the peer-review publishing process in efforts to seek evidence-based research that investigates and addresses these biases and disparities (e.g., Bancroft et al., 2022). Additionally, as issues of access and equity continue to surface in public discourse, funding agencies are increasingly insisting on broader public access to grant funded research findings.

This chapter argues that grey literature has a role in increasing the breadth of voices represented in the behavioral sciences as well as addressing some of the inequities to accessing relevant and timely research. The activities of knowledge translation include transferring knowledge from more formal academic settings (e.g., laboratory, peer-reviewed journal, conference, etc.) to the individuals, communities, and organizations that will benefit from increased access to information. By increasing the reach of evidence-based research findings and practice-based knowledge, grey literature has a role to play in the field of behavioral science, particularly in areas of ongoing education and professional development, community engagement, informing policy decisions, engaging government and organization actors, and timely access to research and practice advancements in the field. Researchers who engage in community-based research often utilize grey literature instruments to communicate findings to their community partners (Hanneke & Link, 2019).

Grey Literature

Grey literature, broadly defined, are materials that are outside of conventional peer review and publishing channels. Often produced by organizations, governments and/or individuals, grey literature does not usually go through a peer-review process and includes instruments such as reports, policy briefs, briefing/working papers (aka white papers), newsletters, speeches, infographics, op-eds, preprints and memoranda (Schopfel & Francis, 2018). "Grey literature can simplify difficult ideas for a non-specialist audience, and it can convey new information earlier than traditional forms of academic publication" (Pappas & Williams, 2011, p. 234). As scholars and practitioners in the behavioral sciences increasingly seek out avenues to share their research findings and practice-based knowledge, dissemination practices increase in complexity to include many forms of grey literature (Hanneke & Link, 2019). A recent example specific to behavioral science is the freely available Sci Comm

Toolkit put forth by the Society for Behavioral Medicine, which provides a plethora of resources for researchers and practitioners to increase public dissemination of their work and "create real-world impact" (https://www.sbm.org/scicomm). The toolkit promotes effective science communication with primers, resources, articles, and more on how to operationalize a variety of instruments from op-eds to social media to increase the reach of public communication.

Generating grey literature instruments as well as traditional scholarly journal articles is an increase in workload, however, scholars who engage in such activities argue the benefits of timely dissemination, increased audience reach and informing public policy making and debates are some of the outcomes that make the extra effort well worth it (Hanneke & Link, 2019). Additionally, researchers who engage in participatory and community-based research argue that grey literature instruments (e.g., blogs, websites, etc.) are an ideal way to share findings with study participants and communities for feedback and ongoing dialogue. The knowledge translation possible with the dissemination of research through grey literature instruments allows researchers to target audiences, engage in community engagement activities, and inform public discourse in timely and efficient ways.

While certainly not an exhaustive list, what follows are some examples of grey literature instruments that can increase the dissemination of behavioral science research and practice beyond traditional scholarly publishing models.

Infographics

Infographics are visual representations of information designed to easily communicate often complex or difficult to understand information or data for quick and concise digestion (see Fig. 16.1). Infographics have been increasing in popularity as access to digital platforms and tools to create them have become more accessible. Often used to disseminate more complex information or data to the public and/or research participants who may not have the technical expertise to wade through professional jargon, the use of pictorial graphics, attractive colors and fonts, and easy to navigate frames can all contribute to conveying complex ideas or information in an easily understood format. The ability of infographics to convey technical information efficiently makes them well suited for multiple applications within the behavioral sciences. For example, infographics can be created to share information with research or treatment teams as well as student and consumers.

Op-eds

An op-ed, which is an abbreviation of "opposite the editorial page," where these pieces would traditionally appear in the newspaper, is an opinion piece that is usually written by subject matter experts or regular columnists. Written from the perspective

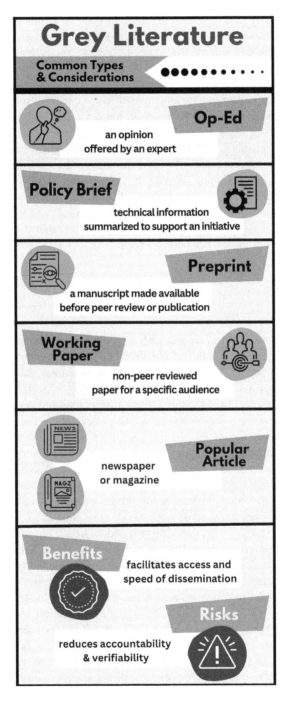

Fig. 16.1 Infographic example

of an expert and providing an informative and convincing perspective, an op-ed is an excellent opportunity to disseminate research. Op-eds should be clear strong arguments from a particular perspective grounded in one's area(s) of expertise. Written in accessible language and with an eye to persuasion, an op-ed should work to make connections outside of a narrow research focus and link to current events and discourse. Op-eds appear in major and minor news outlets and digital publication platforms. While op-eds differ in tone and content from peer-reviewed journal articles, the quality of writing and research should be equal. Op-eds are an excellent way to increase the reach of one's research, have real-world impact and influence public discourse. Op-eds are also a strategic way to balance dissemination activities and are worthy additions to academic CVs and resumes. The Society of Behavioral Medicine's resource Sci Comm Toolkit (https://www.sbm.org/scicomm) offers tips and resources for creating op-eds in the field of behavioral sciences. Op-eds are well suited for members of the behavioral sciences community who wish to share their views with the stakeholders or larger society in a manner that is convincing while avoiding the use of technical behavioral jargon.

Policy Briefs

Policy briefs are concise instruments with the intention of summarizing and communicating complex research and information for a specific audience. Often directed toward nonexpert audiences such as decision makers, bureaucrats, and advocates, policy briefs foreground key facts and/or insights. It is important that the policy brief, like the op-ed be framed within current discussions and debates on the issue in question—relevance is key in constructing policy briefs. Policy briefs have a distinct format, summarizing information into short, digestible segments, with concise headings, working to grab the attention of audiences and delivering enough information/data for one to make an informed decision or advocate for a particular perspective. It is important to keep the audience in mind and offer practical actions and options; it is not written for an academic audience. Limited in size, policy briefs are usually about four pages and do not exceed six or eight at most. Writing in policy briefs needs to be clear and the document should have a clear flow, avoid jargon and unnecessary language. Including short headlines, images, and/or photos can contribute to the attractiveness and utility of a brief. Key elements of a policy brief include: title/headings, executive summary, rationale for action, proposed policy options/recommendations, sources consulted, resources for further information on the topic, links to original research and contact information (American Library Association, n.d; Young & Quinn, 2017). Policy briefs may be useful to members of the behavioral science community who hold leadership positions within academic organizations, research laboratories, or treatment centers and need to concisely convey key information to nonexpert decision makers as part of advocacy campaigns aimed at increased support for an initiative or idea.

The International Centre for Policy Advocacy (ICPA), an independent, nonprofit organization that supports researchers to effectively contribute to policy making and debates, offers a comprehensive set of resources for policy brief development as well as numerous examples of policy briefs (https://www.icpolicyadvocacy.org/resources/policy-brief-resource-page). The ICPA's "Essential Guide to Writing Policy Briefs" (https://www.icpolicyadvocacy.org/sites/icpa/files/downloads/icpa_policy_briefs_essential_guide.pdf) is an excellent point of departure for those new to developing and writing policy briefs.

Preprints

Making preprints of academic articles available is an accessible and timely way to share findings with research participants and stakeholder communities. Preprints are manuscripts made public prior to undergoing peer review and publication in an academic journal. Often made available via the web on preprint servers and author/organizational websites, and free to post and read. Motivations for making preprints available include more rapid and open dissemination of research, increased visibility of research findings and authors' work, opportunities for increased peer feedback, fulfilling granting agency requirements, and increasing community engagement. While there are a variety of potential benefits of preprints, they can be divisive and there are some potential drawbacks, including issues of accountability and verifiability in non-peer reviewed research. Preprints in behavioral sciences are a potential way to make findings fully accessible to research participants and communities without cost or delay. Preprints are increasing in popularity, recently demonstrated with the increased demand for rapid and accessible research during the pandemic.

Working Papers

Working papers are non-peer reviewed papers that share research findings, ideas, or work with an intended audience. Not dissimilar to preprints, working papers may share work publicly prior to submitting an article to a peer-review journal in order to elicit feedback, increase community engagement, inform policy discussions, and/or support timely dissemination of work. Often disseminated via the web on an author's or organizational website, working papers are usually free to publicly access. A working paper may be used as a draft version of a future article or stand alone as a finished product. Including working papers in dissemination of behavior sciences can support collaboration with research participants and bring research and/or a topic into the professional conversation for engagement and debate.

Popular Magazine/Newspaper Articles

Popular magazine or newspaper articles are a suitable way to increase the reach of research to nontraditional communities. Disseminating research findings for a lay audience requires authors to ensure there is minimal use of technical terms and jargon, writing is in line with the style and audience of the publication, and focuses on key findings and/or issues. Like the policy brief, newspaper and magazine articles are best suited to topics that are timely and current. Sharing behavior science research through newspaper and magazine articles can increase the range and reach of audiences, bring awareness to issues and research that may not traditionally be in the public domain, and provide behavioral perspectives on issues in the broader public discourse. The scope and size of newspaper and magazine articles will vary depending on the venue, including shorter more concise articles and long-form journalistic style pieces.

Conclusion

The benefits of using grey literature to disseminate behavioral science research are many. Grey literature can make highly specialized technical information more accessible and digestible for the layperson audience; however, experts within the field of behavioral sciences can also benefit from the inherent flexibility grey literature provides. Grey literature can be disseminated with increased speed and efficiency as compared to traditional, peer-reviewed research. By increasing ease of dissemination, grey literature fosters timely discourse on important issues between behavioral scientists while simultaneously facilitating inclusion of the general public in the conversation. Improved discourse between researchers, applied practitioners, and the consumers they serve may be useful in inspiring more translational research efforts which are best cultivated through reciprocal communication. When conversations centered on behavioral science are open to a larger audience, all involved parties stand to benefit from increased social validity of research efforts and results that are more likely to be adopted as best practice.

While nontraditional dissemination efforts increase the ease of connecting researchers, practitioners, and consumers allowing for increased immediately, relevance, and transparency of discourse, adding to a body of information which is often not tightly controlled or regulated comes with great responsibility. The authors of grey literature must do their due diligence to ensure their contributions to the field of behavior analysis are indeed valuable in that they are honest are humble. Behavioral scientists must be truthful and accurate in the information they provide to others and take care not to mislead the public or exaggerate success or effectiveness of any materials they produce. Furthermore, disseminated information, whether traditionally published or not, should have a foundation in "behavioral conceptualization" that is based in principles, processes, and procedures that have been repeatedly validated under careful levels of informed and structured scrutiny (BACB, 2020).

References

American Library Association. (n.d.). *Guidelines for position papers & issue briefs.* https://www.ala.org/yalsa/aboutyalsa/yalsahandbook/whitepapers

Atkins, L., Vicars, M., Duckwork, F. F., & Phil Rigby, V. (2016). Feminine men and masculine women: In/exclusion in the academy. *Education & Training, 58*(3), 252–262.

Bancroft, S. F., Ryoo, K., & Miles, M. (2022). Promoting equity in the peer review process of journal publication. *Science Education, 106,* 1232–1248. https://doi.org/10.1002/sce.21733

Behavior Analyst Certification Board. (2020). *Ethics code for behavior analysts.* https://bacb.com/wp-content/ethics-code-for-behavior-analysts/

Hanneke, R., & Link, J. M. (2019). The complex nature of research dissemination practices among public health faculty researchers. *Journal of the Medical Library Association, 107*(3). https://doi.org/10.5195/jmla.2019.524

Kelly, J., Sadeghieh, T., & Adeli, K. (2014). Peer review in scientific publications: Benefits, critiques, & a survival guide. *Ejifcc, 25*(3), 227.

Kitchin, R., Collins, S., & Frost, D. (2015). Funding models of open access digital data repositories. *Online Information Review, 39*(5), 664–681.

Komaritsa, V. N. (2022). Benefits of using open access: Citation analysis. *Automatic Documentation and Mathematical Linguistics, 56*(4), 197–202.

Lee, C. J., Sugimoto, C. R., Zhang, G., & Cronin, B. (2013). Bias in peer review. *Journal of the Association for Information Science and Technology, 64,* 2–17. https://doi.org/10.1002/asi.22784

Murray, D., Siler, K., Lariviére, V., Chan, W. M., Collings, A. M., Raymond, J., & Sugimoto, C. R. (2018). Gender and international diversity improves equity in peer review. *BioRxiv,* 400515.

Pappas, C., & Williams, I. (2011). Grey literature: Its emerging importance. *Journal of Hospital Librarianship, 11*(3), 228–234. https://doi.org/10.1080/15323269.2011.587100

Piwowar, H., Priem, J., Larivière, V., Alperin, J. P., Matthias, L., Norlander, B., Farley, A., West, J., & Haustein, S. (2018). The state of OA: A large-scale analysis of the prevalence and impact of Open Access articles. *Peer J, 6,* e4375. https://doi.org/10.7717/peerj.4375

Saifuddin, K., & Mette Jun Lykkegaard, P. (2016). Digital exclusion in higher education contexts: A systematic literature review. *Procedia, Social and Behavioral Sciences, 288,* 614–621.

Schopfel, J., & Farace, D. J. (2018). Grey literature. In J. D. McDonald & M. Levine-Clark (Eds.), *Encyclopedia of library and information sciences* (4th ed.). CRC Press. https://doi.org/10.1081/E-ELIS4

Sigal, A. (2009). The evolution of class inequality in higher education: Competition, exclusion, & adaptation. *American Sociological Review, 74*(5), 731–755.

Walker, R., Barros, B., Conejo, R., Neumann, K., & Telefont, M. (2015). Personal attributes of authors and reviewers, social bias and the outcomes of peer review: A case study. *F1000Research, 4*(21), 21.

Young, E., & Quinn, L. (2017). *An essential guide to writing policy briefs.* International Centre for Policy Advocacy. www.icpolicyadvocacy.org

Dr. A. Delyla Ulm   is a behavioral consultant whose work focuses on improving outcomes for children and adolescents in home, school, and clinical settings. She also works at the graduate level as an educator and fieldwork supervisor to students of applied behavior analysis. She earned her Ph. D. in applied behavior analysis at The Chicago School of Professional Psychology. Her interests include cultural responsiveness, dissemination of behavior analysis to nonexpert audiences, staff training, behavior change programming, problem behavior reduction, and skill building.

Dr. Elizabeth Shaffer   is an Assistant Professor, University of British Columbia School of Information. Her current work and research focus on critical enquiry into how information policy, practices, and systems emerge and evolve in contemporary digital spaces, with particular attention to social justice issues, impacts of colonialism, anti/de-colonial research and pedagogies, and collections that document traumatic human events. Prior to UBC, she was Director of Collections at the Vancouver Holocaust Education Centre, overseeing initiatives focusing on the digitization, preservation, and educational use of Holocaust survivor testimonies and collections in support of anti-racism education and exhibition curation on issues of genocide. She explores tensions and opportunities for policy and practice at the intersections of race, gender, and digital infrastructures and technologies. Elizabeth lives, works, and learns on the traditional, ancestral, and unceded territory of the xwməθkwəy̓əm (Musqueam), Skwxw.7mesh (Squamish), and Səl.[lwətaʔ/Selilwitulh (Tsleil-Waututh) peoples.

Chapter 17
International Dissemination of Behavior Analysis

Dorothy Zhang, Fan Yu Lin, and Neil Martin

Dissemination is the act of "targeted distribution of information and intervention materials to a specific audience" (Kelly et al., 2019; Schillinger, 2010, p. 1.). In Chap. 2, the authors describe the importance and the need for dissemination in the field of Applied Behavior Analysis (ABA) as well as the types of dissemination including the target audience. In Chap. 16, the authors discussed the nontraditional options for dissemination, particularly dissemination via social media. Within these contexts, the focus of this chapter is dissemination on a global scale and the challenges associated with this.

The authors of this chapter are behavior analysts with years of experience engaging in dissemination activities worldwide and supporting countries to establish the professional infrastructure for behavior analysis to emerge as a recognized (and eventually a regulated) profession. To disseminate accurate information as well as contemporary and relevant research, it is important that one understands and responds to the varying cultural contexts that behavior analysis is developing in such that one can navigate and mitigate issues that are unique to global dissemination. We hope that the information provided, and the proposed strategies can provide a framework for others to engage in effective dissemination across different countries and cultures.

D. Zhang (✉)
Department of Behavior Analysis, College of Graduate and Professional Studies at The Chicago School, Chicago, IL, USA
e-mail: dzhang@thechicagoschool.edu

F. Y. Lin
Philadelphia (Ningbo) Education Technology Co., Ltd., Ningbo, China
e-mail: fylin@ibao-aba.cn

N. Martin
Behavior Analyst Certification Board, Littleton, CO, USA
e-mail: neil@bacb.com

© The Author(s), under exclusive license to Springer Nature Switzerland AG 2023   269
A. K. Griffith, T. C. Ré (eds.), *Disseminating Behavioral Research*,
https://doi.org/10.1007/978-3-031-47343-2_17

Current Barriers to the International Dissemination of Behavior Analysis

Lack of Scientific Communication Across Disciplines

A major part of the dissemination of science is through publication in peer-reviewed journals which is considered a permanent product of the units of consensus among behavior analytic researchers (Kranak et al., 2020). Indeed, the primary focus of this book is to provide researchers with a general guide for how to disseminate the steadily increasing applications of behavior analysis through publication and public presentation. However, behavior analysts' reliance on single subject experimental designs, observational data, and visual analysis are at odds with most other scientific fields (Friman, 2014). Even within the broader field of behavior science, the communication between basic, translational, and applied researchers may also be lacking due to disparities between subject-specific knowledge, utilization of knowledge, and knowledge exchange (Mace & Critchfield, 2010). The difficulty of publication outside of behavior analytic journals or across basic, applied and service provision branches could discourage researchers from attempting to publish or even initiating a productive scientific conversation with peers, let alone debate and discussion across disciplines.

Limited Access to Postgraduate Training and Research Support

Disseminating academic innovations and promoting the overall understanding and practice of behavior analysis, requires acquiring and mastering the scientific language and methods. Most (if not all) of this training is completed through postgraduate studies. However, access to such training seems inequitable across the world and is likely seen as a first world privilege by many developing and/or underdeveloped countries. In general terms, the USA has by far the largest share of individuals (between the ages of 25 and 64) holding a doctoral degree, accounting for approximately of 2% of its population, closely followed by Germany and the UK (OECD, 2022). However, only 0.1% of the population in Indonesia has obtained a doctoral degree. If one looks at the number of postgraduate university training programs in behavior analysis using the number of Association for Behavior Analysis International (ABAI) verified course sequences (VCSs) as a proxy measure, then the majority (74%) are based in the USA (ABAI, n.d.-a). While some individuals from countries without access to postgraduate programs may have the luxury/ability to choose to study abroad, some countries are struggling merely to increase adult literacy rates rather than focus on the development of postgraduate training, especially for an unrecognized albeit emerging field.

In recent years, there has been a near exponential rise in the number of behavior analysts joining the field. Using Behavior Analyst Certification Board (BACB) certificants as a proxy measure for this assertion, as of August 2023, more than half of the total number of Board Certified Behavior Analysts (BCBAs), since the BACB started offering certification in 1999, have been certified in the last four years (BACB, n.d.-a). Although such growth should be celebrated in a world where behavior analytic interventions ought to be widely sought (e.g., addressing issues related to climate change, health and safety, an increasingly elderly population, etc.), this growth does not equate to a comparative increase in the numbers contributing to scientific dissemination. According to a survey of BACB certificants, only a small number of BCBAs (0.29%) engage predominantly in dissemination activities and the majority of BCBAs (87%) are based in the USA anyway (BACB, n.d.-a).

Lack of Translated Academic Resources

Researchers over the years have examined the origins of publications in the *Journal of Applied Behavior Analysis* and found that less than 10% of articles were published by non-US authors and institutions (Dymond et al., 2000; Martin et al., 2016). These data correlate with the numbers of BCBAs in predominantly English-speaking countries—certificants from the USA, Canada, Australia and the UK represent 95% of the total number (BACB, n.d.-a) —but this correlation perhaps better represents interest, acceptance and service provision opportunities within those countries more than a measure of research activity and dissemination. However, the lack of academic infrastructure to support behavior analytic publications outside of North America is particularly apparent when it comes to the availability of research funding and prevalence of English-based journals (Lee et al., 2023; Martin et al., 2016). Non-English speaking behavior analysts are hindered by the additional complications involved in publishing in English language journals beyond conducting the research: they must navigate the editorial rules and standards, write in technically and grammatically correct English, and converse with journal editors/reviewers about (often) nuanced and technical subtleties. Of course, there are numerous language translations of some of the behavior analytic textbooks and assessment tools, but for an individual to receive the breadth and depth of training required at postgraduate level to become a behavior analyst requires access to the full range of published, contemporary, academic material and, at least in terms of journals, the vast majority are published only in English.

Misinformation and Mistrust About Behavior Analysis

Effective dissemination is not just about the distribution of information and resources within the scientific community and conversing amicably among colleagues, it also involves the conveyance of accurate, relevant, and understandable content to practitioners, service recipients, and other stakeholders (Welch-Ross & Fasig, 2007). If behavior analysts are unable to explain and illustrate fundamental aspects of the field (along with its associated evidence-based strategies and tactics) to those who do not have the prerequisite postgraduate training, then there is little or no credibility from a lay-person's perspective, and it would be difficult to establish a dialog and widely disseminate important findings. Furthermore, in the absence of being able to do this with compassion and cultural awareness/sensitivity, and in the face of the growing number of criticisms directed towards applied behavior analysts that work with (and *allegedly* harm) individuals with a diagnosis of autism (Graber & Graber, 2023; Kapp, 2020; Milton & Lyte, 2012), the levels of misinformation abound and this has engendered an environment of mistrust and hostility (Kupferstein, 2018; National Council on Independent Living, 2021; Sandoval-Norton & Shkedy, 2019).

Within the field of autism around the world, there are also significantly different cultural views on the etiology and knowledge of effective interventions for individuals with autism who have severe skill deficits. For example, some Asian practitioners and consumers tend to believe only in a genetic etiology of disabilities (Hall, 2005), suggesting that medical guidance is all that is required, and this is at odds with a behavior analytic viewpoint that stresses the importance of environmental contingencies (Skinner, 1938). There also appears to be misinformation about ABA that stems directly from the field of autism specifically, with ABA being characterized as just one of many autism interventions (Chiesa, 2006), equated to animal training (Millman, 2019) and a dated and out of touch philosophy that has not evolved for 50 years (Baron-Cohen, 2014).

Limited Professional Emphasis

The majority of behavior analysts, again, if using the number of BCBAs as a proxy measure, work with individuals with autism, and there is now unequivocal evidence for the effectiveness of behavioral intervention for autism as well as for individuals with other developmental disabilities (Alves et al., 2020). ABA has become the *gold standard* for working with learners with autism (see Larsson, 2012) and has been well adapted in many regions (Tanner & Dounavi, 2020). However, the success of working with individuals at one tail of the normal distribution has both fueled the misunderstanding that ABA is just an intervention for individuals with autism, but also limited the reach of behavior analysts in terms of so many other matters of social significance where human behavior change is vitally significant and pressing. The fact that behavior analysts have, generally, focused their interests on a limited range of applications has been unhelpful in terms of accurate dissemination of a powerful science, and a 'call to action' has been advocated by many over the years (Friman, 2010; Friman, 2014; Normand & Kohn, 2013).

Lack of Dissemination Skills, Competencies, and Strategies

More senior behavior analysts, particularly those who are academics, course instructors and supervisors, may assume or be delegated the responsibility of dissemination, regardless of whether they have the skills and competencies involved to do so. However, effective dissemination, just like supervision, can be considered as a set of skills and competencies which likely require training. Supervisors are expected to undergo specific training in order to provide good and effective supervision (BACB, 2018), but this is not the case for disseminators. The increasing work-related demand for behavior analysts, at least in the USA (BACB, 2023), and the increasing number of behavior analysts (BACB, n.d.-a) does not necessarily lead to an increase in the number of individuals who can effectively disseminate behavior analysis.

Lavis et al. (2003) proposed five critical considerations for the transfer (i.e., dissemination) of scientific information. These considerations are as follows:

(1) What should be disseminated?
(2) To what target audience?
(3) Who should disseminate?
(4) What dissemination methods should be used?
(5) What is the desired effect/outcome of dissemination?

Without such clear strategic considerations, it is easy to see how behavior analytic dissemination could become merely a mechanism to report new or nuanced strategies and tactics (#1) to other behavior analysts (#2) by a select group of academics and researchers (#3), mainly by peer-reviewed publication and conference presentations (#4) and with no specific outcome other than, perhaps, an additional line on someone's curriculum vitae.

Lack of Global Recognition and Regulation

To date, other than the USA and very few exceptions, no country has formally recognized behavior analysts as a distinct professional group and without formal recognition, there can be no regulation. For behavior analysts to become recognized, there needs to be consensus on the need for this from all stakeholders—behavior analysts, other professionals and paraprofessionals, consumers/recipients of applied behavior analytic services, academics, students, etc. In the absence of consensus — especially if even the behavior analysts cannot agree on national standards for training, experience, professional and ethical conduct codes, scope of service delivery etc. —disseminating information becomes difficult, confusing, and potentially contradictory. There are a number of countries that have multiple behavior analytic associations and organizations that operate in isolation from one another, develop their own standards (and perhaps have their own register of individuals that have met those standards), run their own conferences, have specific foci in terms of client groups, and may represent themselves as *the* national behavior analysis association.

Reliance on standards, systems, and even certification from third-party organizations outside of the country may also hinder the development and emergence of a national, cohesive, and culturally sensitive field. It seems unlikely, for example, that a group of professionals will be recognized as a distinct field and regulated within a country based on a third-party credential that is not located within the country and that may not even prescribe postgraduate university training.

Addressing Barriers to the International Dissemination of Behavior Analysis

Increasing Scientific Communication Across Disciplines

Single-subject research design is the most used research design in behavior analysis. Visual inspection of the data provides evidence of functional relations between the independent and dependent variables. Within behavior analysis, there has been an ongoing discussion and a call to action for incorporating statistical analysis into describing behavior (Virues-Ortega et al., 2023; Young, 2018). Learning materials on building statistical skills are available for behavior analysis practitioners and researchers (Cox & Vladescu, 2023) as a step to communicate with other disciplines using a more *common* knowledge base. Of course, the argument here is that behavior analysis should not just use statistics for the sake of establishing communication with other disciplines, but because statistics can bring value to the field in terms of evaluating the effectiveness of the relevant independent variables. Similarly, it seems important that behavior analysts should report outcome measures that are both reliable and valid and, importantly, used by and understandable to others (Martin et al., 2003; Padilla et al., 2023).

Publishing in outlets other than behavior analytic journals is also an important consideration (see Schlinger, 2014), and Reed (2014) proposed three considerations for doing this including (1) evaluating the message to be delivered; (2) ensuring that the message represents the best interests of the field; and (3) determining if publishing "outside the box" is worthwhile. We encourage behavior analysts to consider these issues and disseminate widely.

Starting Postgraduate Training

Completion of postgraduate behavior analytic training and fieldwork experience is widely accepted as meeting the standards required to become an independent behavior analytic practitioner, but as previously noted, the vast majority of university-based postgraduate training programs are in the USA. The solution is conceptually simple, but practically complicated—start more postgraduate training programs within universities around the world. There are several options for doing this:

(1) Create a stand-alone postgraduate certificate, diploma, or specialization program.
(2) Embed sufficiently comprehensive behavior analytic coursework into an existing and appropriate postgraduate degree program (such as applied psychology, education, special education, etc.).
(3) Create a new postgraduate degree program in behavior analysis.

All of these options require instructors who themselves have completed postgraduate study in behavior analysis, and additionally have practical clinical experience, but it is very unlikely that many universities will have faculty that have postgraduate degrees in behavior analysis that can start and teach on such programs, requiring that instructors are sought from elsewhere. This provides the first challenge; persuading a university department to start a program that will not be taught by existing faculty, but by individuals employed as adjunct faculty or external instructors/consultants. There are a number of compelling arguments one could make for such an arrangement. First, universities are interested (or should be) in innovation, marketing, and student numbers, and the case could be made for the prestigious nature of being the first university in a country/region to start a postgraduate program for an emerging field, with the knowledge that existing behavior analytic practitioners within the country/region would have had to go elsewhere to get the required training. Second, the importance of addressing the growing needs of young professionals and, more importantly, consumers of behavior analytic services. Third, the likelihood that there may be individuals already offering behavior analytic services within the country, but with dubious, unknown or no recognized training and experience, and the potential harm to consumers that this may cause. Fourth, the fact that beyond providing a teaching space, administrative support, and issuing academic qualifications upon successful completion of the program, the response effort from the university's perspective is negligible. Of course, all of this is predicated on the assumption that individuals can be found who are willing to teach on such a program (albeit remotely), and anyone reading this who wishes to spend several years in a different country please take note! Starting and teaching a postgraduate behavior analysis training program and, thus, creating the next wave of instructors and supervisors will yield far bigger returns for the country/region than providing individual behavior analytic services locally.

Translating Academic Resources

Translation in a technical sense can be a difficult task and is one of the skills that is relevant to international dissemination and that requires knowledge about the subject matter and the cultural context of the languages that are being translated. Tuomisto and Parkkinen (2012) provide some context for the importance of translating technical terms and use their translation of behavior analytic terms into Finnish, both for terms related to the experimental analysis of behavior, applied and clinical behavior analysis, to discuss the relevance of this to the dissemination of science. Virues-Ortega and colleagues recommend five hierarchical and topographical considerations for the translation of behavioral terms to other languages. First, if a lexemic equivalent for a word is available, then that should be used; second, if no lexemic equivalent is available, then use a non-lexemic equivalent; third, if there is no appropriate non-lexemic equivalent, then use periphrasis; fourth, in the absence of effective periphrasis consider using an integrated Anglicism; fifth, use a non-integrated Anglicism (Virues-Ortega et al., 2015). These considerations were expanded to include semantic and etymological (functional) considerations by Alipov, Qamar, and Martin (2018). Alipov et al. (2018) suggest that such considerations should also include the preservation of historic succession (e.g., Pavlov, Thorndike and Skinner's use of terms, etc.), the preservation of interdisciplinary compatibility (e.g., the terms *reflexivity, symmetry, transitivity,* and *equivalence* come from Cantor's Set Theory, 1874), and the maintenance of the uniqueness of terms if appropriate (Skinnerian neologisms such as *mand* and *tact* are difficult to translate and are better preserved as is).

The four most widely spoken languages in the world are English, Mandarin Chinese, Hindi, and Spanish (World Economic Forum, n.d.). However, English and Hindi are both official languages of India's federal government, thus English, Mandarin Chinese, and Spanish could be argued to be the three most prevalent of the spoken languages. Written Chinese can be either Traditional Chinese or Simplified Chinese, but Simplified Chinese is far more prevalent and used throughout mainland China by more than one billion people (compared to only millions that use and read Traditional Chinese). Many behavior analysis textbooks have already been translated into different languages to encourage learning and dissemination. For example, *Applied Behavior Analysis* (Cooper et al., 2019) has been translated into multiple languages including Spanish and Chinese. *Ethics for Behavior Analysts* (Bailey & Burch, 2016) has been translated into Chinese. *Principles of Behavior* (Malott & Kohler, 2021) has been translated into Spanish and Chinese. While textbooks are an important resource for any training course, access to journals is vital to be able to access the most contemporary research, and the majority of behavior analytic journals are published in English. However, the *Journal of Applied Behavior Analysis* has recently started translating some of its seminal and contemporary articles into Spanish and Chinese (Wiley, n.d.).

Addressing Misinformation Issues and Criticisms

Schlinger (2015) has suggested that one way to reduce misinformation about behavior analysis is through comprehensive training programs that include coverage of the experimental analysis of behavior as well as the theoretical and conceptual foundations of the science. In addition to having knowledge about the subject, those that study behavior analysis should be able to think critically about the science and not only be able to convey information accurately but also defend it against those who are critical, usually because of the misinformation acquired or assumed.

Some of the criticisms of ABA that are centered around its application to individuals with autism and associated skill deficits and behavioral excesses have been addressed by Leaf et al. (2021), who made recommendations based on those concerns. These recommendations include only implementing and advocating for interventions based solely on positive reinforcement-based contingences and ensuring that there is evolution and progression of evidence-based practice rather than the rigid adherence to previously researched and implemented protocols. Generally, there should be more emphasis given to skill building with considerations of the strengths of the learner with the aim being to maximize independence and lead to an improvement in quality of life. The learner should be included in the development of their own treatment plan and their feedback should be solicited and valued throughout intervention. A caring and symbiotic relationship is an important factor for intervention outcome as shown by the evidence and experience from mental health and general health practices (Taylor et al., 2018). It is important to disseminate and promote an applied science that is about development and compassion rather than simply attempt to rebut individual criticism, however hostile such criticism may be, and to incorporate cultural awareness, cultural humility, and the importance of diversity, equity, and inclusion as crucial issues in a fast-developing and increasingly more connected world (Wright, 2019; ABAI, n.d.-b).

Promoting the Many Applications of Behavior Analysis

It is incumbent upon the field of behavior analysis to ensure that every opportunity is taken to accurately explain that behavior analysis is a natural science where behavior (albeit widely defined) is the focus, and that ABA is simply the application of the science to addressing issues of social significance where behavior change is required. Behavioral intervention for autism is only one of the multitude of applications of behavior analysis although clearly many see ABA as being synonymous with this specific application. There are numerous resources that can be utilized to promote the multifarious applications including the wide variety of ABAI special interest groups (ABAI, n.d.-c), ABA subspeciality practice areas including summary fact sheets and videos listed on the BACB's website (BACB, n.d.-b), the Cambridge Center for Behavioral Studies' help centers (Cambridge Center for Behavioral Studies, n.d.).

Behavior analysts should consider working in diverse areas to expand the reach and impact of the science as well as for the sake of dissemination beyond the scope of autism and developmental disabilities. There is no limit to the range of activities/industries that would benefit from behavior analytic intervention!

Teaching Appropriate Dissemination Skills

Effective dissemination, in addition to in depth subject knowledge, requires other soft skills that are not often directly taught in formal behavior analytic courses. For example, public speaking and presentation skills are needed when disseminating orally, are rarely explicitly included as part of a training curriculum, but could be considered important (if not necessary) to achieve widespread and mainstream prominence. Friman (2015) provides a 15-step tutorial to master what he refers to as such "front of the room" skills. Similarly, one must know how best to utilize media to broadcast and display information via different modalities (e.g., slides, videos, live interviews, podcasts, social media, etc.) and, again, the teaching of such skills is typically not part of any behavior analysis course. Indeed, behavior analysts and other scientists still rely on antiquated methods of dissemination such as the printing press that was popularized by Gutenberg in 1440 but that dates back to 3000 BC (American Print History Association, n.d.). Keenan (2016) argues that behavior analysts should embrace the recent advancements in computer technology and appreciate the importance of, for example, incorporating animation and multimedia in order to communicate and disseminate in more sophisticated ways.

Behavior analysts should learn how to speak publicly, learn how to present effectively and with clarity, learn how to use all available media including computer technology. Behavior analysts should learn how to communicate effectively in the twenty-first century. Additionally, when disseminating internationally, Fong et al. (2016) have also stressed that in addition to knowledge about behavior analysis and the other necessary skills involved in disseminating, behavior analysts should develop the necessary cultural awareness skills to disseminate within different global contexts more effectively (also see Benuto et al., 2021).

Supporting Other Countries to Build Professional Infrastructure

It takes many years if not decades to establish a profession. The professionalization of the field on a country-by-country basis requires that a number of factors are addressed: behavior analytic service provision should eventually become regulated, but regulation first requires professional recognition. Professional recognition requires agreed national standards, and agreement requires consensus from the behavior analytic community and support from key stakeholders and organizations. Underpinning all of this is the necessity to develop a professional infrastructure to support the growth of the field including (perhaps most importantly) the availability of university training, and this should be seen as a priority—please refer back to the *Starting Postgraduate Training* section for these recommendations.

In addition to starting and running postgraduate training courses, and perhaps even in advance of this, information about the science, its many applications, and why the development of the profession is important, could be achieved by hosting events with key messages and presentations provided by the national behavior analytic community, with support from the wider community, that are designed to promote interest and awareness in behavior analysis. Ideally such events should be attended by politicians, other healthcare professionals, teachers, potential consumers of services, other stakeholders, and the press, not just behavior analysts or students of behavior analysis.

Conclusion

Dissemination of behavior analysis is not the responsibility of one, or a few, and neither is it a transitory activity. It is a process with clear goals and plans to facilitate a greater understanding of the science and its applications. This process should extend from traditional academic modes such as the publishing of journal articles and books, or presenting at conferences, to the use of new tools and media to a wider audience.

In regions where behavior analysis is relatively (or completely) unknown, building the foundational infrastructure to foster the development of the science/profession would be the top priority. Introduce the science, the terms, and the core concepts to others by any and all means possible. Publish "outside the box" in newspapers and magazines. Speak at other professions' conferences. Demonstrate the power of the science at every opportunity.

In regions where behavior science is already known and established (e.g., there are university training programs and a national association), the focus should be more on addressing misinformation, misinterpretation, and malpractice. Call out unprofessional and unethical practice. Work with other professionals. Utilize the powerful support of consumers, service providers and contractors, key stakeholders.

Behavior analysis as a profession has developed rapidly over the years. However, continuous effort is required to ensure that information about behavior analysis and the scale of its applications are more greatly understood. This is a global challenge but one that must be embraced by the field and embedded within our scope of competence.

References

Alipov, N., Qamar, Z., & Martin, N. (2018). Translating behavior analytic terminology: Semantic and etymological considerations from a Russian perspective. *European Journal of Behavior Analysis, 20*, 1–13.

Alves, F. J., De Carvalho, E. A., Aguilar, J., De Brito, L. L., & Bastos, G. S. (2020). Applied behavior analysis for the treatment of autism: A systematic review of assistive technologies. *IEEE Access*. https://doi.org/10.1109/ACCESS.2020.3005296

American Print History Association (n.d.). *History of printing timeline*, retrieved on August 29, 2023 from https://printinghistory.org/timeline/

Association for Behavior Analysis International. (n.d.-a). *Verified Course Sequence Directory*, retrieved on July 12, 2023 from https://www.abainternational.org/vcs/directory.aspx

Association for Behavior Analysis International. (n.d.-b). *Diversity, Equity and Inclusion Board*, retrieved on August 29, 2023 from https://www.abainternational.org/dei.aspx

Association for Behavior Analysis International (n.d.-c). *Special Interest Groups*, retrieved on August 29, 2023 from https://www.abainternational.org/constituents/special-interests/special-interest-groups.aspx

Bailey, J., & Burch, M. (2016). *Ethics for behavior analysts* (3rd ed.). LEA.

Baron-Cohen, S. (2014). *What scientific idea is ready for retirement?* Radical behaviourism, Edge. https://www.edge.org/response-detail/25473

Behavior Analyst Certification Board. (2018). *Supervision training curriculum outline 2.0*. BACB.

Behavior Analyst Certification Board. (2023). *US employment demand for behavior analysts: 2010–2022*. BACB.

Behavior Analyst Certification Board. (n.d.-a). *BACB certificant data*, retrieved on July 12, 2023 from https://www.bacb.com/bacb-certificant-data/

Behavior Analyst Certification Board. (n.d.-b). *About behavior analysis: ABA subspeciality resources*, retrieved on August 29, 2023 from https://www.bacb.com/about-behavior-analysis/

Benuto, L. T., Newlands, R., Singer, J., Casas, J., & Cummings, C. (2021). Culturally sensitive clinical practices: A mixed methods study. *Psychological Services, 18*, 632–642.

Cambridge Center for Behavioral Studies (n.d.). *Help centers*, retrieved on August 29, 2023 from https://behavior.org/help-centers/

Cantor, G. (1874). Ueber eine Eigenschaft des Inbegriffes aller reellen algebraischen Zahlen. *Journal für die Reine und Angewandte Mathematik, 77*, 258–262.

Chiesa, M. (2006). ABA is not 'a therapy for autism'. In M. Henderson, K. P. Kerr, & K. Dillenburger (Eds.), *Applied behaviour analysis and autism: Building a future together*. Jessica Kingsley.

Cooper, J. O., Heron, T. E., & Heward, W. L. (2019). *Applied behavior analysis* (3rd ed.). Pearson.

Cox, D. J., & Vladescu, J. C. (2023). *Statistics for applied behavior analysis practitioners and researchers*. Elsevier Academic Press.

Dymond, S., Clarke, S., Dunlap, G., & Steiner, M. (2000). International publication trends of JABA authorship. *Journal of Applied Behavior Analysis, 33*, 339–342.

Fong, E. H., Catagnus, R. M., Brodhead, M. T., Quigley, S., & Field, S. (2016). Developing the cultural awareness skills of behavior analysts. *Behavior Analysis in Practice, 9*, 84–94.

Friman, P. C. (2010). Come on in, the water is fine. Achieving mainstream relevance through integration with primary medical care. *The Behavior Analyst, 33*, 19–36.

Friman, P. C. (2014). Publishing in journals outside the box: Attaining mainstream prominence requires demonstrations of mainstream relevance. *The Behavior Analyst, 37*, 73–76.

Friman, P. C. (2015). Behavior analysts to the front! A 15-step tutorial on public speaking. *The Behavior Analyst, 37*, 109–118.

Graber, A., & Graber, J. (2023). Applied behavior analysis and the abolitionist neurodiversity critique: An ethical analysis. *Behavior Analysis in Practice*. https://doi.org/10.1007/s40617-023-00780-6

Hall, G. C. N. (2005). Top 10 recommendations for treating comorbid addictive behaviors in Asian Americans. *The Behavior Therapist, 28*(6), 118–120.

Kapp, S. K. (2020). Autistic community and the neurodiversity movement: Stories from the frontline. In *Autistic community and the neurodiversity movement: Stories from the frontline*. Palgrave Macmillan.

Keenan, M. (2016). The scientific image in behavior analysis. *The Behavior Analyst, 39*, 7–8.

Kelly, M. P., Martin, N., Dillenburger, K., et al. (2019). Spreading the news: History, successes, challenges and the ethics of effective dissemination. *Behavior Analysis Practice, 12*, 440–451.

Kranak, M. P., Falligant, J. M., Bradtke, P., Hausman, N. L., & Rooker, G. W. (2020). Authorship trends in the journal of applied behavior analysis: An update. *Journal of Applied Behavior Analysis, 53*, 2376–2384.

Kupferstein, H. (2018). Evidence of increased PTSD symptoms in autistics exposed to applied behavior analysis. *Advances in Autism, 4*, 19–29.

Larsson, E. V. (2012). *Analysis of the evidence base for ABA and EIBI for autism*. The Lovaas Institute for Early Intervention.

Lavis, J., Ross, S., McLeod, C., & Gildiner, A. (2003). Measuring the impact of health research. *Journal of Health Services Research & Policy, 8*, 165–170.

Leaf, J. B., Cihon, J. H., Leaf, R., McEachin, J., Liu, N., Russell, N., Unumb, L., Shapiro, S., & Khosrowshahi, D. (2021). Concerns about ABA-based intervention: An evaluation and recommendations. *Journal of Autism and Developmental Disorders*. https://doi.org/10.1007/s10803-021-05137-y

Lee, G. T., Jiang, Y., & Hu, X. (2023). Brief report: Publications from mainland China, Hong Kong, and Taiwan in behavioral journals 1980–2021. *Behavioral Interventions*. https://doi.org/10.1002/bin.1947

Mace, F. C., & Critchfield, T. S. (2010). Translational research in behavior analysis: Historical traditions and imperative for the future. *Journal of the Experimental Analysis of Behavior, 93*, 293–312.

Malott, R. W., & Kohler, K. T. (2021). *Principles of behavior* (8th ed.). London and New York.

Martin, N. T., Bibby, P., Mudford, O. C., & Eikeseth, S. (2003). Toward the use of a standardized assessment for young children with autism. *Autism, 7*, 321–330.

Martin, N. T., Nosik, M. R., & Carr, J. E. (2016). International publication trends in the journal of applied behavior analysis: 2000–2014. *Journal of Applied Behavior Analysis, 49*, 416–420.

Millman, C. (2019). *Is ABA really "dog training for children"? A professional dog trainer weighs in*. https://neuroclastic.com/is-aba-really-dog-training-for-children-a-professional-dog-trainer-weighs-in/#:~:text=Dog%20trainers%20understand%20that%20dogs,when%20things%20get%20too%20much

Milton, D., & Lyte, M. (2012). The normalisation agenda and the psycho-emotional disablement of autistic people. *Autonomy, the Critical Journal of Interdisciplinary Autism Studies, 1*, 1. ISSN 2051-5189.

National Council on Independent Living. (2021). Resolution opposing applied behavior analysis (ABA). *The Advocacy Monitor*. https://advocacymonitor.com/resolution-opposing-applied-behavior-analysis-plain-language

Normand, M. P., & Kohn, C. S. (2013). Don't wag the dog: Extending the reach of applied behavior analysis. *The Behavior Analyst, 36*, 109–122.

OECD. (2022). *Education at a glance 2022: OECD indicators*. OECD Publishing. https://doi.org/10.1787/3197152b-en

Padilla, K. L., Weston, R., Morgan, G. B., Lively, P., & O'Guinn, N. (2023). Validity and reliability evidence for assessments based in applied behavior analysis: A systematic review. *Behavior Modification, 47*, 247–288.

Reed, D. D. (2014). Determining how, when, and whether you should publish outside the box: Sober advice for early career behavior analysts. *The Behavior Analyst, 37*(2), 83–86. https://doi.org/10.1007/s40614-014-0012-3

Sandoval-Norton, A. H., & Shkedy, G. (2019). How much compliance is too much compliance: Is long-term ABA therapy an abuse? *Cogent Psychology, 6*, 1–8.

Schillinger, D. (2010). In P. Fleisher & E. Goldstein (Eds.), *An introduction to effective, dissemination, and implementation research: A resource manual for community-engaged research*. University of California, San Francisco: Clinical and Translational Science Institute.

Schlinger, H. D. (2014). Publishing outside the box: Unforeseen dividends of talking with strangers. *The Behavior Analyst, 37*, 77–81.

Schlinger, H. D. (2015). Training graduate students to effectively disseminate behavior analysis and to counter misrepresentations. *Behavior Analysis in Practice, 8*, 110–112.

Skinner, B. F. (1938). *The behavior of organisms: An experimental analysis*. Appleton-Century.

Tanner, A., & Dounavi, K. (2020). Maximizing the potential for infants at-risk for autism spectrum disorder through a parent-mediated verbal behavior intervention. *European Journal of Behaviour Analysis, 21*, 271–291. https://doi.org/10.1080/15021149.2020.1731259

Taylor, B. A., LeBlanc, L. A., & Nosik, M. R. (2018). Compassionate care in behavior analytic treatment: Can outcomes be enhanced by attending to relationships with caregivers? *Behavior Analysis in Practice, 12*, 654–666.

Tuomisto, M., & Parkkinen, L. (2012). Defining behavior-environment interactions: Translating and developing an experimental and applied behavior-analytic vocabulary in and to the national language. *Journal of Experimental Analysis of Behavior, 97*, 347–355.

Virues-Ortega, J., Martin, N., Schnerch, G., Garcia, J., & Mellichamp, F. (2015). A general methodology for the translation of behavioral terms into vernacular languages. *The Behavior Analyst, 38*, 125–135.

Virues-Ortega, J., Moeyaert, M., Sivaraman, M., Rodríguez, A. T., & Castilla, B. F. (2023). Quantifying outcomes in applied behavior analysis through visual and statistical analyses: A synthesis. In J. L. Matson (Ed.), *Handbook of applied behavior analysis. Autism and Child Psychopathology Series*. Springer.

Welch-Ross, M. K., & Fasig, L. G. (Eds.). (2007). *Handbook on communicating and disseminating behavioral science*. Sage Publications.

Wiley. (n.d.). *Journal of Applied Behavior Analysis Translated*, retrieved on August 29, 2023 from https://onlinelibrary.wiley.com/page/journal/19383703/homepage/jaba-translated

World Economic Forum. (n.d.). *Which languages are most widely spoken*, retrieved on August 29, 2023 from https://www.weforum.org/agenda/2015/10/which-languages-are-most-widely-spoken/

Wright, P. I. (2019). Cultural humility in the practice of applied behavior analysis. *Behavior Analysis in Practice, 12*, 805–809.

Young, M. E. (2018). A place for statistics in behavior analysis. *Behavior Analysis: Research and Practice, 18*, 193–202.

Dr. Dorothy Zhang is a program chair and an Associate Professor in the ABA Online department at the Chicago School. She received a Ph.D. in Education from George Mason University in 2015, specializing in Educational Psychology and Applied Behavior Analysis. As a Board Certified Behavior Analyst, she has over 17 years of experience working with children and young adults with special needs and their caregivers and educators. Dr. Zhang is also actively involved in the development of Behavior Analysis in mainland China.

Dr. Fan Yu Lin is a Board Certified Behavior Analyst and International Behavior Analyst. She received her PhD in Special Education from the Pennsylvania State University (USA) in 2004 and had served as a professor, researcher, and advisor. Since 2020 Dr. Lin has started working in China and has first-hand experienc of international dissemination both academically and practically.

Dr. Neil Martin has been working as a Behavior Analyst (as a clinician, academic, supervisor, and researcher), since 1990. He received his Ph.D. from the University of Reading (UK) in 1998 and became a Board Certified Behavior Analyst in 2002. In April 2015, Dr. Martin became the BACB's Director of International Development, and he provides help and support to countries in terms of developing professional infrastructure for the emergence of the field of behavior analysis, including the development of country-specific credentialing programs.

Index